Movies for the masses is a pathbreaking study of the "unknown" Soviet cinema: the popular movies which were central to Soviet film production in the 1920s. Denise J. Youngblood discusses acting genres, the cinema stars, audiences and the influence of foreign films and she examines three filmmakers – Iakov Protazanov, Boris Barnet, and Fridrikh Ermler – who are widely assumed in the West to be of considerable importance but about whom little is actually known. The author also looks at the governmental and industrial circumstances underlying "commercial" filmmaking practices of the era, and provides an invaluable survey of the contemporary debates concerning official policy on entertainment cinema.

Dr. Youngblood demonstrates that the film culture of the 1920s was predominantly and aggressively "bourgeois" and enjoyed patronage that cut across class lines and political allegiance. Thus, she argues, the extent to which Western and pre-revolutionary influences, bourgeois directors and middle-class tastes dominated the film world is as important as the tradition of revolutionary utopianism in understanding the transformation of Soviet culture in the Stalinist revolution.

Movies for the masses is based on an extensive study of rare films, the periodical press, studio archives and fan mail. It makes a major contribution to the little-explored history of Soviet popular culture and will be widely read by students and specialists of film studies, Soviet studies, and popular culture.

Movies for the masses

MOVIES FOR THE MASSES

Popular cinema and Soviet society
in the 1920s

DENISE J. YOUNGBLOOD

Assistant Professor of History, University of Vermont

CAMBRIDGE
UNIVERSITY PRESS

Published by the Press Syndicate of the University of Cambridge
The Pitt Building, Trumpington Street, Cambridge CB2 1RP
40 West 20th Street, New York, NY 10011–4211, USA
10 Stamford Road, Oakleigh, Victoria 3166, Australia

Chapter 1 is based in part on research first published in
The Russian Review, 50, no. 2 (April 1991). Copyright 1991
by the Ohio State University Press.

First published 1992

Printed in Great Britain at the University Press, Cambridge

A catalogue record for this book is available from the British Library

Library of Congress cataloguing in publication data
Youngblood, Denise J., 1952–
Movies for the masses: popular cinema and Soviet society in the
1920s / Denise J. Youngblood.
   p.   cm.
Filmography
Includes bibliographical references (p.   ) and index.
ISBN 0 521 37470 7
1. Motion pictures – Soviet Union – History. 2. Motion pictures –
Social aspects – Soviet Union. 3. Soviet Union – Popular culture.
1. Title.
PN1993.5.R9Y6 1992
791.43′0947 – dc20   91-38272   CIP
ISBN 0 521 37470 7 hardback

For Katharyn Webb,
who sparked my interest in Russia
and for Stuart Grover,
who rekindled it.

CONTENTS

ILLUSTRATIONS

FILMS

CARICATURES OF SOVIET AND WESTERN POPULAR CINEMA

MISCELLANY

TABLES

PREFACE

Movies for the Masses is in some respects a sequel to my *Soviet Cinema in the Silent Era* (1985). While building on the earlier work, it takes a very different look at the period. By focusing exclusively on the popular films which comprised the so-called "commercial deviation," it is my intention to demonstrate that the rhetoric of cultural politics and the emphasis of the historiography on the avant-garde notwithstanding, the film culture of the NEP was predominantly and aggressively "bourgeois" – and enjoyed patronage that cut across class lines and political allegiances. I will argue that the extent to which Western and pre-revolutionary taste cultures and the pre-revolutionary middle class dominated the film world is as central as the tradition of revolutionary utopianism in understanding the transformation of Soviet culture in the Stalin Revolution.

Exploration of the dynamics of cultural politics – and especially of the clash of class, ideology, and culture – has been an important part of the work done in Soviet studies in the last twenty years. These issues were first raised by Sheila Fitzpatrick in numerous works of the seventies and early eighties, beginning with her book *The Commissariat of Enlightenment* (1970). Other noteworthy examples of monographs which have added to our understanding of the complex of contradictions that was NEP society are Kendall Bailes's *Technology and Society under Lenin and Stalin* (1978), Peter Kenez's *The Birth of the Propaganda State* (1985), Alan Ball's *Russia's Last Capitalists* (1987), and William J. Chase's *Workers, Society, and the Soviet State* (1988). Because of the prominent position cinema occupied in Soviet culture and the numbers of people it reached, cinema is an exceptional paradigm for further examination of those issues that are at the heart of early Soviet social and cultural history.

But this work emerged from other historiographical contexts as well. Historians of late Imperial and early Soviet Russia are moving away from the "politics and high culture" focus which dominated research for so long (albeit for very good reasons), and some of the most exciting recent work in the field has been in the area of popular culture. Among these pioneering works which seek to give the past a "human face" and broaden the definition of "culture" are S. Frederick Starr's study of Soviet jazz (*Red and Hot*, 1983), Jeffrey Brooks's examination of popular print culture in the nineteenth and early twentieth centuries (*When Russia Learned to Read*, 1985), Richard Stites's magisterial survey of Russian varieties of entertainment (*Soviet Popular Culture*, 1992), and the collections of essays edited by Hans Günther (*The Culture of the Stalin Period*, 1990) and John Strong (*Essays on Revolutionary Culture and Stalinism*, 1990).

The past several years have witnessed an efflorescence of work on culture and society in the earliest years of Soviet power, especially during the Civil War. Monographs like Zenovia Sochor's *Revolution and Culture* (1988), Richard Stites's *Revolutionary Dreams* (1989), Lynn Mally's *Culture of the Future* (1990), and Christopher Read's *Culture and Power in Revolutionary Russia* (1990) collectively challenge received wisdom. William G. Rosenberg's source book *Bolshevik Visions* (1984) and essay collections such as Abbott Gleason et al., eds., *Bolshevik Culture* (1985) and Diane P. Koenker et al., eds., *Party, State, and Society in the Russian Civil War* (1989) do the same. It seems to me that these studies, which question the extent to which Bolshevik cultural policies were naturally or inevitably "authoritarian," must logically give rise to a reevaluation of the culture of the NEP. *Movies for the Masses* is part of this dialogue too.

Finally, I hope this work is also a contribution to cinema studies, though to its historical rather than its theoretical or critical aspects. In the eighties, cinema studies saw a veritable invasion from specialists in other disciplines, especially from those trained in literature, politics, and history. In the Soviet field, this was inaugurated by Richard Taylor's *The Politics of the Soviet Cinema, 1917–1929* (1979), and since then Taylor has made contributions to the study of Soviet cinema too prolific to do justice to here. Nancy Condee, Peter Kenez, Anna Lawton, Vladimir Padunov, and Richard Stites are other noteworthy exemplars of this "cross-over" phenomenon. While I am aware that these incursions have not always been welcomed by our colleagues in film, the increased interdisciplinary communication in the past few years can only enrich our knowledge and our scholarship.

Though my own work may not adequately reflect it, I have learned a great deal about film and the cinematic way of thinking from the works of David Bordwell, Ian Christie, Vance Kepley, Judith Mayne, Annette Michelson, Vlada Petrić, and Kristin Thompson – scholars on the "other side" of that invisible line that divides cinema history from history. And I am pleased to point out that they have been known to cross the border, too. One of the finest pieces of Soviet cultural history written in the eighties came not from a "real historian," but from a film scholar: Kepley's critical biography of Aleksandr Dovzhenko, *In the Service of the State* (1986).

It gives me pleasure to acknowledge the generosity of my colleagues in helping me bring this project to fruition. Vance Kepley, Anna Lawton, Vlada Petrić, Thomas Saunders, and Richard Taylor assisted me in one or more of the following ways: by writing letters on my behalf, reading chapters, sharing their unpublished research with me, and alerting me to the latest relevant publications before the ink was dry. Lois Becker set aside her research on Herzen to serve as "lay reader" of the manuscript, and, at the eleventh hour, I benefited from Kristin Thompson's careful reading and thoughtful suggestions. My greatest debt is to Peter Kenez and Richard Stites, who not only did all the above, but also read every word of the manuscript – sometimes more than once. Their questions, criticisms, counsel, and encouragement were invaluable.

Additional assistance, both tangible (data and other materials) and intangible (ideas), came from François Albèra, William Chase, Marc Ferro, J. T. Heil, Yuri Tsivian, Maia Turovskaia, and William K. Wolf. The Department of History at the University of Vermont has proven a most congenial working environment, and my department chair, James H. Overfield, has been exceptionally supportive of my scheduling and funding requests. My students Scot Ballard, Kelly Kivler, and Bonnie J. Palifka were able research assistants.

I wish to thank the following institutions for making their resources available to me over the past decade: the All-Union State Institute of Cinematography (VGIK, Moscow), the British Film Institute (London), the Central State Archive of Literature and Art (TsGALI, Moscow), the Hoover Institution, the Lenin Library (Moscow), the Library of Congress, the Museum of Modern Art, the New York Public Library, the Pacific Film Archive, the Stanford University Libraries, and the University of Illinois Library. Linda Artel, Ian Christie, David H. Kraus, Hilja Kukk, and Wojciech Zalewski were especially helpful in obtaining films and print materials for me.

I am grateful to the American Council of Learned Societies, the International Research & Exchanges Board, the National Endowment for the Humanities, and the University of Vermont's College of Arts and

Sciences, Graduate College, and Department of History for their financial support, which permitted me to conduct the research on which this work is based and to attend numerous conferences where I presented preliminary versions of various chapters.

And last, but far from least, thanks are due my husband Stanley and my son Ethan, who have tolerated my obsession with Soviet movies and my hours before the computer with remarkable forbearance.

NOTE ON TRANSLATION, TRANSLITERATION, DATES

All titles (including film titles) appear in the text in English, except for *Pravda* (and its variant *Komsomolskaia pravda*) and *Izvestiia*. In the notes and bibliography, titles are given in Russian, without translation. All translations in the text and notes are my own, unless otherwise stated.

Transliteration is according to the Library of Congress system, except that both hard and soft signs (rendered " and ') have been omitted throughout, and "Eisenstein" is used instead of "Eizenshtein" in the text. The Russian word for film, now *film*, was feminine gender, *filma*, in the twenties. Hyphenation of compound words formed with *kino* was variable; e.g., *kino-promyshlennost* and *kinopromyshlennost* were both correct.

The filmography includes the Russian title for all movies mentioned, cross-referenced with other English variants. Since a primary focus of this study is audience reception, dates for films in the text are release dates, rather than production dates, but both are listed in the filmography. The filmography also includes a list of foreign films cited.

ABBREVIATIONS, ACRONYMS, AND RUSSIAN TERMS

agitprop   Bureau of Agitation and Propaganda
Amerikanshchina   "Americanism" or "Americanitis" (pejorative)
apparat/apparatchik   Soviet bureaucracy/Soviet bureaucrat (pejorative)
ARK   Association of Revolutionary Cinematography
ARRK   Association of Workers in Revolutionary Cinematography
AR(R)Kovtsy   Members of AR(R)K
bedniak   Poor peasant
byt/bytovoi   Noun/adjective referring to "everyday life"
Cheka/Chekist   Extraordinary Commission to Combat Counter-Espionage/member of that body
chinovnik   Tsarist bureaucrat
Glaviskusstvo   Main Arts Administration of the Commissariat of Enlightenment
Glavpolitprosvet   Main Committee on Political Education of the Commissariat of Enlightenment
Glavrepertkom   Main Committee on Repertory of the Commissariat of Enlightenment
Glavvosh   Main Military School for the Physical Education of Workers
Goskino   "State Cinema" (film trust and production studio)
Goskinprom Gruzii   "State Cinema Enterprise of Georgia" (studio)
GTK   State Cinema Technicum
inostranshchina   "Foreignism" or "foreignitis" (pejorative)
Istpart   Institute of the History of the Communist Party
KEM   Experimental Cinema Workshop
Komsomol/*komsomolets*/*komsomolka*   Communist Youth League/male member/female member
kuleshovtsy   Followers or protégés of director Lev Kuleshov
kulak   Rich peasant

kulturfilm   Educational film
kupechestvo   Merchant caste (pre-revolutionary estate)
Leningradkino   "Leningrad Cinema" (studio)
meschane   Petty-bourgeoisie (pre-revolutionary estate)
meshchanstvo   Petty-bourgeois philistinism (pejorative)
Mezhrabpom   "International Workers' Aid" (studio)
Narkompros   Commissariat of Enlightenment
Narkomtorg   Commissariat of Trade
NEP   New Economic Policy
ODSK   Society of Friends of Soviet Cinema
peredvizhki   "Travelling" movie projectors
Politburo   Political Bureau of the Communist Party of the Soviet
    Union
Proletkino   "Proletarian Cinema" (studio)
Proletkult   Proletarian Culture (movement)
protazanovtsy   Protégés of director Iakov Protazanov
Rabis   Art Workers' Union
RAPP   Russian Association of Proletarian Writers
RSFSR   Russian Soviet Federated Socialist Republic
Rus   "Russia" (studio)
Sevzapkino   "Northwestern Cinema" (studio)
Sovkino   "Soviet Cinema" (film trust and studio)
sovkinovtsy   Sovkino employees
Sovnarkom   Council of People's Commissars
spetsy   Bourgeois specialists
Teakinopechat   Theater-Cinema Publishing Company
TsGALI   Central State Archive of Literature and Art
valiuta   Hard currency
VAPP   All-Russian Association of Proletarian Writers
VGIK   All-Union State Institute of Cinematography
Vpered   *Forward* (journal and faction of the Russian Social Democratic
    Labor Party)
VSNKh   Supreme Council of the National Economy
VUFKU   "All-Ukrainian Photo-Cinema Administration" (studio)

INTRODUCTION

Without fear of exaggeration, a wide use can be predicted for this invention [cinema] because of its tremendous novelty ... The thirst for such strange, fantastic sensations as it gives will grow ever greater, and we will be increasingly less able and less willing to grasp the everyday impressions of ordinary life.   (Maksim Gorkii, 1896[1])

In 1896, Maksim Gorkii saw his first moving picture at the great fair in Nizhnii Novgorod and wrote about it eloquently. Shortly after the turn of the century, movies theatres were flourishing in European Russia, enchanting audiences from the Emperor Nicholas II to Vladimir Breslav, the druggist's errand boy who was to become the Soviet director Fridrikh Ermler.[2] Since French money was important in financing the development of capitalism in the Empire and the French dominated the early film industry everywhere, it is not surprising that French production companies (beginning with Lumière) set up shop. Russia obviously had the potential to become a substantial market for French films, but French companies were also interested in making "Russian" movies to show in Russia and in Europe, to take advantage of Russia's exotic cachet abroad.

These French entrepreneurs were eventually joined by Russians, as it became clear that the "novelty" was a permanent one, and that there was a great deal of money to be made in the first truly mass form of entertainment. Many early Russian filmmakers came from the merchant caste (*kupechestvo*), and Moscow's merchant district became the capital of Russian cinema. The business proved to be unstable, and studio failures were common, but some native producers (notably Aleksandr Drankov, Iosif Ermolev, and Aleksandr Khanzhonkov) demonstrated the combination of business sense and instinctive understanding of the audience necessary to compete with French firms for domestic audiences. Although technical aspects of filmmaking, especially cinematography, remained the domain of French cameramen like Louis Forestier,[3] important native directors emerged – Evgenii Bauer, Vladimir Gardin, and

Iakov Protazanov, among others. Talented and photogenic actors were drawn to cinema as well, the most famous being the legendary heartthrob Vera Kholodnaia (who died in 1919 of influenza, at the pinnacle of her popularity).

Russians made their debut films in 1908, twelve years after the first public screenings, and their early forays were, not surprisingly, filled with comic misadventures.[4] Since by 1908 film culture was an international one, Russian filmmakers tended to follow the formulas for entertainment films already established by European and American directors. As was the case in Europe in particular, "art films" like historical epics (especially from the sixteenth and seventeenth centuries) and adaptations of Russian literary classics (especially the works of Lev Tolstoi) appealed to viewers' sensibilities. Comedies were popular too, but these remained for the most part the domain of foreign stars. The French comedian Max Linder was a particular favorite with Russian audiences. But sensational love stories (often based on popular novels) and lurid melodramas also attracted a large movie-going public, drawn from the lower urban classes, especially the petty-bourgeoisie (*meshchane*). This public demanded a rather remarkable level of violence and catastrophe in its entertainment films: romance was better thwarted, especially if ending in death – whether by murder, suicide, or some other tragedy. Multiple deaths were best of all.[5]

The events of August 1914 did not have an immediate effect on the flourishing Russian film industry, but eventually "Germans" (like the prosperous Thiemann and Reinhardt studio) were drummed out of the business. As elsewhere in Europe, the tsarist regime realized that movies could serve a useful service, and feature and documentary films were used to support the war effort. Entertainment directors found it quite easy to adapt the "catastrophe" melodrama so popular in Russia to war themes and stepped up production to fill the void left by the reduction in numbers of foreign films.

The year 1917 saw two revolutions and the end of the old order in a social cataclysm of unmatched proportions. Filmmakers watched events unfolding with mounting nervousness. Their fears were realized when the Bolsheviks nationalized the film industry in 1919, and exceeded when that nationalized industry was placed under the ideological control of the Commissariat of Enlightenment. While the Bolsheviks had no ready-made arts policy (and indeed, quarreled among themselves about cultural policies to the end of the decade), it was reasonably clear to any but the most obtuse of the "bourgeois" directors and producers that the purposes of cinema – and certainly the dispensation of its profits – would change under Bolshevik jurisdiction.

Nationalization, like many other early Bolshevik decrees and proclamations, proved difficult to enforce in the chaos of the Civil War. In any case, most of the production companies had already packed up and headed south, leaving inhospitable Moscow for Yalta, where producers set up makeshift studios and created a temporary Russian Hollywood on the Black Sea (a scheme that was almost resurrected in the thirties, when the Soviet film industry was under the leadership of Boris Shumiatskii). As the fortunes of the White Armies faded, so did those of the Russian movie moguls. By the winter of 1919–20, most members of the Black Sea studios had fled, taking their films, their equipment, and their talent and expertise. These filmmakers joined Russian emigré colonies in Paris and Berlin and formed their own studios or worked for French and German firms.[6] Some of them even made it to America.

At home, in Soviet Russia, the film industry may have been in ruins, but many budding filmmakers and cinéastes believed along with some of the revolutionary intelligentsia that backwardness had its advantages. In keeping with the heady utopianism that accompanied the tragedies of the Civil War and the grinding hardships of war communism, they believed that the destruction of the "rotten, bourgeois" Russian film industry cleared the way for the creation of a totally new film art. Cinema was to be the art of the revolution. As if from nowhere, talented young men and women (some of them, like Grigorii Kozintsev and Leonid Trauberg, actually in their teens) emerged to fill the void left by the emigrés. Colorfully decorated trains, carrying short propaganda films called *agitki*, rumbled through a countryside torn by civil war, bringing the Bolshevik promise of a new world. In a country crippled by mass illiteracy, cinema had enormous potential as a tool for educators and propagandists as well as for the "soldiers" of the cinematic avant-garde.

After the war, the economy slowly stabilized, and the institution of the New Economic Policy enabled more theatres to reopen. Enthusiastic young filmmakers set out to revolutionize cinema in earnest, as like-minded artists continued the revolutions in theatre, painting, poetry, and architecture which had begun early in the century. Some of these new directors had gained filmmaking experience during the Civil War (like Dziga Vertov). Some came from the theatre, especially modernist companies such as the Meierkhold theatres (like Sergei Eisenstein). Still others came from their own filmmaking collectives where they made films "without film" because no film stock was to be had (like Lev Kuleshov or the team of Grigorii Kozintsev and Leonid Trauberg). Many were connected in some fashion with the Proletkult, an ambitious if rather amorphous movement which sought to foster the development of a specifically "proletarian" culture in Soviet Russia.[7] Eisenstein's first feature film, *Strike*, was in fact credited as a production of the Proletkult collective.

Other youthful film enthusiasts left established "middle-class" professions in the arts and sciences for the art of the future, the cinema. (Aleksandr Dovzhenko abandoned painting; Vsevolod Pudovkin, engineering; Abram Room, psychiatry.) These men (and women, like film editor and documentarist Esfir Shub) not only revolutionized Russian cinema – they created *Soviet* cinema. In so doing, they earned a secure place for themselves in the international history of the art of the cinema. Dozens of books and articles (and even films), in many languages, testify to their enduring genius.[8]

The relatively relaxed attitude toward diversity and pluralism that was part of cultural "policies" during the period of NEP encouraged cultural ferment, and the new Soviet cinema appeared to fit in effortlessly. This was the era of the film without a hero (unless that "hero" were the masses) and of a film without a plot (unless that "plot" were the Revolution). This period of glorious, unfettered experimentation came to an ignominious end in 1928, when Joseph Stalin, who had brought his political rivals to heel, looked around and did not like what he saw in any aspect of the arts, let alone in cinema. By 1932, film directors, like all other artists, lost all vestiges of artistic independence and entered the service of the state. Directors who could not or would not make "movies for the millions" according to the rigid formulas of Socialist Realism did not make movies at all. Soviet cinema entered a new and terrible phase of its history, but a phase understandably overshadowed by the titanic struggles at the top of society, and the misery below.

This interpretation of Russian and early Soviet film history, which has enjoyed remarkable longevity in Western historiography, is quite problematic.[9] But while the triumphs of the artistic innovators in the twenties and their apparent demise in the thirties are a true and important part of the story, they are perhaps the smallest part. Certainly no one can deny the significance of the contributions of the Soviet avant-garde to world culture, and the film classics of the twenties are central to that legacy. Analysis of the history of the cinema avant-garde (and the reasons for its demise) has told us much about Soviet cultural politics, the problems of the Russian intelligentsia, the pervasiveness of revolutionary utopianism during the NEP, and the dynamics of the Stalin Revolution.

But urban life in the twenties looks very different when viewed through the prism of popular culture, and an analysis of popular cinema serves as a counterbalance to the utopianism of some Soviet cultural circles. Just as Soviet high culture in this period had obvious antecedents in the Russian past, so Russian popular culture lived on after the Revolution. By the time revolution broke out in 1917, the Russian popular filmmaking tradition was an intrinsic aspect of urban life and exhibited exceptional resiliency in the face of crushing adversity.

It is true that many of the biggest names of Russian cinema had left by 1919, but a substantial number of experienced directors, assistants, cameramen, scenarists, editors, and players stayed. Moreover, a few who emigrated, like Iakov Protazanov, returned to the Soviet Union to great fanfare (on a scale only slightly more modest than the fanfare accompanying Maksim Gorkii's return). These men and women not only brought decades of collective technical experience to the "fledgling" Soviet film industry, they also served as a bridge to a past that at times in the twenties seemed all too distant. Most of them were well-educated members of the numerically small Russian middle classes (primarily the *kupechestvo* and the *meshchane*), but, regardless of class background, they were all successful commercial artists. Their contributions to Soviet popular culture were significant, and their work reinforced the "bourgeois" values and tastes which predominated in the cities, existing side by side with utopian vestiges from the Civil War period.

Young Soviet filmmakers may have changed the face of world cinema, but the unvarnished truth is that Soviet audiences in the twenties did not like the pictures that made film history, finding them dull and difficult to understand. Few pictures from the revolutionary avant-garde can be labelled box-office successes with any degree of confidence, not even *Potemkin*, although there was a concerted effort undertaken at the time to correct the record.[10] Soviet audiences, like Russian audiences before them, went to the movies for entertainment – not for "art," and certainly not for education. If they could pick up a little history at the same time, or see a screen adaptation of one of Pushkin's tales, all the better, but the entertainment factor was paramount. The "old specialists" from the pre-revolutionary cinema understood this very well. Despite the best efforts of the "revolutionaries" – whether artists or politicians – socialist values had not percolated down to the level of popular culture (even if one could agree on what the values of socialism were).

More evidence that this was true can be found in the reception accorded foreign films, which Soviet audiences preferred to native productions in most cases. The extraordinary popularity of foreign films attests to the persistence of the pre-revolutionary Westernized "bourgeois" taste cultures in early Soviet society, as well as to the inability of Soviet directors to fill the demand for "Western-style" films. Although first German, and then American, films replaced the French in terms of popularity, they all had their afficionados among audiences. Delays in the arrival of the latest Western hits caused much angst among regular movie-goers, so it seems certain that at least some Soviet citizens still felt themselves very much part of an international community, even if it were only a cinema community. Through movies and movie magazines, they religiously kept up with the "news" from abroad.

Movies for the Masses is the history of this "forgotten" Soviet cinema, the popular cinema. "Popular" has several different definitions when applied to culture; here we will be using it to mean the commercial culture of the urban classes, Pierre Bourdieu's "middle art."[11] In cinema, it refers to those entertainment films whose primary appeal with audiences may be attributed to their conformity to conventional visual styles and narrative structures. Didactic or aesthetic elements were always secondary to the plot and characterization.

Despite formidable political and economic obstacles which hamstrung the popular directors from making such commercial films, they managed to turn out movies which dominated the box-office in the breathing space between the Civil War and the Stalin Revolution, from approximately 1924 to 1930. As narrative and descriptive history makes a comeback, it is once again possible to assert without embarrassment that some stories are worth telling because they are intrinsically interesting, and for what they can reveal about the mentality of the times. This history of the commercial cinema of the NEP seems to be one of them, but it is worth telling for other reasons as well.

The three most important of these additional factors – the time frame, the nature of the audience, and the character of the films – relate to specific concerns in Soviet history. This period in which the commercial cinema flourished roughly corresponds to the life of the state film trust Sovkino, whose administrators championed films of this type, but it also fits the approximate parameters of the New Economic Policy (1921–28) and the Cultural Revolution (1928–32). These are, of course, two of the most pivotal – and most controversial – periods in Soviet history, as historians seek to unravel the origins of Stalinism and understand the dynamics of Stalinization. The NEP has undergone especially intensive scrutiny in the Gorbachev era for a different reason – as a "road not taken" and a potential "native" model for *perestroika*.

The demographics of the movie business in the twenties are also significant, though in one sense they deflate Lenin's maxim that "cinema is for us the most important of all arts." In terms of theatres, audiences, and numbers of films produced, mainstream film culture in the USSR was definitely centered in the RSFSR. For these reasons, although films from the republic studios do make occasional appearances in these pages, the focus here is Russian for the most part.[12] But even in the RSFSR, we cannot argue that film at this time was a mass phenomenon. The audience represented a small proportion of the population; perhaps no more than 2 million Russians were regular movie-goers.[13] In 1927 there were fewer than 1,500 movie theatres (scarcely more than had existed in Russia in 1913); most were located, moreover, in the largest cities of European Russia.[14] And yet small though it was, this target population was a critical mass, the urban advance guard in a society on the brink of rapid urbanization.

Finally, as had been the case before the Revolution, popular cinema was defined by models that were labelled "Western" and seen to be a reflection of a "bourgeois" or "petty bourgeois" culture not believed to be fully "Russian." Foreign movies nearly always beat the Soviet competition at the box-office, and Soviet popular directors not surprisingly attempted to emulate the products that sold. By studying popular cinema culture, we have an opportunity to examine the continuing impact of European cultural influences on Soviet society, the effect of the introduction of American influences, and the responses to this new wave of "cultural imperialism."

Yet although there was considerable foreign influence on early Soviet cinema culture, "Western" did not necessarily mean foreign, and the class element cannot be overlooked, especially given the role of class in Bolshevik ideology. Despite the formation of new cadres, the commercial film industry was still dominated by native directors from the pre-revolutionary middle class. Analysis of the cinema culture of the twenties also gives us a chance to explore the continuing influence of the old bourgeoisie on the development of Soviet culture, as well as the possibilities for social mobility during the NEP. In this process, the validity of class conceptions of culture – and the definition of "Russianness" as something divorced from any European trends – must be carefully scrutinized.

Because my fundamental purpose here is to recreate the cinema culture of the twenties in order to explore these interrelated issues, rather than to demonstrate change over time (which was the focus of *Soviet Cinema in the Silent Era*), the work is thematically organized. My guiding principle in arranging the material was to move from the general to the specific, although it proved impossible to adhere to that principle with absolute rigor. Given the web of interconnections and my desire to select representative rather than arcane examples, it was sometimes necessary to use the same film as illustration in more than one chapter.

The book is divided into three sections. Part 1 provides the contexts – historical, ideological, and international – in which Soviet popular cinema developed. The first chapter is a historical summary which focuses on these conditions which led to a flowering of popular cinema, particularly the policies of the state film trust Sovkino. It also describes the characteristics and evolution of the cinema culture of the 1920s. Despite the success with viewers of Sovkino's policy of support for entertainment films, the revitalization of a native commercial cinema faced serious obstacles, both abstract and concrete, which will be the subjects of the second and third chapters. Chapter 2 focuses on the controversies about the nature of "mass" art in a socialist society, to wit, whether the purpose of cinema should be to entertain or to enlighten, a debate which had parallels in other Soviet cultural institutions as well. Chapter 3 examines the influence of foreign films, and particularly the impact of the American cinematic leviathan on a nascent national film industry, a problem Soviet Russia shared with other European countries.

Part 2 presents an analysis of the Soviet popular film industry in practice. Chapter 4 is devoted to a discussion of the most popular genres, and the most popular films within those genres, in order to examine the ways in which "bourgeois" filmmakers accommodated themselves both to the Soviet regime and their Russian past. Chapter 5 analyzes recurring images from the popular cinema to see how Western "types" were modified to fit Soviet social and political reality. It also seeks to explain, first, why the popular cinema failed to create convincing heroes among the types – and second, why it failed to foster the careers of actors who could compete with foreign stars in the competition for the audience. Chapter 6 centers on the career of the king of Soviet popular cinema. Iakov Protazanov (1881–1945), whose work exemplifies the strengths and weaknesses of the Soviet entertainment film industry – and whose person provides a compelling link between past and present.

Part 3 presents three Soviet alternatives to the "bourgeois" entertainment film to determine the degree to which it was possible to "politicize" entertainment and still entertain. Chapter 7 focuses on the work of a young director who, like Protazanov, worked for the premier commercial studio, Mezhrabpom. Boris Barnet (1902–65) experimented with genres but did his best commercial work in comedy. Chapter 8 examines the social melodramas of Fridrikh Ermler (1898–1967), perhaps the quintessential Soviet director in terms of biography: a proletarian, a Bolshevik, and a former member of the secret police. Finally, chapter 9 discusses the transmogrification of the entertainment film into "factory and tractor" films, primarily during the Cultural Revolution.

The popular cinema of the New Economic Policy period was firmly rooted in the Russian past with strong connections to the European present. Its history has the potential to serve as a paradigm for analysis of a nation in transition. As such it can contribute to the analysis of class culture in the classless society and of the socio-cultural functions of "the most important of the arts."[15] But on another level, the human level, it also provides us with a fleeting glimpse of how ordinary people (movie-goers) and fairly ordinary people (filmmakers) engaged in everyday pursuits and attempted to cope in a time of turbulent change.

PART 1

CONTEXTS

CHAPTER 1 A HISTORICAL OVERVIEW "FROM BELOW"

Cinema exists for the masses, not the masses for the cinema.

(Ippolit Sokolov, 1929[1])

Soviet Russian cinema rose from the ashes of world war, revolution, and civil war in the early twenties. The cinema revolutionaries believed that film as the "last born" of the arts, has been less contaminated by bourgeois ideology than the other arts. It therefore had the most possibilities for development in a socialist society.[2] Stimulated by the economic recovery engendered by the New Economic Policy, a cultural climate amenable to diversity, and the capable leadership of Sovkino administrators I. P. Trainin and M. P. Efremov, in 1924 Soviet cinema began a period of rapid growth. The results were, however, not quite what the aesthetic radicals had hoped for.

True, some remarkable experimental films were made, primarily under the aegis of Sovkino, but most Soviet films were unabashedly commercial products. These popular movies, designed to cater to the tastes of the mass audience, made a respectable showing against the formidable popularity of foreign films. The cinema culture of the twenties was a multifaceted one, but one based on "bourgeois" entertainment films of foreign and Soviet origins. It was the profits from these films which funded the work of the avant-garde.

PREHISTORY: 1921–1924

The Civil War was over by November 1920, but the Bolshevik government immediately met a new series of crises: famine in the Volga, rebellion at Kronstadt, and the peasant uprising in the Tambov region. Behind this turmoil was the irrefutable fact that the economy had totally collapsed. Facing calamity in 1921, Lenin decided that the only way forward was backward, and he began his great retreat – the return to a partial market economy known as the New Economic Policy. The

New Economic Policy lasted until 1928 and gave its name to an era: NEP.

The NEP was to have a profound impact on the revitalization of the film industry and on its evolution in the twenties. Distribution and most production remained nationalized, but foreign investment was encouraged, and many theatres were run by private entrepreneurs.[3] Until cinema revenues surpassed those from other sources, notably vodka, the government expected it to depend on its profits from sales and rentals to fund future productions.[4] This new market orientation led to a diversification of the repertory, since few doubted that the agit-films which had been the staple of production during the Civil War would not attract paying audiences.

In 1921, however, any advantages to be gained from the NEP for cinema appeared to be far in the future; indeed the period from 1921–1924 is "prehistoric" in terms of our concerns. A mere twelve feature films were produced in 1921; only sixteen in 1922. Although the latter figure represents a 33 per cent increase over the previous year, it should be compared with the fifty-seven films made in 1919.[5] (While it is true that most movies produced in 1919 were "shorts" of one to four reels, seven of the sixteen films made in 1922 fell into this category, still a substantial proportion.) Recycled pre-revolutionary films, in well-worn copies, played ramshackle theatres (if the projectionist deigned to show up and the projector worked).[6] A few foreign films, of ancient vintage, also began to appear.[7]

In 1922, in recognition of the "crisis," the Council of People's Commissars (Sovnarkom) authorized the establishment of a new state cinema enterprise, called Goskino, which would have a distribution monopoly.[8] The monopoly was necessitated by the fact that the nationalization decree of 1919 had proven difficult to effect, and three quasi-private studios were still in operation in the RSFSR: Sevzapkino (which made seven of the sixteen pictures produced in 1922), Proletkino, and Rus. A fourth studio, Mezhrabpom, which subsumed Rus in 1924, was essentially independent and supported financially by the German socialist organization, International Arbeitershilfe (International Worker's Relief) though its style remained in essence that of the Rus studio.[9]

This distribution monopoly (which had its counterparts in other sectors of the NEP economy, like the publishing industry) did not, however, achieve the desired results, and Goskino was never able to establish itself as a power in filmmaking. At the end of 1923, Goskino supposedly had only 27,000 rubles left in its treasury, not enough to finance even one film.[10] While it is true that production increased almost

50 percent from 1922 to 1923 and more than doubled the following year, the number of films was still too small to make a significant impact on the market.

In 1924, approximately 95 percent of the films in distribution were foreign – "petty bourgeois, stupid, and dull," in the words of a contemporary critic.[11] These foreign films were certainly "petty bourgeois"; some of them may even have been "stupid," though classics like *Dr. Caligari's Cabinet* were among their number. It was obvious, however, that Soviet audiences did not find them "dull." Viewers believed virtually any foreign picture to be more entertaining than a Soviet film and clamored for more. Until 1924, German films predominated, but after that there was an apparently insatiable demand for the latest American hits.[12]

The movie theatres were in deplorable condition, especially in Moscow. One of the most vivid early descriptions came from the English journalist Huntly Carter. Carter reported on the basis of observations made in 1922 that only 90 of Moscow's 143 movie theatres were still in operation – and just barely:

I visited the "Mirror" kino in Tverskoi, another of Moscow's fashionable thoroughfares ... The decorated ceiling had been newly decorated by shot and shell and had a special ventilation system introduced by the method of dropping eggs from aeroplanes. The windows were patched with odds and ends of timber, and the seats were in splints and looking unusually frowsy. Most of them were just plain wooden benches. Two dim lights made their appearance during the intervals, which were pretty frequent. An ancient screen, suffering from jaundice, and a worn-out projector, buried in an emergency cement structure and half hidden by a dirty curtain, as though ashamed of itself, completed the fitments.[13]

None of the contemporary Soviet sources was as colorful as Carter; after all, Soviet film writers had to maintain a modicum of national pride. But they confirmed that theatres were extremely run-down and noted with embarrassment the shocked reaction of foreigners to the best Soviet Russia had to offer.[14]

The situation in provincial theatres, not surprisingly, was much worse. Managers had no choice of films, and the shortages were acute enough that theatres frequently had no films at all to show. Rental rates were much higher than before the Revolution; it was difficult for theatre owners to make a living, let alone a "bourgeois" profit.[15]

Ticket prices were also high. At the Mirror theatre, which Carter described so fetchingly, the price of a single ticket for a one-hour show ranged from 700,000 to 2 million rubles. This was caused in large part by the extraordinary inflation that accompanied the first phase of the NEP and was exacerbated by the steep luxury tax on movie tickets (30 percent in 1922). Nonetheless, as Carter noted, "notwithstanding the prices and the brevity, the proletarians rolled up."[16]

This, then, was the situation in 1924, which was a turning-point in Soviet film history, and the true start to our story.

THE SOVKINO ERA: 1924–1928

Sovkino and the studios

In 1923, the government had created the so-called Mantsev Commission to study the problems of film production. At the 13th Party Congress in 1924, the Commission recommended the abolition of Goskino. Due to political infighting, this recommendation was not put into effect until December 1924. At this time, a new state cinema enterprise called Sovkino was organized as a joint stock company held by the Commissariat of Trade (Narkomtorg), the Commissariat of Enlightenment (Narkompros), the Leningrad and Moscow Soviets, and the Supreme Council of the National Economy (VSNKh). Sovkino took over the distribution monopoly.[17]

Centralization of film production continued over the following two years as unprofitable studios like Proletkino and Sevzapkino folded (although Sevzapkino had made some successful pictures). The process was complete by the end of 1926. At that time there were three major studios in the RSFSR: Mezhrabpom-Rus, the Moscow Sovkino studio (the former Goskino studio) and the Leningrad Sovkino studio (first called Leningradkino, this studio had emerged from the remains of the bankrupt Sevzapkino).[18] The most important non-Russian studios were Goskinprom Gruzii, the Georgian studio, and VUFKU, the Ukrainian studio.) (Because of a feud between VUFKU and Sovkino over distribution rights, relatively few Ukrainian films enjoyed first-runs in major Russian theatres.)

Sovkino took its financial dealings seriously and never forgot that cinema had to pay for itself. From its inception, Sovkino pursued a two-pronged policy of support for big-budget entertainment films and importation of the latest foreign hits. Domestic production was intended to succeed abroad as well as at home, and hence these films were labelled by their detractors as "export" films. The rationale behind the policy was that by giving audiences what they wanted in large doses, Soviet cinema could become self-sufficient. Some of the profits earned through the commercial sector of the industry would then be channeled into the production of films less likely to succeed with the mass audience.

When Sovkino took over, Soviet films for the most part were not perceived as entertaining. Ilia Trainin, a member of Sovkino's collegium, and a leading propagandist for entertainment films, characterized the situation Sovkino faced this way in a speech to the Moscow Art Workers' Union (Rabis):

With agit-films, [viewers] expect [to see] pretentious films in which the agitational side predominates, in which numerous intertitles abound, often very revolutionary, but at the same time very boring. This "revolutionary" zeal often drives them back to foreign "art" pictures, and so in this fashion, the whole point of such agit-films is lost. We need to begin a struggle for a really artistic film, in which its own action and entertainment would be agitational.[19]

For the first time, a state film trust executive had acknowledged that entertainment might have an official role in Soviet cinema, if only to "agitate."

The studios' limited financial resources was a critical factor in the poor quality of most Soviet films, as Trainin freely admitted. Productions costing 50,000 rubles (the typical budget for a Soviet movie) could not be expected to compete with the lavish scale of Hollywood films, so Trainin proposed several solutions that were at the time rather radical: solicit foreign investment, develop joint ventures, and concentrate production on a few big-budget films that could be sold on the foreign market.[20] Trainin wanted Sovkino to continue importing foreign films, but in a selective and timely fashion to ensure the best return on the investment.

Sovkino's policies had a dramatic impact, and cinema recovered quickly. Sovkino followed through with Trainin's promise to fund big-budget films, and Trainin's prediction that such films would generate good box-office both at home and abroad proved accurate. Domestic films which were touted in the film press and in audience surveys as box-office successes are the subject of this book; they resembled Western pictures in terms of style, though most were at least superficially Soviet in content. Those that succeeded (or were purported to have succeeded) abroad were usually "exotic" – costume dramas tended to fare well. With the consolidation of the studios in 1926, the commercial orientation of Soviet cinema became even more pronounced.

Trainin's hopes for foreign investment in Soviet film production bore some fruit, as the curious case of Mezhrabpom demonstrates. Mezhrabpom's history, like Sovkino's, illustrated that profits and socialism were not considered mutually exclusive in some quarters. The German capital that funded it was communist money, to be sure, and Mezhrabpom had a number of "revolutionary" directors in its stable, producing one of the legendary pictures of the Golden Age, Vsevolod Pudovkin's *Mother.* Yet despite its impeccable revolutionary lineage, Mezhrabpom was also home to director Iakov Protazanov, the most bankable director of the pre-revolutionary Russian cinema, and, for many, the studio epitomized the "bourgeoisification" of Soviet cinema. The studio turned out hit after hit, and even its "revolutionary" films were reasonably enjoyable. Its record of commercial success (for which studio chief Moisei Aleinikov must be given substantial credit) was remarkable under the circumstances.[21]

Domestic production

With Sovkino and Mezhrabpom at the apex of Soviet filmmaking, production soared, and there was no longer a shortage of movies. The three-year period from 1926 to 1928 was the peak of commercial film production, with 148 feature films in 1928 (see table 1). Of course, only a few of these were hits, and fewer still were the cinematic masterpieces for which the era is known. Most Soviet movies were inexpensive films sent off to second-run theatres, provincial theatres, travelling shows (*peredvizhki*), or workers' clubs. If Soviet-made films were released to first-run houses, they generally played from two to three weeks. Avant-garde films frequently disappeared from the screen in a week or less.[22]

Although Dziga Vertov and his supporters liked to complain that Sovkino and theatre managers plotted to keep his films off the screen, the public's reaction to the films of Eisenstein, Dovzhenko, Vertov, and Kozintsev and Trauberg is well documented and unambiguous. Films "without scripts" or with a battleship as a hero generally did not appeal to the ordinary movie-goer, however much they appealed to critics. Yet there are some exceptions: Eisenstein's *Strike* was an avant-garde hit, running for thirty-seven days.[23]

The perception that avant-garde films were unprofitable and inaccessible to mass audiences persisted throughout the decade. In a 1929 interview, a theatre manager discussed the effect "revolutionary" films had on revenues. He noted that "the public watched [Dovzhenko's *Arsenal*] with great difficulty," and that attendance had dropped to 50 percent of normal when his theatre screened *New Babylon*, Kozintsev and Trauberg's famous picture about the Paris Commune. Asked about the reaction to Vertov's *The Man with the Movie Camera*, he replied sar-castically, "One hardly need say that if *New Babylon* didn't satisfy the spectator's requirements and 'lost' him, then *The Man with the Movie Camera* didn't satisfy him either."[24]

The films that did satisfy could not have been more different from the Young Turks' masterworks, and all will be discussed in some detail in subsequent chapters. Two lavish costume dramas, *The Decembrists* and *The Poet and the Tsar*, and the stunningly overwrought melodrama *The Bear's Wedding*, dominated the box-office for domestic fare. These three pictures were enormously expensive, but also enormously popular with Soviet viewers. *The Bear's Wedding* was novel enough to enjoy some success abroad as well.

Other Soviet pictures which were hits at home were a crime caper, *The Case of the Three Million*; a clever spoof of movie mania, *Mary Pickford's Kiss*; a three-part adventure serial, *Miss Mend*; a "three-handkerchief" Armenian story of love and betrayal, *Honor*; a comedy about the housing shortage, *The Girl with the Hatbox*; and a Civil War adventure-romance, *The Forty-First*.[25] Although the genres of such commercially successful films differed, all combined in varying measure two or more of the tested ingredients for popular entertainment – love, sex, violence, humor, action, human interest, and happy endings (though tragic endings could be satisfying, too, as they had been in the pre-revolutionary cinema). Such characteristics were generally absent from most avant-garde films. These pictures conformed to the conventions of narrative realism, a characteristic which also distinguished them from the majority of the avant-garde classics.[26]

Foreign imports

In terms of sheer volume, importation of foreign films reached its peak in 1924, Goskino's final year of operation, and dropped steadily thereafter (see table 1). It was a point of pride for the Soviets that in 1927, for the first time, Soviet productions topped the imports in number of titles. Numbers do not, however, necessarily coincide with popularity, and they did not in this case, as Soviet film critics and directors were painfully aware.

Sovkino imported the latest hits with less delay than earlier, and their popularity was unabated, even though Soviet cinema had entered its fabled Golden Age. Foreign films played the premier theatres in the major cities for months on end (sometimes at several theatres

Table 1. *New" films shown in the USSR, 1921–1933*

	Foreign	Soviet	Total
1921	3	12	15
1922	63	16	79
1923	278	28	306
1924	366	76	442
1925	347	90	437
1926	128	105	233
1927	72	141	213
1928	62	148	210
1929	68	106	174
1930	43	146	189
1931	5	103	108
1932	0	90	90
1933	0	35	35
Unknown	258	0	258
TOTAL	1,693	1,096	2,789

Sources: Figures on imports are based on Vance Kepley, Jr., and Betty Kepley, "Foreign Films on Soviet Screens, 1922–1931," *Quarterly Review of Film Studies* 4, no., 4 (Fall 1979): 430, which was in turn based on the Kartseva, Egorova, and Greiding catalogues in *Kino i vremia,* no. 1 (1960) and no. 4 (1965). For the 258 foreign films listed as "unknown," specific date of release in the USSR could not be determined. Figures on Soviet features are based on my analysis of *Sovetskie khudozhestvennye filmy,* vols. I and II (Moscow: Iskusstvo, 1961–64). (See appendix 1 in Youngblood, *Soviet Cinema,* for more details.) Soviet film production has also been analyzed in Taylor and Christie, *Film Factory,* p. 424 and Steven P. Hill, "A Quantitative View of Soviet Cinema," *Cinema Journal* 11, no. 2 (1972): 18–25; rpt. Richard Dyer MacCann and Jack C. Ellis, eds., *Cinema Examined: Selections from Cinema Journal* (New York: E. P. Dutton, 1982), pp. 76–83.

simultaneously) and were heavily advertised, even in *Pravda* and *Izvestiia.* The American film *The Thief of Baghdad,* starring Douglas Fairbanks, ran for years at various locations around the country and was probably the biggest box-office hit of the decade, with more than 1.7 million viewers in its first six months.[27]

In varying combinations of foreign and domestic productions, Soviet audiences now had some 200 new titles to choose from annually (see table 1). Although this was a substantial decline from 1924, the quality of the choices had improved considerably. This balance of native and foreign movies provided a solid foundation for the growth of a genuine film culture in the USSR, with revitalized theatres, a lively film press, and ardent fans."

Theatres

Now that there were movies to screen, the theatres, especially in Moscow and Leningrad, began to revive and from 1925 to 1927, the number of theatres across the country more than doubled. They regained something of their former splendor, though anyone familiar with the magnificent movie palaces in the West might justifiably regard Moscow's pride as pale imitations. So while it is worth remembering that Moscow was not Berlin or New York, it is also worth noting that Moscow cannot be considered a typical Soviet city by any means. With its well-established film culture from pre-revolutionary days and its fifty theatres (compared to two or three for most provincial cities),[28] Moscow set the standard provincial capitals sought to emulate.

Theatre management was decentralized and varied, although the best appointed houses tended to be run by NEPmen or leased to studios. The Mezhrabpom studio, for example, controlled three elegant first-run theatres in Moscow: the Ars, the Koloss, and the Artes.[29] A few of the first-run theatres retained their evocative pre-revolutionary names – Fantomas, Magical Reveries, Splendid Palace (in English!). These Soviet movie palaces featured as standard accoutrements orchestras, snack bars, and souvenir stands selling movie memorabilia. The grandest boasted champagne buffets and pre-show music in the foyers (usually a string quartet, but sometimes a jazz band). The First Goskino Theatre had a reading lounge; the Malaia Dmitrovka was famous for its seventeen-piece orchestra, its dance floor, and its repertory of foreign films.[30]

Tickets at these first-run theatres were expensive (though a far cry from the prices in the days of runaway inflation not long past). They averaged from 35 to 90 kopeks, but the choicest seats at the luxury theatres typically went for 1.50 rubles. At these prices, the palaces catered to the *nouveaux riches* – NEPmen and *apparatchiki* and their families, friends, and entourages. In one survey, 86 percent of movie-goers felt movie tickets were too costly.[31]

To understand the fate of the popular cinema at the end of the decade, we must keep in mind that while it may truly have been a cinema for the masses in terms of its repertory, in practice it was a cinema for the few, for the middle- and lower-middle classes in Moscow and

Petrograd/Leningrad. Since Soviet film critics in the twenties wrote constantly about the "crisis" in this or that aspect of cinema, one needs to take their tendency toward hyperbole into account when evaluating sources. But many reports corroborate that conditions in non-commercial and provincial theatres were distinctly inferior to those in the big city theatres. While at least two theatres in working-class districts in Moscow ("Labor" and the "Krasnaia Presnia") met the standards of the bourgeois palaces, the proletariat mainly saw films at clubs, after the first-run, when the prints were well worn.[32] If workers did go to the palaces, ticket prices forced them to sit high in the upper balconies, which naturally exacerbated class resentment against the privileges of the new bourgeoisie.

We see even worse reports from the small towns, where movie patrons were threatened by hooligans roaming the streets.[33] One doleful reporter characterized the majority of the country's theatres as having "a poor little projector, a dirty counterfeit screen, and a third-rate projectionist."[34] Most theatres offered no more music during shows than could be extracted "from a single broken-down piano."[35] A practice that seemed to have occurred in its most extreme form mainly in provincial theatres was to run movies so quickly that the titles could not even be read – in order to pack more screenings (and therefore more viewers) into a single evening.[36]

The most serious problem was that while the shortage of films had abated in Moscow and Leningrad, provincial towns often had no movies at all to show.[37] While a citizen of Kharkov could complain in 1925 about not having seen popular Soviet films like Protazanov's *Aelita* (1924) or even Razumnyi's *Commander Ivanov* (1922), one in Penza noted that not a single Soviet film had ever played in the town.[38] And these people were lucky compared to peasants, who did not have theatres at all and saw movies at travelling shows. None of this, however, seemed to discourage cinéastes in the provinces (where cinema was "tsar"), and their enthusiasm for films continued apparently unabated (and probably unsatisfied) to the end of the decade.[39]

The film press

The popular film press is another means by which to evaluate the cinema culture of the time. Anyone seriously interested in movies had to subscribe to a film journal or newspaper, since the official press, like *Pravda* and *Izvestiia*, and even the general press, like the *Moscow Evening*

News, covered movies infrequently and selectively. The spiritual ancestor of the popular film press of mid-decade was a short-lived journal entitled *Cinema Life*, the maiden issue of which appeared in May 1922, the last in March 1923. *Cinema Life* featured the late pre-revolutionary star Vera Kholodnaia on its first two covers. Inside, readers found reports on the activities of the cinema emigrés (such as Ivan Mozzhukhin, now a star abroad), lamentations that Kholodnaia was no more, and photomontages spotlighting popular actors of the pre-revolutionary screen. *Cinema Life* also had amusing advertisements for movies with names like *The Human Beast*, and "colossal mass scenes," and for beauty products and miracle medical remedies.[40]

In 1925, there were four film periodicals from which to choose. The stodgy *Soviet Cinema*, published by the Cinema Section of the Commissariat of Enlightenment's Main Committee on Political Education, was a "thick journal" in the pre-revolutionary tradition. Although one could occasionally find good film criticism therein, it focused on the "cinema to the countryside" campaign and on promoting educational films (*kulturfilmy*). The other periodical designed for those in the business was the Association of Revolutionary Cinematography (ARK)'s journal *ARK*, retitled *Cinema Front* in 1926. ARK, founded in 1924, counted virtually all prominent directors, scenarists, and critics among its membership. Until 1929, when it became the Association of Workers in Revolutionary Cinematography (ARRK), ARK was the locus for the most interesting critical debates in Soviet cinema, in its meetings and on the pages of *ARK* and *Cinema Front*.[41]

It is unlikely, however, that too many laypeople subscribed to either of these journals, since two other periodicals were intended for a popular readership. *Cinema Gazette*, founded in September 1923 and renamed *Cinema* in 1925, had articles of interest to professionals in the industry, but was also oriented toward the "masses."[42] It regularly ran readers' letters until mid-1926 and provided comprehensive theatre listings. *Soviet Screen*, which had a circulation of 70,000 in 1928, most approached the defunct *Cinema Life* in style and spirit, featuring many full-page publicity photos of stars and extensive coverage of Western movies.[43] But while *Soviet Screen* was certainly the most "Western" Soviet movie magazine, its level of sophistication should not be exaggerated, as a comparison with as minor a European counterpart as the Russian emigré journal *Cinema-Creation* (published in Paris on heavy glossy stock) demonstrates.[44]

The press was also an important factor in film attendance, with many

Table 2. *Biographies of foreign and Soviet film personalities published in the USSR, 1922–1932*

Years	Foreign subject	Copies	Soviet subject	Copies
1922–25	3	17,000	0	0
1926–27	55	1,479,650	12	260,000
1928–29	22	416,000	15	280,000
1930–32	0	0	0	0
TOTAL	80	1,912,650	27	540,000

Sources: Data for both tables 2 and 3 are based on my analysis of titles in *Knigi o kino (1917–1960): Annotirovannaia bibliografiia* (Moscow: Izd-vo Vostochnoi literatury, 1962). Programs for individual films were generally printed in quantities of 10,000–30,000 copies; other books in 3,000–5,000 copies.

regular movie-goers using newspapers or magazines to decide on which films to see. In one survey, 17 percent reported that they decided on which films to see based on advertisements in the press; 35 percent relied on reviews.[45] Another survey reported that half relied on reviews (the rest on word-of-mouth).[46] A number of first-rate critics reviewed films in *Cinema* and *Soviet Screen* as well as in *Cinema Front* – Mikhail Levidov, Khrisanf Khersonkii, Mikhail Shneider, Viktor Shklovskii, and Ippolit Sokolov. Film criticism was a rather incestuous business, however, with definite conflicts of interest. For example, Shklovskii and Sokolov both worked for the Sovkino studio, and Khersonskii often reviewed the same films for *Pravda* or *Izvestiia* as well as for *Soviet Screen* or *Cinema*.[47]

The state theatre/film publishing company Teakinopechat, which published *Soviet Screen*, had a healthy book business, focusing on popular biographies of film stars, especially European and American stars. These paperback books were short, simply written, and inexpensive. In 1926–27, the heyday of Soviet popular cinema, fifty-five different titles on foreign stars appeared, with a press run (in an era of chronic paper shortages) of nearly 1.5 million copies.

Biographies of Douglas Fairbanks and Mary Pickford went through several printings, so, given the market conditions of the NEP, it is logical to assume that Teakinopechat was responding to actual demand for the 245,000 copies produced on these stars alone. Teakinopechat also published biographies of Soviet actors, but the contrast is startling: only

Table 3. *Other film books published in the USSR, 1922–1932*

	1922–25	1926–27	1928–29	1930–32
Programs	2	19	14	0
History/theory	4	11	6	5
Soviet film history	2	1	4	2
Dramaturgy	1	3	1	1
Scripts	1	1	2	0
Directing	0	3	3	1
Acting	0	1	6	0
Camera	0	2	1	0
Sets	0	0	0	1
Foreign	2	8	4	0
Reference	1	18	10	11
Sound/music	0	1	2	4
Children	1	0	4	0
Animation	0	0	0	1
Documentary	0	1	1	0
Scientific	0	1	2	3
TOTAL	14	70	60	29

twelve titles for a total of 260,000 copies (see table 2). The biggest Soviet draw was apparently the comic actor Igor Ilinskii, whose biography went through several editions totaling 60,000 copies.[48] Teakinopechat also published film history and theory, technical manuals (intended to help amateurs break into the movies as well as to advise professionals), and programs for individual films, but in much smaller quantities (see table 3).

Audiences

Who were the people who flocked to the theatres, and bought all those books about Douglas Fairbanks? It is difficult to characterize the Soviet film audience of the 1920s, which numbered approximately 1 million viewers a day, with absolute assurance.[49] The most concrete evidence we have of viewers' preferences is connected to lengths of runs and reported box-office returns, but even there we must rely on evidence which may be superseded as more archival materials become available to research-ers.[50] The film press reported receipts from time to time, and studios boasted of their successes in advertisements and polemical pamphlets. Film-goers wrote letters to the editors of the movie magazines, and critics recorded comments overheard in the theatres. Theatres sometimes conducted voluntary exit surveys, and there were a number of "scientific" viewer studies and audience surveys sponsored by ARK, the Komsomol, and the amateur Society of the Friends of Soviet Cinema (ODSK).

Some audience characteristics are reported fairly consistently from survey to survey. Audiences were evenly divided in terms of class or occupation between workers, civil servants, and NEPmen, although most theatres appear to have catered to one group or another.[51] The audience was, however, substantially youthful: 45 percent consisted of viewers in the 10–15 years age bracket.[52] Few significant class-related differences concerning preference on style, genre, or stars emerged. Half the viewers liked melodramas and comedies best in one survey; another survey confirmed viewers' strong preference for comedy (46 percent).[53] Igor Ilinskii and Mary Pickford emerged as the favorite stars (though proletarians did not like Pickford as much as did office workers, which seems plausible).[54]

There is an element of ambiguity on the important issue of attitudes toward foreign films due to the fragmentary nature of the information, and the real possibility that figures were inflated to serve nationalist aims. The major published investigation – Troianovskii and Egiazarov's *A Study of the Cinema Spectator* – claimed that 50 percent of workers and 67 percent of Party members preferred Soviet films over foreign.[55] An ARK poll reported a similar figure – that some 45 percent of a general sample preferred Soviet films. (It is not clear whether the question posed was generic or whether specific titles were offered for comparison.)[56] None the less, the circumstantial evidence flatly contradicts the assertion that audiences would rather see Soviet films if there were a choice. As a typical example of many such observations, A. I. Krinitskii from the Party's Bureau of Agitation and Propaganda (Agitprop), reported that workers found Soviet films "boring" and in all ways demonstrated tastes identical to those of the petty-bourgeoisie.[57]

Other areas in which it is difficult to interpret the data are entertainment preferences and attendance patterns. It is somewhat deflating to note that after all the hullabaloo about cinema as the art of the future, the Troianovskii and Egiazarov survey shows that cinema barely edged out theatre as first choice for an evening's entertainment among Muscovites – 23 percent ranked cinema first, 22 percent, theatre.[58] But an ARK poll yielded significantly higher results, showing that 79 percent preferred movies, while a Komsomol survey in Kharkov (Ukraine) indicated that 62 percent favored movies.[59] These variations might be explained by bias (for or against movies) or by the relative youth of the subjects in the ARK and Komsomol surveys.

The wider array of entertainments available in the capital might also be a factor, as the following comparison suggests. According to Troianovskii and Egiazarov, 40 percent of Moscow's movie-goers attended two to four times a month; 43 percent went five or more times a month (and 22 percent of these saw eight or more films a month). In the provincial city of Tula, by contrast, 60 percent went five or more times a month (with 37 percent seeing eight or more films a month).[60] It seems safe to assert that movies were quite popular among a certain segment of the population.

Gender and age-related differences should be noted. Women (who comprised only 12 percent of the Kharkov survey) responded much more favorably to Mary Pickford than did men, while young (working-class) men preferred adventures over other genres.[61] Teenagers comprised a disproportionate share of the audience, and they were also much more likely to admit that they went to the movies for entertainment. For example 63 percent in the Kharkov survey said they attended films for one of the following reasons: "enjoyment," "home is boring," "want to," "films are interesting."[62]

Important class differences emerge when looking at frequency of attendance. Troianovskii and Egiazarov's attendance patterns were unusually high, indicating that their subjects may have been well-heeled. (A competing Glaviskusstvo study showed that no more than 22 percent of Muscovites attended films as often as one to four times a month.)[63] Efraim Lemberg gave a far different picture of working-class attendance. Lemberg stated that the average proletarian family in Moscow had 1.98 rubles a month for recreation, and spent 44 kopeks of that on cinema (enough for one cheap ticket at a commercial theatre). He pegged workers' attendance at a scant 1.7 times a month in 1927, including free screenings at clubs, and claimed that men went to the movies twice as often as women.[64] The Kharkov study showed that 80 percent of its sample of proletarian adolescents attended three or fewer times a month and confirmed that film-going was a male-dominated activity for the proletariat.[65]

Access to movies was obviously a problem for the "masses" due to distribution patterns favoring first-run theatres and the price of tickets, but if people could go, they seemed to want the same things from the experience. To use the expression of the day, the tastes of the Soviet movie audiences were definitely "philistine." Critics found to their horror that: "The viewer does not search for life as it is in the cinema, but for life as he wants it."[66] Most spectators, workers included, sought pleasure, relaxation, and entertainment from cinema.[67] Critics also worried about the mental health of young people reared on a diet of films like *The Bear's Wedding* and *Robin Hood* – and feared the spread of "cinema-psychosis."[68] Proof positive that the psychosis had reached epidemic stage could be seen in the frenzied reaction to Mary Pickford's and Douglas Fairbank's visit to Moscow in 1926 – but given the treatment of the royal couple in the press, it is hard to imagine that even the most hard-bitten opponent of "philistinism" in cinema would have turned down a chance to meet them.

THE CULTURAL REVOLUTION, 1928–1932

The Party Conference on Cinema Affairs

Soviet cinema on the eve of the Cultural Revolution had some weaknesses – most notably the predominantly urban character of the distribution network and the repertory – but its growth over four years had been phenomenal. The quality of Soviet films was impressive, considering the enormity of the problems the industry had faced. The audience, though not demographically representative, seemed to like what they got, and it was reasonable to assume that given enough time, the bounty would be shared across the country.

Sovkino had, however, run out of time. The "snail's pace" approach to socialist reconstruction had lost Stalin's support – and the support of many in the *apparat* and the working class. The film industry had begun to wean itself from dependence on foreign films, but not from foreign-made equipment and film stock. With the inauguration of the First Five Year Plan in 1929, the country's limited resources were almost exclusively devoted to industrialization. Under these circumstances, spending precious hard currency on films and film equipment was viewed as nothing short of counterrevolutionary. The abrupt end of the NEP would have jolted the fledgling Soviet film industry under the best circumstances, but the invention of sound had already thrown it into turmoil. Because of economic politics in the USSR , Soviet cinema was left standing still in a moment of technological revolution in world cinema, a revolution which required, in the words of a contemporary film activists, "colossal capital."[69]

The First Five Year Plan was accompanied by an orgy of cultural and social criticism known as the Cultural Revolution.[70] Ideological attacks on cinema during the Cultural Revolution focused on alleged deficiencies in the repertory, notwithstanding that based on what we know of the box-office, audiences enjoyed Sovkino's and Mezhrabpom's films. But as important as ideology was at that time, the most deadly accusations were couched in economic terms. Considering that the country was about to embark on a program of crash industrialization, this is quite understandable. In the 1926–27 fiscal year Sovkino ran an enormous deficit and projected another for 1927–28. Both deficits were related to costs incurred in the construction of new studios.[71] Layoffs followed, as did other cost-cutting measures.[72] As justifiable as these deficits may have been in a period of expansion, they contributed to the general impression that Sovkino did not manage its resources very carefully, and in 1927 sixteen filmworkers were brought to trial for economic crimes.[73] And despite Sovkino's protestations to the contrary, the foreign factor in their strategies was still strong. As late as the 1927–28 fiscal year, foreign films accounted for over 85 percent of Sovkino's gross revenues, although they comprised only 33 percent of the titles.[74]

Although the Cultural Revolution did not officially begin in cinema until March 1928, after the All-Union Party Conference on Cinema Affairs, Sovkino's "philistinism" had been a subject for public debate for some time. Throughout 1927 and 1928 Sovkino was denounced in the pages of the film journals, in books, and in meetings called to discuss the "crisis." Sovkino was a "monopolistic putrescence"; its administrators were "slaves of adultery" wallowing in a "swamp of petty-bourgeois philistinism."[75] Mezhrabpom came under similar fire for its supposedly "vulgar" artistic standards, its major hits like *The Case of the Three Million, Aelita, The Bear's Wedding*, and *Miss Mend* attacked as "pseudo-Soviet experimentation made under foreign influence."[76]

The Party Conference on Cinema Affairs in March 1928 established new goals for Soviet cinema and decided not only Sovkino's fate, but also the fate of the entertainment film in Soviet cinema. The conference resolutions called for cinema to take part in socialist reconstruction, class warfare, and the cultural revolution. In order to do so, it would have to strengthen itself economically, as well as politically and ideologically. All bourgeois vestiges had to be eradicated. Although Sovkino was not abolished until 1930, the course of Soviet cinema began to change quickly and dramatically. Cultural pluralism was no longer to be tolerated. Cinema was to be pressed into the service of industrialization and collectivization, and in a way that could easily be "understood by the millions."[77] The Cultural Revolution was under way.

Phase 1, 1928–1930

Shortly after the Party Conference on Cinema Affairs, Politburo member Stanislav Kosior, not previously known as an expert on film, wrote an article on the future of cinema in *Revolution and Culture*. Kosior's words were to be taken as a warning both to Sovkino and its opponents:

[Cinema is] not only a tool [enabling] the cultural and political influence of the proletarian government on the masses, but together with this, a mighty and important state commercial enterprise. A purely cultural approach to cinema would be incorrect.[78]

Producers and audiences faced hard times.

Sovkino's production plan, announced in July 1928, was devoted to the new line. In the past, the majority of its budget had been apportioned for entertainment films, but now it planned to focus on "new socialist relations, the struggle against the survivals of the past, the enlightenment of the masses, economic and political problems, achievements of culture, class illumination of history, the organization of leisure . . . " etc.[79] Based on box-office patterns throughout the twenties, films of this sort were unlikely to attract audiences. Since Sovkino was the major producer, its studios responsible for about 40 percent of Soviet films, this was ominous news indeed.

Despite these new formulas, if one considers film production only, nothing seems amiss during the first two years of the Cultural Revolution, 1928–29. Soviet production in fact increased slightly, to 254 films, and good Soviet entertainment films were still being made. Some of them were very good, as popular directors adjusted to changing times and began to make theme films responding to the various "campaigns" under way. For example, Iakov Protazanov's *Don Diego and Pelageia* and Fridrikh Ermler's *The Parisian Cobbler* (to be discussed in chapters 6 and 8, respectively) demonstrated that it was possible to make films that were both topical and entertaining; consequently they were well received by critics and apparently by the public as well.

But although domestic film production did not immediately respond to the "general line" of the Stalin Revolution, changes were under way which had an immediate impact on viewers, especially the working-class audience. Beginning in May 1928, continuing to the end of the year, film

libraries were purged of foreign and domestic pictures supposedly dedi-
cated to the glory of "prostitution and debauchery ... and criminal
activity,"[80] in other words, the most entertaining movies circulating the
clubs and second-run houses, where proletarians generally saw their
movies. We have no evidence that this purge corresponded to the desire
of the proletariat to see more "wholesome" pictures.

Even worse, foreign imports continued to drop – to 130 titles – a sign
that hard currency was being diverted to the industrialization campaign
and that the xenophobia and "proletarianism" of the Cultural Revolution
were taking their toll as well. Because Soviet audiences preferred foreign
films, this fairly substantial decrease (representing a decline of 35
percent) had an even greater negative impact than the numbers indicate.

Changes in the press were so sweeping that they would have been
immediately obvious even to the most casual fan. Although crude and
strident language had begun to make its appearance in the film press late
in 1926, after the Party Conference on Cinema Affairs in March 1928, it
became the rule rather than the exception. "Reviews" for the most part
were violent diatribes couched in the vituperative jargon which characterized the Cultural Revolution.[81]

By the end of 1928, both *Soviet Cinema* and *Cinema Front* had been
liquidated, indicative of the trouble in which their respective publishers,
the Commissariat of Enlightenment and the Association of Revolutionary Cinematography, found themselves. The newspaper *Cinema* was
transferred to the control of the Society of Friends of Soviet Cinema
(ODSK), one of the many voluntary societies organized in the twenties to
promote mass participation in cultural activities.[82] Although *Cinema*
survived, it cannot be considered a popular organ from this point on.
Soviet Screen, the most "Western" of all Soviet film periodicals,
struggled on. Its publisher Teakinopechat, which had been specifically
excoriated at the March Party conference for its supposedly anti-Soviet
line, responded by dramatically reducing both the space allotted to
foreign films in *Soviet Screen* and the numbers of biographies of foreign
stars it printed. Nonetheless, the twenty-two titles (416,000 copies)
published in 1928–29 on foreign actors still surpassed the fifteen titles in
280,000 copies that Teakinopechat devoted to Soviet stars in the same
period (see table 2).

Early in 1929, Teakinopechat's crisis came to a climax. V. P.
Uspenskii, the Old Bolshevik who had been Teakinopechat's founder
and director, was demoted to editor-in-chief of *Soviet Screen* and committed suicide shortly thereafter. *Soviet Screen* was purged in November

1929 and transformed into *Cinema and Life,* a dismal mouthpiece for the rhetoric of the Cultural Revolution. The only surviving organ of popular cinema in print culture was no more, and, not surprisingly, the purge of Teakinopechat soon followed.[83]

Early Soviet film critics had never been particularly charitable. Yet despite their many failings, the first Soviet critics were a talented lot who genuinely loved movies. As film criticism became part of an official political agenda in the late twenties, such attributes were no longer valued. Leading critics like Khersonskii, Levidov, Shklovskii, Shneider, and Sokolov now found themselves displaced by new "cadres." These men exemplified by Boris Bek, I. F. Popov, and Ia. Rudoi, knew little about film and couched what little they knew in execrable prose. It is also painfully obvious from their "reviews" how little they liked movies.[84]

Phase 2, 1930–1932

By the end of 1930, although a final important "formalist" silent picture (Dovzhenko's *Earth*) graced the screen that year (and experimental sound films were under way), it was clear that some fairly major changes had taken place in the film world. The cinema culture of the twenties, a vibrant amalgam of entertainment films of Western and domestic production and native avant-garde classics, had been badly damaged. Though it was possible to make an entertaining film in the Stalin era, it was difficult. Though it was possible to make an avant-garde film, it could not be screened.[85] Many directors active in the silent period saw their reputations shattered, and a few never rebuilt their ruined careers. It would take decades for Soviet cinema to recover fully from the débâcle.

Production figures tell the story best: 147 films were made in 1930, 103 in 1931, 90 in 1932, 35 in 1933. As startling as this last figure is, its true meaning becomes apparent only when one looks at foreign imports at this time: zero (see table 1). After the purge of foreign films and the demise of *Soviet Screen*, which had championed the Western entertainment picture, the cessation of importation was a foregone conclusion. One of the goals of the First Five Year Plan in cinema had been achieved; Soviet movies now accounted for 100 percent of the pictures on Soviet screens. It was a pyrrhic victory.

The decline in production, while striking, does not tell the entire story of the change in line that was part of the Stalin Revolution in cinema. Proportional representation of genres also shifted quite noticeably at this time. In 1926–27, five genres dominated, in rank order: contemporary

Table 4. *Soviet production by selected genre, 1922–1933*
(No. of titles is followed by % of total production in parentheses)

	Comedy	Contemporary	Historical	Revolutionary	Literary adaptation
1922–23	6(14)	7(16)	6(14)	3 (7)	11(25)
1924–25	32(19)	27(16)	10 (6)	28(17)	8 (5)
1926–27	38(15)	52(21)	32(13)	48(20)	31(13)
1928–29	34(13)	72(28)	17 (7)	42(17)	19 (7)
1930–31	23 (9)	117(47)	3 (1)	28(11)	2(11)
1932–33	11 (9)	52(42)	6 (5)	17(14)	2 (2)

Source: Adapted from Youngblood, *Soviet Cinema*, appendix 2, which is based on analysis of *Sovetskie khudozhestvennye filmy*, vols. I and II.

melodrama (usually about love), the Revolution/Civil War film (in popular cinema, a substitution for the adventure), comedy, historical costume drama, and adaptation of literary classics. Melodramas were quite popular throughout the twenties, averaging 21 percent in 1926–27, but in 1930–31 we see a very dramatic change both in content and numbers. The contemporary melodrama was redefined at this time in a significant way. Depiction of the concerns of private life (the typical content of melodrama) was labelled "bourgeois," and the new Soviet melodrama focused on public life (tales of *kulaks* and industrial saboteurs for the most part). These hackneyed films accounted for nearly half of Soviet film production – making for monotonous viewing indeed for the public (see table 4). Not surprisingly, there was virtually no export market for such a cinema.

The periodical press now consisted of *Cinema, Cinema and Life, Cinema and Culture,* and *Proletarian Cinema,* the Association of Workers in Revolutionary Cinematography's journal.[86] These journals discussed movies as little as possible; "campaigns," purges, and slanderous personal attacks on critics, directors, and scenarists were foremost. When cinema was a topic, it was usually a scientific-technical treatise on sound or a tendentious "sociological" discussion of audience reception far removed from reality. It seems almost superfluous to add that in 1930–32 the sum total of popular biographies, whether on Soviet or Western stars, was also – zero. (There were, however, twenty-nine titles printed on other film subjects at this time; see tables 2 and 3.)

Why was Soviet cinema destroyed, apparently systematically, from 1928 to 1932? Why was popular cinema, which seems to be a relatively harmless frivolity, anathematized in the USSR by the late twenties? Part of the answer lies in the conflicting concepts of "mass" culture in early Soviet society; part lies in the feelings of cultural inferiority and xenophobia that the influx (and popularity) of foreign films engendered. These are the subjects of the next two chapters.

CHAPTER 2

THE ENTERTAINMENT OR
ENLIGHTENMENT DEBATE

It's boring, comrade editor, in a country busy replacing the plough with the tractor,
where peasants and cooks run the government, where lovers of the electric light bulb
don't understand the tales of Baghdad ...

(Letter to Teakinopechat, 1927, [to be continued][1]

Debates about the form and purpose of cinema were not unique to Soviet
society. Such controversies can also be found in the film press of other
European countries, most notably in France and Germany, where "high
culture" was highly developed and therefore, highly esteemed.[2] But
because of the state's central role in film production and distribution, the
Soviet "entertainment or enlightenment" debate differs from its European counterparts in several respects. First, it was quite politicized:
members of two Bolshevik factions staked their political futures on the
outcome, and though the enlighteners' aims were not in themselves
narrowly political, their ideals were so close to those of the Cultural
Revolution that they could easily be incorporated. Second, it can be
understood as a struggle between haves and have-nots. (Sovkino gave,
and the blessed – mainly representatives of the old order – received.)
Finally, it dealt a seemingly crushing blow to popular cinema, ending in
1931 with the apparent victory of the enlighteners.

HIGH CULTURE, LOW CULTURE

When the Bolsheviks began formulating their cultural policies, they
quickly recognized the advantages cinema had over theatre as a mass art.
Not only was it mechanically reproducible, it was potentially more
intelligible to the marginally educated, an important advantage in a
country like Russia.[3] Even if Lenin did not really say that "cinema is for
us the most important of all arts," it can be verified that as early as 1913
he had noted cinema's value as an educational medium.[4] It was soon
obvious that "mass art" did not necessarily mean "popular art" to the

new regime, and many Bolsheviks believed, like Lenin, that cinema was valuable primarily for its didactic potential. As already noted, when cinema was nationalized in 1919, it was placed under the titular control of the Commissariat of Enlightenment (Narkompros). That same year Narkompros published the first Soviet cinema manifesto, a slim and sober volume which called on the moving picture to become a "book for the illiterate," and mentioned entertainment films infrequently and disparagingly.[5]

Almost from the moment of cinema's inception in the 1890s, pedagogues and social reformers, even in the US, had attempted to use movies to propagandize worthy causes.[6] This tendency was pronounced in the USSR, both because it was a partially nationalized (rather than commercial) industry – and because of the "cultural baggage" the Bolsheviks brought to the institutionalization of culture. There was a hallowed radical tradition in Russian aesthetics dating back to the critic Vissarion Belinskii, who in the 1830s and 1840s applied social and utilitarian criteria to his analyses of Russian literature. His methods and philosophy were perfected by the radical critics of the 1860s, notably Nikolai Chernyshevskii and Nikolai Dobroliubov. Russian populists from the 1870s onwards concocted numerous projects, most of them unappreciated by the recipients, to carry "progressive" culture to the countryside.[7]

In 1898, the Russian Social Democratic Labor Party (out of which emerged the Bolsheviks and the Mensheviks) was founded. Because the social democrats had Marx as well as Belinskii to contend with, cultural politics became exceptionally complicated. Marx's attitudes toward art and culture were quite ambiguous and have been the subject of numerous and often conflicting interpretations. While Marx believed that art like everything else grew out of the economic superstructure, he also recognized that art had the disconcerting ability to transcend the superstructure. Perhaps because art was intrinsically resistant to being systematized, Marx wrote relatively little about art and aesthetics, giving his followers a great deal of scope to develop their own interpretations.[8]

The Bolsheviks took advantage of that opportunity; there was no single "correct" approach to the arts in place before the Revolution (nor was there in the twenties). Lenin did not provide much guidance. His tastes in art were "classical" in the tradition of the intelligentsia, but to his credit he exhibited little inclination to arbitrate in this arena. It is interesting to note, however, that even before the Revolution, post-revolutionary culture was a burning issue in social democratic circles. Two of the most prominent "deviations" connected with Bolshevism –

the *Vpered* and Proletkult groups – focused on culture: the *Vpered*ists
believed that the new culture of socialism would develop spontaneously
after a socialist revolution, while the Proletkult supported the idea of a
specifically proletarian culture created by the proletariat.[9]

Cinema as it had evolved before the Revolution certainly seemed to
support an orthodox Marxist interpretation: a business as well as an art,
it had become a "tool" of capitalism with remarkable ease. But one must
be careful not to read too much Marxist influence into the Soviet dislike
of the "Gold Series" of pre-revolutionary blockbusters. Disdain for
popular culture is neither particularly Soviet nor particularly Marxist;
elite groups over time and across national boundaries have divided the
arts into "high" and "low." Elites have historically tended to believe, to
paraphrase Patrick Brantlinger, that mass culture represents social decay
and decline.[10] Indeed, this is particularly true of cinema, which was
almost instantly recognized as an agent of "corruption" when it appeared
in Europe and the US at the turn of the century. Cinema's endless
repertory of adventure and romance and its technical novelty combined
to mesmerize audiences. Nicholas II, who enjoyed films and employed a
court cinematographer, nonetheless made these annotations to a police
report about the latest menace to the Empire:

I consider that the cinema is an empty, totally useless, and even harmful form of
entertainment. Only an abnormal person could place this farcical business on a par
with art. It is complete rubbish, and no importance whatsoever should be attached to
such stupidities.[11]

This same view was widely held after the Revolution in Soviet
educational and cultural circles, especially in Narkompros's Main Committee on Political Education (Glavpolitprosvet) and the All-Russian
Association of Proletarian Writers (VAPP), and among avant-garde
artists and critics like Dziga Vertov and Aleksei Gan. In 1922, for
example, Gan spoke of a cinema in the "hands of cinema junk dealers,
cinema gout sufferers, cinema speculators [as] ... poisoning the masses,"
while Boris Arvatov proclaimed that "high and low art" had been
replaced by "revolutionary and reactionary art." In 1924, VAPPist
Albert Syrkin characterized the majority of Soviet films as "hastily made
nonsense, petty-bourgeois, philistine, narrow-minded, loosely draped in
red rags." Numerous other examples making exactly the same point
could be found.[12]

I am not, of course, seriously trying to argue that Nicholas II and
Albert Syrkin held identical views about cinema. The early Soviet

pedagogues and the "proletarian" artists, unlike Nicholas II, did believe
that "popular" art (art for the masses) was to be encouraged. But they set
about, with misplaced idealism and phenomenal energy, to transform
"popular cinema" from those pictures which appeal to the lowest
common denominator (through a combination of action and sentiment),
to an agent of social, political, and cultural enlightenment.

1921–1924

The Civil War prevented Narkompros from putting its program for
cinema into effect. As we know, cinema served almost exclusively as an
agent of propaganda during the Civil War, but afterwards, although
cinema remained under Narkompros's nominal control, official support
(whether economic or moral) for the idea of using film exclusively for
enlightenment purposes dissipated. Party and government essentially
lost interest in film, since it no longer seemed quite so necessary to tap its
propaganda potential. Under the terms of the New Economic Policy,
cinema became a commercial commodity on the cost-accounting system.
This set-up was tailor-made for conflict. Who would determine the role
and purpose of cinema in Soviet society – the "people" (as consumers in
the cinema marketplace), the theatre owners, the state film trust, or
Narkompros?
   The debate over how Soviet cinema should best serve the masses was
involved and protracted, and some simplification of the issues and the
actors is necessary here. There were three basic "camps" and two major
issues. Glavpolitprosvet was actively engaged in cinema affairs
throughout the 1920s. Glavpolitprosvet organized the cinefication of the
countryside campaign, founded the first "mass" cinema organization, the
Society of Friends of Soviet Cinema (ODSK), and published its own
journal, *Soviet Cinema*. In some arenas, Glavpolitprosvet's aims were
close to those of "proletarian" organizations, especially to VAPP, many
of whose members wrote screenplays. Its policies also enjoyed the
support of some documentary filmmakers, like Grigorii Boltianskii and
Nikolai Lebedev. Glavpolitprosvet cinema activists Vladimir Meshcheriakov and Aleksandr Katsigras tirelessly promoted the educational film
and the cinefication campaign, and just as indefatigably attacked both
avant-garde ("art") and entertainment films as incompatible with the
aims of a socialist society. But their main villain was certainly the
entertainment film; "fun" and "relaxation" did not appear to be in their
vocabularies.

The avant-garde also vociferously attacked entertainment films as "bourgeois," "petty-bourgeois," and much worse. Under this general rubric, I include directors, scenarists, and critics who made or liked elite films variously labelled "avant-garde," "abstract," "formalist," etc. They were not a coherent group; indeed, they sometimes fought bitterly with each other (Eisenstein's and Vertov's mutual dislike and noisy public feuding was notorious).[13] But they believed that their films would raise the artistic consciousness of the masses and deplored the continued "narcotic" influence of the pre-revolutionary and Western taste cultures on film audiences. They also scorned the drab "formula" films that the pedagogues and "proletarianists" (to borrow Richard Stites's apt term) believed suitable for the masses.[14]

The third group consisted of studio heads and film trust administrators, whose charge was to keep the industry solvent. Since no foundations or philanthropists existed to subsidize worthy but dull film projects, the industry had to rely on its own, limited, resources. Sovkino's plan for setting the industry right was to give people the movies they wanted, whether that meant importing the latest foreign hits or making their Soviet equivalents. Some of the profits from these commercial endeavors could then be channeled into the production of movies less likely to succeed at the box-office. Sovkino's Ilia Trainin was a frequent and effective spokesman for the cause of the entertainment film. Other prominent Sovkino officials – Konstantin Shvedchikov, Pavel Bliakhin, and Mikhail Efremov – also staunchly supported the primacy of the entertainment film (indeed, Bliakhin was the scenarist for one of the most popular Soviet films of the decade, *Little Red Devils*).

This tripartite debate took many forms and was played out in many forums (on the screen, in the pages of the press, in the associations). The main focus here will be on the conflict between Narkompros and the producers, with the avant-garde's contributions to the debate serving as counterpoint. Glavpolitprosvet and Sovkino agreed on one thing – that "futurist" or "formalist" art was not what people wanted to see – but they disagreed on whether serving the masses meant entertaining them or enlightening them. Those very people who talked loudest and most often about "the masses" seemed to listen to them the least and to distrust their instincts the most. Sovkino's Trainin was perfectly willing to tolerate diversity not only in theory, but also in practice, by offering viewers real choices. For a revolutionary idealist like Glavpolitprosvet's Vladimir Meshcheriakov, on the other hand, cultural pluralism was an unacceptable compromise with the older order.

Table 5. *Leading feature film directors, 1921–31*
(in terms of number of films; 8 or more films)

	No. of films	Birthdate	In cinema since
Ivan Perestiani	17	1870	1916
Vladimir Gardin	16	1877	1913
Petr Chardynin	14	1878	1907
Cheslav Sabinskii	13	1885	1908
Petr Malakhov	13	1892	1923
Mikhail Verner	12	1881	1915
Iakov Protazanov	11	1881	1907
Iurii Zheliabuzhskii	11	1888	1915
Vladimir Barskii	10	1889	1919
Amo Bek-Nazarov	10	1892	1914
Abram Room	10	1894	1924
Vladimir Shmidtgof	10	1899	1924
Iurii Tarich	10	1885	1907
Aleksandr Panteleev	9	1881	1918
Olga Preobrazhenskaia	9	1881	1913
Aleksandr Ivanovskii	8	1881	1918
Aleksandr Razumnyi	8	1891	1915

Sources: Data on number of films are based on my analysis of *Sovetskie khudozhestvennye filmy*. Biographical data come from *Kino-slovar; Kino: Entsiklopedicheskii slovar;* "Rezhissery sovetskogo khudozhestvennogo kino," *Kino i vremia*, vol. III (1963); and *Stsenaristy sovetskogo khudozhestvennogo kino, 1917–1967: Spravochnik* (Moscow: Iskusstvo, 1972).

Cinema "revolutionaries" like Meshcheriakov faced formidable obstacles. Foreign films dominated the country's decrepit movie theatres, attracting enormous audiences, especially for American pictures. Directors who had been active in Russian cinema began making films again, films which were "Sovietized" versions of their former work. As early as 1925, it was obvious that these directors (Iakov Protazanov, Cheslav Sabinskii, Peter Chardynin, Konstantin Eggert, Vladimir Gardin, Aleksandr Ivanovskii, Iurii Tarich, and Iurii Zheliabuzhskii) constituted a formidable "bourgeois front" (see table 5). Their works were, in fact, the only Soviet products which could hope to compete with foreign films, and they enjoyed considerable success.

By late 1924, the ideologues of cultural enlightenment knew that if they did not take action soon, the battle for the cinema audience would be lost. Glavpolitprosvet established a Cinema Section specifically for the purpose of agitating for a cinema "for the masses," which it defined as peasants rather than proletarians.[15] Gifted young directors like Dziga Vertov, Sergei Eisenstein, and Lev Kuleshov had made their first pictures, so Soviet cinema no longer had to rely on "remnants" from the old regime. Sovkino had just replaced Goskino. In short, conditions seemed right at the end of 1924 for an ideological coup d'état in cinema, but it took four long and bitter years before this actually occurred.

1924–1928

Trainin, Lunacharskii, and entertainment cinema

Economic (and to a certain extent, political) factors were important impediments to the enlighteners in Glavpolitprosvet, but so were the two articulate and persuasive supporters of the entertainment film who emerged to do battle. One was Ilia Trainin, in his capacity as an administrator of the state film trust, Sovkino. The other was Anatolii Lunacharskii, Commissar of Enlightenment, whose attitudes about film and activities on the cinema front put him at odds with members of his own commissariat, Narkompros.

Lunacharskii, one of the best-known figures in early Soviet culture, needs no introduction. Yet, despite the appearance in 1965 of the document collection *Lunacharskii on Cinema*, little attention has been paid to his role in film. Given what has been written about this Bolshevik man of letters, however, it seems that the part he played in cinema was in keeping with his character.[16] Lunacharskii's interest in film, no doubt encouraged by his marriage to actress Natalia Rozenel, apparently was as genuine as his interest in the other arts. He wrote his first screenplay, *Overcrowding* (an agit-film about the housing shortage), in 1918. A number of popular films of the twenties were either based on Lunacharskii's plays or on screenplays that the commissar had written.[17] He appeared in several films playing himself with boyish enthusiasm; the most charming example was his "role" in the cartoon *Tip Top in Moscow*, where he can be seen with the animated character "Tip Top."[18] Lunacharskii also wrote an interesting and well-informed book, *Cinema in the West and in the USSR*, and numerous articles about film.[19]

Ilia Trainin is a figure of an entirely different order of magnitude than Lunacharskii. Little is known about Trainin, and his role in Soviet culture was confined to the period from 1924 to 1930. What we do know about him provides important connections to Lunacharskii, apart from their mutual enthusiasm for movies. An Old Bolshevik who joined the Party in 1904, Trainin (like Lunacharskii) had been an "oppositionist," a member of the *Vpered* deviation, which flourished before World War I. During the Civil War, Trainin joined the Proletkult, and wrote several articles arguing against experimental art. Trainin's first recorded jobs in the new government were minor posts in the Commissariat of Nationalities, but in 1924 he entered Narkompros as a deputy director of the publications censorship department. That same year, he became the chair of the Main Committee on Repertory (Glavrepertkom), which was responsible for film censorship, and he held this key post until 1930. Concurrently he was a member of the board of directors of Sovkino, the state film trust.[20] In these two positions, he was uniquely placed to influence the direction of Soviet cinema.

Trainin's and Lunacharskii's cinematic policies proved to be very much in the *Vpered*ist and Proletkult traditions of encouraging cultural change by non-authoritarian means, though they did not share the Proletkult's high culture bias.[21] They began laying the groundwork for the revival of the "Russian" entertainment film late in 1924, with articles in *Cinema Week* which argued against propaganda, and for entertainment.[22] They embroidered on their arguments, ironically enough, in the maiden issue of *Soviet Cinema*, the organ of their arch-enemy, Glavpolitprosvet's Cinema Section.[23] Shortly thereafter Trainin began developing his program for the salvation of Soviet cinema in earnest.

His idea for setting the industry right was straightforward: give the people what they want to see. Since audiences loved foreign films, if Soviet cinema were to survive Soviet directors would have to replicate the Western style. "Old-fashioned" pictures with heroes like *Stepan Khalturin*, a picture that Trainin cheerfully labelled "pseudo-Soviet," were essential to attract paying audiences to the theatres. Trainin just as forthrightly denounced the cinema avant-garde, although he admired their technical accomplishments, because their pictures did not make enough money.[24]

Throughout 1925, Trainin repeated his assessment of the problem (crude ideology and "incomprehensible" form) and the solution (entertainment) at every opportunity. Occasionally he would piously intone that Soviet cinema was a "weapon of culture," but he had thrown down the gauntlet.[25] Trainin was not the first person to argue against simplistic (or naive) emphasis on revolutionary content in Soviet films.[26] Neither was Trainin the first person to complain that "revolutionary" form was inaccessible to the general audience.[27] Trainin was, however, the first person to be in a position to do much about the style and content of Soviet films, and from 1925 to the beginning of 1928, Soviet cinema was transformed – in a way that seemed to mock everything the Revolution stood for. The new Soviet film culture was directed toward the middle classes in the major urban centers and concentrated on foreign films and domestic hits. Film-lovers could choose among dozens of lively films which showed them the world and entertained them at the same time.

The problem was that these were exactly the kinds of movies Glavpolitprosvet's Cinema Section hoped to purge from the repertory. The Cinema Section proposed that Soviet directors counter such bourgeois "propaganda" with films about the "rationalization of production and industrialization," "mechanization and collectivization," the "struggle with arson," or the "struggle to establish a Soviet community." Yet how could movies on these topics possibly compete with escapist entertainment like *Rosita* or *Bella Donna*, two American pictures popular with Soviet audiences?[28] The American cinematic juggernaut, which had taken over the world market after the Great War (and the Soviet market after 1924), inhibited the development of virtually all national cinemas, including those much better funded than Soviet cinema.[29] Soviet audience surveys confirmed the external evidence – Soviet viewers, including proletarians, strongly preferred foreign films or their domestic equivalents, that is, movies that were action-packed and entertaining. Trainin's program might be politically suspect in some respects, but, on the other hand, it made sense under the circumstances. Sovkino was responding to audience demand, making movies for the masses.

Enlighteners on the offensive

Opponents of the entertainment film were not passively watching Sovkino's activities on the cinema front. Because Glavpolitprosvet seemed to have had an endless supply of reinforcements, their initial forays were not well coordinated, and it is not as easy to single out the entertainment film's chief opponents as it is to identify its star supporters. There were, however, two key figures consistently involved in the enlightenment campaign. One was the architect of the Cinema Section's all-important cinefication campaign, Aleksandr Katsigras, a Narkompros functionary who held minor posts in Glavpolitprosvet and later in the Art and Literature Section. The other leading figure in the movement, and certainly the man with the most political clout, was Vladimir

Meshcheriakov, Glavpolitprosvet's director. An Old Bolshevik like Trainin and Lunacharskii, Meshcheriakov was a member of the Narkompros Presidium and in 1929 was elected to the Party Central Committee.[30] Although Meshcheriakov wrote less frequently than did Katsigras, it was clear that unlike his fellow Bolsheviks Lunacharskii and Trainin, he was no *Vpered*ist. In Meshcheriakov's opinion, the masses were too backward to be allowed a choice in their film fare.

The objects of Glavpolitprosvet's scorn were established early: foreign movies, film critics, the Association of Revolutionary Cinematography (ARK), and Sovkino.[31] There were also lengthy discussions in Glavpolitprosvet's journal *Soviet Cinema* of practical problems (such as the production of projectors of film stock), studio finances, the amateur society ODSK, film education, and the "right" kinds of films (on health and sanitation, or other edifying subjects).[32]

Soviet Cinema's obsession, however, was the "cinefication" (*kinofikatsiia*) of the countryside campaign; officially announced in 1924, it was featured in every issue.[33] An ideologically acceptable repertory for the countryside would consist of educational films (*kulturfilmy*), newsreels, and documentaries; entertainment feature films, whether of foreign or domestic origin, were condemned as "bourgeois." Glavpolitprosvet's recipes for rural cinema became the butt of jokes in the popular film press:

The priest and the rich peasant [*kulak*] hurt the poor peasant [*bedniak*]; the poor peasant wants to wed his daughter forcibly to a man she does not love. The rich peasant sets the cooperative on fire. The rich peasant and the priest always appear with a bottle of moonshine [*samogon*] in their hands.

The teacher and the Komsomol member give a speech before a gathering ... As a result, everything ends happily: the rich peasant in prison, the priest discredited, the poor peasant satisfied, the daughter marries her lover.[34]

Directors tended to avoid these assignments, perhaps because they did not have talent enough or patience enough to infuse them with life, perhaps because it would have subjected them to the scorn of their peers.

Because of directors' reluctance to make the "right" kind of films, even a die-hard enlightener like Katsigras admitted that some Soviet-made feature films would have to be approved for rural screenings, and suggested pictures that are fairly "bourgeois" by anyone's standards: *Cross and Mauser*, *The Station Master*, *The Palace and the Fortress*, as well as the picture Trainin admired, *Stepan Khalturin*.[35] But *The Bear's Wedding* (the story of an ursine vampire based on a Lunacharskii script) was strictly forbidden, along with foreign films which featured "sadism, naked lewdness [and] depravity."[36]

Katsigras's partial "capitulation" did not mean that Glavpolitprosvet had given up on its plans to revolutionize the repertory, yet it did seem fairly clear by 1926 that the enlighteners would not prevail on the strength of ideological arguments alone. Vladimir Meshcheriakov therefore launched a new campaign directed against Sovkino in the polemical pamphlet *Cinema Ulcer*. Meshcheriakov, Katsigras, and M.S. Veremienko now side-stepped ideology to focus on economic issues: Meshcheriakov accused Sovkino over and over of being too commercial-minded, while Katsigras and Veremienko claimed that Sovkino was not savvy enough to recognize the business opportunities awaiting it in the country. According to Meshcheriakov, Sovkino's shortsighted commercialism, exemplified by their alleged slogan, "To the pocket!" had led to a policy which "harms the Republic's [RSFSR] cinema affairs and should be radically changed."[37]

The tactic worked and drew unwelcome attention to Sovkino as it was struggling to establish itself. Ideological shortcomings might be overlooked in the relatively free cultural climate of the mid-twenties but the country was too poor for economic questions to go unanswered. Sovkino's administrators had to spend more and more time compiling statistics about their rural distribution networks and preparing rebuttals to such accusations. No matter how often Sovkino "proved" that its fiscal policy was sound, Glavpolitprosvet countered with a fresh set of figures.

The conflict between Glavpolitprosvet and Sovkino eventually spilled over into the pages of other film journals and thereby, into the cultural community as a whole. Sovkino, like Goskino before it, had few friends (at least, few outspoken friends). Many thoughtful observers of the film scene were genuinely alarmed at the box-office success of a blatantly "bourgeois" film like *The Bear's Wedding* and by the ample evidence of the audience's fanatic devotion to Western movie stars.[38] In 1927, Sovkino added to the furor by releasing two colossally expensive costume dramas, *The Decembrists* and *The Poet and the Tsar*. Both were judged to be horrifying affronts to good taste, the former to the revolutionary tradition, and the latter to Pushkin.

Film critics and social commentators were not the only ones dissatisfied with the direction of Soviet cinema. Young directors felt they were not getting the support they needed as they watched the big money going to middle-aged filmmakers who in general had made their names before the Revolution. At this point the "artists" formed an informal alliance with the "enlighteners." The most vivid (because it is the most extreme) example of avant-garde opposition to Sovkino came from Dziga

Vertov. Vertov had spoken out early and often against the entertainment film. In 1922, he proclaimed: "WE [*sic*] declare the old films, the romantic, the theatricalized, etc., to be leprous." In 1924, he stated that "the fiction film should occupy the place in a film show that is now occupied by the newsreel." In 1926, he predicted that "the proletarian audience will gradually come to realize the *impossibility* of salvaging the decrepit and degenerate 'acted' film."[39] Now Vertov had ulterior motives: he had failed to produce a box-office success, although *Cinema Eye, Forward, Soviet!*, and *One-Sixth of the World* found supporters among some of the more "advanced" critics. Vertov's followers felt that his films were being mishandled by Sovkino, and these charges crescendoed after Vertov was fired from Sovkino for alleged budget overruns on *One-Sixth of the World*. The aggrieved Vertov believed himself to be at the mercy of "specialist[s] in the lace on Mary Pickford's pantaloons."[40]

Other influential artists, like poet Vladimir Maiakovskii, joined the anti-Sovkino bandwagon. Maiakovskii also had had problems with Sovkino, and he attacked Sovkino in *New Lef* for failing to approve a screenplay he had written, singling out Trainin, Efremov, and Shvedchikov in his denunciation.[41] Maiakovskii attended a conference in fall 1927 organized by ODSK and the Komsomol, the ostensible purpose of which was to discuss the future of Soviet cinema. Again Sovkino came under scathing attack. When the *sovkinovtsy* charged Maiakovskii with seeking to abolish commercial moviemaking, he said:

Rubbish ... We're merely saying that the masses who pay to see the films are not the upper stratum of NEP or the more or less well-to-do strata, but the many tens of millions of the masses [...] And however much you try, however much profit you make from the public by catering [to] their tastes, you are doing something foul and nasty.[42]

Ilia Trainin, Pavel Bliakhin, and Mikhail Efremov did not emerge from this conference unscathed; they were humiliated again and again by their "colleagues." Efremov in particular was badly shaken, if his abject apology in *Cinema* is any indication. He declared that Sovkino's new slogan was: "100 percent ideology, 100 percent entertainment, 100 percent commerce."[43]

Trainin, however, quickly rebounded. In *Cinema on the Cultural Front*, he made his last stand. He argued vigorously against the utilitarian aesthetics of his opponents, and pointed out that workers and peasants, no less than the "petty-bourgeoisie" went to the movies to be entertained.[44] Offering them diverse genres and subject-matter (adventures and domestic melodramas) was truly serving the people's needs, not "pandering."[45] Furthermore, Trainin argued that Sovkino was serving the interests of state and Party, because "a dry and conventional approach to the problems of life has frequently turned the viewer (as in the case of the reader) to things and ideas alien to us . . ."[46]

Throughout all this Anatolii Lunacharskii had more or less stayed on the sidelines (having other problems in the Party and the Commissariat to contend with as well), but he had made very strong cinematic statements through his screenplays for *The Bear's Wedding* and *Poison*, the latter a film about a young man who succumbs to the blandishments of a beautiful woman and joins a spy ring. Lunacharskii insisted that an entertainment cinema could and should be distinct from something he termed "abominable commercial cinema," because "a consciously propagandizing cinema that wants to teach is like someone with their [*sic*] legs in irons." (He is surely right about "propagandizing cinema," but it is difficult to see how his own movies differed from "abominable commercial cinema.") Lunacharskii continued:

One thing is true, namely that [the Soviet public] loves brilliance, a variety of experiences, romance, beauty, rapid actions, an interesting plot, and there is nothing to fear in that.

When the greater and lesser pedants of Soviet cinema start to teach us grandiloquently that all this is essentially trash, and that we should pass as quickly as possible to films without a plot and without a hero, without eroticism, etc., they will be serving us very badly.[47]

Unfortunately for advocates of entertainment films like Lunacharskii and Trainin, the "greater and lesser pedants" were on the ascendancy.

1928–1932

The Party Conference on Cinema Affairs began 15 March 1928. Lunacharskii, who was conspicuously absent, was one of the main targets, and the conference was as much an indictment of Narkompros and its commissar as it was of Sovkino. The rift between Lunacharskii and his deputy Meshcheriakov was out in the open. Although Meshcheriakov did not give a keynote address, this was his week of triumph. He spoke of the two Lunacharskiis – the one who passed resolutions condemning Sovkino when he was in the sanctuary of Narkompros, and the one who would not dare do the same in public, presumably because his record as a scenarist would not stand up to scrutiny. Most speakers supported Meshcheriakov's views on the future of Soviet cinema, and the *sovkinovtsy*, even Trainin, were handily subdued.[48]

recap

While Sovkino's enemies could not technically claim victory until the organization's dissolution, we know that the Party Conference marked the turning-point in the development of Soviet cinema. The Commissariat of Enlightenment lost a number of the institutions under its control in 1929, and Lunacharskii and several of his supporters resigned that year in protest.[49] The Cultural Revolution engulfed the cinema industry, sweeping away the film press and other "cadres" in highly publicized purges which led to the abolition of Sovkino in spring 1930.

Under the aegis of Soiuzkino, Sovkino's successor, cinema became a tool to support the goals of the First Five Year Plan and the ideals of the Cultural Revolution. The rhetoric was that of the enlighteners: cinema became a weapon in the "class struggle" taking place in city and countryside. Soiuzkino promised to focus production on making "the high quality-art-mass film which satisfies the basic demands of the proletarian viewer."[50] Films became overwhelmingly "contemporary," addressing the problems of the day (that is, "wreckers" and tractors).[51] Yet victory for the enlighteners proved elusive, as film production plummeted. After 1932 they had outlived their usefulness, and many vanished from the cinema front.

The "entertainment or enlightenment" debate in popular cinema is a microcosm of Soviet cultural politics in the twenties, illustrating its pervasive cultural elitism and incipient authoritarianism very well.[52] This debate shows us that in the most relaxed period of Soviet cultural history (excepting the present), many believed that as lowly an aspect of culture as popular cinema had to be "directed" – in the best interests of the masses, of course.

The interorganizational conflict between Glavpolitprosvet and Sovkino which was at the heart of the debate also demonstrates the political, economic, and intellectual tensions that shattered Soviet society at the end of the twenties. Vladimir Meshcheriakov was a representative of the Party's left wing, that is, an opponent of NEP. Ilia Trainin, on the other hand, was apparently a rightist, a supposition supported by the frequency with which he quotes Bukharin in *Cinema on the Cultural Front*.[53] And Glavpolitprosvet's claims to monopolize political rectitude notwithstanding, Trainin was not Sovkino's token communist. At a time when approximately 15 percent of the work-force was Party/Komsomol, 28 percent of Sovkino's 3,200 employees were members.[54]

Finally, the debate introduces what will be a recurring theme in this book: that perceptions are at least as important as "reality" in understanding the past. In this case, both Sovkino and Glavpolitprosvet's Cinema Section believed they represented the interests of the masses. The evidence they marshalled against their opponents was "real," but it was too slanted to be "true." Glavpolitprosvet cinema activists, for all their talk about the masses, rarely demonstrated much inclination to find out what the people wanted. It is also odd that the mainstay of the Revolution, the proletariat, did not figure into their plans to bring movies to the masses.

The *sovkinovtsy* were pragmatic by comparison, but they too saw only what they wanted to see. Like most businessmen, they were interested in people – if they had the wherewithal to buy tickets for the movies. This left out the class which comprised the vast majority of the country's population: the peasantry. In the end, Sovkino proved to be as removed from Soviet reality as was Glavpolitprosvet. The next chapter, on the *inostranshchina* in Soviet cinema and the cult of foreign films (which served as the cornerstone of Sovkino's policies), demonstrates that quite convincingly.

CHAPTER 3 THE *INOSTRANSHCHINA* IN SOVIET CINEMA

I'm bored, and I'm tired of life. That's why I love [Harry] Piel and Doug [Fairbanks] and Conrad [Veidt].   (Letter to Teakinopechat, 1927 [conclusion][1])

In 1922, the following statement appeared in the radical journal *Cinema-photo*:

Anyone who systematically frequents film theaters, viewing all the films that are released from Russian as well as foreign studios, anyone who has noticed which films cause the audience to react to cinematic action would conclude the following: 1. foreign films appeal more than Russian ones; 2. of the foreign films, all the American ones and detective stories appeal most.

 Both superficial people and deep-thinking officials get equally frightened by "Americanitis" [*amerikanshchina*] and "detectivitis" [*detektivshchina*] in the cinema and explain the success of particular films by the extraordinary decadence and poor tastes of the youth and the public of the third balcony.[2]

The author of this article, the young director Lev Kuleshov, called this "phenomenon" *amerikanshchina*. A related and more generic term that was frequently used to characterize the popularity of foreign films was *inostranshchina*: "foreignitis" or "foreignism." (The Russian suffix *-shchina* may be used to add an extremely negative connotation to many words.)

The relationship of foreign movies to Soviet film culture was an integral part of the entertainment and enlightenment debate. Goskino and its successor Sovkino made importation of foreign films a cornerstone of their policies to resurrect the Soviet film industry. As a result, there were so many foreign films playing Soviet theatres that it is not hard to understand why filmworkers felt they were in the midst of a veritable invasion from the West, hence the use of the term *inostranshchina*. And since foreign films were assumed *de facto* to be more entertaining than the domestic product, opposing entertainment automatically meant opposing the imports.

But the significance of foreign films in Soviet cinema goes beyond their role in the entertainment or enlightenment debate. A surprising number of Soviet filmmakers learned the craft from reediting foreign films to make them suitable for domestic consumption.[3] The popularity of foreign films also revitalized the historic debate about Russia and the West – was Russia a part of Europe, or a world apart? Among film critics in particular we see signs of a deep-seated cultural inferiority complex that had a profound impact on Soviet cinema. As critics began to define both cinematic success or failure in terms of foreign models, Soviet film production could not help but be affected – and in a way that was not conducive to the development of a national cinema.

THE CULT OF FOREIGN FILMS

From the beginnings of the NEP to the end of the Cultural Revolution (1921–31), the Soviets imported about 1,700 American, German, and French films. Foreign films accounted for almost two-thirds of the titles screened in the twenties. American films alone amounted to 35 percent of the total, scarcely less than the Soviet percentage. Nearly as many American as Soviet films were shown in this period (944 to 971).[4] At present we have limited box-office information for the period, and empirical data are hard to come by. It seems to me, however, *prima facie* evidence that 1,700 foreign films did not enter the USSR in the 1920s to play to empty houses.[5] While it is true that imports declined sharply after 1925, this was a factor of cultural rather than economic politics – no one ever suggested that these American, French, and German films did not make money. Sovkino's head, K. M. Shvedchikov, claimed in 1927 that Sovkino would be bankrupt were it not for the success of its import policy.[6] Even a staunch opponent of foreign films could freely admit as late as 1928 that Sovkino made at least a 100 percent profit on foreign pictures while taking a 12 percent loss on the average Soviet film.[7] In a socialist society, however, profits were not supposed to determine policy (or so the argument went).

If the evidence at hand is impressionistic, it is nonetheless ample and unambiguous. Foreign movies played the best theatres, exerting a virtual monopoly in the city centers. The Douglas Fairbanks picture *The Thief of Baghdad* ran for three and a half months at Moscow's largest theatre, the Malaia Dmitrovka (which seated more than 1,000), and played Moscow for more than a year.[8] Two Soviet critics declared it so entertaining that all Soviet pictures were boring by comparison, and in a 1928 survey it was listed as fifth among ten all-time favorites.[9] A 1929 survey of children's viewing habits found it to be the most seen film (followed by Fairbanks's *The Mark of Zorro* and the Soviet adventure picture *Little Red Devils*) and third favorite (after *Little Red Devils* and *The Mark of Zorro*).[10]

Fairbanks's popularity was phenomenal. Another of his movies, *Robin Hood*, played fourteen of Moscow's fifty theatres simultaneously. While this was an extraordinary case which testified to his drawing-power, it was a common practice for foreign films to be booked in more than one first-run theatre.[11] Other major box-office successes were also American films: *The Mark of Zorro*, *The Sea Hawk*, and the adventure serial *Speed*.[12]

The Party newspaper *Pravda* ran few advertisements and paid film relatively little attention, but a glance at any issue of other major newspapers or periodicals indicates that foreign films were promoted much better than Soviet pictures. Advertisements for foreign films were numerous, large, and well placed. They usually quoted from reviews in foreign magazines like *Moving Picture World* or *Cine-World*.[13] As late as 1929, well into the Cultural Revolution, the *Moscow Evening News* was filled with advertisements for Fairbanks's *Son of Zorro*.[14]

Promotion was not limited to advertisements and posters. *The Thief of Baghdad* had an elaborate, "Western-style" campaign. In Leningrad, for example, streets were strewn with colored leaflets announcing the film, and there was an amusing telephone promotion as well. When Leningraders answered the phone, they might hear a voice whisper "thief of Baghdad" and nothing else – before hanging up![15]

An especially poignant example of the favoritism toward foreign films can be found in *Izvestiia* in 1924. A Soviet picture, *Vasilii Griaznov*, received an unusually good review (for a Soviet film) – on the same day that it closed at the Splendid Palace. It was being replaced by an American film, *The King of the Circus*, a four-year-old Universal production starring Eddie Polo. *The King of the Circus* was also opening the next day at the Goskino and the Ars theatres.[16]

Enthusiastic promotion of foreign films was not limited to Moscow. If anything, foreign films and foreign stars seemed to be even more popular in the provinces, which perhaps can be attributed to the fact that there was less to do in Nizhnii Novgorod than in Moscow or Leningrad. The following advertisement, styled in the old orthography, appeared in 1926, in the town of Mikhailov, Riazan province:

Light in the Darkness
The international artist
Mary Pickford
In a new, never-before-seen role
Hurry to see her!
The Empress of the screen
In Soviet Mikhailov
Cinema "Armored Car"
Only with us, almost monopolistically![17]

   The cinema press, especially *Soviet Screen*, heavily promoted foreign film stars, rather than foreign films *per se*. Just as foreign films served as the financial foundation of Sovkino, so did the 1.5 million copies of biographies of foreign film stars anchor Teakinopechat, the theatre and cinema publishing company. Again, one sees important differences in the promotion of foreign stars *vis-à-vis* their Soviet counterparts. These paperback biographies favored foreign stars by nearly a 6:1 ratio, with only Igor Ilinskii approaching the Pickford and Fairbanks sales. Publicity photos of foreign stars were also sold, and the best-sellers – Fairbanks, Pickford, Ilinskii – paralleled the book sales.[18] Yet despite Ilinskii's undeniable popularity with the Soviet public, there is an important difference in the way he was handled in the press. His films *Mary Pickford's Kiss* and *The Tailor from Torzhok* were never called "Igor Ilinskii's films." On the other hand, it was always Douglas Fairbanks's *Robin Hood*, *The Thief of Baghdad*, *The Mark of Zorro*, *Son of Zorro*, and so on.
   Film-goers' love of the Western stars was legendary. While the young woman quoted in the epigraph to this chapter (and the one preceding) expressed her love for Harry Piel, Douglas Fairbanks, and Conrad Veidt in more extreme terms than would most, there is no doubt that her feelings were shared by many (and not just by women). A young boy could speak of his admiration for "Doug" and the Komsomol in the same breath, and an adult male noted that "We need artists like Douglas Fairbanks. After [seeing his] life-loving, gay, and dexterous acting . . . we feel new strength and energy for work."[19] Rudolph Valentino, Charlie Chaplin, and Mary Pickford were also frequent subjects of readers' letters to *Cinema*.[20]
   American movie actors had many followers, but the most popular of all the foreign stars seems to have been Harry Piel, a German actor featured in numerous adventures. Piel even had an epithet coined in his honor in inimitable Russian fashion: "Harry Pielitis" (*Garri Pilevshchina*) – a

dreaded variant of "cinema psychosis." Piel's popularity in the Soviet Union can be traced back to 1922 (when German films predominated), in an unlikely source: the constructivist journal *Cinema-photo*.[21] A *Pravda* critic noted in 1924 that healthy substitutes needed to be found for "Harry Piel & Co."[22] A survey conducted in Krasnoiarsk to determine the influence of "American [*sic*]" films on children suggests that Piel's screen persona appealed to children in particular. The anonymous reporter indignantly noted that "quite a few of the girls" answered the question "What has cinema taught you?" by saying: "[That] I would like to marry Harry Piel," while "the boys expressed the hope of *being* Harry Piel."[23] Finally, Piel's popularity received filmic tribute in several Soviet movies. In *The Cigarette Girl from Mosselprom*, for example, we see a Harry Piel poster in the film studio, and in *Mary Pickford's Kiss*, Igor Ilinskii's character "Goga" is introduced to Fairbanks and Pickford as "the Soviet Harry Piel."[24]

Despite the adulation of the ubiquitous Harry Piel, the incident which most dramatically illustrates the cult of the foreign film in the USSR was the much-anticipated visit of Douglas Fairbanks and Mary Pickford to Moscow in July 1926. The cinema press carried articles on the visit weeks in advance, and announced their arrival with 4-inch headlines. Their every move was reported, and their apparent lack of interest in the "most Western" products of Soviet popular cinema was a major disappointment.[25] Their every move was also recorded on film, giving Sergei Komarov enough footage to make it appear that Pickford and Fairbanks had actually taken part in his clever spoof of movie mania, *Mary Pickford's Kiss*.

SUPPORT FOR FOREIGN FILMS

Theory

Audiences could unabashedly declare their love for foreign films and their stars, but the attitude of industry professionals was much more complex. For most, admiration for foreign films meant recognition that foreign pictures appealed to Soviet audiences, while Soviet pictures apparently did not.[26] Rather than disparage the tastes of the Soviet viewer as "philistine" or to find ways to "educate" them (as did the enlighteners), most popular filmmakers and many critics wanted to find the answer to that question. They believed that domestic filmmaking could be strengthened only through careful analysis of the structure of foreign films, especially the "classics."[27]

The cult of foreign films had a particularly puzzling aspect, one which Soviet critics and directors felt they had to unravel: why was it that of all foreign movies, American films in particular enjoyed such broad appeal, effortlessly cutting across cultural and class boundaries? Soviet critics and directors were well aware that they were not alone before the American juggernaut, that all European countries screened a significant percentage of American movies.[28] Lev Kuleshov was one of the first Soviet filmmakers to tackle this question, and his article "Americanitis," quoted at the beginning of this chapter, is a good example of the thoughtful approach some Soviet filmworkers took to the *inostranshchina*. In "Americanitis," Kuleshov determined that the basic reason for the success of American movies was that they were truly moving pictures, that is, they depended on action to attract viewer interest. They were also more visually interesting and emotionally appealing than the typical Soviet film.[29]

Many Soviet critics agreed with Kuleshov that American films provided better escapist entertainment than Soviet films (and considering what Soviet citizens had been through since 1914, their need to escape from reality from time to time is easily understandable). American films were seen by their admirers as more "cheerful" and "life-affirming" than the Soviet, regardless of genre.[30] This was especially true, however, of American comedies, which had few rivals in any other national cinema. The films of Charlie Chaplin, Buster Keaton, and Harold Lloyd were much loved for this reason.[31] "Harry" Lloyd was especially appealing to Soviet audiences, even more so than "Charlie" and the native favorite Ilinskii (whom the German critic Walter Benjamin dubbed "an unscrupulous, inept imitator of Chaplin").[32]

The "happy ending" of American films reinforced their overriding optimism. Critics recognized the psychological punch of the happy ending, but viewed it as a phenomenon so "alien" to the Russian cultural tradition that the term was sometimes transliterated, rather than translated, into Russian – as "*kheppi end.*"[33] Audiences, however, did not share this reserve toward the "happy ending," belying the stereotype of the anguished "Slavic soul" and once again indicating that the critics were a populace apart. *Soviet Screen* reported receiving many letters from viewers who claimed that the happy ending was the main reason they preferred American films to Soviet.[34]

Another characteristic which distinguished the movies of the *inostranshchina* from those of Soviet production was their believable characters. Americans really knew how to create a hero, while the characters in Soviet films were seen to be stereotyped and not very interesting.[35]

Closely related to this was the fact that American and European studios seemed to have an abundance of charismatic actors to play these good roles. The American studios were renowned for their star system, and it was recognized that Hollywood actors were much better paid than Soviet actors (in relative as well as absolute terms). That Hollywood's stars also enjoyed fame the world over added to the appeal of American movies in a country as "isolated" as the USSR.[36]

Soviet movie actors, in stark contrast, did not receive the recognition they deserved, and the public was hard pressed to come up with names of native stars.[37] The pay was so low that many found work in the theatre more lucrative as well as more "respectable," artistically speaking. Some held two jobs simultaneously – acting on the film set during the day and on the stage at night. Scenarist and critic Valentin Turkin blamed actor Vladimir Fogel's recurring bouts with depression on stress and lack of acclaim, and contrasted this situation to the acclaim movie actors enjoyed abroad.[38] (Turkin's analysis conveniently ignored the highly publicized problems of American stars with drugs, alcohol, and sex.)

The artistic aspects of foreign filmmaking were not the only ones to receive attention from Soviet critics. The economics of American film production received extensive coverage as well. Evgenii Chvialev, in his book *Soviet Films Abroad*, gave three reasons for the financial success of American cinema on the international market: (1) its broad domestic distribution base (the 21,000 American movie projectors accounted for nearly half the world's total, generating enormous income); (2) the heavy capitalization of the Hollywood studios and their attractiveness to investors; (3) production of films, designed for mass audiences, which were not narrowly "nationalistic."[39] (Chvialev thereby implied that Soviet films, known to be unappealing, were narrowly nationalistic.)

Another writer carried out an interesting cost comparison of twenty-one American and twenty-one Soviet films to see how production funds were allocated (given in percentages):[40]

	American	Soviet
Screenplay	10	1
Film stock	5	13
Sets/costumes	22	6
Actors	25	21
Director/cameraman	10	10
Miscellaneous	28	49
TOTAL	100	100

Some important points of contrast emerge. First, according to these calculations, Americans spent ten times as much on the screenplay, which certainly would be a significant factor in understanding why American films had better plots, characters, and were overall considered more interesting. Ippolit Sokolov argued that economizing on screenplays was false economy, since a properly written screenplay, such as those for *A Woman of Paris* and *The Mark of Zorro*, would lead to an efficiently and economically produced film.[41] Second, Americans spent nearly four times as much on the decorations, and Soviet audiences were known to enjoy experiencing the "good life" vicariously. It was hard for them to suspend disbelief in the typical Soviet film, whose sparsely furnished sets and poorly clad actors reflected Soviet reality all too painfully.

Third, it is difficult to imagine why miscellaneous expenses should amount to nearly half a film's budget, as they supposedly did in the Soviet case. This accounting reinforced the widely held belief that Sovkino did not monitor the studios very carefully, and that administrators were lining their pockets. A later analysis, which compared ratios of production personnel to administrators and "service" people, indicated that the Soviet film industry was heavily bureaucratized by the late twenties, despite its youth and small number of employees. Hollywood studios had a 3:1 ratio of production workers to administrators (300,000: 100,000), while the Soviet industry had a 15:1 ratio in the other direction (2,000: 30,000).[42] Yet all these "managers" did not lead to greater efficiency: Soviet filmmakers shot only 12 takes a day (compared to 30 to 40 for the Americans), while editing lasted from 90 to 100 days (compared to 3 to 7 for the Americans and the Germans).[43]

In short, the costs of Soviet films were seen to be abnormally high to little end – at least by comparison with results in the West. These calculations are probably exaggerated, perhaps deliberately so. They certainly overlook the fact that total investment in the film was more critical than how the funds were allocated, but the hyperbole illustrates the anxiety the issue produced very well. As another example of such exaggeration, one critic asserted that the average Soviet film cost 100,000 rubles, which would produce a "grandiose" film in the West.[44] This figure is inaccurate on both counts: 30,000 to 40,000 rubles per picture was more typical in the USSR, while $100,000 to $500,000 per picture was the norm in Hollywood.[45]

By 1926, we can see that reasoned and pragmatic comparisons of Soviet and Western films (like Kuleshov's) were in short supply in most sectors of the film community. Instead, Soviet film critics engaged in a self-defeating competition with the *inostranshchina* that betrays a strong sense of national inferiority. It is this sense of inferiority which distinguishes Soviet efforts to come to terms with American films. In Germany, for example, critics spilled rivers of ink in their zeal to counteract Americanism, but one never doubts their belief in the superiority of German films over any other.[46] The Soviet reaction was that everything was done better in the West, especially in Hollywood. Americans spent more money on movies and spent it more wisely, their women were prettier, their comedians funnier, their heroes more dashing, their stories more interesting, their lives more – lively. The many shortcomings and abuses of the Hollywood system were ignored, as were the many achievements of the Soviet studios. Significantly, the "skeptics" who believed a Soviet entertainment cinema was impossible (or at least quite improbable) under current circumstances were labelled "cinema-westernizers" (*kino-zapadniki*) by their opponents, recalling the debates of the 1840s.[47]

Practice

The "cinema-westernizers" put their ideas into practice in two basic ways – making pictures on American themes and making pictures on Soviet subjects in the "Western" style. It was hoped that the latter could be sold abroad, hence their label "export films." The former had no resale value at the time (though they would be fascinating curiosities today), and most of them have not survived. Some of the "American" pictures spoofed popular American films: *The American Girl from Baghdad*, *A Thief, but Not from Baghdad*, *The Mark of Zorro in the Village*. Others featured "American" characters: *Miss Katie and Mister Jack*, *The Horseman from the Wild West*, *Jimmy Higgins*, *Columbus Discovers America*.[48] Most of these films received little notice at the time of their release, but there were a few which were successful, like Boris Barnet and Fedor Otsep's *Miss Mend* and Nikolai Khodataev's *One of Many*. *Miss Mend*, an American-style adventure serial with action ranging around the globe, was a major box-office hit and will be discussed in more detail in connection with Barnet's work. *One of Many* combines acted, animated, and documentary footage in a charming spoof of movie mania. A young girl, infatuated with Doug and Mary, longs to go to America to meet her idols. She dreams that she is on a Hollywood set, where she meets D. W. Griffith, Charlie Chaplin, Harold Lloyd, and Buster Keaton. Doug comes to her "rescue," first as the thief of Baghdad, then as Zorro, but alas, he abandons her when Mary calls.[49]

The example best known in the West, however, comes from Lev Kuleshov, a director whose work is not ordinarily considered "popular," and indeed, his pictures were not box-offices successes. Yet he put the ideas he developed in "Americanitis" to good use in his most popular film *The Extraordinary Adventures of Mr. West in the Land of the Bolsheviks*, a zany comedy which satirizes both American fears of Bolshevism and the NEP's low-life. Mr. West (Porfirii Podobed), the President of the YMCA, ventures to Soviet Russia accompanied by his bodyguard, Cowboy Jeddy (Boris Barnet). He is immediately set upon, not by Bolsheviks, but by nefarious dregs of the Empire led by an "adventurer" (Vsevolod Pudovkin) and a "Countess" (Aleksandra Khokhlova). This film has had great staying power, but critics rejected it for many reasons, not the least of which was that it was not truly "Russian," that is, it had too many American characters. As urbane a critic as Viktor Shklovskii wrote that "a real Russian picture is more interesting than Mr. West against the background of the Kremlin."[50] Unlike most directors, who merely flirted with "Americanism," Kuleshov stubbornly continued to make films on American themes, like _By the Law_ (based on a story by Jack London) and *The Great Consoler* (with O. Henry as the protagonist of the framing narrative), and continued to be attacked for so doing.

As interesting as these overtly American films were, the so-called "export film" was the fullest manifestation of the *inostranshchina* in Soviet cinema. As we have seen, the export film was the cornerstone of Sovkino's production policy. As early as 1924, Ilia Trainin proposed making long entertainment films, for the specific purpose of competing with foreign hits.[51] Export films received more or less equal treatment with their foreign counterparts in terms of advertising and bookings. They were screened in several theatres simultaneously, and newspaper advertising celebrated their virtues *vis-à-vis* American hits. For example, Vladimir Gardin's *Cross and Mauser* supposedly earned a higher box-office than *The Thief of Baghdad*, and Amo Bek-Nazarov's *Honor* allegedly set a Soviet attendance record (whether for a domestic or foreign picture, as the advertisement pointedly noted): 34,000 in three weeks.[52] Nikolai Okhlopkov's film *The Sold Appetite* was actually advertised in Moscow as a foreign movie to add to its box-office appeal.[53]

These blockbusters were accorded "American-style" advertising campaigns, such as the one for Protazanov's science fiction movie about a revolution on Mars, *Aelita*. In the weeks before the film opened, in order to pique curiosity, the Martian "radio signals" *Anta-odeli-uta* appeared in newspaper advertisements without mention of the movie's title.[54] Even *Pravda* ran much bigger notices for *Aelita* than it did for other films.[55] Provincial towns like Voronezh celebrated the film's opening by having airplanes shower the streets with fliers bearing the legend *Anta-odeli-uta*. (This gimmick was described as being "almost American [in] style.")[56] *Aelita* played two major theatres, the Forum and the Ars. At the Ars, Dmitrii Blok (the premier Soviet composer of movie music) conducted a 30-piece orchestra in his own, specially written score.[57]

The export films were quite successful at home, invariably appearing in viewers' surveys as favorites, because of their resemblance to Western films. Export films comprised five of the ten most popular films in the Troianovskii and Egiazarov survey: *The Bear's Wedding* (no. 2), *The Forty-First* (no. 3), *The Decembrists* (no. 4), *The Case of the Three Million* (no. 7), and *The Collegiate Registrar* (no. 8).[58] Critics praised them in "Western" terms; for example, Nikolai Volkov admired *The Case of the Three Million* as a film "up to good Western standards."[59]

It is obvious from reading the press that it became increasingly common for the "cinema-westernizers" to value Soviet films to the extent that they were well received abroad, and perhaps even to exaggerate claims of foreign success. As one critic joked, the best way to promote a Soviet film was to announce that it had been an "enormous hit in Europe and the Sandwich Islands."[60] The allegedly "colossal" European successes of the historical melodramas *The Collegiate Registrar*, *The Palace and the Fortress*, and *The Wings of a Serf* were reported with a great deal of pride; "failures" with a certain amount of embarrassment.[61] (*The Wings of a Serf*, ironically, was praised for being "of a higher order" than the Western costume drama while at the same time criticized for its "American" montage.)[62] The Sevzapkino studio took out a two-page spread in the Russian emigré journal *Cinema Creation* (Paris) to advertise its productions, but the presence of the emigré colony notwithstanding, Soviet movies did not do particularly well in France, primarily due to its stringent censorship.[63] Soviet films enjoyed the greatest popularity in the Baltic states and in Germany (where censorship was laxer than in France), and it is interesting that Soviet and German audiences seemed to have similar tastes in Soviet pictures. The most popular films exported to Germany according to one early report were, in rank order: *The Collegiate Registrar*, *The Bear's Wedding*, *Potemkin*, *The Wings of a Serf*, *Aelita*, *Abrek Zauer*, *The Ninth of January*, *Minaret of Death*, *Wind*, *Death Bay*, and *Strike*.[64]

Despite all these "colossal" successes, the export industry proved to be no more than a minor source of income in the period from 1921 to 1928. Only sixty-three titles were sold, and only seven of these earned more than 50,000 rubles in royalties.[65] These disappointing figures were explained in a number of ways. It was argued that Soviet films could not possibly be attractive to the "bourgeois and petty-bourgeois" European and American audiences.[66] Sovkino complained that European distributors conspired to bid low for Soviet films (which may well have been true) and that Hollywood studios monopolized theatres in the US (which was definitely true).[67] Interestingly enough, censorship of Soviet films abroad was rarely mentioned.

Supporters of an "export cinema" argued nonetheless that the movies were good advertising for the Soviet Union. America had become an international economic giant (or so this line of reasoning went) because of the Hollywood film industry. For example, American goods were in demand in Argentina because they had been subtly promoted in American films seen there.[68] Yet it was never clear what "product" the Soviets had to sell in the late twenties other than ideology, and as popular directors well knew, entertainment films were by their very nature ill-suited to "marketing" ideology.[69]

OPPOSITION TO FOREIGN FILMS

Problems

By 1926–27, there were many points of opposition to the import-export policy. One of the most compelling arguments against foreign films was a familiar and not uniquely Soviet one. They allegedly were pornographic and "mystical." They supposedly corrupted youth and promoted crime, "hooliganism," and violence. Gloria Swanson's picture *Society Scandal* was charged with "stimulat[ing] the world view of hooliganism."[70] Other American films also seen as enticements to anti-social activities included the comedies of Ben Turpin and the film *The Sea Wolf*.[71] Douglas Fairbanks's films supposedly taught children to steal and admire violence; while this is not exactly the message of *The Thief of Baghdad*, *Robin Hood*, and the *Zorro* movies, it is perhaps not surprising to find semi-official opposition to movie heroes who are "good" outlaws helping the oppressed.[72]

The case of Harry Piel provides the best illustration of the widespread belief that foreign films "corrupted." Piel had never been popular with the moralists and the pedagogues, but, beginning in 1927, a veritable campaign was opened against him. Yet despite the numerous attempts to condemn Piel and his stunt films as "vulgar" and "deceptive," there is compelling evidence of spectator resistance to strong-arm tactics. *Pravda* reported on the mock trial of Harry Piel, where his films were found to be "stupid, trashy, and profoundly harmful." Yet less than half the audience voted with the judgment of the "court," though the circumstances must have been highly coercive.[73] Textile workers marshalled to denounce Piel at a public "debate" (as these inquisitions were sometimes called) also demurred. One worker even dared to point out how profitable Piel's pictures were![74]

Piel and "all such adventure trash" were condemned along with Sovkino at the ODSK–Komsomol Conference in October 1927, and attacks accelerated with the onset of the Cultural Revolution.[75] He was excoriated as a "fashionable adulterer" in the pages of *Revolution and Culture*, his films characterized as an admixture of "criminal wiliness, idealization of banditry – and [as] the apotheosis of apacheism."[76] When film libraries were purged of foreign films late in 1928, it was seen as especially important to track down and destroy all of Piel's movies – but it was feared that some continued to be shown in "remote corners" of the USSR.[77] (Piel was not the only German attacked; his compatriot, director Richard Oswald, was also popular enough to be so honored during the Cultural Revolution.)[78]

The domination of Soviet screens by foreign films posed other dangers, more specifically connected to the Soviet context. The most critical of these special dangers was the ideological threat. According to this line of reasoning, Western films were intended to strengthen capitalism, to bewitch audiences with dreams of material wealth.[79] They depicted, after all, characters supposedly as far removed from reality as happy farmers and philanthropic millionaires.[80] Or as Viktor Pertsov pithily stated: "Los Angeles doesn't coordinate its production plans with Soviet political education!"[81]

The predominantly American orientation of the import policy caused great alarm, since America epitomized everything the Soviets opposed.[82] Director Sergei Vasilev asserted that 70 percent of American films were totally unsuited for Soviet audiences; the rest needed further (and fairly drastic) editing.[83] According to Osip Brik, there was no reason for Soviet citizens ever to see Douglas Fairbanks, Mary Pickford, Pola Negri, Priscilla Dean and their ilk parading about on Soviet screens.[84] The worker-correspondent Bystritskii summarized this point of view best:

"The social-educational value of the picture *The Mark of Zorro* for our worker audience equals zero."[85] (*The Mark of Zorro*'s entertainment value for workers was pointedly ignored.)

Rational opponents of the *inostranshchina* like Aleksandr Dubrovskii voiced concern not so much over the numbers of foreign films on Soviet screens, but over the way they were determining the character of Soviet film production.[86] Osip Beskin charged that films which were not judged "exportable" faded into oblivion, while native directors turned out "pseudo-Soviet" films like *The Road to Damascus*.[87] Just as the cinema-westernizers praised Soviet films for being "as good as" foreign films, so did opponents of the *inostranshchina* trash Soviet pictures for being "as bad as" foreign films. Khrisanf Khersonskii and Boris Gusman charged Protazanov's *Aelita* with being a Western picture made for the foreign viewer.[88] Vladimir Gardin's *Cross and Mauser* was lambasted as a "boulevard-European hit" in the pages of *Izvestiia*.[89] There were many, many examples of this practice, but perhaps the most pitiful is Khersonskii's characterization of Grigorii Kozintsev and Leonid Trauberg's avant-garde adventure *The Devil's Wheel* as a "sick" picture – and an example of "*3rd-class* Americanism [emphasis added]."[90] It seemed Soviet directors could not be first-rate at anything.

Until about 1927, most of these criticisms bore some relationship to reality, even if the connection were tenuous, that is, films labelled "American" or "European" usually showed at least a trace of foreign influence. But by 1928, such epithets were employed rather indiscriminately. For example, *The Wandering Stars* (a much-criticized film based on a screenplay by Isaak Babel) was called "American" for supposedly "ignoring the interests of the viewer."[91] That, of course, is exactly what American films did not do, unless one assumes that Soviet and American audiences had different interests.

And what sort of message was the Soviet Union sending to the workers of the world with its export films? *Commander Ivanov* was shown in New York as *The Beauty and the Bolshevik*.[92] *Third Meshchanskaia Street* was retitled *Bed and Sofa* or *Menage à trois*, *The Minaret of Death* as *The Harem from Bukhara*, either by Sovkino or by their foreign distributors.[93] If such retitling made sense (or so opponents of the *inostranshchina* argued), then it was a serious indictment of the content of these supposedly "Soviet" films.[94] Soviet films were commonly reedited when shown abroad, especially in Germany. Reediting ranged from the counterrevolutionary (moving the execution scene in *Potemkin* to after the mutiny) to the merely insulting (changing the nationality of the peasant inventor in *The Wings of a Serf* from Russian to German).[95]

Given that during the period of the NEP, ideology never seemed to carry as much weight as did economic arguments, opponents of the *inostranshchina* began to develop and exploit an economic angle. They claimed, not that foreign and domestic "export" films were unprofitable, but that ideologically correct Soviet films could be as profitable. Paradoxically, they also argued that profit could be too costly: was 100,000 rubles in hard currency for *The Thief of Baghdad* a sensible expenditure of *valiuta*, since the profits came back in rubles?[96] Many "truly Soviet" films could be made for the budget of one "export" film.[97] In 1928, when a concerned viewer wrote *Soviet Screen* to find out why so few Chaplin pictures currently played the theatres, he was informed that Soviet citizens would have to make such sacrifices to build socialism. (In other words, the First Five Year Plan had not allocated hard currency for Chaplin pictures as a line item.)[98]

Soviet cinema was still heavily dependent on imports for revenue, despite the steady decreases in the numbers of foreign films entering the country. Vladimir Kirshon reported that for the 1926/27 fiscal year Sovkino's income was 11.8 million rubles from Soviet films, 18.7 million from foreign films.[99] Soviet cinema was also totally dependent on the West for film stock and some equipment; while Hollywood studios did not manufacture their own stock, the American film industry as a national industry was self-sufficient.[100] About the time of the war scare of 1927, concern over Soviet cinema's dependence on foreign markets for raw materials and finished films reached a crescendo.[101]

Solutions

Since opponents of the *inostranshchina* now claimed that Soviet films were as good technically as Western pictures, should not Soviet film production become Soviet?[102] Critics of the *inostranshchina* called for "the Soviet film on the Soviet screen!"[103] While some cautioned against the cultural chauvinism implicit in this statement directed against Protazanov's *The Forty-First* – "Every camel participating in a Soviet film should carry a little piece of ideology at the end of its tail" – most embraced it.[104] Sovkino and Mezhrabpom would have to reform, which would be especially difficult in the case of latter studio. Could Mezhrabpom really keep its foreign backers happy if it became "100 percent Soviet"?[105] It was believed highly unlikely, however, that Mezhrabpom could ever become "Soviet," since the studio made movies for a "public [who] loves women and the beautiful life, exactly as in Europe."[106] Mezhrabpom's production chief Moisei Aleinikov was singled out for his allegedly "foreign ideology"; it is possible that anti-Semitism may have played a part in this charge.[107]

Film critics who supported diversity on the screen were also going to have to change their ways. The "cinema-westernizers" among them came under heavy fire, as the example of Ippolit Sokolov demonstrates. Sokolov, the critic whom avant-garde director Dziga Vertov had attacked as "a specialist in the lace on Mary Pickford's pantaloons" was now excoriated for his book on Lillian Gish (a serious analysis of Gish's artistry) as well as for his "misguided Americanism."[108]

Studios and critics were handy targets, but even their enemies realized that easy as it was to attack them, such attacks did not contribute much toward the construction of a new Soviet cinema. Was there any solution to the conundrum? A cartoon which appeared in *Cinema* on the eve of the 1928 Party Conference on Cinema Affairs showed the following: three movies, labelled "*Such a Woman*," "*Mary's Kiss*," and "*Foreign Trash*" are running away from "cultured rental," the "peasant and worker film" and the "cultured critic." The latter three are carrying a large banner which says "Give us a truly Soviet film!"[109] If *Such a Woman* and *Mary Pickford's Kiss* were not "truly Soviet," then which pictures were? Were there no acceptable models from native filmmakers?

Anyone who reads the Soviet press coverage of Soviet movies in the twenties has to be struck by the prevailing tone of negativism and the constant carping over the supposedly abysmal quality of native filmmaking. Export films were "bad" because they were too "foreign," so they failed to meet ideological standards. Avant-garde films were "bad" because ordinary viewers could not understand their formal attributes, so they failed the popularity test. The mass of long-forgotten "B" (and "C") grade pictures was also uniformly attacked as being exceptionally poor in technical terms, so they failed to pass muster in terms of quality.

Grandfather Knysh's Gang was "slow"; Georgian and Armenian films had too much "love and adventure."[110] *Machinist Ukhtomskii* featured excessive "shooting and killing," while *The Struggle for the Ultimatum* was so "incompetent" that Nikolai Lebedev claimed "one doesn't want to write about it."[111] *Evdokiia Rozhnovskaia* was "earnest but primitive"; *The Whirlpool* was "not a real rural film"; *On Life and Death*'s nature scenes were the only things in the film that could be praised, and, of course, that was Russia's due, not the director's.[112]

Some lesser films did receive fairly decent reviews, though few were lavished with praise. It is instructive to note how this was done and what characteristics film critics believed desirable. Even opponents of the *inostranshchina* tended to evaluate their "good" films by reference to the Western model. "Good" movies were not good because of their superior direction, acting, script, or cinematography, but because they were not like Western pictures. A review of Ivan Perestiani's *The Suram Fortress* approvingly concluded that it was far removed from the "stereotyped, sugary beauty of Italian films and the Gold Series."[113] Mikhail Koltsov praised Protazanov's *His Call* for not being "psychological," an invidious characteristic of Western films, yet both Koltsov and Khrisanf Khersonskii seemed concerned that *His Call* be well received by foreign workers.[114] Vladimir Solskii even argued that "second-rate" but politically correct Soviet films like *Wind* or *The Ninth of January* would do better abroad than "Western imitations," because foreign viewers would enjoy the novelty.[115]

We see a critical shift in this pattern of "negative praise" by the time of the Party Conference on Cinema Affairs and the onset of the Cultural Revolution. As early as fall 1927, a concerted effort to articulate a new film aesthetic, drawn mainly from the views of the enlighteners, was apparent. This change in course was reflected in the positive terms now used to praise the "middling" films: *Two Days* featured "living people"; *The Right to Life* was a "simple story" with "life-affirming humor"; *Katka the Apple Seller* was "melodramatic but not theatrical."[116] These themes were continued at the conference, where entertainment films (both domestic and foreign) were condemned.

Purges of film libraries and dramatic curtailment of imports followed shortly thereafter; the many liabilities of foreign films were now seen as far outweighing their entertainment value. The need to retool the industry for sound made the time seem right for a break with the "primitivism" of American style.[117] And yet the attributes of the "new" cinema – simplicity, humor and optimism, lack of theatricality, focus on "real" people – were all characteristics admired in American films. But subtract the love, sex, violence, angst, and beauty – and what one is left with is not "Americanism," of course, but Socialist Realism.

Foreign films disappeared from Soviet screens for three major reasons – economic, nationalistic, ideological – but despite the importance of ideology, I think the first two outweigh it. The economic exigencies of building "socialism in one country" meant that the situation could not remain as it was. Closely related to "socialism in one country" was the revival of Russian nationalism in opposition to the proletarian internationalism of Marxism-Leninism. In such a milieu, the dominance of foreign films and the sycophantic fawning of some film critics over them were pure embarrassments. The continuation of an overtly bourgeois taste culture in the USSR was also intolerable, but an acceptable alternative to revolutionary avant-gardism had to be devised. Audiences did not like experimental cinema, whether political or apolitical.

Socialist Realism has a complicated genesis, but it emerged from the same context – both contemporary and historical – as our cinematic debates. It drew in equal measure from Russian utilitarian and Marxist aesthetics and developed its practical applications from the endeavors of the various "proletarian" groups, including VAPP (later RAPP) and Glavpolitprosvet's Cinema Section (as illustrated in the entertainment or enlightenment debate).[118] In cinema, it also drew from the debate over the *inostranshchina*, taking certain characteristics observed to be popular in American films and discarding others for moral and ideological reasons. The problem was that these characteristics were inextricably entwined; the American "recipe" for success could not be altered to such an extreme degree. No matter how much "life-affirming" humor remains in a film, without the joys and trials of private life, human interest in Soviet cinema was diminished.

The impact of the *inostranshchina* remained in Soviet memory long after foreign films departed from Soviet screens, in the hearts of viewers who lost sight of cherished American "friends" and through the work of popular directors, who had not forgotten the lessons of American films (though it was not easy to put them into practice, especially in the late forties). But the heyday of the *inostranshchina* in Soviet cinema was during the twenties, and so its most tangible manifestation may be found in the films which are the subject of the next three chapters. These were the films of the "commercial deviation" – Soviet movies that Soviet audiences actually liked.

PART 2

PRACTICE

CHAPTER 4 GENRES AND HITS

We don't want to go back to *The Station Master* [*sic*]; *The Bear's Wedding* can be made even better in Hollywood. We don't want to give anyone the right to judge questions of art by today's accurate or inaccurate figures at the accountant's.

(Viktor Shklovskii, 1927[1])

Given the historical, political, and "international" contexts described in part 1, Soviet filmmakers faced an unusually complex situation in their efforts to create a viable popular cinema. In the twenties, every European cinema struggled against the American leviathan, but Soviet cinema faced formidable competition from German and French films as well. Moreover, Soviet popular filmmakers faced a unique set of problems related to the Revolution which generated uncertainty and conflict.

The industry was extremely impoverished and almost totally dependent on foreign sources for equipment and raw material. The partial nationalization of the industry resulted in an amalgam of public and private theatres, a major semi-private studio (Mezhrabpom), and an array of regulatory agencies – which engendered considerable confusion. And because of the politicization of culture, filmmakers were not only subject to the censorship restraints familiar to all national cinemas, but also to a microcosmic analysis and direction of their activities from "outsiders" and self-proclaimed "experts." In addition, filmmakers became unwitting pawns in intra- and inter-institutional struggles, such as that within Narkompros and that between Glavpolitprosvet and Sovkino.

THE PROBLEMS OF FORMULA FILMMAKING

Cinematic genres were well established by 1921, the fourth decade of film production. They represented variations of their literary or theatrical counterparts: drama, tragedy, satire, and so forth – so there was nothing especially Marxist or Soviet about them. But mass audiences exhibited marked preference for the "basest" of the bourgeois genres – melodrama, adventure, slapstick comedy – preferences which the enlighteners believed demonstrated how "uncultured" the people were. If tragedy and drama were "bourgeois" – at least they were also "art."

Could a truly Soviet cinema be created merely by pouring new wine into old bottles? This had been a key question in cinematic politics since the Revolution, and as filmmakers struggled to answer it, the generational and political divisions in Soviet cinema were painfully obvious. Young directors like Eisenstein, Vertov, Pudovkin, and Kuleshov responded to the question with a resounding no – both in their films and in their voluminous polemical and theoretical writings. The "old specialists" who dominated popular cinema, on the other hand, engaged in few public debates but briskly went about their business, turning out "pseudo-Soviet" films made in a "cultured, semi-theatrical, European" style.[2]

Soviet popular cinema in the twenties can be divided into four genres: comedy, melodrama, adventure, and historical (costume) drama.[3] Soviet filmmakers found it reasonably easy to "Sovietize" adventure by making Civil War movies which emphasized adventure over politics. While few pictures in this category were genuine hits – that is, films with box-office takes or attendance figures comparable to those of foreign films – they formed a substantial and fundamentally satisfying proportion of what the Soviets called "middling" films ("B" movies).

Other Soviet filmmakers, albeit those who almost exclusively hailed from the pre-revolutionary cinema, did a good job "Sovietizing" the historical film by selecting incidents from the nineteenth-century revolutionary movements for dramatization. Although comparatively few in number – never accounting for more than 11 percent of Soviet film production – these movies consistently enjoyed good box-office returns. The relative success of the adventure and historical genres is reflected in the import figures. Only 6 percent of the French films which entered the USSR, from 1921 to 1928, were adventures; only 4 percent of German imports of the same period fell into this category (see table 6 for breakdowns). Virtually no historical pictures were imported (but on the other hand, Soviet costume dramas proved to be a modestly successful export product).

Comedy and melodrama were an entirely different matter. Although melodramatic elements could be infused into other genres (a practice in which Iakov Protazanov, the subject of chapter 6, excelled), the constraints of cultural politics and the revulsion against the cinematic depiction of private life meant that the pure melodrama was rare indeed

Table 6. *Major film genres screened in the RSFSR, 1921–1928*

	Adventure	Comedy	Historical	Melodrama
American	149	324	8	180
French	8	26	3	116
German	16	32	22	262
Soviet	29 (137)	100	60	128 (62)
TOTAL	202 (339)	482	93	686 (748)

Note: The figures for Soviet adventure and melodrama require additional explanation. For adventure, the first figure is *SKhF*'s (see source note) "pure adventure"
category; the second is the figure for the "revolutionary" film. Because most
revolutionary films were in fact "adventures," adding the two numbers enables a
more accurate comparison with the foreign adventures. I have applied the same
principle for melodrama. The first figure is for the contemporary melodrama; the
second for the "literary adaptation," which was virtually always melodrama as well.
Sources: These figures are based on my analysis of *Sovetskie khudozhestvennye filmy*;
Kartseva, "Amerikanskie nemye filmy"; Egorova, "Nemetskie nemye filmy";
Greiding, "Frantsuzskie nemye filmy."

in Soviet cinema. Few critics protested.[4] Until Fridrikh Ermler began
making his series of socially critical melodramas in 1926 (see chapter 8),
the melodrama was invariably labelled "salon melodrama" or "boulevard
melodrama." As these tags suggest, most critics considered melodrama a
shockingly bourgeois product directed at foreigners, NEPmen, *spetsy*,
and unreconstructed elements of the petty-bourgeoisie (*meshchane*). But
the import figures tell us that audiences – workers included – responded
quite warmly to such films. Of both French and German imports
between 1921 and 1928, 67 percent were melodramas (see table 6), and
when a Soviet melodrama up to Western standards finally reached the
screen – *The Bear's Wedding* – it was a runaway hit, the twenties
equivalent of Protazanov's legendary 1913 box-office bonanza, *The Keys
to Happiness*.

Comedies proved even more difficult to make than melodramas, which
is not hard to understand since the USSR was a society whose appointed
and self-appointed spokesmen took themselves exceptionally seriously.
As always we see that a sharp divergence between mass elite opinion
permeated Soviet society. Comedies were very popular among audiences,
especially youth and children. Since there were few "good" Soviet
comedies, American comedies, Hollywood's most formidable product,

were firmly entrenched in Soviet theatres, much to the dismay of critics
and native filmmakers. Of American imports between 1921 and 1928, 43
percent were comedies, as well as a substantial minority (22 percent) of
French imports; more importantly, the 324 American comedies imported
were more than three times the number of Soviet comedies screened in
the same period (see table 6).

Given all these problems, it should not be too surprising that even
well-established Soviet filmmakers faced formidable pitfalls practicing
their craft, and that genre filmmaking posed especially thorny issues. To
illustrate both the difficulties directors had to overcome and the solutions
they devised, I have chosen fifteen films which represent the best of
Soviet entertainment cinema. They were demonstrable box-office hits –
and more often than not subjected to prolonged and widespread controversy for that very reason.

FORMULAS FOR SUCCESS

Comedy

Though a few funny films were made, comedy was the perennial sore
spot of Soviet silent cinema. More was written about it than about any
other genre: while critics were constantly declaring comedy the most
important genre of the most important art, they just as constantly carped
about the results.[5] Relatively few major directors were willing to risk
being abused more than once for making the "wrong" kind of comedy;
the most notable exceptions were Iakov Protazanov and Boris Barnet,
whose film comedies will be discussed later, as part of their *œuvres*.

Early attempts at comedy like *Commander Ivanov* (Aleksandr Razumnyi, 1922) and *The Tailor from Torzhok* (Iakov Protazanov, 1925) were
derided in the press as "bourgeois" and undoubtedly they were, if we are
to understand "bourgeois" as a synonym for "apolitical." The former,
successful with the "non-cinema public," was a sly little romantic
comedy about a Red Army officer who breaks down the sexual inhi-
bitions of a priest's daughter;[6] the latter a chaste variant of a bedroom
farce. Despite the apparent difficulties in "Sovietizing" comedy, cries for
a "new" comedy became more insistent in 1926–27, which probably
reflects the growing popularity of American comedies as much as any
perceived weaknesses in Soviet production.

Critics urged filmmakers to "work" and "study" in order to develop a
Soviet variation of the comedic genre, but, in their franker moments, it is

clear they understood the problems very well. One (pseudononymous) critic wrote, for example, that it was much more difficult to make a comedy "ideological" than it was to insert some ideology into a drama.[7] Ippolit Sokolov sagely noted: "At whom and how to laugh is the main thing" in comedy, but Osip Brik went further, writing with tongue-in-cheek candor: "Comedy without laughter is impossible. It's difficult to make a Soviet comedy because we don't know what to laugh at."[8]

Directives issued on what comedy should not be were naturally as numerous and specific as those telling directors what it should be. Comedy should not, for example, feature an "idiot" hero like American comedies, nor should it be "physical."[9] It should be infused with "ideology" and "social significance," though no one speculated how this could be achieved without robbing a comedy of its humor.[10] Small wonder that Sovkino had so much trouble fulfilling its own production plans for comedy and lamented the shortages year after year.[11]

Funny films were made; one of the best, Kuleshov's *Mr. West*, has already been discussed. But while it is possible to read *Mr. West* as veiled political criticism,[12] more typical comedies like *The Cigarette Girl from Mosselprom* and *Mary Pickford's Kiss* were neither "ideological" nor "socially significant." Given the cultural climate, it is also not surprising that they were popular with audiences, but not with critics. *The Cigarette Girl from Mosselprom* (Iurii Zheliabuzhskii, 1924) is a charming and stylish romantic comedy that is among the most polished and "Western" films of Soviet production. The cigarette girl Zina (Iuliia Solntseva) is wooed by a fumbling accountant (Igor Ilinskii), a dashing cinematographer (Nikolai Tsereteli), and a corpulent American businessman (M. Tsibulskii) who is bringing "high fashion" to the USSR. The film is also a cleverly executed spoof of movie mania as Zina is "discovered" by the film crew and becomes a somewhat inept "star."

Although Khrisanf Khersonskii liked *The Cigarette Girl*, most critics panned it in the niggardly fashion all too common in early Soviet film criticism.[13] These criticisms are telling ones. Reviewers admitted that the film was funny, but vigorously denied that it was a Soviet comedy. Sokolov claimed the only thing "Soviet" about it was the citizenship of most of its characters.[14] Edgar Arnoldi, a critic who specialized in writing about genre films, and Vladimir Kirshon, a leader of the proletarian writers' association RAPP, both used "cigarette girls" as a generic term for comedies made according to "capitalist standards."[15] *The Cigarette Girl from Mosselprom* came in number five, however, in a list of "most seen" films, with overwhelmingly positive viewer reactions recorded.[16]

Sergei Komarov's 1927 comedy *Mary Pickford's Kiss* has already been mentioned in connection with the cult of foreign movie stars. Like *The Cigarette Girl from Mosselprom*, *Mary Pickford's Kiss* was a romantic comedy and a spoof of movie madness. It also starred the popular comedian Igor Ilinskii – this time as Goga Palkin, inept movie usher in a luxurious, modern movie palace. After a series of bungling adventures, Goga literally lands in front of Mary Pickford and Douglas Fairbanks as they are touring a Moscow film studio. Introduced to them as a film star, Goga receives Mary's gracious kiss. As a result, Goga finds himself a sex symbol, lionized not only by his skeptical girlfriend (A. Sudakevich) but by screaming, fainting hordes of female admirers until he wipes the lipsticked kiss off his cheek. His fans fade away, but he gets his girl.

Mary Pickford's Kiss was not any more "decadent" than *The Cigarette Girl from Mosselprom*, but the strife in the film community had intensified considerably in the three years that separated the two films. The critics pounced, and, interestingly enough, the reviews in the cultural press were much harsher than those in organs like *Pravda*, where S. Ermolinskii dismissed it as being "of little interest."[17] Kirshon called it "completely alien"; Nedobrovo, "vulgar" and "artless."[18] It was also seen as an "export film" produced for foreign audiences, a fantastic accusation given that the film's humor is so specific to time and place.[19] *Mary Pickford's Kiss* was excoriated so often in the press as the exemplar of the "disastrous" state of Soviet film comedy that it is hard to believe the press would have wasted its time if the film had died a natural death at the box-office.[20]

Adventure

No other popular genre posed quite as many problems as did comedy. Adventure pictures attracted relatively little adverse attention from cinema critics (unless they were the films of the infamous Harry Piel). This was probably because in its Soviet form the adventure genre was so well suited to adaptations of politically correct Civil War themes for the screen. In his book *The Adventure Genre in Cinema* (1929), Edgar Arnoldi touted the adventure film as the most truly popular of all popular genres, since it was accessible and enjoyable to the "ignorant" and "cultured" alike. Arnoldi differentiated between the Soviet and bourgeois variants of the adventure film by claiming that the action in Soviet adventures depended on the hero's class situation, while that in bourgeois adventures was predicated on defense of the hero's property or lover.[21] This distinction, however ingenious, was not always evident in Soviet adventures, which often had a love interest.

The adventure genre in Soviet cinema can be divided into three categories. The Civil War film dominated, but the espionage film (very close to the Western model) and the "Eastern" (primarily Georgian) adventure were also popular. One of the best-known early Soviet adventure films is Ivan Perestiani's Civil War picture *Little Red Devils* (1923), which Arnoldi correctly labelled "the founding point of the adventure genre in Soviet cinema."[22]

The films of Ivan Perestiani, the Georgian actor and director who was the most prolific feature filmmaker of the NEP (see table 5) usually attracted sizeable audiences in the RSFSR. Perestiani, like most directors of the "commercial deviation," had had pre-revolutionary filmmaking experience, in his case in the Khanzhonkov studio.[23] In 1921, Perestiani made an entertaining "Eastern" adventure entitled *Arsen Dzhordzhiashveli*, which featured plenty of violence, intrigue, and especially romance. Its handsome hero (winningly played by Mikhail Chiaureli, later famous for his Stalin films) comes to the tragic end so beloved in the pre-revolutionary cinema. It was *Little Red Devils* which earned Perestiani an indisputed place in the pantheon of Soviet filmmakers and in the hearts of Soviet audiences. The film tells the tale of three children (a brother and sister and their black friend "Tom Jackson"), following their adventures – alternately hair-raising and humorous – dodging the evil Ukrainian anarchist Makhno and his sinister gang of thugs. Disaster follows disaster (the children's father is murdered; the little girl is tortured with hot coals), but good triumphs. *Little Red Devils*, with its skillful combination of humor, violence, and whole-hearted support for the Reds, became a Soviet adventure classic.

Perestiani's film appeared at precisely the moment when the Soviet film community seemed to be in its death throes. *Little Red Devils* created a sensation, and *Cinema Gazette* enthusiastically proclaimed it the "first film of Revolution," a picture which every citizen should see.[24] *Little Red Devils* enjoyed considerable popularity among the public as well as among critics. When Khersonskii saw it, he reported enthusiastic applause from the audience and loud "Hurrahs!"[25] It played at least a month in Moscow, first at the Khanzhonkov, and then at the Kolizei.[26] It was selected for distribution at workers' clubs and was an overwhelming favorite among young spectators. In a 1925 survey, 50 percent named it their favorite film (the nearest competitor, the popular costume drama *The Palace and the Fortress*, got only 13 percent of the vote). By 1926 *Little*

Red Devils had returned 200,000 rubles on a 35,000 ruble budget and so was often touted as an example of how good and profitable a film made on a modest budget could be.[27]

Little Red Devils was an exceptional example of the Soviet adventure film – well plotted, original, droll. More typical of the "B" films which dominated the genre were the CiDl War films *Wind* (Leonid Sheffer and Cheslav Sabinskii, 1926) and *The Tripole Tragedy* (Aleksandr Anoshchenko, 1926). *Wind* concerns a Red Army officer, Vasilii Guliavin (Nikolai Saltykov), who falls obsessively in love with a Cossack vamp, Lelka (O. Podlesnaia), who is an *atamanka*, a leader of a Cossack band. Lelka is beautiful, but vicious and amoral (demonstrated by her sultry glances and cigarette smoking). She intends to betray her lover to the Whites, but, naturally, the only person perceptive enough to see through her schemes is a communist, the unit's political commissar (E. Nadelin). The commissar underestimates his adversary, however, and Lelka kills him in a scene well crafted for suspense. When Guliavin finds his friend lying in a pool of blood, he comes to his senses. He executes his mistress and her followers, and publically apologizes to his comrades. The Reds ride off to take on the Whites; "To horse!" is the final title.

Wind was quite violent, and its depiction of sex and seduction was unusually frank for a Soviet movie, but it received a fairly friendly critical reception.[28] This may have been due to the popularity of its "bourgeois" co-director Sabinskii, but a more plausible explanation is that an even more violent adventure film, Anoshchenko's *The Tripole Tragedy*, was released at approximately the same time. *The Tripole Tragedy* is a veritable orgy of murder and mayhem. The sketchy and thoroughly unbelievable romance between a sweet young girl (Petrova)[29] and a bestial Cossack *ataman* (G. Astafev) is completely overwhelmed by executions, arson, rape, robbery – one after the other. Some of them are ludicrous (as when the Cossacks dance on the graves of soldiers they have buried alive), others sickeningly realistic (like the close-up of a woman's face as she is being raped). The film ends with the girl shooting her lover, after which she is murdered by the Cossacks. The concluding title reads: "Thanks to them we can freely celebrate 1 May," rather an understated ending given the film's general extravagance. *The Tripole Tragedy* became the centerpiece of a campaign against violence on the screen – called in Soviet jargon the "bloody deviation" (*krovavyi uklon*) – and its violence even prompted an outraged letter from a viewer.[30]

Vladimir Gardin, like Sabinskii, was an established "bourgeois" director with many pre-revolutionary films to his credit. He specialized in

"exploitation" films, films which sensationalized Soviet material by
focusing on the villains rather than the heroes. *Locksmith and Chancellor*
(1923, based on a Lunacharskii script) is a good example, but Gardin's
"boulevard, European hit" *Cross and Mauser* (1925) best exemplifies his
style.[31] An espionage variant of the adventure film, *Cross and Mauser* stars
Soviet cinema's leading villain, Naum Rogozhin, as a Catholic priest
(backed by fascists, of course) who plots to destroy the Soviet Union. It is
very similar in theme to Weimar conspiracy films like Fritz Lang's *Spies*,
but with a level of gratuitous violence rare in German films of the period.
There are beatings, fights, murders, a pogrom, arson, and even – very
rare in early Soviet cinema – bare breasts. It opens in 1912: a nun kills a
baby the priest has fathered; they make it appear to be the work of Jews,
and a pogrom rages. In the second part (set in 1922), the priest comes to
justice. He is distracted from his espionage activities by the discovery
that witnesses to his crimes still live. As he plots to murder one witness,
he himself is killed (by being set on fire). There seems to be little doubt
that critics skirted the issue of this film's excessive violence because of the
"correctness" of its attitude toward religion and the church as being the
source of much of the world's evil. Nonetheless, Nikolai Lebedev
claimed that everything about the picture was bad (including the fact that
the film had been oversold when he saw it, leading to a stampede for
seats).[32]

Lebedev's opinions notwithstanding, *Cross and Mauser* was advertised
as a "colossal success," which it no doubt was. The film opened at the
first and second Goskino theatres, and a week later was playing the fourth
Goskino theatre as well. Advertisements in *Izvestiia* proclaimed its
revenues were greater than those for *The Thief of Baghdad* (always the
benchmark for success).[33] As Viktor Shklovskii predicted in his tongue-
in-cheek review, viewers would enjoy *Cross and Mauser* because it told
them everything about "the inner secrets of monasteries."[34] Less nakedly
exploitative (but just as melodramatic) were the "Eastern" adventure
films, set in the Caucasus, and often featuring Robin Hood-like outlaw-
heroes. Perestiani's films *Arsen Dzordzhiashveli* and *The Suram Fortress*
are good examples of this kind of adventure, but an even better one is
Boris Mikhen's *Abrek Zaur* (1926). The dashing mountaineer Zaur
(B. Bestaev) kills a Russian "imperialist" thereby becoming an *abrek*,
member of a roving band of outlaws. This *abrek*, however, never steals
from the people, only from the imperialists. Time and again, Zaur comes
close to being captured, but he always outwits the Russians and their
Cossack minions, who "steal from all equally," according to one title.

Zaur, who hopes "to die fighting," survives to take on the Russians yet another day. *Abrek Zaur* is not especially noteworthy in terms of its technical attributes, but it is interesting to observe that a fairly militant Caucasian nationalism was considered acceptable at this time (as long as the film was set in the tsarist past, as *Abrek Zaur* was). The hyper-critical film press found nothing exceptionable in *Abrek Zaur*, quite an achievement for its director.[35]

Costume drama

Adventures served to satiate the public lust for violence, but historical dramas appealed to different desires. Again we see the divergence between elite and mass opinion. Critics heartily despised the costume dramas and attacked them vigorously, but audiences made their views known at the box-office – and films like *The Palace and the Fortress* (Aleksandr Ivanovskii, 1924), *Stepan Khalturin* (Ivanovskii, 1925), and *The Wings of a Serf* (Iurii Tarich, 1926) were demonstrable commercial successes.[36] For the purposes of this chapter, however, I have selected the two historical films which were the "most" of everything – most popular, most expensive, and most controversial: *The Decembrists* (Ivanovskii, 1927) and *The Poet and the Tsar* (Vladimir Gardin and Evgenii Cherviakov, 1927).

Complaints about the "bourgeoisification" of revolutionary history had been levelled against the historical films since *The Palace and the Fortress*, a film which set the tone for the costume drama by using the revolutionary epoch as a vehicle for exploring the lives and loves of the gentry. It enjoyed the distinction of attracting Politburo member Grigorii Zinovev's ire for its excessive emotionality.[37] The critical controversy over the bourgeois cooption of the past reached a crescendo with the appearance of *The Wings of a Serf*, quite an atypical Soviet historical picture set during the reign of Ivan IV. This film, which was reported to do well abroad although its audience reception at home is uncertain, was charged with being "counterrevolutionary" in a scandal manufactured by opponents of its producer, Sovkino.[38]

Perhaps unaware of the gathering storm, Aleksandr Ivanovskii and historian Pavel Shchegolev had spent nearly two years preparing their blockbuster, *The Decembrists*. (Shchegolev, a well-known specialist on the populist movement, served as scenarist on all three of Ivanovskii's historical films – as well as others, like *The Ninth of January*.) *The Decembrists* was probably the costliest picture produced in the USSR in the silent period. Two sources confirm that it came in at 340,000 rubles, while another claimed that its colossal expense had led to the bankruptcy of the Sevzapkino studio, which then became the Leningrad Sovkino studio.[39] To a certain extent *The Decembrists* does support the old saying that there are virtues in economy. Costing nearly twice as much as its predecessor, *Stepan Khalturin* (an overlong dramatization of one of the unsuccessful plots to assassinate Alexander II led by the People's Will), it was twice as flawed.

Ivanovskii and Shchegolev made little pretense at recreating the Decembrist uprising of 1825, focusing almost exclusively on the love affair between the Decembrist Ivan Annenkov (Boris Tamarin) and Pauline Gueuble (V. Annenkova). Social commentary was minimal (though the Decembrists did not seem particularly admirable – and Grand Duke Konstantin and his Polish wife certainly were not). Ivanovskii paid loving attention instead to details of costume and set, emphasizing glamour, heavy-handed irony, and coy brutality. Despite the participation of a *bona fide* historian as scenarist, the uprising appears to be no more than a badly staged afterthought.

There was no chance that the Soviet critics, with their stiletto pens and critical acumen, would miss this opportunity. The most scathing review appeared in *Cinema* unsigned, a practice which became more common as cultural politics became more uncivilized. In it *The Decembrists* was charged with being a film designed to appeal to the superficiality of the:

continental public ... but for people raised on contemporary cinema, this cine-opera with its agonizingly long and theatrical montage elicits only unpleasant memories of the "psychological" fairy-tales of the time of Ermolev and Drankov.[40]

In other words, *The Decembrists* was an "export" film constructed on the principles of the pre-revolutionary cinema, an accurate assessment. Vladimir Nedobrovo was equally harsh, accusing Ivanovskii of using his material "exploitatively, extravagantly, stupidly"; Vladimir Korolevich called for an end to pictures about "St. Petersburg"; Arsen charged it with historical inaccuracy.[41] *Pravda*'s Boris Gusman concurred that it was "literary-theatrical" but predicted it would be a big hit for that very reason. Gusman's prediction was borne out in the Troianovskii – Egiazarov survey where it was listed as fourth among the ten most popular pictures.[42] And yet it was asserted in 1929 in *Soviet Screen* that the film had recouped only 64 percent of its production costs. Given *The Decembrists*' apparent popularity, which would have translated into paid attendance of well over 1 million at ticket prices ranging from 0.60 to 1.50 rubles, this seems unlikely.[43]

The Poet and the Tsar had the misfortune to appear the same year as The Decembrists, but after it, at precisely the moment when the backlash against "bourgeois" cinema was gathering force. It also did not help that the picture's cavalier treatment of Pushkin attracted the ire of the poet Vladimir Maiakovskii, a formidable force in Soviet cultural circles and an outspoken critic of Sovkino and its policies. Indeed, The Poet and the Tsar became his personal cause in 1927, and he used it as an example of everything that he perceived to be wrong with Soviet cinema. At the ODSK-Komsomol-Komsomolskaia Pravda conference in October 1927 which laid the polemical groundwork for the Party Conference on Cinema Affairs the following spring, Maiakovskii said with a flourish: "Take the film The Poet and the Tsar. You may like the picture . . . but if you think about it, what rubbish, what an outrage this picture is."[44]

Perhaps The Poet and the Tsar is not worth "thinking about" (certainly its appeal was not intellectual), but it is not an "outrage." Vladimir Gardin and actor Evgenii Cherviakov collaborated on the screenplay and co-directed, and Cherviakov starred as Pushkin. Cherviakov looked a fine Pushkin, but unfortunately the screenplay, which centers on the last year of Pushkin's life, is as uncinematic as it is melodramatic. The narrative focuses on Pushkin's unhappy marriage to his unworthy wife (I. Volodko), and Gardin and Cherviakov gave full credence to the old story that Nicholas I (K. Karenin) engineered Pushkin's duel with the nefarious d'Anthès (Boris Tamarin). When Cherviakov's Pushkin is not glowering disapprovingly at various social gatherings, he is wandering about "reading" poems, letters, and so on (and on). Gardin lived up to his reputation as one of the leading directors in both the pre-revolutionary and Soviet cinemas in the well-staged duel scene, but then ruined the dramatic tension by having poor Pushkin linger on forever.

Maiakovskii was not alone in his scathing denunciation of the film, although a fairly judicious review appeared in Cinema in which P. Nezna-mov concentrated on formal attributes, criticizing the static tempo and other technical weaknesses. More typical of the tenor of the reviews was the solemn setpiece in Soviet Screen, where Pushkin scholars were assembled to rail against The Poet and the Tsar's "completely false" portrayal of Pushkin.[45] Adrian Piotrovskii labelled The Poet and the Tsar a film which epitomizes the "petty-bourgeois belief" that history trans-lates into "poeticalness" and "beauty."[46]

This beauty had a high price – at 200,000 rubles not only was the movie four times more expensive than the typical Soviet film, but it had overrun its budget by nearly 25 percent.[47] *The Poet and the Tsar* was therefore not just part of a "front" of reactionary pictures, but also touted as proof of the existence of a "commercial deviation" in cinema which involved Sovkino as well as Mezhrapbom.[48] The public, however, did not share these jaundiced opinions of the picture, and it was apparently a commercial success.[49]

The Poet and the Tsar marked the turning-point in the development of the Soviet costume drama. The final major historical dramas of the silent period appeared in 1928 – Iurii Tarich's *The Captain's Daughter* (about the Pugachev Rebellion) and Konstantin Eggert's *The Ice House* (concerning the scandalous reign of Anna Ivanovna) – but their swift demise was a foregone conclusion. After the Party Conference on Cinema Affairs, the film press focused on promoting "economical," "contemporary," and "ideological" works. Historical pictures certainly could not be contemporary, and their ideological content was superficial at best. Because of the costumes and sets needed to recreate the past "accurately," it was highly unlikely that a "good" historical picture could ever be made as economically as a film about Soviet life. Consequently, only sixteen costume dramas were made in the five-year period from 1929 to 1934 (and none in 1935), accounting for a mere 3 percent of total production.[50]

What the historical film could do better than any other popular genre (because of the constraints of the censorship) was give Soviet audiences a way to enjoy "high life" vicariously – beautiful clothes, lavish homes, plentiful food, leisure time. Despite the romanticization of the Soviet twenties, life during the NEP was not particularly easy; while a few lived well (notably NEPmen and *apparatchiki*), most did not. The costume drama, therefore, served much the same function in Soviet society in the twenties as did those movies about millionaires that were so popular in the US during the Great Depression of the thirties.

Melodrama

The costume dramas had many melodramatic elements, but the melodrama without any historical window-dressing had a distinctive set of problems and imperatives. Adrian Piotrovskii wrote that while melodrama in and of itself was not intrinsically anti-Soviet, most Soviet makers of melodramas had revealed themselves "slaves to bourgeois art" in their focus on the inner workings of private life.[51] If Piotrovskii were correct, then the best-known "slave to bourgeois art" had to be the Commissar of Enlightenment, Anatolii Lunacharskii, for the melodrama in early Soviet cinema is inextricably linked to his name.

Lunacharskii co-authored the screenplays for *The Bear's Wedding* and two other infamous variations on melodrama – *Poison* and *The Salamander*. Until 1928, Lunacharskii managed to rationalize his involvement with these films and avoid undue criticism, but his role was not a passive one. According to Georgii Grebner's contract with Lunacharskii for *The Salamander*, Lunacharskii wrote a libretto which Grebner then translated into a shooting script. Lunacharskii also stipulated in this contract that his wife, Natalia Rozenel, be given the female lead – at a time when directors were being fired for nepotism.[52]

The Bear's Wedding (co-directed by veteran filmmaker Vladimir Gardin and by its star, Konstantin Eggert, 1926) was easily the most sensational Soviet film of the twenties. Critics found very little good in it, but it enjoyed an enormous following and was the number two title in Troianovskii and Egiazarov's "top ten" chart.[53] Its popularity with mass audiences was confirmed in numerous other sources, one viewer writing to *Cinema* that it was a "colossal victory on the cinema front."[54] It was apparently successful abroad as well, and from 1926 on, "bears' wedding" became a synonym for the so-called "export" films.[55]

Why did Soviet audiences find this screen adaptation of Prosper Mérimée's variation of the vampire story so appealing? It is not up to the standards of filmmaking which earned Soviet silent cinema its international reputation. But it is certainly one of the most defiantly apolitical productions of the period, and its emphasis on perversion places it squarely in the pre-revolutionary tradition. Co-director Eggert played the deranged Count Shemet, cursed to have seizures which transform him into a bear on the prowl. The count falls in love with an innocent, awkward young girl (the very popular Vera Malinovskaia, in a part which provides a little comic relief, at least at first). The wedding of the doomed pair is followed by an uncontrolled, sexually charged celebration which becomes more sinister as the night progresses. Tension mounts. The film climaxes in a frightening and gruesome scene in which Count Shemet, besotted by passion and madness, savagely mutilates his bride in their wedding-bed. When he comes to his senses, the count is overcome with anguish, but he attempts to flee the vengeful mob of villagers all the same. Eventually he is murdered by his sister-in-law, and his castle is torched.

The Bear's Wedding had the usual ingredients of popular entertainment – love, sex, violence, action, horror – but in baroque excess. The film is so extreme that this synopsis makes it sound like a parody of a melodrama, but it was not. Eggert managed to make the improbable believable in his portrayal of Count Shemet, and he and Gardin pulled this cinematic pastiche off with style. Critics attributed the film's success to Eggert's performance and to the "romance," linking it to the pre-revolutionary "Gold Series" of big-budget films.[56] It was a common practice among the radical critics to smear films they did not approve of by labelling them part of the Gold Series, but here they were on target. Gardin had been Iakov Protazanov's partner in some of the Gold Series' leading hits, and Protazanov had made what was widely regarded as the most decadent picture in pre-revolutionary cinema, *Satan Triumphant*. For its part, *The Bear's Wedding* was considered so scandalously immoral that Glavpolit-prosvet's Aleksandr Katsigras ordered it banned in the countryside as unsuitable fare for peasants.[57] And its overblown budget was regularly used by opponents of the NEP in the attacks they launched against the "commercialism" of its producer, Mezhrabpom.[58]

The Bear's Wedding* is not a "typical" Soviet melodrama, but it is probably the most pivotal film discussed in this chapter because it challenged the revolutionary mythology so thoroughly. If Soviet audiences loved a picture like this, if a Soviet director made a movie like this, if the Commissar of Enlightenment wrote a screenplay like this, if a Soviet studio financed a film like this ... then had there really been a revolution? There seemed to be only one answer to that question.

Though *The Bear's Wedding* stands apart from all other Soviet attempts at film melodrama, two more examples from the pen of Luna-charskii – *Poison* (Evgenii Ivanov-Barkov, 1927) and *The Salamander* (Grigorii Roshal, 1928) – cover the same ground, a little less extravagantly. *Poison*, which critic S. Ermolinskii aptly labelled a "melodramatic intrigue," concerns Valerii (V. Gerasimov), a Komsomol member whose lover Rimma (O. Malysheva) draws him into a counterrevolutionary espionage circle headed by the foreign agent Johnson Scott (Naum Rogozhin). At Scott's suggestion, Rimma persuades Valerii to murder his father, but before the deed can be carried out, she betrays the plot. Scott then murders her, whereupon Valerii attempts suicide. Valerii is rehabilitated by a good woman (Nina Shaternikova), daughter of a worker.[59] The reviews were uniformly negative, but although K. Denisov wondered why it was necessary to make the "psychopath" (that is, Valerii) a *komsomolets*, the cost of the film was as much an issue as its content.[60] Osip Beskin (the "General" of the Socialist Realist art critics of the thirties)[61] and Vladimir Kirshon (erstwhile architect of

Socialist Realism) had trouble understanding how it was that Sovkino could find 89,000 rubles for *Poison* (24,000 rubles over budget) – and yet plead poverty when it came to producing ideologically suitable films.[62] But Lunacharskii received another reprieve.

By the time *The Salamander* was released, however, it was increasingly obvious that Lunacharskii had little authority left (he resigned the following year), and so there was no longer any effort made to separate the commissar from the films based on his works. *The Salamander*, which was the first Soviet–German co-production (a Mezhrabpom–Prometheusfilm joint venture), turned the true-life tragedy of Paul Kammerer, the Austrian biologist accused of scientific fraud, into a melodramatic conundrum set in Berlin.[63] In the words of an *Izvestiia* critic, it was a "nice old melodrama" which trivialized serious questions of science and religion.[64] The Catholic church (in the person of Sergei Komarov who plays a Jesuit priest) plots to crush science and communism with the help of fascist noblemen (Vladimir Fogel and N. Khmelev, both of whom are heavily made-up). The scheme enables the baron who heads the cabal to seduce Kammerer's beautiful and faithless wife (Lunacharskii's wife, Natalia Rozenel). Lunacharskii, apparently unconcerned about the appearance of nepotism, even gave himself a part in *The Salamander* as Lunacharskii, protector of the world's beleaguered scientists.[65] *The Salamander*, unlike *The Bear's Wedding*, was at least partially "Sovietized" in that the fascists were quite repugnant, but the critics were not fooled; Khersonskii, for example, labelled it "decadent."[66] The importance of *The Bear's Wedding*, *Poison*, and *The Salamander* in the dossier being compiled against Lunacharskii should not be exaggerated, but there can be no doubt that these three movies contributed to the growing impression within the Party and among the "proletarianists" that he was not a suitable advocate for the state's cultural enlightenment goals.

Two other types of melodrama were popular enough to warrant inclusion here, and they illustrate the different methods Soviet filmmakers employed in their attempt to make commercial pictures within the somewhat narrow parameters necessitated by the political climate. When Iurii Zheliabuzhskii embarked in 1925 on a screen adaptation of Pushkin's short story "The Station Master," he may have thought it a safe source for a popular film, given Pushkin's heroic stature as a Russian cultural icon. The film, about an ordinary civil servant who watches his pretty daughter become the mistress of a handsome, rich young officer, maintains its elegiac tone throughout, and Zheliabuzhskii cast three highly regarded actors – Ivan Moskvin, Vera Malinovskaia, and Boris Tamarin – in the leading roles. *The Collegiate Registrar* proved to be quite successful with audiences (garnering the number eight slot on the Troianovskii and Egiazarov survey), but safe it was not. The controversy over the picture probably explains why its official title was *The Collegiate Registrar*, not *The Station Master*. (This led to endless confusion, and the film more often than not was referred to as *The Station Master*, as it is in the epigraph to this chapter.)

Again we see the sharp division between critical opinion and public reception clearly illustrated. Khrisanf Khersonskii, for one, was right when he noted that Pushkin's elegant minor tragedy had been distorted into a "petty-bourgeois melodrama," which he found both "operatic and picturesque." He was wrong, however, when he declared *The Collegiate Registrar* "solidly false," for audiences responded positively to Ivan Moskvin's extravagantly theatrical acting style as well as to the film's sentimentality and glimpses of colorful by-gone days.[67] *The Collegiate Registrar*'s advertisements proclaimed it the film "the whole world has been waiting for," and indeed, it was exported for an unusually high sum.[68] It was a money-maker at home, too; earning a profit of 108,000 rubles in its first four-and-a-half months, more than double the net proceeds from another financially successful picture, Gardin's *Cross and Mauser*.[69]

The "Eastern" variant of the melodrama, unlike melodramatic adaptations of Russian literary classics, tended to fare quite well.[70] Russian critics generally gave much more leeway to directors like Ivan Perestiani and Amo Bek-Nazarov (another veteran of the Khanzhonkov studio) than they ordinarily would to Russian directors, although a few "Easterns," like *The Female Muslim* and *The Eyes of Andoziia* were attacked as "frightening and false."[71] Perestiani's *Three Lives* (1925) was a two-part film about a love triangle, starring Nato Vachnadze, a Georgian actress who was a guaranteed box-office draw in the Russian republic. Although an early intertitle announces that the film is an attack on the "feudal-patriarchal lifestyle of the Georgian princes," viewers were treated to an elaborate melodrama which was not at all tendentious. Bakhva (M. Gelovani), who has risen from shepherd to millionaire, falls in love with Esma, a young hatmaker who is the daughter of a prostitute. Ensign Tsarba (D. Kipiani) lusts after Esma, kidnaps her, and cuts her throat. Tsarba is acquitted at his trial through the wiles of his cousin, the "tsaritsa of dirty thoughts," Princess Valide (T. Valkvadze), and enjoys the good life in Tbilisi. Bakhva, in the meantime, begins an agonizingly slow decline into sloth and alcoholism, but eventually he finds the strength to avenge Esma. In many ways, this film was the antithesis of *Little Red Devils* – it was slow and derivative instead of quick and imaginative. But it has the characteristics which invariably proved popular with Soviet audiences: a surfeit of sex, violence, murder, and coincidence. *Three Lives* was highly profitable, returning three times its investment, and it got decent reviews as well.[72]

Bek-Nazarov's *Honor* (1926) was a variation on the theme of *Three Lives*. Another elaborate tale of thwarted love, murder, and vengeance, its pacing and pathos were similar to that of *The Bear's Wedding*, as was its overt sexuality. The plot is solidly melodramatic: the heroine Zuzanna (M. Shakhubatian-Tatieva) is murdered by her husband Rustam (G. Nersesian) because another man Seiran (S. Mkrtchian) can describe the birthmark on her breast. (Seiran, who also loves Zuzanna, saw this in the devastating earthquake which serves as the first of the film's several very bloody disasters.) When Seiran realizes that his malicious remark has led to his innocent beloved's death, he kills himself. Khrisanf Khersonskii, who attacked the much less melodramatic *The Collegiate Registrar* as too melodramatic, warmly championed *Honor* – and as an example of the incestuousness of the cinema press, he reviewed it for both *Cinema* and *Cinema Front*.[73] *Honor* was proclaimed the biggest hit of 1926, with box-office receipts supposedly greater than those for *The Thief of Baghdad*. While this is undoubtedly an exaggeration (given that *Honor* was released after *The Bear's Wedding*), it is a telling one about the nature of the Soviet audience the very year *Potemkin* reached the screen.

These popular genre films offered Soviet viewers a great deal that the avant-garde classics and *kulturfilmy* did not. Entertainment seems to be a universal human need under the best (and worst) of circumstances, and these films were entertaining. They had easily understandable stories. They looked real (although they were in their own way more fantastic than any product of the avant-garde). They had larger-than-life heroes – and villains to match. What distinguished them from European films of the twenties was not so much the addition of Soviet stock characters or politically correct intertitles – but the recurring motifs of obsessive love, sadistic violence, and tragic or partially resolved endings. These were motifs which came straight from the pre-revolutionary cinema.

Yet these popular genre films were too few in number to offer serious competition to the accomplished and well-financed productions of American and European studios. Soviet studios had directorial talent, but their coffers were quickly depleted. In addition the content restrictions imposed by the vagaries of cultural politics made the reception of any production problematic. As serious was the fact that the studios had another shortcoming which adversely affected commercial film production during the NEP: reluctance to develop a star system to showcase the impressive array of Soviet acting talent.

CHAPTER 5 IMAGES AND STARS

If cinema is the best means of agitation and propaganda among all the arts, then within cinema, the actor is more powerful than directorial form as a means of affecting the viewer.

I know opponents of acted films, but they are constantly going to the cinema to see –

Rod La Rocque or Gloria Swanson. (Valentin Turkin, 1929[1])

Scenarist and critic Valentin Turkin was probably the Soviet film actor's most devoted friend, yet even he used foreign stars to illustrate his point, the surest sign of the actor's sorry position in Soviet cinema.[2] Though only Igor Ilinskii and Nato Vachnadze were widely recognized as stars, there were a considerable number of first-rate actors working in film. Names which immediately come to mind are Nikolai Batalov, Vladimir Fogel, Aleksandra Khokhlova, Anatolii Ktorov, Elena Kuzmina, Fedor Nikitin, Ludmila Semenova, Iuliia Solntseva, Maksim Shtraukh, and Anna Sten, but there were others. Yet despite the obvious talents of these individuals, none of them saw their names emblazoned in lights or promoted to any great extent in the advertisements for their films.[3] And only Fogel worked with the frequency usually connected with star status.

Actors quite naturally found this a frustrating state of affairs, one that had to be changed. By mid-decade, it was painfully apparent to film-makers and critics that Soviet popular cinema was ill-equipped to compete with its foreign counterparts for the Soviet audiences. Even the most popular domestic films rarely garnered the box-office returns of the latest American hits. As this perceived crisis in Soviet cinema deepened, some film critics and film activists turned to the actor to lead Soviet cinema out of its "blind alley." It was hoped that the actor would bring the "living man" to the screen – and audiences to the theatres for Soviet pictures.

How Soviet cinema reached the blind alley is the subject of this chapter. The star problem was real, but it cannot be discussed without reference to characterization in Soviet films, because few actors can transcend their roles. These two factors – the rigidity of permissible stereotypes and the inability of cinema as an institution to create a star system – seriously inhibited the development of Soviet popular cinema. Perhaps no other aspect of popular filmmaking was as deeply politicized as this one.

THE POLITICS AND HISTORY OF THE ACTED FILM

After the Revolution, cinema's Young Turks (especially Dziga Vertov, Sergei Eisenstein, and Lev Kuleshov) began to search for new alternatives to the "bourgeois" actor as well as to the "bourgeois" theatrical film. Rejection of "theatrical" actors, whether old or young, became an article of revolutionary faith in avant-garde circles. Dziga Vertov may be placed at the extreme left of the Leftists, since he completely repudiated the acted (or fiction) film as unalterably bourgeois; his idealized Soviet cinema left no room for stories or impersonations.[4]

Eisenstein and Kuleshov did not go so far. They believed that the fiction film could be the foundation of revolutionary cinema, if acting were revolutionized along with other aspects of filmmaking. "Typage," the practice of selecting people for roles who looked their parts whether or not they were professional actors, was fashionable in the Soviet film world throughout the decade. The anti-professional bias inherent in typage appealed to radical egalitarians who despised reliance on "specialists."[5] Typage also attracted a following because of its connection to Eisenstein, who enjoyed considerable prestige as an artist regardless of his doubtful popularity with audiences. Although Eisenstein did not invent typage, he was its foremost practitioner, and his example lent an added measure of authority to this idea.[6] Directors at one point were actually urged to cast from portfolios, rather than through auditions or screen tests.[7]

Kuleshov's program for reforming film acting was less radical than Eisenstein's, but to the generation of actors and directors raised on the precepts of Stanislavskii as still practiced in the Moscow Art Theatre, it was quite radical enough. Kuleshov espoused the training and deployment of professional film actors he called "actor-models" (*akternaturshchiki*). Kuleshov's actor-model was in some respects a "type" – but one subjected to rigorous physical training.[8] His unorthodox methods produced interesting results, and his influence was an important step forward in the professionalization of Soviet film acting. Aleksandra

Table 7. *Popular Soviet silent film actors, 1920s*

	Birth and death dates	First work in theatre	First work in cinema	Soviet films 1921–31
Nato Vachnadze	1904–1953	n/a	1924	13
Vladimir Fogel	1902–1929	n/a	1925	12
Igor Ilinskii	1901–?	1917	1924	11
Naum Rogozhin	1879–1940	1904	1925	9
Iuliia Solntseva	1901–?	1922	1924	9
Anatolii Ktorov	1898–1980	1919	1924	8
Vera Malinovskaia	1900–?	n/a	1924	7
Konstantin Eggert	1883–1955	1912	1924	6
Ivan Koval-Samborskii	1893–1962	1922	1924	6
Fedor Nikitin	1900–?	1917	1926	6
Vera Baranovskaia	?–1935	1903	1916	5
Nikolai Batalov	1899–1937	1916	1924	5
Maria Bliumental-Tamarina	1859–1938	1887	1916	5
Veronika Buzhinskaia	1895–1983	n/a	1924	5
Vera Maretskaia	1906–1978	1924	1925	5
Nikolai Okhlopkov	1900–1967	1918	1924	4
Ludmila Semenova	1899–?	1920	1920	4
Anna Sten	1906–?	?	1927?	4+
Evgenii Cherviakov	1899–1942	1918	1925	3
Nikolai Tsereteli	1890–1942	191?	1916	3
Valerii Solovtsov	1904–1977	n/a	1926	3+

Sources: Data are drawn from *Kino-slovar*, vols. I and II and *Kino: Entsiklopedicheskii slovar*. Data for Anna Sten (who emigrated in 1932 and is still *persona non grata*) and Valerii Solovtsov are incomplete, but on Sten, see Khersonskii, "Dve biografii." Vera Baranovskaia and Vera Malinovskaia emigrated in 1928; Vladimir Fogel committed suicide in 1929; Konstantin Eggert was arrested during the Great Terror; Nikolai Batalov died in 1937 from tuberculosis. As of 1986 (the publication date of *Kino: Entsiklopedicheskii slovar*), Ilinskii, Malinovskaia, Nikitin, Semenova, and Solntseva were still living.

Khokhlova and Vladimir Fogel were the best-known actors to emerge from the Kuleshov school, but it should not be forgotten that directors Boris Barnet, Sergei Komarov, and Vsevolod Pudovkin were also fine actors who launched their film careers in the collective. Kuleshov's emphasis on acting was mirrored in two other prominent filmmaking collectives of the period: Grigorii Kozintsev and Leonid Trauberg's

Factory of the Eccentric Actor (FEKS, which featured future director Sergei Gerasimov, Elena Kuzmina, Sofia Magarill, and Petr Sobolevskii) and Fridrikh Ermler's Experimental Cinema Workshop (KEM, which "produced" Veronika Buzhinskaia, Iakov Gudkin, and Valerii Solovtsov).[9]

The "bourgeois" directors of popular films issued no proclamations, conducted no acting classes, and did not roam the countryside looking for "types."[10] They typically cast recruits from the theatre. Most of the best (and best-known) actors in the popular cinema – Vera Baranovskaia, Nikolai Batalov, Maria Bliumental-Tamarina, Konstantin Eggert, Igor Ilinskii, Anatolii Ktorov, L.M. Leonidov, Vera Maretskaia, Nikolai Okhlopkov, Ludmila Semenova, and Iuliia Solntseva – had begun their acting careers in the theatre (see table 7).[11] Many continued to work in theatre and cinema concurrently, and a few, like Igor Ilinskii, reprised roles created for the stage when they were adapted for the screen. Yet it was no more true that the "old specialists" only used well-established theatre actors for casting their films than it was that young directors never used them.[12] Vladimir Fogel, to name one prominent example, was cast in many "bourgeois" films, despite his youth and his "revolutionary" credentials as a former member of the Kuleshov collective. Another example may be found in the case of Ada Voitsik, who was "discovered" by Protazanov while still an acting student at the State Cinema Technicum (GTK).

By the mid-twenties, the critics' ardor for the avant-garde had cooled quite noticeably. It became increasingly clear that non-acted films and films featuring casting by typage did not attract viewers, despite a few well-publicized though problematic successes like *Potemkin*. Dziga Vertov's films had long been "dismissed" by critics for not speaking to the masses (and implicitly or explicitly, for not making money), but it was only a matter of time before Eisenstein's fortunes also became linked with the debate over the actor.

The turning-point for Eisenstein was *October*. He committed many "sins" in *October*, but weak narrative development and absence of a hero were foremost. (Of course, Eisenstein and his critics were operating on different aesthetic imperatives.) Eisenstein had cast as Lenin a worker so anonymous that we are not even sure what his surname was; in the press of the time it appeared as either "Nikandrov" or "Nikanorov." Whatever his name, the man's wooden impersonation of the founder of the Soviet state offended many, including Lenin's widow Nadezhda Krupskaia.[13] The fact that Lenin's nemesis Kerenskii (N. Popov) was the most vivid character in *October* did not help Eisenstein's situation (even though the depiction of Kerenskii is undeniably negative).

Eisenstein compounded *October*'s casting "errors" in his next Soviet film, *The Old and the New*. He selected for his heroine a "type," a peasant woman named Marfa Lapkina, just as there was a loud campaign calling for "prettier women" in Soviet cinema.[14] Whatever Lapkina's virtues as a "type," she certainly did not conform to the ideal of feminine beauty held by urban movie critics, and presumably, by audiences.[15]

By the onset of the Cultural Revolution, "sterile" formalist exercises without stories and heroes (and actors) had been rejected. Putting "man" back into films was seen as a key element in the process of transforming cinema from a medium for the "masses" into one for the "millions." Critics recognized that unadorned ideology bored everyone, even the already converted (as Turkin sarcastically noted in the epigraph to this chapter). But critics seemed not to understand that the institutional edifice they themselves had helped create discouraged both actors and scenarists, and that it would not be a simple matter to effect an about-face and develop "real" characters for the screen.

IMAGES AND STEREOTYPES

Most Soviet film critics of the twenties believed Soviet cinema to be exceptionally clichéd, evidence that they did not fully understand the function of stereotyping in popular cinema. A good example of this attitude comes from Ippolit Sokolov, who wrote:

Generals always take bribes; rich peasants (*kulaks*) set fire to cooperatives; poor peasants (*bedniaks*) support cooperatives. NEPmen always have angora cats, White soldiers dance in prison, etc. Is this really "life as it is?" No, this is simply nonsense. This is lack of talent. This is a harmful state of affairs that discredits Soviet pictures in the eyes of the mass viewer.[16]

There are numerous other examples of critics attacking the prevailing stereotypes, especially the "primitive" delineation of heroes and villains.[17] But genre cinema is clichéd by definition; stereotypes provide spectators security. Audiences for popular films like knowing what they are going to see, especially if they have to pay for the privilege. After all, the Hollywood films that Soviet audiences so loved were replete with stock types – the vamp, the Latin lover, the girl-next-door, the cowboy, the gangster (or "good" outlaw), the prostitute, etc. – and so were French and German films. Since it is not axiomatic that stereotypes are boring,

why did Soviet cinematic stereotyping seem less interesting than the
Western?

Soviet cinema, whether avant-garde or traditional, first- or second-
rate, had created variations on old themes drawn from both Russian and
Western sources. The "new" villains were people whose activities com-
promised the Soviet regime or were antithetical to its ideals: foreigners,
imperialists, capitalists, black-marketeers, priests, nobles (or "Whites"),
discredited radicals (Kadets, Socialist Revolutionaries, anarchists),
kulaks, hooligans, non-Party bureaucrats. Heroes (whether male or
female) were: revolutionaries, commissars (or other Party members), Red
Army officers, workers, *bedniaks*, Komsomol members, Chekists. In the
cinemas of the union republics, "outlaws" who opposed tsarist rule were
also acceptable "heroes." "Gray" characters, like Fedor Nikitin's hapless
intelligent in *Katka the Apple Seller* or Ivan Koval-Samborskii's White
officer in *The Forty-First*, rarely made it to the screen.

Soviet stereotypes proved considerably harder to vary than Western
stock characters because they were politically dictated, not determined by
audience tastes. Although the rules were unwritten, directors and scenarists seemed to understand that they had a limited range of possibilities,
with boundaries beyond which variation was impermissible.[18] For
example, a priest could never be a positive or even a neutral character
because the state encouraged atheism, while a communist could have no
flaws unless he were "unmasked" as an enemy (and therefore revealed
not to have been a believer after all).

Soviet directors were quite resourceful, and even these strictures
might have been overcome if there had not existed another critical
restriction which inhibited character (and narrative) development. These
black-and-white characters were supposed to operate almost exclusively
in the public sphere.[19] As a result, romance (a staple of popular fiction, no
matter the form) could never be the overt subject of a film. Communists
did fall in love in Soviet films, but, as a rule, ever so chastely; love was not
supposed to interfere with union organizing or revolution (especially not
for women). Passionate love between communists and non-communists
had to end in the violent death of the latter (as it does in *Wind*, *His Call*,
The Forty-First). The bourgeois directors tended to prefer the tragic
ending to cutting the romance altogether and so avoided making egre-
gious "errors."

As a result of all these factors, most screen heroes were frankly dull,
and it was difficult for even the best actors to breathe vitality into their
roles. Three who could were Nikolai Batalov, Vladimir Fogel, and Igor

Ilinskii. Ilinskii was the most successful of the three in that his impersonations of the "little man" against the world consistently attracted audiences, but nonetheless, it does not appear that he stole their affections away from Charlie Chaplin. Batalov could infuse the conventional heroes of Soviet Russian cinema with life, as he did in *Aelita*, *Mother*, and *A Start in Life* (and in his unconventional roles, like that in *Third Meshchanskaia Street*). He did not, however, look like a "leading man" to audiences used to the regular-featured heroes with pomaded hair who graced foreign and pre-revolutionary films, and so he did not offer Douglas Fairbanks any real competition. Fogel was the leading male actor of the NEP in terms of numbers of pictures, but he played so many different kinds of roles that he never established a recognizable screen persona.

Actors who better resembled Western matinée idols were more likely to be found in the Georgian and Ukrainian cinema of the period (although the Protazanov regular Anatolii Ktorov is an obvious exception). Georgian actors, like Mikhail Chiaureli in *Arsen Dzhorzhiashveli*, used the greater latitude given Georgian filmmakers to create more glamorous heroes in the Douglas Fairbanks style. And the Ukrainian actor Semen Svachenko (who earned a permanent niche in the history of Soviet cinema for his performances in Dovzhenko's *Arsenal* and *Earth*) was among the most charismatic actors to appear on the Soviet silent screen.

Though the lip-service paid to feminist principles in the twenties should have opened new possibilities for women in the movies, the situation for actresses was depressingly similar. Heroines had to be "wholesome," like Vera Popova in *His Call*, Vera Maretskaia in *The House on Trubnaia Square*, or Emma Tsesarskaia in *Peasant Women of Riazan*. Since glamour signified villainy (as in Olga Zhizneva's role in *The Case of the Three Million* or O. Malysheva's in *Wind*), actresses like the beautiful and talented Iuliia Solntseva found their acting careers cut rather short.

Those actresses who did succeed in working regularly found women's parts to be defined in a distinctly traditional way. Vera Malinovskaia (*The Collegiate Registrar*, *The Man from the Restaurant*, *The Bear's Wedding*) managed to carve out a career playing victims, especially in costume dramas where some handsome but corrupt nobleman could take advantage of an innocent young woman's virtue. As a variation on this theme, Veronika Buzhinskaia (*Katka the Apple Seller* and *The Parisian Cobbler*) specialized in proletarian heroines victimized by NEP types. A few others, like Anna Sten (*The White Eagle*, *The Girl with the Hatbox*), Natalia Glan (*Miss Mend*), and Ada Voitsik (*The Forty-First*) found more active roles as spunky working women who take charge of their lives. Yet two of the staple types of genre filmmaking, full-fledged romantic heroines and sex symbols, were practically non-existent.

One important exception to these generalizations came from Georgian, not Russian, cinema. Presumably because as a Georgian she was a "passionate" Easterner, Nato Vachnadze could depict private life on screen (especially as the flagrantly wronged woman) without arousing the anxieties of Russian critics.[20] The other major exceptions can be found in the work of the avant-garde – Marfa Lapkina in *The Old and the New* or the roles Elena Kuzmina played in Kozintsev and Trauberg's *New Babylon* and *Alone* (as a Paris communard and a struggling teacher in Central Asia, respectively).

But in the main villains were far more interesting then heroes, and those actors who devoted their careers to personifying iniquity consistently earned the "admiration" of audiences. Some of the masks of villainy were completely repugnant, like the corpulent capitalist or the drunken hooligan, but in other cases, spectators rooted for the villains in a film because they were "stronger and more clever" (and sometimes more handsome) than the heroes.[21] Naum Rogozhin, a sophisticated character actor with a long and impressive stage career, served up deliciously wicked villains in films like *Cross and Mauser* and *Poison*. (Rogozhin was also popular enough to be seen playing himself as film star in *Mary Pickford's Kiss*.) A few younger actors followed this route to fame as well, notably the debonair Anatolii Ktorov, dashing anti-hero in *The Case of the Three Million* and *St. Jorgen's Feast Day* (and out-and-out rogue in *His Call*), and Valerii Solovtsov, who specialized in speculator roles in Fridrikh Ermler's films.

Critics were horrified that mass audiences preferred these negative types – and they blamed scenarists. They claimed that better-qualified and more talented scenarists could create more interesting Chekists and poor peasants (*bedniaks*). Even critics as knowledgeable as Valentin Turkin (the scenarist whose words opened this chapter) and Ippolit Sokolov (author of a book on Lillian Gish and many works on various aspects of Soviet cinema) believed that the acting "problem" in Soviet cinema chiefly resulted from poor scripts with cardboard characters.[22]

Yet whenever directors and scenarists attempted to "shade" the black and white, however slightly, they were invariably attacked by the same critics who complained about excessive stereotyping. For example, the

American businessman Oliver McBride in Zheliabuzhskii's *The Cigarette Girl from Mosselprom*, while far from complex, strayed too far from the norm. Yes, he was fat (as capitalists had to be) and carried too much luggage (like all Americans), but he was also ever-so-slightly sympathetic. He hoped to marry Zina, not to make her his mistress. Likewise, Ivanov-Barkov's depiction of a *komsomolets* as a potential traitor and murderer in *Poison* and Sheffer and Sabinskii's of a Red Army officer blinded by lust (*Wind*) raised negative comments from the ever-vigilant critics.[23]

If there was indeed a "scenario crisis," it was part of the larger crisis in Soviet cinema, the question of control over the production process. It could not be resolved in isolation – and certainly not without taking into account the complex and symbiotic relationship between the image and the image-maker.

ACTORS VS. "STARS"

Fridrikh Ermler, one of the few directors who consistently succeeded in injecting life into the stock characters of Soviet cinema, did so against type. Ruggedly handsome Valerii Solovtsov was always the villain in Ermler's films, while the gentlemanly Fedor Nikitin was the hero. While other directors (notably bourgeois directors) understood the function of actors in films, few critics seemed fully to appreciate the power of the actor to enrich an ordinary script – and to overcome mediocre directing. Ironically, Valentin Turkin revealed this particular blind spot in his book *The Cinema Actor*, a book which in most respects celebrates the art of film acting.[24] Turkin was puzzled by the popularity of Vera Kholodnaia, the fabled star of the pre-revolutionary Russian screen, because she was not (in his view) a real actress. Turkin's opinion of her acting ability is arguable but irrelevant; the point is that he did not seem to understand why she was a star. Kholodnaia was a star because she had "it" – whether "it" is defined as sex appeal, charisma, or simply star quality. Actresses as diverse as Clara Bow, Greta Garbo, Lillian Gish, Pola Negri, Mary Pickford, and Gloria Swanson had it. Charlie Chaplin, Douglas Fairbanks, Harry Piel, and Rudolph Valentino had it. Aleksandra Khokhlova and Fedor Nikitin – both important talents – did not, nor did most of the many gifted performers of Soviet cinema.

Yet despite their evident uncertainty as to the potential of the actor to enliven a film, Soviet film critics were concerned about the failure of Soviet actors to attract followings of the same magnitude as Western

movie stars.[25] Their concerns were well-founded, because although
scholars, critics, and cinéastes categorize films in terms of directors, mass
audiences think of them in terms of stars. There was not, of course, some
defect in the national character that prevented Soviet actors from becoming stars. Although more obvious examples of Soviet stardom come from
the thirties (Liubov Orlova was a star by any standards), two of the most
prolific actors of the twenties, Nato Vachnadze and Igor Ilinskii, were
also *bona fide* stars. They worked constantly, their names sometimes
appeared in the advertisements for their films, and spectators mentioned
them in letters and surveys.

Nato Vachnadze made thirteen movies from her debut in 1924 to the
end of the Cultural Revolution and was the only "ethnic" actress who
was as popular in the RSFSR as she was in her native republic.
Advertised as the "Soviet Vera Kholodnaia" (which really says it all),
Vachnadze was honored by two pulp Russian-language biographies
printed in nearly 100,000 copies.[26] References to movies in Soviet
memoir literature are disappointingly (though understandably) rare, but
it is not mere coincidence that one of these few concerns Nato Vachnadze, whom Evgeniia Ginzburg remembered as "dovelike heroine" and
eternal victim.[27]

It is worth noting that most of Vachnadze's pictures were steamy
genre melodramas on the love-betrayal-vengeance theme which had been
immensely popular in the pre-revolutionary cinema, but which were
practically non-existent in Soviet Russian filmic variants. Vachnadze's
abilities as an actress were real though her range was limited, and she
infused all of her vulnerable and doomed heroines with a great deal of
passion and emotion. Yet reviewers had little to say about her acting in
their critiques, other than to note sadly that her presence guaranteed
another hit for the Goskinprom Gruzii studio and that she was "accidentally photogenic."[28]

Igor Ilinskii was the only other actor in Soviet cinema who was known
to be a guaranteed box-office draw. His biographies were printed in a
mere 75,000 copies, and he made "only" eleven films, but one must
remember that he was a constant presence on the stage of the time as
well. Despite Walter Benjamin's snide references to Ilinskii as an imitation Chaplin (echoed by many contemporaries, including Viktor
Shklovskii), Ilinskii made a considerable difference to the troubled
comedy genre.[29]

While Vachnadze acted exclusively in film, Ilinskii was a well-
established theatre star (trained by Meierkhold) who worked in the

theatre as often as in film. The undeniable cachet of the "legitimate" theatre doubtless contributed to his appeal among Russian audiences, who retained high culture biases, Revolution or no Revolution.[30] Movie-goers could rely on Ilinskii as they could on Vachnadze to give them a character they wanted to see; in Ilinskii's case, a sly but lovable buffoon. Soviet critics disliked him with varying degrees of intensity, but it is surely another sign of his popularity that they deigned to notice him at all.[31]

Despite the examples of Vachnadze and Ilinskii, stardom proved virtually impossible for other Soviet film actors to achieve. Nikolai Batalov and Vera Malinovskaia had as much talent and charisma as Ilinskii and Vachnadze (if not more), yet they were not stars. The numbers of films they made in the twenties (five and seven, respectively) reflect this, although they had quite respectable careers. The fact was that film actors, even those with impressive credentials like Batalov's (*Aelita*, *Mother*, *Third Meshchanskaia Street*) and Malinovskaia's (*The Collegiate Registrar*, *The Bear's Wedding*, *The Man from the Restaurant*), had to struggle to maintain position in the twenties. Director Abram Room claimed that Batalov earned so little from his film work that he was forced to hold two jobs.[32] By the end of the decade, many felt the struggle was not worth it, and several prominent film actors (Malinovskaia, Vera Baranovskaia, Mikhail Chekhov, and Anna Sten, among others) emigrated to uncertain futures.[33]

Actors faced a number of institutional factors which prevented the development of the kind of "star system" that catapulted Hollywood actors into a life of fame and luxury – and Hollywood films to dominate the world market. These institutional impediments – lack of promotion, depressed salaries, inability of studios to sign actors to exclusive multi-picture contracts – were ideologically motivated as well as financially predetermined.

The ideological reasons for the lack of a star system hark back to the debate about keeping professional actors out of cinema altogether. Since socialism is intended to benefit the group over the individual, ensemble acting and production collectives were encouraged in early Soviet cinema as ideologically correct. Stars, on the other hand, must be promoted as individuals and paid according to their name recognition. The prejudice against personal display and unequal treatment was so strong in the twenties that even the Mezhrabpom studio, which was essentially autonomous and had its own studio style, hesitated to deviate from the unwritten rule. When Mezhrabpom did dare to depart from the norm –

as when the studio paid the astronomical salaries of 500 rubles a day to
Vasilii Kachalov and Vsevolod Meierkhold for their parts in Protazanov's film *The White Eagle* – critics did not hesitate to make an issue of
it.[34]

Ordinary actors were poorly paid by comparison. Typical salaries for
a shooting day were 3.50 rubles for an extra, 6–7.50 rubles for a
speaking part, and 10–20 rubles for a leading part. The Kamernyi
Theatre's Nikolai Tsereteli, a major theatre star who occasionally
appeared in films (like *The Cigarette Girl from Mosselprom*), commanded
the substantial figure of 75 rubles a day.[35] Working conditions were
poor: long hours without overtime pay and unregulated use of child
actors ("He's little – he won't talk!") are only a few examples.[36]
Unemployment among film actors (even experienced actors) was high,
and it was believed that directors were always looking for "new faces"
rather than promoting the careers of experienced actors.[37]

Another problem Soviet film actors faced was that their work was
unheralded. Unlike foreign stars their names almost never appeared in
advertisements and film posters, and often only their first initial was
used. Publicity photos or articles about them were likewise uncommon.
The quality of their performances was discussed only infrequently in
reviews, especially true in the reviews appearing in the general press,
which tended to summarize plots. But although it would have been
quite insulting enough to be underpaid and ignored, film actors suffered numerous other petty humiliations that made working in the
theatre a more attractive as well as a more prestigious alternative.[38]

Movie actors felt themselves pawns in a system dominated by a
"dictatorial" director. Actors had to do battle with the director to be
allowed to see any of the script before shooting began, which reinforced
their impression that the director was the "dictator" on the set, and
they were mere flunkeys.[39] Critics openly stated that if a director were
really good, then the actor was no more than a "mirror" reflecting the
director's will, a "cheap thing" to be exploited.[40] Actors even faced the
indignity of searching for a lavatory that they were allowed to use, since
some were posted "No actors allowed!"[41] Not surprisingly, mature and
well-established actors like Vera Baranovskaia and Naum Rogozhin
complained bitterly about directors' attitudes and working conditions
in the studios.[42] Even a star like Igor Ilinskii clearly preferred to work
in theatre.[43]

THE ACTOR DURING THE CULTURAL REVOLUTION

The Cultural Revolution proved a turning-point in this as in every other aspect of Soviet cinema, and the pattern is by now a familiar one. There were real shortcomings in Soviet cinema and genuine reasons for discontent, but the issues quickly took unexpected turns as they were exploited for political and personal ends. Yet, despite the fact that the ends achieved did not always promote human interest in films, this conflict demonstrates apparently genuine ideological commitment among the cinema rank-and-file for change.

The debate over actors was redefined as part of the class and generational struggles resurfacing throughout society by 1927, in this case as a battle between the "old specialists" (theatre actors) and the "new" (cinema actors) – or more cynically, as a competition between successful and unsuccessful actors for jobs. The stakes were high. As one *Cinema Front* editorial put it: "Who created Soviet cinema? Not old, pre-revolutionary specialists [*spetsy*], but new people." Yet "new people" were out of work, while the *spetsy* enjoyed full employment. Studio administrators were seen to be bedfellows of those directors with pre-revolutionary experience who produced "comfortable and safe trashy films" relying exclusively on the assistance of their bourgeois cronies.[44]

Certain actors, invariably minor names, believed that it would be in their interests to curtail directorial independence in casting. Chief among them was Olga Tretiakova, secretary of ARK's Acting Section and an actress whose career had faltered after her early success in *Commander Ivanov*. Tretiakova led the charge against "nepotism" and "protectionism" in cinema. Many directors faced these charges – among them Lev Kuleshov, Lili Brik, and Boris Barnet – but the best example is the case manufactured against six directors from the Leningrad Sovkino studio – Evgenii Cherviakov, Fridrikh Ermler, Aleksandr Ivanovskii, Grigorii Kozintsev, Cheslav Sabinskii, and Leonid Trauberg.[45]

These directors were charged with "protectionism," specifically with refusing to hire professional actors for their films. One has only to look at the list to know that this "case" was fraudulent and politically motivated. Ivanovskii and Sabinskii were among the most venerable of the "bourgeois" entertainment directors and as such relied heavily on big names for their films; Kozintsev and Trauberg and Ermler, as noted earlier in this chapter, had founded their own filmmaking collectives on the principle of ensemble acting; Cherviakov was himself an actor (as well as a director). The "crime" of the Leningrad directors was that they persisted in casting their films as they chose, without regard for "proletarian" credentials.[46]

The radicals insisted that "bourgeois" actors (meaning, theatre actors) no longer be considered "professionals" since it was impossible to expect such actors convincingly to portray peasants and workers, the exclusive subjects of the new Soviet cinema.[47] The fact that the bourgeois specialists in the acting community were also the best and most popular actors working in Soviet cinema was ignored – as was the fact that urban audiences apparently had already had enough of peasant-heroes, given their preference for Western and native "bourgeois" films.

Yet who was to replace them? The Association of Revolutionary Cinematography (struggling to keep pace with more authentic "proletarianist" organizations like the Russian Association of Proletarian Writers) advanced three propositions: (1) that the definition of "stars" needed to be revised to mean those who understood "Soviet" principles of work, foreign to actors in "capitalist American cinema"; (2) that a "strong" cadre of film actors needed to be constituted; (3) that theatre actors could work in cinema only if they demonstrated through "long and diligent" effort that they were not dilettantes.[48] But could any "star system" be truly Soviet? Many critics believed star systems by their very nature were alien. Khrisanf Khersonskii, for example, understood the relationship between the star system and the popular appeal of Hollywood films, but he felt that the price – individualism and careerism – was too high to pay, even if it meant better movies.[49]

Those actors who had sought to curb directorial independence in casting and establish professional standards for film acting had achieved some of their aims, but their "victory" was analogous to that of the enlighteners. True, directors were humbled, and typage was formally rejected. Types might serve as "background," but only the "literate film actor" could be expected to bring the "living person to the screen."[50] Peasants needed to stay on the farms "where they belong," rather than flocking to the city to look for movie roles (a chilling, though faint reflection of the collectivization campaign then underway).[51]

But the outlines of Socialist Realism were now becoming apparent, and its emphasis on public life and relentless optimism meant that the "new hero" was more circumscribed in his activities and emotional range than was the old. The "imported" hero who epitomized petty-bourgeois values was firmly rejected.[52] Stereotyping became even more rigid, as this extract from a satire on a meeting between a screenwriter and his producer demonstrates:

"Where's the rich peasant [*kulak*], I ask you? Shame! A picture without a rich peasant
...? Shame! Rewrite it. Correct it. And also write in a light cavalry, it's impossible not
to have one. It's the hit of the season!" And as I was leaving, he shouted after me,
"And the RKI [Workers-Peasants Inspectorate]! And don't forget a wall newspaper
[*stengazeta*]! What about a cultural outing [*kultpokhod*]?"[53]

As disquieting for the young radicals who had hoped to displace the
"bourgeois" cadres of established film actors was the fact that those very
same specialists were now marshalled to support the new path. For
example, "bourgeois" critic Mikhail Levidov called for "new" heroes,
while the Moscow Art Theatre-trained film actor Fedor Nikitin urged
actors to serve as the "emotional organization of the masses of Soviet
society."[54] Olga Tretiakova, the actress who had hoped to oust these
spetsy, does not even have an entry in any of the standard biographical
directories.

Given the complicated conditions governing genres, characterization,
and casting, it is not surprising that there were so few hits and so few
stars in early Soviet popular cinema. Yet it was possible to succeed as a
"commercial" filmmaker, if one had talent, luck, and perseverance – and,
especially, the financial backing of the Mezhrabpom studio. Iakov Protazanov had all of these. Although he was not the most prolific popular
director of the period (an honor belonging to Ivan Perestiani), Protazanov was the "bourgeois specialist" most consistently in the limelight.
Even critics who despised his work proclaimed him Soviet cinema's most
popular director.[55] Protazanov's career was exceptional in its level of
achievement, but paradigmatic in other respects. It illustrates how one
director navigated the obstacles to popular filmmaking to emerge from
the twenties with ten hits to his credit.

We're building cinema art anew and guarding Soviet prestige. It's only in Protazanov's pictures – whether Moscow or Paris – that [Soviet cinema] is being rebuilt in a
border station. He sat three years for nothing – ugh! he understands the French
Revolution better than "October."   (Ia. Galitskii, 1927[1])

Among the many filmmakers who left Russia during the Civil War was
Iakov Protazanov (1881–1945). Protazanov had been one of the
flourishing pre-revolutionary film industry's most prominent directors,
and the more than eighty movies he had made since his directorial debut
in 1911 included box-office hits like *The Keys to Happiness*, *The Queen of
Spades*, and *Satan Triumphant*. From 1920 to 1923, Protazanov lived in
Paris and Berlin, making a name for himself in both French and German
cinemas – so he hardly "sat three years for nothing," as Galitskii
charged.[2] In 1923 in Berlin, he received a visit from Moisei Aleinikov, a
producer from the Rus studio (soon to be subsumed by Mezhrabpom).
Aleinikov persuaded Protazanov that the time was right to return home.[3]
Three weeks later Protazanov was back in Moscow, and shortly thereafter at work on his first Soviet film, *Aelita*.

The history of Soviet popular cinema cannot be understood without a
discussion of the director whom one Soviet film scholar has dubbed the
"Russian Griffith."[4] Iakov Protazanov made ten silent films for the
Mezhrabpom-Rus studio in six years, beginning with *Aelita* in 1924 and
ending with *St. Jorgen's Feast Day* in 1930.[5] His work epitomized what
was known as the "Mezhrabpom film," that is, pictures which were
widely distributed, enjoyed runs of several weeks in the largest theatres,
invariably profitable, and frequently named in viewer surveys.
Throughout his long career in cinema, Protazanov seemed to have an
uncanny understanding of what movie-goers liked, whether they were
Russian, French, or Soviet.

To the young cohort, however, Protazanov was a figure of altogether
different significance. He epitomized everything they perceived to be

wrong with the Soviet film industry in the twenties – its emphasis on profits, its lack of financial support for experimentation (regardless of the lipservice paid the avant-garde), its "pandering" to the tastes of the masses. Why was Soviet cinema banking on "old specialist" directors like "the little Moscow merchant" instead of on Kuleshov, Vertov, or Eisenstein?[6]

PROTAZANOV AND RUSSIAN CINEMA

Protazanov's background is worth going into in some detail because the personal characteristics and experiences which enabled him to succeed as a director in the pre-revolutionary period served him well in the Soviet period. He was pragmatic, efficient, and discreet – attributes which set him apart from those younger Soviet directors who sometimes seemed to be as interested in courting controversy as they were in making films.

Iakov Aleksandrovich Protazanov was born in Moscow in 1881, on his mother's side the member of a well-to-do merchant family named Vinokurov.[7] Several of Protazanov's relatives were in the theatre business, and Protazanov early evinced an interest in stagecraft.[8] Though he had hoped to attend engineering school, he was sent instead to the Moscow Commercial School; after his graduation in 1900, he was employed as a clerk in an office, an experience he found quite disagreeable. The long-awaited opportunity to "escape from [the] slavery" of job and family came in 1904 when he received a 5,000 ruble inheritance from his father's aunt. Protazanov left the country in June of that year. While in Paris, he added the Pathé studio, center of pre-war European cinema, to the standard tourist itinerary. To the surprise and horror of his family and friends, Protazanov fixed suddenly and irrevocably upon movie-making as his career of choice.[9]

Protazanov did not return permanently to Russia until 1907, whereupon he went to work for the Russian-owned "Gloria" film studio as an interpreter for a Spanish cameraman (notwithstanding that he spoke French, not Spanish). "Gloria" failed (as did many studios in the early days of cinema), and Protazanov offered his services to the more established concern of Thiemann and Reinhardt.[10] Protazanov quickly learned all the aspects of movie-making as Thiemann and Reinhardt's jack-of-all-trades, and his "big break" was not long coming. In 1911, he dashed off a script called *Convict's Song* which he sold to Thiemann for 25 rubles. The film, Protazanov's directorial debut, was a rousing success.[11]

The production practices that Protazanov developed in his pre-revolutionary career reflect early developments in the Russian industry that survived into the Soviet period. Perhaps most important was the close relationship which existed between Russian theatre and cinema. Many early Russian movie directors came to cinema from theatre – Vladimir Gardin (with whom Protazanov frequently collaborated), Peter Chardynin, and Evgenii Bauer, to name only a few. Similarly, actors and set designers moved from theatre to film and back, depending on where the jobs were. Throughout his long career in the movies, Protazanov preferred to use actors with theatre training and to hire production personnel he had known in the pre-revolutionary cinema.

Protazanov enjoyed an excellent working relationship with actors and was an astute judge of talent. His ability to attract actors of the stature of Ivan Mozzhukhin and Nataliia Lisenko doubtless contributed to the popularity of his pre-revolutionary movies with a public which had heard of these stars but could not afford to attend the theatre.[12] He did not depend exclusively on established names, however, and gave Olga Preobrazhenskaia, then a little-known provincial stage actress in her early thirties who was deemed "too old" for major roles, the chance that made her a star.[13]

Protazanov came to be known for his big-budget screen adaptations of famous literary works, an especially popular genre in the Russian cinema, which was seeking respectability and a middle-class audience. Protazanov directed his share of these lavish costume dramas and screen adaptations, the best known being his mammoth version of *War and Peace* (1915, co-directed with Vladimir Gardin) and *The Queen of Spades* (1916).[14] But the film that placed Protazanov at the forefront of Russian film directors did not bring a serious work of literature down to the lowly screen. It was instead his 1913 adaptation of one of the most popular works of Russian *boulevard* fiction, Anastasiia Verbitskaia's sensational novel about a liaison between a Russian girl and an older, Jewish businessman, *The Keys to Happiness*.[15] Protazanov's instinct for the entertaining rarely failed him, and *The Keys to Happiness* was a legendary box-office success. In direct response to the phenomenon of *The Keys to Happiness*, Thiemann and Reinhardt, established its famous "Gold Series" of full-length feature films, mainly directed by Protazanov.[16] Although Protazanov continued making movies based on the classics, his biggest hits were usually derived from popular fiction, a practice he continued in his Soviet work.

With the outbreak of World War I, the "German" firm of Thiemann and Reinhardt was attacked by mobs, and in 1915 Protazanov left Thiemann to join the Ermolev studio, at the princely salary of 20,000 rubles.[17] Protazanov was drafted at the age of thirty-five in September 1916, an event which had no effect on his ability to make movies.[18] Since the war had led to a shortage of foreign films, Protazanov was able to accelerate his rate of production to meet increased demand: nineteen pictures in 1914; twelve in 1915; and fifteen in 1916.

After the February Revolution, the Ermolev studio effortlessly adjusted to the revolutionary mentality and began producing works on revolutionary themes. Protazanov adapted as well and among the eight films he made in 1917 were two about revolutionary martyrs: *Andrei Kozhukhov* and *We Don't Need Blood* (about Sofia Perovskaia). More to his taste, certainly, was his *succès de scandale Satan Triumphant*, a film about demonism.[19] Revolution also made it possible for Protazanov to adapt Lev Tolstoi's *Father Sergius* (1917, released 1918), a story which he had wanted to film for some time, but which the pre-revolutionary censors had repressed as a movie script. This picture, starring Ivan Mozzhukhin as the tsarist officer who becomes a monk, is usually considered the last great work of Russian (as distinguished from Soviet) cinema.[20]

EXILE AND RETURN

Sometime during the winter of 1918–19, Ermolev studio head Iosif Ermolev (like Protazanov, scion of a Moscow merchant family) became alarmed at the direction the Revolution was taking. Concerned for the health and safety of his company in cold and hungry Moscow, he persuaded the entire group, including Protazanov, to move with him to Yalta and set up shop there. The Ermolev studio's sojourn in Yalta was a short one and at the beginning of February 1920, the troupe was again on the move, this time ending up in Paris.[21]

Professionally speaking, Protazanov effortlessly adjusted to emigré life. From 1921 to 1923 he made six movies, five in France and one in Germany. By the time Aleinikov contacted him in Berlin, Protazanov had joined the ranks of established European directors. There can be little doubt that Protazanov, like others from the Ermolev and Khanzhonkov studios, could have had a successful career in exile in the West. It is not clear, therefore, why the maker of *The Keys to Happiness* and *Satan Triumphant* chose to return to Soviet Russia, abandoning a potentially lucrative European career. Protazanov was a circumspect individual, who wrote virtually nothing for publication and responded to interviews as laconically as possible.[22] Even his Soviet biographers make no effort to claim a political awakening for him.[23]

Fig. 1 Iakov Protazanov, Iurii Zheliabuzhskii, Vladimir Gardin

Fig. 2 Fridrikh Ermler

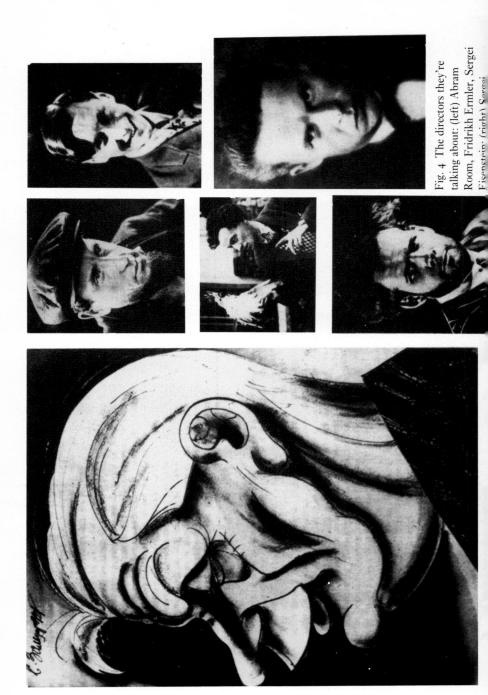

Fig. 4 The directors they're talking about: (left) Abram Room, Fridrikh Ermler, Sergei Eisenstein; (right) Sergei

Fig. 6 Igor Ilinskii, Mikhail Chekhov, "Actress X", Anatolii Ktorov (right)

(left)

Fig. 5 Boris Barnet

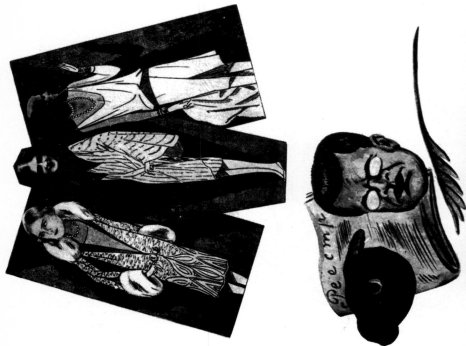

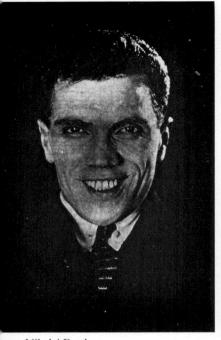 

g. 9 Nikolai Batalov   Fig. 10 Igor Ilinskii

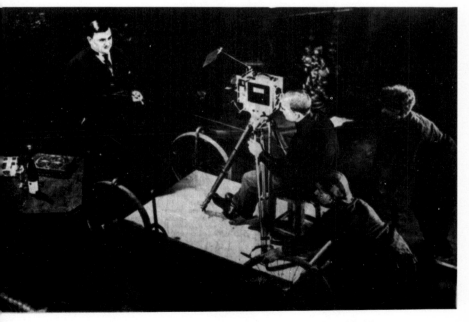

g. 11 On the set of *The Man from the Restaurant* (M. Narokov, misidentified in
e original as Mikhail Chekhov)

Fig. 12 Fedor Nikitin in (left) *The Fragment of the Empire* and (right) *Engineer Elagin*

Fig. 13 Iuliia Solntseva

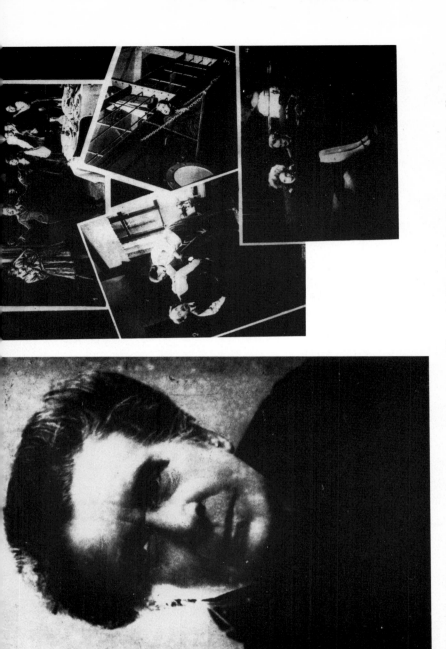

Fig. 14 Maria Bliumental–Tamarina

Fig. 15 (1) *Mary Pickford's Kiss*, (2) *Poison*, (3) *Ivan Kozyr* (released as *Mr. Lloyd's Voyage*), (4) *Your Acquaintance*

Fig. 16 *Poison*

Fig. 17 *The Man from the Restaurant*

Fig. 18 *The Poet and the Tsar*

Fig. 19 *Peasant Women of Riazan*

Fig. 20 *The Parisian Cobbler* (note that Veronika Buzhinskaia's surname has been misspelled *Puzhinskaia*)

Fig. 21 *The House on Trubnaia Square* (note that Vera Maretskaia's surname has been misspelled *Moretskaia*)

Fig. 22 *The White Eagle*

Fig. 23 *Lace*

Fig. 24 Our heroines (left);
heroines in films that are not
ours (right)

Fig. 25 The soul of the American film

Fig. 26 The standards of foreign pictures

Fig. 27 The standards of Soviet *bytovoi* pictures

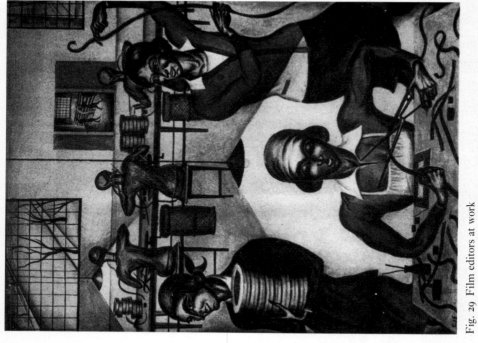

Fig. 29 Film editors at work

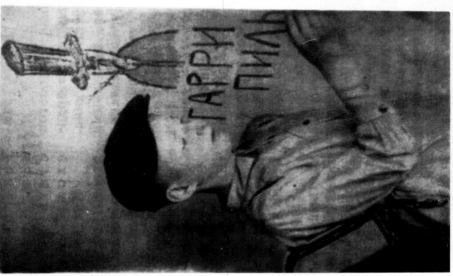

Fig. 28 Cinema madness: a young cinema-maniac drawing graffiti of Harry Piel

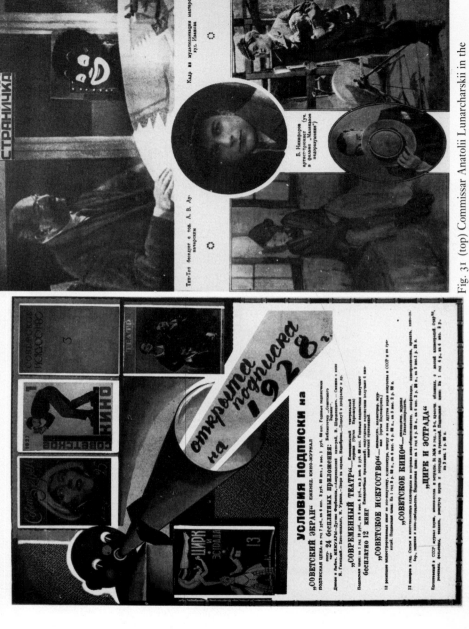

Fig. 31 (top) Commissar Anatolii Lunacharskii in the company of Tip Top, (center) the Soviet stuntman B. Nikiforov, (bottom) Lillian Gish, Buster Keaton, and Lloyd Hamilton

Fig. 30 Subscription advertisement for cultural magazines, including *Soviet Screen* and *Soviet Cinema*

When Protazanov made the crucial decision to return to Soviet Russia in February 1923, the debates over entertainment films and "foreign" influences in cinema had not really begun. Given his youth as a rebel against family tradition, though, it is reasonable to surmise that Protazanov might have been a bit bemused to find himself at the center of a controversy in which he was cast at the age of only forty-two as a representative of the "old order."[24] This controversy was set off on the release of his first Soviet film, the science fiction fantasy *Aelita*.

Aelita was a loose adaptation of Aleksei Tolstoi's popular novel, too loose for the exacting standards of his critics.[25] In Protazanov's version, the Soviet engineer only dreams of building a spaceship, taking off for Mars, and falling in love with a Martian princess named Aelita. Because this fantasy is but a dream, critics accused Protazanov of stripping the proletarian revolution on Mars of its ideological value, thereby making the film like any other "Western picture."[26] Further confirmation of this "charge" could be found in the addition of a melodramatic framing story, in which the engineer is depicted as a violently jealous husband who tries to shoot his wife.

The production history of *Aelita* indicates that Protazanov prepared for his Soviet debut with great care and forethought, but without political foresight. Though schooled in the breakneck pace of pre-revolutionary filmmaking, averaging more than ten films annually before the Revolution, he took over a year to complete *Aelita*. According to the handsome program that was distributed at screenings of the picture, Protazanov shot 22,000 meters of film for the 2,841-meter movie (a 3:1 ratio was the norm) and employed a cast and crew of thousands.[27]

This cast and crew may not actually have numbered in the thousands, but it was certainly one of the most impressive assembled in the twenties for a single picture. Fedor Otsep, the head scenarist, and Iurii Zhelia-buzhskii, the cameraman, had had considerable pre-revolutionary film-making experience (and both became Soviet directors). Protazanov also paid tribute to new artistic trends by having Aleksandra Ekster and Isaak Rabinovich design the Constructivist costumes and sets for the Martian scenes.

The casting was stellar, and according to Protazanov's custom in his Russian work, drawn almost exclusively from the ranks of theatre actors. The troupe included the director Konstantin Eggert, Vera Orlova, Valentina Kuindzhi, Olga Tretiakova, and Nikolai Tsereteli, and introduced to the screen Igor Ilinskii, Nikolai Batalov, and Iuliia Solntseva (all three of whom became leading movie actors). The promotional campaign suited the star-studded cast and has already been discussed as a model of the preferential promotion accorded "export" films. There can be no doubt that Protazanov intended to make his presence felt in his Soviet debut. The director of *The Keys to Happiness* had returned! *Aelita* did cause a sensation, but not quite the one that the Mezhrabpom studio and Protazanov had hoped for.

No other film of early Soviet cinema was attacked as consistently or over so long a period as *Aelita*. From 1924 to 1928, it was a regular target for film critics and for the many social activists who felt that the film industry was not supporting Soviet interests. The movie that the British critic Paul Rotha labelled "extraordinary," though theatrical, was greeted quite differently in the pages of the Soviet film press, excoriated on ideological, economic, class, and national grounds. Even the relatively moderate newspaper *Cinema Gazette* was unrelenting in its opposition to *Aelita*, going so far as to call it "ideologically unprincipled" and to warn that the potential danger of a "rallié" like Protazanov might outweigh the benefits of his experience and professionalism.[28]

These criticisms were echoed elsewhere, especially (but not exclusively) in "proletarianist" circles. *Proletarian Cinema* claimed *Aelita* had cost the equivalent of ten films in money, workers, and raw materials; another newspaper with a proletarianist orientation, *Cinema Week*, attacked *Aelita*'s scriptwriters as individuals "alien to the working class" and advised that the Party keep bourgeois specialists like Protazanov under close watch.[29] But the following examples, similar in tone, came from sources who were usually sympathetic to entertainment films. Viewers in Nizhnii Novgorod allegedly criticized its "petty-bourgeois" (*meshchanskii*) ending and complained that the hardships of the Civil War years were absent from the film.[30] Even a "bourgeois specialist" like Ippolit Sokolov deemed *Aelita* excessively complicated, Soviet in content but not in form, and "too Western."[31] As late as 1928, *Aelita* was still used as a negative example.[32]

FROM *HIS CALL* TO *THE WHITE EAGLE* (1925–1928)

Aelita's aftershocks jolted Protazanov. Except for his first movie (a never-released short for which he served as scenarist), every picture he had made had been a critical as well as a popular success. Protazanov learned from this experience, and from this point on, both the style of his films and their manner of production changed to conform to Soviet reality better. He eschewed special effects, expensive sets, and fanciful scripts in favor of realistic contemporary films with modest productions (but he never abandoned his preference for seasoned crews and theatre actors, preferably those with pre-revolutionary experience).

Despite these important efforts in the "right" direction, content continued to pose problems for him (as it did for other directors). But Protazanov recognized that he was living in a new world, and he was adaptable enough to be able to make good films in different genres on different subjects. Whether knowingly or not (and I suspect that it was intentional), Protazanov alternated between making films which his critics found acceptable and those which they found unacceptable. Though the critical reception of his films in the Soviet period might be unpredictable, their public reception was quite predictable and more than compensated Mezhrabpom for any criticisms.

His Call (1925), the director's next film after *Aelita*, baffled Protazanov's opponents and helped explain his long-term survival. How could the director of *Aelita* have made such a "truly Soviet" film? *His Call* appealed immediately to Soviet audiences and appeared on a "top ten" list in 1925.[33] In *His Call*, Protazanov succeeded where other Soviet directors had not – he had made an entertaining but indubitably "correct" film about Soviet life.

The melodrama begins in the final days of the Revolution; a rich industrialist and his son Vladimir (Anatolii Ktorov, who was to become a regular in Protazanov's films) hide some of their fortune before fleeing abroad. Although Protazanov dwells with obvious pleasure on the scenes of their lavish life in Paris, he took care to contrast this "decadence" with the suffering that Soviet citizens, especially children, were simultaneously undergoing. Five years after the Revolution, the pair has spent all their money, and so Vladimir returns to Soviet Russia to retrieve the cache (enlisting the obligatory *kulak* as his accomplice). In true melodramatic style, coincidence follows coincidence. Young Katia (Vera Popova, a starlet from the Vakhtangov Theatre who embodied proletarian beauty)[34] and her grandmother (Maria Bliumental-Tamarina, a famous stage actress) now occupy the very room where the treasure was stashed. Katia, attractive but quite naive, is easily seduced by the depraved Vladimir (who also happens to have killed Katia's father during the Revolution). Though his seduction is successful, Vladimir finds the going too slow to satisfy his lust for gold, so he murders Katia's grandmother in his desperate efforts to retrieve it. He ends up, fittingly, with a bullet in his back. In the meantime, Lenin has died, and the Party has issued its "call" for new members, dubbed the "Leninist enrollment." The "fallen woman" Katia hears the call – but unworthy to join the Party's ranks, resists it. Eventually she is convinced that joining the Party will redeem her sins.

His Call had everything social critics wanted – contemporary subject-matter and precise details of everyday life, and everything the public wanted – love, violence and a happy ending. The usually dour reviewers could find little about which to complain (except for Khersonskii, who thought the film should have included more scenes of workers' life).[35] His Call played three major first-run theatres – the Ars, the Kolizei, and the Forum – simultaneously.[36]

The formula of this picture seems simple, but few Soviet filmmakers were able to replicate it successfully. Protazanov did not try in his next two Soviet pictures, The Tailor from Torzhok (1925) and The Case of the Three Million (1926), both of which enjoyed audience acclaim while drawing the critics' ire. The Tailor from Torzhok is a farce which is distinguished mainly by its stars, Igor Ilinskii and Vera Maretskaia. Petia (Ilinskii) needs to wrest his winning lottery ticket from the landlady, an unattractive, but well-off "older woman" whom he was supposed to marry and with whom he has quarrelled. Petia and his true love, a poor shopgirl named Katia (Maretskaia), embark on a series of comic misadventures in the course of trying to retrieve the lottery ticket. In the spirit of the NEP, it seems that only wealth will ensure them a happy life together. Yet Protazanov protected himself by giving the film an anti-NEP message as well. Katia is being horribly exploited by a cruel relation, a minor NEPman who owns the shop in which she works.

The Tailor from Torzhok, with its light-hearted materialism and fairy-tale ending, struck a responsive chord with Soviet audiences. It recorded a healthy profit only two months into its run.[37] Critics generally disapproved, but not too strenuously (although they clearly were not fooled by the superficial "Sovietization" of the story). The worst review came from the pen of Khrisanf Khersonskii, who found the picture only sporadically funny, its style eclectic, and its tailor (Ilinskii) "psychologically alien."[38] Nevertheless, The Tailor escaped any serious opprobrium until the Cultural Revolution; Protazanov was probably still reaping the benefits of His Call.

His next comedy, The Case of the Three Million (1926), was a different matter. More "bourgeois" in setting and style and more overtly acquisitive than just about any other film of Soviet production, The Case of the Three Million is a crime comedy-adventure that is virtually indistinguishable from Western productions of the era. Yet The Case of the Three

Million does have a "class-conscious" theme. It concerns a banker who has sold his house for 3 million rubles so that he will have the capital necessary to speculate on food shortages. The famous "gentleman thief" Cascarillia (played by the debonair Anatolii Ktorov), seduces the banker's lascivious wife Nora (Olga Zhizneva, who literally rips her clothes apart as she pants in passion). With Nora's assistance, Cascarillia steals the money (which has conveniently been left at the house) – only to have his glory stolen from *him* by the "common thief" Tapioca (Igor Ilinskii). When the police arrive, the hapless Tapioca was at that very moment trying to rob the banker's house, so they assume that he took the 3 million. The problem is that Tapioca did not have the money on him, and since no one can imagine where the fortune is, Tapioca becomes a folk hero for having outsmarted the police. Unable to stay out of the limelight, Cascarillia makes a dramatic appearance at Tapioca's trial, tossing the 3 million to the wildly cheering crowd.

Despite the potential of the theme to "expose" bourgeois decadence, this stylish film was played for entertainment value, and Ktorov's Cascarillia must have reminded viewers of the gay and dashing thieves Douglas Fairbanks immortalized. It is not surprising, therefore, that 90 percent of the audience surveyed in one study like it. The public embraced *The Case of the Three Million* wholeheartedly, and, like *His Call*, it made Troianovskii and Egiazarov's "top ten" list.[39] Though Lunacharskii called it "a victory for Soviet cinema" and " an elegant European farce," most critics glowered, attributing *The Case*'s popularity to its "Western-adventure" genre, its "primitive Americanism," and its emphasis on sex and greed.[40] Even Sergei Eisenstein, who did not much concern himself with Protazanov or other bourgeois specialists, singled out *The Case of the Three Million* as an exemplar of the "Western-local" film that was in his opinion anathema to a revolutionary cinema.[41] A few critics gave credit for the film's popularity to Ilinskii (who was reprising the role he had created for the Kommissarzhevskii Theatre's adaptation of the same story), but no credit at all was given Protazanov for having made a film that was more graceful, amusing, and accomplished than most Soviet entertainment pictures.[42]

Protazanov was too astute not to have recognized the awkwardness of his position and may well have felt the time right for another "safe" film. But whatever his reason for choosing to film Boris Lavrenev's popular Civil War novella, *The Forty-First* was a rousing success. Although flatly written, Lavrenev's story contained the elements which had made *His Call* so entertaining: Soviet subject + melodrama + love interest. In

Protazanov's capable hands, the simple formula was transformed. The *Forty-First* became a classic of Soviet commercial filmmaking.

The picture has a deceptively slow start as a camel train wends its way across the desert seemingly forever, but high melodrama fortunately takes over. A poetry-writing Red Army sharpshooter (who notches her "kills" on her rifle) and the White officer who is her prisoner are stranded on a desert island after a storm. Once on the island, separated from the rest of her Red Army company, Mariutka (played by the engaging Ada Voitsik, then a student at GTK, the state film institute) saves the young aristocrat (Ivan Koval-Samborskii from the Meierkhold Theatre) from cholera. They fall in love, and at this point the story becomes a kind of reverse "Admirable Crichton" (with Mariutka occupying the Crichton role). She teaches the lieutenant how to survive, and he helps her with her poetry. One day they see a ship on the horizon – rescue at last! But when Mariutka realizes that the rescuers are Whites, mindful of her duty as a Bolshevik, she claims her lover as her forty-first victim.

The Forty-First had everything a film-goer could desire for enter-tainment – a pretty woman, her handsome lover, humor (as the odd couple works out their differences), and true romance (when the mésalliance seems to turn out happily). But the stunning climax added a dimension to the *The Forty-First* which can best be appreciated by comparing the film's ending to the novel's. Lavrenev handled Mariutka's murder of her lover very matter-of-factly; not so Protazanov. He ends the picture with a visual question mark: is this her victory as a Bolshevik or her defeat as a person? (Protazanov's answer seems to be the latter.)

The Forty-First was accorded an advance ticket sale (rare for a Soviet production) and announced in advertisements as a hit before it had even opened.[43] It made Troianovskii and Egiazarov's top-ten chart in 1928, listed as the third-most-popular film.[44] But in 1927 (the year of the film's release), critics were much more cautious than they had been two years earlier when *His Call* appeared. Although *The Forty-First* was generally quite well received for all the reasons mentioned above,[45] there were some disquieting notes that portended problems soon to come. "Arsen," one of the most censorious of the new breed of "hard-line" critics, labelled it a "socially primitive" and "decadent" example of the "Western adventure" picture – all the more "dangerous" because it was so well done.[46] Fortunately for Protazanov, Arsen's view of *The Forty-First* was in the minority.

Protazanov made three more films in the following two years, but only one was a critical success *Don Diego and Pelageia* (1928). Two other films from this period, *The Man from the Restaurant* (1927) and *The White Eagle* (1928), were uncharacteristically "serious" works, lacking the adventure, romance, and humor of his previous work. *The Man from the Restaurant* takes place in 1916–17 and concerns the social awakening of a poor waiter (played by the Moscow Art Theatre actor Mikhail Chekhov). The waiter's musically gifted daughter (Vera Malinovskaia) must leave school to help support the family. She plays the violin in the restaurant where her father works, and there she is exposed to the way of life of the demimondaine. Her innocent beauty attracts the unwelcome attentions of a wealthy industrialist who hopes to make her his mistress. The contrasts between the haute-bourgeoisie (greedy, profligate, immoral, and cruel) and the proletariat (as depicted by the waiter and his daughter – hardworking, humble, and honest) are sharply drawn. Protazanov's efforts to evoke the waiter's growing sense of outrage were apparently sincere, but the film suffers from a number of shortcomings.

The plot and mise-en-scène are strongly reminiscent of F. W. Murnau's *The Last Laugh* (1924) which leads to an inevitable comparison between the talents of Murnau and Protazanov on the one hand and those of Emil Jannings and Mikhail Chekhov, on the other. (Protazanov and Chekhov do not come off the better.) But more important to the Soviet context, at a time when there was an ever-increasing clamor for a positive Soviet hero, the protagonist of *The Man from the Restaurant* is far from positive. The waiter is so tediously humble that the picture lacks dramatic focus, a problem intensified by Chekhov's mannered performance. Moreover, the waiter's "political" transformation seems to spring from purely personal sources. His son dies at the front; his wife dies from grief; his beloved daughter, now the only remaining member of his family, needs to be protected; and he himself is in dire financial straits after breaking a stack of dishes at the restaurant.

It certainly did not help *The Man from the Restaurant*'s reception, considering the political climate in 1927, that the plot had been derived, not from a popular Soviet novel like *The Forty-First*, but from a pre-revolutionary story by Ivan Shmelev. Like Protazanov, Shmelev was a member of the Moscow *kupechestvo* who had emigrated to the West. Unlike Protazanov, he had not returned, so there were dubious "foreign" and "counterrevolutionary" overtones to the film as well. Despite its implied criticism of prostitution, the hubbub over the film continued into 1928, exacerbated by the fact that its star, Mikhail Chekhov, chose that moment to emigrate. (Vera Malinovskaia left the following year.)

In 1927, on the eve of the Party Conference on Cinema Affairs,

Protazanov's studio Mezhrabpom found itself (like Sovkino) under heavy fire. Protazanov's films *The Man from the Restaurant*, *The Tailor from Torzhok*, and *The Case of the Three Million* became ammunition in the assault on Mezhrabpom.[47] *The Man*, in particular, was specifically attacked, over and over, as too theatrical and "reactionary" (but Nikolai Volkov was honest enough to admit that people would go to see Chekhov anyway).[48]

It was again time for a change of pace, and *Don Diego and Pelageia* (1928) provided it. Based on a *Pravda feuilleton* by Bella Zorich called "The Letter of the Law,"[49] *Don Diego and Pelageia* tells the story of an old woman's unwitting attempts to circumvent Soviet power, personified by "Don Diego," a foolish daydreamer who is the village station-master. Don Diego (Anatolii Bykov), who would rather act out his fantasies than do his job, is stirred into action when he witnesses a heinous crime. Pelageia (Maria Bliumental-Tamarina once again) has illegally crossed the railroad tracks, and the fact that she is illiterate and therefore could not read the warning sign is no excuse. Don Diego arrests her. After a farcical trial, she is sentenced to three months in jail. Enter the Party – two Komsomol members and the local Party secretary come to the rescue of Pelageia and her bewildered husband. Although the rude and incompetent bureaucrats snap to when the Party secretary arrives, he is not fooled, and they are all fired.

Protazanov's depiction of provincial life is scathing, revealing much about the problems of Soviet society: a decade into the Revolution, peasants are more than a little mystified by its ideals and goals. And why not, for what sort of revolution do we see? The bureaucracy has changed in name only. Tsarist *chinovniki* have been replaced by rigid, lazy, and insolent Soviet *apparatchiki* who obviously understand the Revolution no better than do the peasants. This movie, which coincided with the campaign against the "bureaucratic deviation," demonstrated that it was possible to make a topical movie that could transcend the concerns of the moment and entertain at the same time.

Don Diego and Pelageia enjoyed widespread accolades at home as a fine example of what the film comedy could and should be; Nikolai Iakovlev went so far as to praise it as the "first [Soviet] comedy."[50] It was also singled out for the efficiency and economy of its production. *Don Diego and Pelageia* was completed in three months at a cost of only 40,000 rubles, whereas Vertov's documentary *One-Sixth of the World* (1926) had taken nineteen months and 130,000 rubles.[51] But film critics, whatever their stripe, were fairly nervous in 1928 and the more astute among them wanted to be sure they had protected themselves. Some felt compelled, therefore, to assert that the role of the Party in solving problems had been insufficiently developed, and that the great evil of bureaucratism had been too individualized in the unlikely person of Don Diego. Despite these reservations (and a fear that the film might be edited abroad in an unflattering fashion), *Don Diego and Pelageia* continued to be hailed as a "great event" in the development of Soviet comedy.[52]

When Protazanov's next film, *The White Eagle*, was released, the Cultural Revolution was definitely under way. Whatever its flaws, it illustrates that Protazanov was not – as his critics often charged – a "formula" film-maker; certainly he was not an "epigone of *Khanzhon-kovshchina*," as the futurist critic and scenarist Sergei Tretiakov claimed.[53] *The White Eagle* is an adaptation of Leonid Andreev's story about a provincial governor during the Revolution of 1905 (and we must keep in mind at this point that Protazanov was abroad during the Revolution). The governor (Vasilii Kachalov) orders troops to break up a street demonstration by firing on a crowd – and three children are among those killed in the ensuing mêlée. Rewarded for his success at crowd control with the Order of the White Eagle, the governor is tormented by his bad conscience, and his struggle to come to terms with his deed is the crux of this psychological drama. The corollary to the governor's angst is that of the governess-cum-revolutionary (Anna Sten), who cannot bring herself to assassinate the governor although she is convinced that it would be just retribution for the massacre.

The American critic Dwight MacDonald admired the film enormously, going so far as to call Kachalov's performance "the high water mark of movie acting,"[54] but his opinion was assuredly not shared by his Soviet contemporaries, at least not by those who dared to go on record about the film at a time when "lines" were changing almost weekly. *The White Eagle* was castigated by critics from different points on the cultural–political spectrum for humanizing the "class enemy," for being only superficially revolutionary, for being "like a prison sentence" to watch due to its "subjective psychologism," and for appealing to the petty-bourgeois viewer.[55] It was regularly used as a stick with which to beat Mezhrabpom and was seen as too "dangerous" to export.[56]

The White Eagle – and its spiritual predecessor, *The Man from the Restaurant* – are curiosities in the *œuvre* of a director who devoted his career in film to making crowd-pleasers. Although they were far from "prison sentences" to watch, *The White Eagle* and *The Man from the Restaurant* were not the kind of action pictures contemporary critics expected from the war-and-revolution genre. Their drama depends on the internal, rather than the external, struggle, and given what we know about audience tastes at this time, specifically their preference for elaborately plotted or fast-moving films, it is difficult to imagine long lines at the box-office for these two pictures.[57] Nonetheless, *The White Eagle* had a very respectable run of at least three weeks in one of Mezhrabpom's deluxe theatres, the Koloss, and the studio commissioned a full orchestral score from Dmitrii Blok.[58]

PROTAZANOV DURING THE CULTURAL REVOLUTION

And yet despite all his troubles, in the darkest days of the Cultural Revolution Protazanov not only avoided a sustained personal attack (a major achievement in itself), he continued to work. No doubt his resolute silence on the burning questions of the decade (regardless of his motivations) served him well. After the *Aelita* "scandal" in 1924, Protazanov kept a low public profile (although he was once singled out in the press for enjoying a higher standard of living than did other filmworkers).[59]

His absence from the debates raging throughout the decade about actors and acting, plots and scripts, montage, rationalization of production, etc., while not unique, was noticeable because of his fame. Perhaps the most amusing example of Protazanov's fabled reserve can be found in a two-part series which appeared in *On Literary Guard*. Directors and others prominent in Soviet cinema were called upon to answer several questions about film and literature posed by the journal's editors. Sergei Eisenstein's response to the three questions was about 1,300 words: Protazanov's, exactly 84. His attitude toward his critics was nonetheless quite clear: "I like to read literary criticism because it doesn't criticize me. For that reason, I read film criticism with less pleasure."[60]

Since Protazanov had neither written nor said anything for the record, nothing could be held against him except his movies. While, as we have seen, there was much that the new "proletarianist" critics (who eventually took over the cinema press) found to dislike in these films no one had ever charged Protazanov with the crime of technical innovation. And luckily for Protazanov, it was the "formalists" – the code word for youthful avant-garde directors – who were the chief targets of the Cultural Revolution in cinema.

Given the political climate and Protazanov's apparent political acumen (despite *The White Eagle* and *The Man from the Restaurant* fiascoes), it is not surprising that his final two silent films, *Ranks and People* (1929) and *St. Jorgen's Feast Day* (1930), are cautious ones. *Ranks and People*, based on three stories by Chekhov, represents Protazanov's return to Russian literary classics as a source for his films for the first time since *Father Sergius*. The vignettes stay very close to the stories on which they were based – "The Order of St. Anne," "Death of a Bureaucrat," and "Chameleon," and feature good performances from Ivan Moskvin (as the unlucky *chinovnik* whose sneezing on a superior at the opera eventually leads to his death) and Maria Strelkova (as the unhappy young woman trapped in a marriage of convenience). Yet as unremarkable as this film seems, it is possible to read a veiled criticism of Soviet society in Protazanov's choice of vignettes, most particularly in "The Death of a Bureaucrat," but also in "Chameleon," a satire of rank-consciousness as townspeople try to determine the "status" of a dog who bit a man.[61] *Ranks and People* was quite popular, one of the few hits of 1929.[62]

St. Jorgen's Feast Day represents a return to Protazanov's patented style. A lively anti-religious comedy, it stands out among the film comedies made during the Cultural Revolution, a time when there was little to laugh at. Anatolii Ktorov and the irrepressible Igor Ilinskii play two escaped convicts masquerading as nuns on a pilgrimage. Ktorov, in a variation of his role as Cascarillia in *The Case of the Three Million*, is an "international thief" by the name of Michael Korkis, who seizes the unexpected opportunity to claim the pretty "bride" (Maria Strelkova) chosen for the saint on his feast day. Korkis sheds his habit and "appears" to the worshipful throng as the saint. *St. Jorgen's Feast Day* displays a much lighter touch than many films that were part of the campaign against religion, a small but important achievement.

To the disinterested observer viewing these two films more than sixty years later, *Ranks and People*'s portrayal of pre-revolutionary life differs little from that of *The Man from the Restaurant*, and yet the former picture received only half-hearted criticism for its "soft" portrayal of hard times. The mystery deepens when *St. Jorgen's Feast Day* is compared to *The Case of the Three Million*. The movies are quite similar – satires set abroad featuring the type of thief-hero popular in films as well as folklore. Yet *The Case* was much-maligned, while most critics termed the *Feast Day* "valuable and well-made."[63]

This anomaly might be explained by referring to the chaos of the times – much was happening that was ambiguous, confusing and contradictory. Yet even as the Cultural Revolution was playing itself out, the outlines of the second phase of post-revolutionary culture were discernible. This new culture was, as we know, based on the tenets of Socialist Realism, fulfilling at least part of the program espoused by the enlighteners and the proletarian radicals for simplicity, realism, and optimism in film-making.

But post-revolutionary culture had another component that increased in importance in the thirties – traditionalism. In the thirties, the "new traditionalism" that was a corollary to Socialist Realism manifested itself in the arts in two ways: by a call for a "return to the classics," and by establishing Soviet ties to the Russian past. Considering the short span of cinema history, Protazanov himself was a "classic," and he had long been accused of being too "traditional."[64] In most respects his films con-formed to the new aesthetic criteria quite well, laying the foundation for his survival as an artist into the thirties and forties and an eventual reevaluation of his work.

Protazanov's story is significant in a number of respects. Because he came to Soviet cinema as a mature artist who had been a key figure in pre-revolutionary cinema, his career illustrates connections between Russian and Soviet popular culture which are often overlooked. By virtue of his family background, education, and professional experience, he was also the quintessential "bourgeois specialist" – so his career sheds light on the role of the "former" middle classes in the formation of the new society. That this director, labelled in his time a "reactionary," "socially primitive" maker of "shallow entertainment" pictures, not only survived but prospered as a Soviet filmmaker is a testament to the tenacity of the old tradition and the adaptability of its leading practitioner. That he did this while producing a varied and unpredictable *œuvre*, continuing to grow as a filmmaker, makes his story even more remarkable.

In his person and through his art, Protazanov carried on the bourgeois tradition of pre-revolutionary Russian cinema. All Protazanov's pictures are realistic. Story development was not an area of particular strength, but his plots were easy to follow, with enough action and human interest to engage the viewer. He excelled in characterization and casting, a key in understanding the popularity of his films with a public already in love with Western stars like Fairbanks and Pickford. Protazanov infused his Soviet films with a "Russianized" version of the "Western" style of filmmaking that audiences found so appealing. He also proved to the "nationalists" among critics that a Russian could make movies that they believed were as good as American films (whether they liked them or not).

As attractive as these attributes were to critics in the thirties and beyond, in the twenties even those who admired Protazanov found him too European and "a little out of date."[65] The supporters of entertainment films hoped to give their cause a boost by encouraging a "Soviet" alternative to the popular cinema created by bourgeois specialists like Protazanov and others of his cohort. It was hoped that the new generation of popular filmmakers would embody Protazanov's positive attributes as a filmmaker without any of his "faults" – and that their films would be "truly Soviet" and absolutely entertaining. The struggle to achieve this dream is the subject of the final three chapters.

PART 3

ALTERNATIVES

CHAPTER 7

BORIS BARNET: SOVIET
ACTOR/SOVIET DIRECTOR

[*On the work of the actor and the director*]: I can say only one thing: this work is incredibly difficult.   (Boris Barnet, 1927[1])

Iakov Protazanov was the quintessential bourgeois specialist and the quintessential Mezhrabpom director. But as Mezhrabpom's chief Moisei Aleinikov somewhat disingenuously pointed out whenever he had the opportunity, the USSR's premier entertainment studio was not merely a nest of "old specialists." It was also home to two prominent young directors who had gotten their starts in film in the Kuleshov collective: Vsevolod Pudovkin and Boris Barnet. Pudovkin, the darling of proletarianist critics since *Mother* (1926), was Mezhrabpom's token "avant-gardist," a label he bore uneasily (though he could not be considered a commercial director either). Barnet, on the other hand, was being groomed as the studio's young Protazanov.

Barnet directed seven silent films (if one counts each of the three parts of *Miss Mend*, which were full-length pictures screened consecutively, as separate titles). In five of the seven (the exceptions being the disastrous *Moscow in October* and the little-seen *The Ice Breaks*), he displayed the Russian master's versatility and vitality, but with a zest that was undeniably youthful and totally Barnet. This was an appealing combination of characteristics that suggested a new possibility for Soviet popular cinema – that young directors might be as capable as the old specialists like Protazanov of making entertaining films. Yet although the studio and the public were pleased with Barnet's productions, the critics held him up to the same impossible standards the old-timers faced.

EARLY YEARS

Like Protazanov, Barnet was a Muscovite from the commercial classes who wrote little and cultivated a certain air of mystery about his past. The personal resemblance ends there (but as we shall see, their professional ties were strong). Born in 1902, Barnet was of a different generation, a man of the twentieth century.[2] His family traced its origins not to the *kupechestvo*, but to an English printer named Thomas Barnet, who emigrated to Russia in the mid-nineteenth century.[3] Barnet's father, Vasilii (Thomas's son), ran a typographical concern with twelve employees. Although Barnet (cognizant of the potential danger of being identified with the propertied classes) once described the family business in deprecatory terms as "extremely small," the shop was confiscated after the Revolution.[4] Both Barnet and his biographer Mark Kushnirov delicately avoided naming Barnet's pre-revolutionary estate, but it was most probably the petty-bourgeoisie (*meshchane*).

Small or not, the business was highly successful. It enabled the Barnet family (which included Boris and his three siblings) to enjoy a very comfortable, upper-middle-class standard of living. Their way of life provides an interesting illustration of the breakdown in caste distinctions so typical of late Imperial society. Barnet attended the private Mazing Real-Schule and frequented the movies, especially to see the French comedian Max Linder, who enjoyed great popularity in the pre-revolutionary period. He also attended the Moscow Art Theatre on a regular basis. His gift for drawing, a talent shared by all the members of his family, was recognized early and encouraged. In 1916, he entered the very traditional Moscow Arts Academy to study architecture; he eventually transferred to the painting section.[5] The Great War had little obvious impact on the family, but the Revolution changed their fortunes and way of life forever. Most importantly, at least as far as the history of Soviet cinema is concerned, it altered the young Barnet's conception of "art."

After the confiscation of the family business, Barnet was forced to abandon the formal study of art to find a job, though he was only fifteen years old. He became a set painter for the experimental First Studio of the Moscow Art Theatre, work which enabled him to combine his vocation with his avocation. Before long, Barnet felt he had found a new calling, but as an actor, not as a theatrical set designer. He soon ran into a major stumbling-block due to a minor speech impediment. His lisp, an inability to pronounce the letter "r," meant that he could not pursue his dream of becoming a stage actor.

In 1920, at the age of eighteen, Barnet enlisted in the Red Army and left Moscow for the Front, caring for typhus patients in a medical detachment. His stint as a soldier-medic lasted until the summer of 1922; he contracted cholera and spent time in a nursing home before being demobilized.[6] On returning to Moscow, his life took a surprising and fateful turn. On a whim, the young artist entered the Main Military School for the Physical Education of Workers (Glavvosh), where he enthusiastically learned boxing.[7] A natural athlete, Barnet quickly attained enough proficiency to turn professional, though by all accounts he was not championship quality (and so, as he jocularly noted, he never broke his nose). Barnet found more than a new trade at Glavvosh; the school also served as a bridge to his career in films. For there he met two of his closest future collaborators in cinema: actor/director Sergei Komarov (who taught gymnastics) and the imaginist poet and movie scenarist Vadim Shershenevich (who conducted the school's cultural evenings).[8]

From 1922 to 1924, Barnet earned his living as a professional athlete; he was a boxing instructor at Glavvosh and fought publicly in demonstrations and competitions. In January 1923, Lev Kuleshov and Aleksandra Khokhlova saw Barnet in the ring and were entranced by the grace of his movements.[9] Barnet entered the Kuleshov collective shortly thereafter (though he continued teaching boxing), joining a stellar cast, including Kuleshov, Khokhlova, Komarov, Pudovkin, Vladimir Fogel, and Ada Gorodetskaia (who became Barnet's first wife). As part of the collective, Barnet was introduced to a cultural world far removed from that of Stanislavskii and the academic traditions of the Arts Academy. Kuleshov's was the brave new world of culture in revolution – of films without film, Meierkhold, the futurists, and American action pictures – and Barnet was soon cast in his first motion picture, *The Extraordinary Adventures of Mr. West in the Land of the Bolsheviks*. While *Mr. West* launched Barnet's career in films in a most spectacular fashion, it also, paradoxically, ended his formal association with the Kuleshov collective, and thereby with the avant-garde and radical aesthetics. But it did begin his fruitful relationship with collective members like Sergei Komarov and Vladimir Fogel.

FROM *MR. WEST* TO *MISS MEND*

Barnet's ties to Kuleshov were short-lived and ended badly. Given Kuleshov's seminal importance in the history of Soviet cinema, however, it would be a mistake to dismiss *Mr. West* altogether as a factor in Barnet's artistic evolution. When Kuleshov first saw Barnet boxing, the young director who was the "old man" of the avant-garde was planning his first important film, which has already been discussed as an example of "Americanism." Although Kuleshov had initially cast Vsevolod Pudovkin in the role of the YMCA President's bodyguard Cowboy Jeddy, seeing Barnet inspired him to change his mind. He asked Barnet to play the part of Jeddy, and Pudovkin became the diabolical Zhban, wily protector of the "Countess" (Aleksandra Khokhlova) and mastermind of the scheme to extort money from the innocent Mr. West, who has been caught tangled up with the Countess in a most compromising position.

Kuleshov had lived through too many lean years to waste money, so the shooting proceeded quickly. (Beginning on 15 December 1923, it ended less than four months later, on 7 April 1924.) Barnet was a perfect Cowboy Jeddy – handsome and robust, he looked American (or at least, not especially Slavic) and his talent and charisma transformed a relatively small role into one of the best-loved comic characters in early Soviet cinema. Although Barnet had an explosive temper, he and Kuleshov apparently worked amicably together until the day that Cowboy Jeddy had to walk a tightrope, strung seven stories high between two buildings. Barnet fell. What happened next is open to some dispute. Barnet says he was dangling for some 30 minutes while Kuleshov berated him for not having trained well enough; Kuleshov recalls that he immediately called the fire department to help rescue the fatigued and frightened actor. In any case, Barnet refused to try the stunt again, and the agile Vladimir Fogel doubled the scene without incident (a substitution shot so cleverly that no one noticed, despite the fact that Fogel was a much different physical type).[10]

Barnet left the collective, and from 1924 to 1926 he continued working at Glavvosh as a boxing instructor. He was unable, however, to forget about movies altogether. He wrote a film script with a plot reminiscent of *Mr. West*'s spirited highjinks which he offered to the Mezhrabpom-Rus studio in Moscow. Discouraged by its rejection, he swore to quit films for good, but he was unable to live up to his hasty promise. The script had been good enough to attract the attention of Valentin Turkin, the prominent scenarist and sometime critic who was employed by Mezhrabpom. Turkin offered Barnet a job writing the screenplay for a film adaptation of a series of popular novelettes, Marietta Shaginian's *Mess Mend* (which had been published under her "American" pseudonym "Jim Dollar").[11] The original material was both highly entertaining and consciously cinematic, and the assignment proved ideal for Barnet's talents. Barnet's adaptation was a very free one, and by the time shooting started, the title (and the heroine's name) had changed to *Miss Mend*. (In

the books, "Mend mess/mess mend" is the password the proletarian
Mess Mend alliance uses to identify its members.)

Barnet was attracting the right kind of attention at Mezhrabpom.
Although Fedor Otsep, the successful scenarist who had written scripts
for the popular films like *The Cigarette Girl from Mosselprom* and *The
Collegiate Registrar*, had been slated to direct, Barnet was added as
co-director at the last minute. Barnet apparently proved more capable on
the set than Otsep, and Otsep served as junior to Barnet during the
shooting.[12]

When Barnet became a Mezhrabpom director, the studio was a
flourishing concern, its commercial style already well established.
Despite its dependence on "leftist" German capital, it turned out
unabashedly "bourgeois" films – films with the dash and glamour which
had characterized the pre-revolutionary cinema. This is not as surprising
as it seems, given that Mezhrabpom had the corner on the old talent. The
studio employed most of the best pre-revolutionary directors, scenarists,
and cinematographers, including Iurii Zheliabuzhskii, Louis Forestier,
Sergei Kozlovskii, Petr Ermolov, as well as Otsep and Turkin. Despite
Mezhrabpom's embarrassment of talent, no one had any doubt that its
star was Iakov Protazanov, who set the studio's standards for excellence
and entertainment. Although Barnet never explicitly acknowledged any
Protazanovian influence in his work (which would not have been
especially politic in the twenties for a young director), it is quite clearly
there, in terms of subject, treatment, and visual style.[13]

Although Protazanov's influence is apparent as early as *Miss Mend*, it
should not be overemphasized in this film. *Miss Mend* also reflected a
Kuleshovian influence more obvious than in any other film Barnet
directed. *Miss Mend* was a rarity in Soviet cinema – a three-part adventure serial, with unabashedly Western antecedents and strongly satirical
overtones. Barnet was reluctant to give up acting, and he joined the
kuleshovtsy Vladimir Fogel and Sergei Komarov and the *protazanovtsy*
Ivan Koval-Samborskii and Igor Ilinskii as male leads, while Anatolii
Lunacharskii's wife Natalia Rozenel and Barnet's soon-to-be wife
Natalia Glan served as female leads.[14] The story-line is that of the
prototypical serial: a reporter (Barnet), a news photographer (Fogel), a
bumbling clerk (Ilinskii), and the secretary Miss Vivian Mend (Glan)
band together to foil millionaires (Koval-Samborskii and Rozenel) and
assorted anti-Soviet conspirators (including Komarov) both at home and
abroad. These villains are planning to launch chemical warfare against
the Soviet Union, to name but one of their grandiose schemes.[15] *Miss*

Mend's revolving series of plots, subplots, and counterplots provide ample opportunity for action – brawls, murders, car chases, body snatchings, and real "cliff-hangers."

Although in the third part, set in the Soviet Union, Barnet adds social relevance by having Fogel help out some homeless children, *Miss Mend* was sheer escapist entertainment which drew heavily from the conventions of German spy films and the acting style of American comedy. Its satirical depiction of class enemies also drew from Kuleshov's *The Extraordinary Adventures of Mr. West*.[16] Barnet had already revealed himself an actor with screen presence in *Mr. West* (which he demonstrated again in *Miss Mend*). Now he proved himself a director who could make a movie move.

While there is much in *Miss Mend* that reminds the viewer of *Mr. West* (notably its wit and its frenetic action), Barnet's film was considerably more popular than Kuleshov's. In fact, *Miss Mend* was one of the most-seen films of the twenties, with a recorded audience of more than 1.7 million in its first six months.[17] It played at least two months at the deluxe Ars theatre in Moscow.[18] While it does appear that viewers enjoyed *Mr. West*, it would be impossible to claim that it had been a major hit, so the differences between the two films are more important than the similarities. First, the very "Westernness" of *Miss Mend*'s fantastic plot would have been a selling-point with audiences, since it was reminiscent of the American films they liked so much. Second, the fact that the action mainly took place abroad was another important attraction; the foreign settings made it possible for Barnet to show a life both exotic and glamorous. Third, the acting style of Barnet's talented cast was naturalistic (in sharp contrast to the deliberately eccentric style of Kuleshov's no-less-talented players). Moreover, they were a handsome lot (and one must remember that the campaign for "prettier women" on the screen had been largely directed against Aleksandra Khokhlova, the Countess in *Mr. West*). So although *Miss Mend* is less "Protazanovian" than *The Girl with the Hatbox*, its resemblances to Protazanov's patented style are the keys to understanding its success.

Successful though it was with audiences, *Miss Mend* was one of the most criticized movies of the twenties, which should come as no surprise, given what we have seen about "official" attitudes toward entertainment. The reviews ranged from the dismissive ("naive and stupid" and "varnished barbarism") to the denunciatory (accusations that the film's cheerful antics promoted "hooliganism," a sign that critics read films much more seriously than did audiences).[19] Its advertising campaign was also criticized – for being "too Western" and very "noisy," although this is somewhat of an exaggeration.[20] It was believed to typify Mezhrabpom's "general line" of producing "naked entertainment" movies.[21] Eventually *Miss Mend* joined excellent company – Protazanov's *The Case of the Three Million*, Fridrikh Ermler's *Katka the Apple Seller* – as an exemplar of the "petty-bourgeois" deviation in Soviet cinema.[22]

THE GIRL WITH THE HATBOX

If the critical outrage over *Miss Mend* affected Barnet, he did not let it show. It certainly had no effect on Mezhrabpom, for Barnet immediately went to work on another film for them, the comedy *The Girl with the Hatbox* (1927). Though less ambitious than *Miss Mend* (it barely met the minimum footage for a full-length film), *The Girl* was just as "Western" and could therefore be expected to arouse much the same controversy. Barnet's debut as solo director, this film demonstrated his move away from Kuleshov's "Americanism" toward the development of a personal style more closely tied to Soviet life and therefore better suited to the Mezhrabpom standard.

The plot and theme of the film are strongly reminiscent of Protazanov's *The Tailor from Torzhok*, not surprising since Valentin Turkin served as scenarist for both films. Like *The Tailor*, *The Girl* is on the one hand a gentle satire of the annoyances of NEP society and on the other, a romantic comedy. A young milliner Natasha (Anna Sten) lives in a village outside Moscow with her grandfather, despite the fact that she has a Moscow residence permit. This permit is part of a ruse contrived by "Madame Irène" (Serafima Birman), who owns the chic shop where Natasha sells her wares, to get an extra room for her husband Tager (Pavel Pol), who seems to have no occupation other than reclining on his sofa and listening to the radio. Natasha takes pity on a poor peasant Ilia (Ivan Koval-Samborskii, in an untypical guise) who has come to Moscow to study but sleeps on park benches at night (in winter), since he cannot find even a "corner" to rent. They enter into a "fictitious" marriage so that he can live in Natasha's room at Madame Irène's.

Madame is naturally outraged at the intrusion, and sends Tager to the housing inspectors to report the deception. Of course, Natasha happens to arrive just as the inspectors are grilling Ilia about his "so-called wife." Madame then retaliates by firing Natasha, and Tager pockets her pay, giving her a lottery ticket instead. When Tager finds out that Natasha's ticket has won 25,000 rubles, he dashes to the village to retrieve it. After a series of mishaps and pratfalls – which include Natasha's "rescue" by the railroad clerk (Vladimir Fogel) who adores her – Ilia and Natasha realize they have fallen in love and want their fictitious marriage to be real. Fortunately, their domestic bliss is assured. Not only do they have a room in Moscow, they have the 25,000 rubles.[23]

Though attempting to capitalize on bankable formulas was as common in early Soviet cinema as it is in Hollywood today, *The Girl with the Hatbox* is not just a tired remake of Protazanov's *The Tailor from Torzhok*. Barnet brought in his old friend from Glavvosh, Vadim Shershenevich, to freshen Turkin's script. Shershenevich, known in the West as a poet, was by this time making a name for himself in film circles as a satirist of the cinema community's many foibles, and his jokes in this film about the NEP "types" are particularly cutting.[24] They also work well because Barnet specifically tailored the parts to showcase the talents of his cast, and fine-tuned the script after making his casting decisions. Barnet recognized that one of the chief reasons the films of the older generation succeeded with audiences was their emphasis on acting, which in turn created human interest. As an actor himself, he not surprisingly approved this tendency and wanted to make his own contributions to the development of an actors' cinema.[25]

While we have no hard evidence at present of the popularity of this film, it had all the ingredients for success – popular actors, a slick production, a story with a happy ending, romance, and so on.[26] It was a film without grand pretenses, but by Soviet standards it was well done. Mezhrabpom promoted it accordingly; one poster read:

How can there be disagreement!
We'll put the question in two parts:
(1) To be late seeing *The Girl with the Hatbox* is a disgrace!
(2) Not to see it at all is misery.[27]

Though he certainly recognized that being a Soviet director was in many respects a thankless occupation (as I think his laconic statement at the beginning of this chapter indicates), Barnet was stubbornly committed to the creation of Soviet film comedy.[28] As we have already seen, there were ample opportunities for mis-steps and wrong turns in this genre in particular, and Barnet's troubled career in the twenties illustrates these difficulties very well. He continued to make the "wrong" kinds of films, even though he attempted to tone down his proclivity for "Western" stylistic devices. We can discern this in *The Girl with the Hatbox*, which avoided many of the "shortcomings" in *Miss Mend* that had raised the critics' ire. It was set in Soviet Russia rather than abroad, with Soviet rather than foreign characters. It dealt with Soviet problems – NEP and NEPmen had proved a fertile subject for filmmakers, ripe with melodramatic and comedic possibilities. But as the critical reception of Protazanov's comedies indicated, treating a Soviet subject in a Western style could lead to even more critical opprobrium than dealing with a purely foreign theme – and that was certainly the case with *The Girl with the Hatbox*.

The vitriolic energy with which the film was attacked was disproportionate to its relative weight – and greatly exceeded the degree to which Protazanov's work was denounced. *The Girl* was held up as the epitome of a "Mezhrabpom film" – "in coarse taste," "completely neutral," and, ironically, "straight from Paris."[29] *The Girl* occupied the same role in the cultural politics of spring 1927 as did Abram Room's *Third Meshchanskaia Street*; the former was the stick with which to beat Mezhrabpom, the latter – Sovkino. *Soviet Screen*'s editor-in-chief Nikolai Iakovlev made this eminently clear when he said in his review of *The Girl* that it was so bad that *Third Meshchanskaia Street* looked good by comparison.[30] The only reasonably accurate reviews appeared in *Pravda* and *Izvestiia*, where *The Girl*'s cheeriness and acting and cinematography were praised.[31]

Why was Barnet attacked more vigorously than Protazanov? In this case it was Barnet's very youth that seemed to make him especially vulnerable. Protazanov, though constantly criticized, was nonetheless a cultural icon, even among the radical critics, and he had managed to intersperse a few "truly revolutionary" films in his *œuvre*, like *His Call* and *The Forty-First*. Barnet, who as a child of the Revolution should have known better, had only *Mr. West*, *Miss Mend* (in triplicate), and *The Girl* to his credit.

MOSCOW IN OCTOBER

The reception of *Miss Mend* and *The Girl with the Hatbox* may explain why Barnet accepted the commission to make a film honoring the tenth anniversary of the October Revolution – released as *Moscow in October* – but it does not explain why he was offered the commission. Among the young realist directors, Fridrikh Ermler would have been a more logical choice, but Ermler worked for the Leningrad Sovkino studio. *Moscow in October* was a disaster for Barnet, antithetical to his style in every way. Barnet's Soviet biographer appropriately titled his chapter on the history of this production as "Barnet against Barnet" and ended it by saying: "In this film – made by Barnet – there was no Barnet."[32]

Barnet was presented with a script by Oleg Leonidov that had been approved by the Party's Institute of History (Istpart). The director faced the unenviable task of trying to create major drama where there was virtually none to be found; the decisive Bolshevik coup had taken place in Petrograd, not Moscow. Barnet, moreover, had to stretch this little flurry of activity into a full-length film on a shooting schedule of only forty days without modifying the Istpart-sanctioned script.[33] As an actor and an actor's director, Barnet must have found working with the inept non-professional Nikandrov as Lenin (the same Nikandrov who appeared in Eisenstein's *October*) exceptionally painful. *Moscow in October* was exactly the kind of film Barnet most disliked: a grandiose epic without real people or a real story.

Barnet's discomfiture with this film is reflected in the finished product. Only three reels of *Moscow in October* are extant, which makes it difficult to form a coherent impression.[34] Nonetheless, each scene is so badly staged that it is difficult to imagine that seeing even more of them could force a different evaluation. The film is not, however, entirely devoid of interest, since Barnet attempted to make up for the lack of story by resorting to "formalist techniques" – cross-cutting, fast-cutting, and fancy camera angles. Some of it works, but as the infamous telephone scene illustrates, Barnet had a lot to learn. Cutting from telephone operators mixing up lines to Bolsheviks listening in on the Provisional Government's plans is probably one of the more ill-conceived attempts at parallel action in Soviet silent film. And his mass scenes, which mainly consist of crowds of people aimlessly milling around, provoked an inevitable (if unfair) comparison to the work of Barnet's contemporaries, Eisenstein and Pudovkin, and especially to their anniversary films *October* and *The End of St. Petersburg*.

Certainly *Moscow in October* represented Barnet's sincere effort to make a "political" film, and so it was a radical departure from his previous pictures *Miss Mend* and *The Girl with the Hatbox*. Yet Barnet clearly realized before the film's release that more trouble was ahead. Although he rarely contributed to the film press, he wrote a pre-release apology for *Moscow in October* in which he consistently referred to the picture as "our" film, and used "I" only once (in contrast to his liberal use of "I" in previous writings). He pointed out that he was given very little time to make the film. He also objected to the constraints of historical reconstruction, noting (quite correctly) that the methods and purposes of history and cinema rarely coincide and that "many historical facts are not interesting from a cinematographic point of view."[35]

The Mezhrabpom studio always supported its directors, and so despite Barnet's misgivings, *Moscow in October* opened in three theatres in Moscow.[36] This unusual level of promotion notwithstanding, Barnet's views on his work were essentially the same as those of his critics. Previously Barnet's films had been criticized as being all surface and no substance; this one was attacked for exactly the opposite reasons. *Moscow in October* was not entertaining enough! It was seen instead as being "false" and "confused."[37] Although all the jubilee films were disappointments to the faithful, *Moscow in October* had the dubious distinction of being considered the greatest of the "failures."[38] It is small wonder that no particular care was taken to preserve the film in its entirety.

THE HOUSE ON TRUBNAIA SQUARE

Barnet did not lose his confidence and quickly rebounded, following *Moscow in October* with his most accomplished silent film, *The House on Trubnaia Square* (1928). This picture holds its own among the best Soviet silent comedies and deserves to be far better known than it is.[39] Here Barnet reworked motifs and styles that he had learned from Kuleshov and Protazanov in such a way that they became truly his own. He also incorporated some of the stylistic devices he had experimented with in *Moscow in October* to a better end. He demonstrated that it was possible to make a film that was funny and serious, accessible yet formally interesting, all at the same time.[40]

Barnet was being watched very closely, and he ran into a number of serious difficulties while making *The House*. The film industry was in the midst of the nepotism scandal discussed in chapter 5, and Barnet's cast had been purged of allegedly "unqualified" actors.[41] The number of scenarists who worked on the script (Bella Zorich, Anatolii Mariengof, Vadim Shershenevich, Viktor Shklovskii, and Nikolai Erdman) also indicates trouble – and the Shklovskii connection almost guaranteed it.[42] Given these problems, the film must be considered a remarkable success.

Barnet dealt with a number of themes in *The House* – the disparity between cultural standards in the city and the country, the craven pretenses of the NEP petty-bourgeoisie, and the decay of urban life – and interwove them skillfully. The film opens with its funniest and most famous scene, one which Noel Burch used to good effect in his 1985 television documentary on Soviet silent film, *Born Yesterday: USSR*,

1924–28. By means of a long travelling shot, the viewer is treated to a bird's-eye view of the activities on the staircase of a tenement-like apartment building. People are sawing wood, dumping garbage, fighting, and so on, despite the numerous signs admonishing them not to do this, that, and the other. A naive country girl, Parasha (Vera Maretskaia), will soon find herself in this place as a maid because she has come to Moscow looking for her uncle, with whom she was to stay while she found work.

After spending a day trying to decipher directions from city slickers, Parasha locates her uncle's flat, but he has gone back to the country. The bewildered girl has to brave big-city life alone. Poor Parasha ends up in the clutches of the hen-pecked and mean-spirited barber (Vladimir Fogel in one of his last roles) and the barber's pretentious and lazy wife (E. Tiapkina). Parasha becomes a virtual slave to the Golikovs, but not to the extent that she would be prevented from falling in love with a handsome chauffeur (Vladimir Batalov, Nikolai Batalov's brother) or from being recruited to union membership (by Ada Voitsik) or from attending a hilarious parody of "revolutionary" drama at a worker's club.[43]

The comic conceit around which the action of the last half of the film is constructed is especially biting. The Golikovs, who have attempted to prevent Parasha from taking part in union activities, believe that she has been elected to the City Soviet. Because this will add to their status in the eyes of the denizens of their tenement, they plan a big party for Parasha – only to be humiliated when they learn it was a case of mistaken identity.[44] Parasha loses her job, but goes on to a better life, with her man and the union.[45]

When this film was released in fall 1928, the Cultural Revolution was well under way. The Party Conference on Cinema Affairs had led to a self-criticism campaign within the film industry that in turn had led to "specialist baiting." This specialist baiting mirrored the campaign against NEPmen and the petty-bourgeoisie which was taking place in society at large. *The House on Trubnaia Square* seems on the surface to coincide very nicely with political concerns then current. It also epitomized the kind of socially committed films the critics were claiming Soviet society needed, with the added value of being both appealing and accessible to mass audiences.

But Barnet found himself under fire once again. The film was attacked in an ARRK discussion for supposedly *not* being funny, with special attention drawn to alleged deficiencies in the script. Viktor Shklovskii, one of the script doctors called in to tinker with the screenplay, shamelessly and enthusiastically joined critics in denouncing *The House on*

Trubnaia Square, an act reminiscent of his "betrayal" of Iurii Tarich in the scandal over *The Wings of a Serf*.[46] Invidious (and rather unfair) comparisons were drawn between *The House* and *The Girl with the Hatbox*. The Golikovs do resemble Madame Irène and her husband in *The Girl*, but the critique of the NEP was much sharper in Barnet's newest effort.[47]

BARNET'S "FALL"

Protazanov responded to the criticism over *The White Eagle* by retreating to the classics (his Chekhovian almanac, *Ranks and People*). Barnet simply retreated, although Kushnirov says he was offered a number of scripts.[48] He did accept a part in his former co-director Fedor Otsep's picture *The Living Corpse* (1929), and he also directed two experimental sound shorts.[49] In 1931, he reemerged from his quasi-retirement to undertake his final silent film, *The Ice Breaks*, a screen adaptation of K. Gorbunov's story about class struggle in the countryside prior to collectivization.[50] The Mezhrabpom studio, increasingly politically conscious from necessity, apparently saw *The Ice Breaks* as its answer to *Earth*. It was to be a film about village life, but without any of the technical or aesthetic attributes which might leave it open to charges of formalism. Why Barnet was chosen to direct it is again a mystery; the tale of a drunken village Soviet chairman under the sway of local *kulaks* fits neither the studio's style nor Barnet's.[51] Perhaps the question that was posed was: why not Barnet? It is even more difficult to imagine other Mezhrabpom directors, like Protazanov or even Pudovkin, filming such a story.

Barnet succeeded in one respect – *The Ice Breaks* was not charged with the dreaded "formalism" (although Bernard Eisenschitz describes it as a "truly formalist film").[52] It did not, however, add to his reputation as a director. Critic K. Feldman accused Barnet of schematic development of the main characters and unsuccessful resolution of the action (the *kulaks* murder the chairman and are brought to trial by the *bedniaks*).[53] The film quickly disappeared from the screen.[54]

Barnet disappeared as well, but only temporarily. In 1932, he began working on his first full-length sound film, the anti-war movie released in 1933 as *Outskirts*.[55] *Outskirts*, one of the few Soviet masterworks of the early sound period, marked a new stage in Barnet's career as well as a new stage in Soviet film history.[56]

The suspicion and intolerance with which Protazanov's work was greeted at least were understandable if unjustified. Protazanov represented the old school in every way: he came from a wealthy upper-middle-class family. His *œuvre* exemplified Russian cinema's flamboyant past. His loyalty to the new regime had wavered. He kept his critics off-balance as he alternated between the perfectly political (*His Call*) and the perfectly neutral (*The Case of the Three Million*).

While it was true that Barnet was far from "proletarian" (despite his protestations about that supposedly inconsequential family business), he had paid his dues. He had worked since he was fifteen and had served in the Red Army. While he learned the filmmaking trade, he had continued to support state defense (and himself) by teaching boxing in Glavvosh. The critics wanted young, really Soviet directors; he was one. They wanted simple, inexpensive, and entertaining films; he made them. *Miss Mend* was only superficially concerned with Soviet problems, and then only in the final of the three parts of the serial, but Barnet, unlike Protazanov, did not repeat that particular "mistake."[57] That Barnet's level of "engagement" and technical mastery was increasing is obvious by comparing *The Girl with the Hatbox* with *The House on Trubnaia Square*. Yet throughout his silent film career, Barnet was subjected to relentless attack, and to a proportionately greater degree than was Protazanov.

The lesson for aspiring young filmmakers, especially those who had no artistic pretensions, was a troubling one.[58] Barnet was a director with a gift for comedy and clear potential for professional growth. But in 1928 it appeared unlikely that he would have a future as a popular filmmaker in the Soviet society. Closely connected to Barnet's problems were questions with sweeping implications for cinema, for popular culture, and, ultimately, for Soviet society. If Barnet's films were not acceptable entertainment, which movies were? Were there no safe subjects? Would Soviet directors have any input into the movies they made? Was the Soviet Union turning into a state where even entertainment had to be directed?

Looking at the career of another young director, Fridrikh Ermler, provides us with a rather different way to assess the pitfalls and possibilities of a Soviet alternative to "bourgeois" entertainment cinema in the 1920s. Like Barnet, Ermler was young and talented, but unlike Barnet, he was a rarity in Soviet cinema. Ermler was not a "proletarianist," but an indubitably genuine proletarian.

CHAPTER 8 FRIDRIKH ERMLER AND THE SOCIAL PROBLEM FILM

The semi-literate druggist's boy from Rezhitsa [Rezēknē], next a fighter for the Revolution, the producer of the most talented cinematic chronicles of the Party, a director of world-wide fame – surely one hears in this fairy-tale biography the mighty wind of October. (Fedor Nikitin, 1970[1])

In 1926, the Leningrad Sovkino studio released a movie which embodied all the characteristics that socially and politically active Soviet film-workers and critics had demanded for the new Soviet picture. Like the works of the "old specialists," it had a plot and a hero and realistic montage and mise-en-scène. Audiences found the film both entertaining and easily comprehensible. But unlike most films of the "commercial deviation," this film also dealt with contemporary Soviet problems in a serious way. The pedigree of its obscure young director, moreover, was a propagandist's dream. He could not have been more unlike a Protazanov, a Gardin, a Sabinskii. Not only was he a genuine proletarian, he was also a Party member, and a former Chekist.

The film was _Katka the Apple Seller_, the director – Fridrikh Ermler. Before the decade ended, Ermler produced three more movies which established him as a leading talent among Soviet cinema directors. But Ermler's _œuvre_ was more than an attractive alternative to bourgeois entertainment films. Taken together, his movies present a coherent critique of Soviet society from the point of view of a political activist. They also lay the basis for the genre known as the _bytovoi_ film, that is, movies dealing with the problems of contemporary Soviet society.

And yet despite the fact that Ermler seemed to personify the ideal – a talented, socially responsible cinematic realist – he met many obstacles in his quest to realize his vision. His problems mounted during the Cultural Revolution, especially following the release of his final silent film, _The Fragment of the Empire_. Some time in 1930, Ermler announced his retirement from film and entered the Communist Academy as a student.

ERMLER'S EARLY YEARS

Ermler's friend and competitor, director Grigorii Kozintsev, has written that he never understood why Ermler, after making the highly praised *The Fragment of the Empire*, attempted to quit the cinema. Others who knew him well, like the scenarist and critic Mikhail Bleiman, also found him (and his work) enigmatic.[2] Ermler was indeed an elusive figure, but what we know of his life provides a compelling portrait of the opportunities for upward social mobility the Revolution offered some of its supporters. Protazanov had been a child of privilege; he made his own way because he wanted to, and was helped immeasurably in his struggle for independence by the 5,000 ruble bequest from his aunt, a considerable sum of money. Barnet had made his own way out of necessity, but he, too, had had a privileged upbringing. Ermler was an outsider in every way, and yet despite the vast gulf in class, privilege, and education that lay between these men, they share striking similarities as well.

Ermler was born Vladimir Markovich Breslav in the Latvian river town of Rezēknē in 1898.[3] His family was Jewish; their pre-revolutionary estate, *meshchane* (petty-bourgeois). His father was a skilled tradesman, a cabinetmaker who emigrated to America in 1905, never to return. Ermler's mother was left behind to raise five children on her own. Ermler apparently never attended school and learned to read and write at home. He was, in his own words, "almost illiterate." He went to work as an errand-boy for a druggist when he was twelve. The job apparently was not too onerous, for he had time to pore over cheap novels – and to sneak off to the movies at the "Diana" theatre in Rezēknē. In 1915, he travelled to Moscow to pursue his dream of movie stardom; when he innocently asked a policeman where the movie studios were, his heavy accent betrayed him. Since he could not produce a passport, he was put on the next train back home, feeling lucky that he had not been arrested.

Ermler was drafted in 1916, deserted shortly thereafter, and went to Petrograd, where he was caught and sent to Krasnoe Selo as part of the 171st Infantry.[4] He was vague about his activities during 1917, and we know nothing of his political attitudes or how he was recruited to the cause of the Revolution. By 1918, he was working for the Revolutionary Military Commissariat as a spy. He spoke German, and as "Fridrikh Ermler" he carried out more than twenty missions behind enemy lines, mainly in German-occupied Latvia and Poland, and spent some time in prison in Wilno. Although he apparently never wrote about this period, maintaining a spy's discretion, he retained his "German" pseudonym to the end of his days.

In late 1919, he was invited to join the Party, and in 1920, he entered the Cheka, working first in intelligence. He was sent to Samara in 1921, where he served as assistant to the head of the Special Section and as a member of the Revolutionary Military Tribunal.[5] Given the activities of the revolutionary tribunals at this time, it is virtually certain that Ermler was involved in some nasty business, a subject about which he once again maintained complete silence. Yet it was during this tumultuous period of revolution and civil war that we see his first steps to end his active involvement with the Revolution. Never before had he had the chance to read seriously, and, unschooled though he was, he became a voracious reader, especially of Lev Tolstoi.

But new-found pleasures did not deter him from pursuing his dream of becoming a movie actor. In 1923, he arrived at the door of the Leningrad Institute of Screen Arts, intending to study acting. The student-policeman guarding the portals (future director Sergei Vasilev) informed the upstart that he could not just walk in, that he had to apply and be chosen to matriculate. Ermler's response became an institute legend – he pulled out his Browning pistol and said, "*This* has selected me."[6] Ermler continued to work for the internal security police (reorganized as the GPU) for an unspecified time after he enrolled in the film institute,[7] and he was treated with considerable caution by his fellow students. He was believed always to be armed, and Aleksandra Glama-Meshcherskaia, the redoubtable doyenne of the institute, never extended him her hand to kiss.[8] He even had one student, Iakov Gudkin, arrested on theft charges which turned out to be unfounded, but it is a measure of Ermler's brash charm that Gudkin too eventually became a member of Ermler's loyal following.[9] Ermler also found the time, between his classes, to organize and serve as secretary of the institute's Party/Komsomol cell.

In 1924, his nearly decade-old dream was realized when he was cast in two films, *Tea* (a one-reel agit-film) and *Red Partisans* (a full-length Civil War adventure).[10] The parts were small, but Ermler was bitterly disappointed in his performances. With characteristic decisiveness, he gave up acting to become a film director.

To attain his new goal, Ermler organized his own production collective, the Experimental Cinema Workshop (KEM). KEM's stated aims were in keeping with Ermler's political background and personal aspirations. KEM was formed to guard the film institute from counterrevolutionary influences, to prepare cinema actors, and to make only strictly contemporary films. In practice, KEM's primary focus was definitely on acting, reflecting the interests of its organizer. Its slogans were "No feelings! No transformations!" and "Down with Stanislavskii! Long live Meierkhold!," which reflects the spirit of the times more than it does Ermler, a quintessential realist. As Ermler later admitted with wry humor, all he knew was that Stanislavskii was a gentleman (barin) and that Meierkhold was a Jew and a communist.[11]

Ermler had no illusions about film as "art," nor any high-flown theories. His ideas were simple, direct, pragmatic. He wanted film acting – and indeed, all aspects of filmmaking – to be considered a trade. Using a simile which recalled his father's profession, he wrote in one of the original KEM manifestoes that a filmworker should be "like a cabinet-maker, who knows his wood, tools ..."[12]

The year 1924 was a busy one for Ermler. Not only did he begin and end his career as an actor and found KEM, he left the Leningrad Institute of Screen Arts, apparently without graduating, and worked first for Sevzapkino as secretary to the Scientific-Art Council, and then as an assistant to director P. P. Petrov-Bytov, an ideologue of "proletarian films" whose work and ideas will be discussed in chapter 9. After Petrov-Bytov fired him, Ermler persuaded Sevzapkino to finance a one-reel educational film called *Scarlet Fever*, which Mikhail Bleiman says was a bizarre comedy done in an extreme avant-garde style. It was "scandalously unsuccessful" – literally never booked by theater agents.[13]

This could well have been the finale of a very short career in film, if it had not been for Ermler's Party membership. Lenin's widow Nadezhda Krupskaia had just approved a script for a Civil War adventure, so Sevzapkino (soon to become Leningradkino) was looking for a Party member to direct. Ermler got his second chance. By all accounts this film, *Children of the Storm* (1926), was rather ordinary, although Bleiman in his review in *Leningradskaia pravda* saw promise in the direction despite the "terrible" script.[14]

FROM *KATKA THE APPLE SELLER* TO *THE HOUSE IN THE SNOWDRIFTS*

This promise was realized in Ermler's next film, *Katka the Apple Seller* (1926), the true start of his career as a film director and chronicler of Soviet life. Narratively, the film is a simple melodrama exposing the "dark side" of society during the NEP. A naive peasant girl named Katka has come to Leningrad looking for factory work. Instead, she falls in with a gang of thieves and blackmarketeers and has a child by Semka, the gang's ringleader. Being a cad as well as a criminal, Semka of course refuses any responsibility for Katka and his child, and so Katka is reduced to selling apples on the street to make a living. Yet the kind-hearted Katka can still take pity on someone worse off than herself – the former *intelligent* Vadka, who serves as a look-out for the street vendors. Vadka moves in with Katka to help take care of her baby. Meanwhile, the nefarious Semka and his new girlfriend Verka (a shopgirl who bootlegs perfume) are busy.[15] After inadvertently killing an old woman in a bungled robbery, Semka decides to plan a less risky crime, the robbery of a cattle-dealer from Tambov whom Verka has charmed. The naive provincial has promised to open a perfume store for her (thereby making her an honest woman), but Verka prefers crime to work. After she drugs him, Semka bashes him on the head. Then Semka decides he is going to kidnap his child, giving Vadka (a rather ineffectual character who has tried to commit suicide) the chance to become a man of action at last. Vadka foils the villains, and he and Katka decide to go to work in a factory, their decision sealed with a kiss.

From this plot outline, *Katka the Apple Seller* sounds like another in a series of primitive Soviet melodramas peopled by caricatures instead of characters. Yet with the exception of a clichéd ending that in Soviet cinema is the equivalent of the heroine getting her man in Western movies, *Katka* is an original look at the problems of NEP society. It was also deftly directed and beautifully photographed, shot on location in Leningrad, rather than in a studio.

But the real strength of the film lay in its casting. Ermler's instincts in this important aspect of filmmaking were as good as Protazanov's and contributed to a large degree to *Katka*'s success. Like Protazanov, Ermler drew actors from theater as well as from the movies (mainly from his own collective), but he added a twist. Semka is played not by a debauched "bourgeois" character actor but by the attractive and athletic Valerii Solovtsov. His sidekick (Iakov Gudkin) and his girlfriend Verka (the sullenly pretty B. Chernova) are also meant to be members of a specific-ally Soviet underclass, rather than the depraved remnants of the tsarist lumpenproletariat. Veronika Buzhinskaia, who made a specialty of such parts, brought a fresh naturalism to the somewhat one-dimensional role of Katka. The flatness of her character was more than counterbalanced by the vividness of Vadka, the quintessential superfluous man, affectionately portrayed by Fedor Nikitin. Nikitin, who had studied acting at the

Moscow Art Theatre before moving to Leningrad, dominates every scene he is in, and his Vadka is perhaps the oddest hero of the Soviet silent screen.[16]

Ermler demonstrated that by using the same "tools of the trade" employed by the old specialists and adding a dash of imagination, it was possible for a young director to craft an entertaining melodrama from Soviet life – and cheaply too. The plot featured believable characters with clearly delineated heroes and villains, and Ermler skillfully created dramatic tension as the viewer watches to learn if the villains will be brought to justice or not. The quirky, understated romance between Katka and Vadka also contributed to the film's inherent human interest.

But the Katka–Vadka romance and the oddity of the Vadka character illustrate quite well the originality that brought Ermler trouble. Ermler was not just a proficient hack who could be counted on to make the same movie time and again. He intended to use film to criticize Soviet life, and *Katka the Apple Seller* is the first clear-cut critique in Soviet cinema of NEP society and the market economy that supported hooligans like Semka and Verka. The film also reveals a society in considerable disarray almost ten years after the Revolution, a society unable to integrate not only disaffected elements like the *intelligent* Vadka, but one of the masses, the peasant girl Katka. A non-productive member of the new Soviet society, Katka is an unwed mother on the fringes of a crime network. No social services exist to help Katka and Vadka – and the Party is certainly nowhere to be seen – so they help each other in a reversal of traditional gender roles. She is the breadwinner, as it were, and he the caretaker of home and child.

Soviet critics found Ermler's depiction of Soviet society quite troubling, although they recognized that in many ways the film was an important step forward in creating a "truly Soviet" melodrama. Glavpolitprosvet's organ *Soviet Cinema* applauded the way Ermler created believable characters in a film that could be easily understood by the masses.[17] Writing for *Pravda*, Khrisanf Khersonskii also admired the film, especially its simplicity, humor, and good acting, but he found Katka's sudden transformation into a staunch proletarian fairly unbelievable.[18] *Izvestiia*, on the other hand, criticized it for the very reasons that *Soviet Cinema* had praised it – that it was a simple melodrama.[19] The worst review appeared in *Cinema Front*, where K. Ganzenko admired only the cinematography. He thought the characters unbelievable, the acting poor, and the direction "naive and empty" and labelled the picture a "stereotyped, poster-like agit-film [based on] an alien way of life."[20]

As time passed, these negative reactions faded, and it is important to note why. Audiences liked it, to be sure, but more importantly it made money. Scenarist and critic Adrian Piotrovskii, no friend of entertainment films, singled out *Katka* as a film unusual for being both ideologically correct and profitable.[21] This refrain was repeated at the Party Conference on Cinema Affairs, where *Katka* was praised as much for its low cost and profitability as for its contemporary theme.[22]

Ermler completed two movies in 1927, the year following *Katka*, but neither opened until 1928. *The Parisian Cobbler*, his fourth film to be released, seemed a logical progression in his work. Where *Katka* had been a slightly tentative attempt at a *bytovoi* film, *The Parisian Cobbler* was an assured and didactic melodrama, with topical subject-matter and an unusually violent climactic scene.

This film had received an unusual amount of pre-release publicity for an Ermler film, since Ermler, like Protazanov, maintained a low profile and did not engage in aesthetic controversies or otherwise promote himself or his views. Ermler had co-authored the script with Nikolai Nikitin (a member of the Serapion Brothers literary group), after which Nikitin wrote a novella based on the scenario. The novella was published in *Red Virgin Soil* in fall 1927 under the title "Kirik Rudenko's Crime" and enjoyed a certain reputation.[23]

Like *Katka*, *The Parisian Cobbler* depicted an unmarried pregnant girl whose fate was connected (in this case, involuntarily rather than voluntarily) with hooligans. Unlike Katka, which examined NEP's street society, *The Parisian Cobbler* focused on a specific social campaign – the campaign against loose sexual mores and abortion, which was part of the rejection of "revolutionary" social values characterizing the late twenties. This campaign against illicit sex was inextricably connected with an attack on the Komsomol youth, among whom sexual license was supposedly rampant.[24]

Once again, Ermler used vivid villains and complicated "positive" characters to good advantage. He reprised *Katka the Apple Seller* by casting Veronika Buzhinskaia and Fedor Nikitin in the lead roles. Buzhinskaia's innocent demeanor was well suited to the role of Katia, the small-town working-class girl in trouble (a far weaker character than Katka). Nikitin, however, played not a struggling intellectual, but the tradesman Kirik – a shoemaker. But this change could not be taken as any sign that Ermler had learned his "lesson" about how to create a positive hero. Kirik may have been a worker, but, like Vadka, he was an outsider – a deaf-mute scorned by the village youth. Moreover, the very NEP-like name of his shop, the "Parisian Cobbler," testified that the love of things foreign had even penetrated rural backwaters.

Ermler continued to employ Soviet villains, rather than relying on emigrés, foreigners, or other accepted class enemies. Valerii Solovtsov found new and subtle ways to portray iniquity – this time not as a petty thief, but as Andrei, a *komsomolets* who hails from the petty-bourgeoisie (as a title warns the viewer early on). Iakov Gudkin, who had served as one of Semka's nameless underlings in *Katka*, here occupies center stage as Motka Tundel, local hooligan chieftain.

Once again, the plot is simple: Katia learns she is pregnant and is rejected both by Andrei (when she refuses to have an abortion) and by her "traditional" (bourgeois) father. Andrei seeks counsel from his Komsomol cell leader (portrayed as an effete intellectual) to no avail; the cell's discussion of the situation also yields no result. The calculating young roué will do anything to get rid of his unwanted child; now desperate, he falls in with Motka Tundel and his thugs. The hooligans busy themselves spreading malicious rumors about Katia's supposed promiscuity, and they finally concoct a scheme to gang rape Katia so that she will miscarry.[25] Hovering on the sidelines is Kirik. He loves Katia, and knows everything, but because of his disability seems helpless to assist her. Yet in the violent conclusion, the watchful Kirik does save Katia, by attacking Motka Tundel.

Shot in the fluid, realistic style that was Ermler's hallmark, *The Parisian Cobbler* is well crafted and well acted by all the principals, but especially by Nikitin, in a difficult and rather thankless role. To an even greater degree than *Katka the Apple Seller*, *The Parisian Cobbler* showed audiences that for Ermler, unlike most other Soviet directors dealing with contemporary themes, there were not only Soviet heroes, but Soviet villains and Soviet problems as well. Ermler was emerging as a moralist with a dark view of Soviet life, yet a moralist who could make the message palatable. Though the work relies heavily on melodramatic conventions, it also had nuances which distinguished it from lesser melodramas, such as the imaginative use of a deaf-mute as a hero and the relatively complex characterization of the selfish young anti-hero Andrei. *The Parisian Cobbler* made it plain that Soviet cinema had another star – a first-class director who produced socially relevant films that were intelligible and entertaining.

Reviewers, though much more enthusiastic than they had been for *Katka the Apple Seller*, were still critical. Again, if we are to evaluate the viability of a Soviet alternative to the bourgeois entertainment film, it is important to note what contemporary critics liked and did not like about the film. Khersonskii praised *The Parisian Cobbler* in *Pravda* as the most socially relevant picture of the winter season and drew attention to its fine acting.[26] Mikhail Shneider in *Cinema Front* labelled it the first true *bytovoi* film, a "breath of fresh air" falling between "trashy" commercial pictures and the inaccessible avant-garde films which he saw dominating the Soviet screen.[27] In *Soviet Screen*, K. Feldman underscored the picture's use of "living material" as an important virtue.[28] But even given all this, one suspects that it was the film's profitability which went farthest in absolving any shortcomings.[29] As a result, even though *The Parisian Cobbler* was released only shortly before the Party Conference on Cinema Affairs, it was favorably mentioned there several times.[30]

Despite *The Parisian Cobbler*'s good fortune in being praised at the Party Conference, all was not quiet on the cinema front. Both the Association of Workers of Revolutionary Cinematography (ARRK, the Association of Revolutionary Cinematography's new name) and the Friends of Soviet Cinema (ODSK) held screenings and discussions of the film, in which we see a disquieting shift in tone, a portent of things to come. Although Khrisanf Khersonskii (and *Izvestiia*'s Nikolai Volkov) had been concerned about the brutal ending to the film, ARRK and ODSK took a much harder line on the violence.[31] ARRK's resolution on the film praised *The Parisian Cobbler*'s realistic depiction of Komsomol and worker life, as well as its cinematography and acting, but discerned elements of "aestheticism" in it. ARRK also found troubling the lack of definitive answers to the problems raised and puzzled over the meaning of the film's title.[32] (This line was continued in ARRK, and in 1929 the film was attacked for being melodramatic.)[33] While ODSK found the film artistically significant, it criticized Kirik's ambiguous class position, the strange title, and the "aestheticism" perceived in the film's beautiful shots of the outdoors.[34]

But considering the difficulty Soviet directors had getting any positive remarks from the critics about their work, Ermler had done well. In terms of plot and theme *The Parisian Cobbler* seemed a logical successor to *Katka the Apple Seller*, yet it was not actually the next film Ermler made. That film, *The House in the Snowdrifts*, the story of a musician struggling to survive the bitter winter of 1919, was suppressed. When it was finally released, late in March 1928, it played a few second-run theaters before disappearing again.

The House in the Snowdrifts is a difficult film to situate thematically in Ermler's *œuvre*. This is exacerbated by the fact that half the film is no longer extant, and contemporary descriptions of Ermler's work can be quite misleading, since such descriptions tended to focus on plot rather than on characterization and visual style. Loosely based on Evgenii Zamiatin's very brief short story "The Cave," *The House in the Snowdrifts* concerns the battle of a member of the pre-revolutionary intelligentsia, a nameless musician (Fedor Nikitin), for physical and spiritual survival after the Revolution.

In contrast to *Katka the Apple Seller* and *The Parisian Cobbler*, this film does not have any representatives of the laboring classes in central roles. Although there is a subplot about the machinations of a speculator-counterfeiter (Valerii Solovtsov creating yet another memorable villain), and one about a proletarian family, *The House in the Snowdrifts* is above all else a moving and sympathetic portrayal of an individual devastated by the Revolution. The musician's increasing desperation drives him to steal not only wood, as in Zamiatin's story, but also a pet parrot (a communist sympathizer who chirps "To the barricades!") with which he cooks soup for his sick wife. This tragio-comic device skillfully serves as a metaphor for the musician's total degradation – what could be more loathsome to an artist than such an act?

The House in the Snowdrifts broke Ermler's pattern of strict contemporaneity in subject-matter, but in most ways it can be considered a part of his *œuvre*. Although set in 1919, it is not in any respect a "Civil War" movie, and in fact does not even refer to the Civil War, a great heresy in the twenties.[35] *The House* is a film about a recognized social problem; once again, the inability of Soviet society to integrate its populace. Overtly the theme of *Katka*, this idea was part of the subtext of *The Parisian Cobbler*.

The House apparently did not have a first run and received little coverage in the film press. Khrisanf Khersonskii, a cagey critic who did not go out of his way to support films in trouble, nonetheless championed it in *Pravda*. He admired its "profound simplicity and truthfulness" and its humor and irony, calling Ermler a "director-lyricist of people, everyday life [*byt*] and revolution." Khersonskii castigated Sovkino for attempting to suppress the picture by relegating it to showings in workers' clubs and suburban theaters.[36] *Izvestiia*'s Nikolai Volkov, on the other hand, described *The House in the Snowdrifts* noncommittally as a film about how "various social groups survived the terrible winter of 1919" and faintly admired its realistic treatment of the period. He felt, however, that it was a film which the mass viewer would find irrelevant, presumably because its main character was an intellectual.[37]

The discussion of *The House* in ARRK revealed much about the picture's problems. The scenarist, Boris Leonidov, reported that the script had been savaged in Sovkino's artistic (censorship) section, which understandably unnerved Ermler. Leonidov, however, vigorously defended the picture for showing that while the intelligentsia were inherently passive, they were not beyond the Party's salvation. This somewhat disingenuous defense apparently had not fooled the censors, since Leonidov admitted that the picture had been extensively reworked and permission for its release withheld for nearly a year. Despite Leonidov's pleas, and K. Feldman's report that Ermler liked it best of all his films, *The House* was thoroughly condemned in ARRK, even by Ermler's old friend and associate Sergei Vasilev.[38]

ERMLER IN THE CULTURAL REVOLUTION

Ermler's final silent – released in 1929 when the sound era and the Cultural Revolution were beginning – was *The Fragment of the Empire*. Co-authored by Ermler and the prominent scenarist Katerina Vinogradskaia, the script is based on the supposedly true story of an amnesiac's recovery of his memory ten years after the Revolution.[39] *The Fragment of the Empire* opens in the Civil War, with a worker-soldier Filimonov (Fedor Nikitin) and a peasant women who has befriended him stealing the boots from a dead soldier. Ermler eschews heroism and romanticism. For him, the Civil War is not signified by Cossacks cheerfully singing and dancing on the graves of Reds they have buried alive (as in *The Tripole Tragedy*), but by a truly nightmarish panoply of images of death and destruction.

The story then leaps from the darkness of civil war to the light of Soviet power, as Filimonov regains his memory. Nikitin makes the unbelievable transformation believable; Paul Rotha has described it best (although he attributed the impression entirely to the direction and editing, and not to the acting);

From a psychological point of view, the direction of Ermler was amazing. The subconscious process of the man's mind, particularly in the return of his memory through an association of latent ideas was portrayed with an extraordinary power. From death to emptiness, from emptiness to perplexity, from perplexity to understanding, the changing mental states were subtly revealed. As a representation of mental images, of reactions, of subconscious thought, the film was remarkable.[40]

Still unaware what the Revolution has meant for Russia, Filimonov goes to "Peter" (Leningrad) to search for his wife. Stunned by the wondrous and strange transformations in his city – skillfully wrought both by Ermler (through what he shows) and by Nikitin (in how he reacts) – Filimonov manages to find his former employer, now living in poverty. The ex-boss directs the puzzled Filimonov to the factory to look for work. Although the factory is clean, well lit, modern, the workers leave much to be desired. We see them mocking the befuddled Filimonov in one scene; in another, Filimonov prevents a drunken worker from attacking an inspector. When Filimonov finally does locate his wife (Veronika Buzhinskaia), she has married a Soviet *apparatchik* (Valerii Solovtsov). The *apparatchik*, a "cultural worker" who lectures to unreceptive workers about women's rights, is crude and sullen, a hypocrite who preaches women's rights but regards his wife as a drudge. Filimonov, confronted by this scene of domestic discord, sees in the face of the *apparatchik* the drunken factory worker and the murderous White soldier merged into one, a powerful condemnation of the new bureaucracy. Yet, despite Filimonov's pleas, his former wife decides that the material comfort of her present life is worth its spiritual degradation.

Filimonov has found a new start in life under Soviet power as a clean-shaven "modern" worker. But what of most of the others in the film? The crafty peasant woman continues to scratch out a marginal existence; the oddly sympathetic "former person," Filimonov's old employer, is sunk in poverty; Filimonov's wife (now a "new" Soviet woman) endures abuse for creature comforts; the model factory is a scene of taunts, drunkenness, and assaults; the hypocritical *apparatchik* is surely no improvement on a tsarist *chinovnik*. More than any other Ermler film, *The Fragment of the Empire* shows Ermler's pride in Soviet industrialization. But also more than any other film by Ermler, this picture displays his critical, politically left-wing view of Soviet society in painfully sharp relief.

The Fragment caused Ermler a great deal of trouble and became a *cause célèbre* of the Cultural Revolution, pitting the innovative Leningrad filmmakers against the "reactionary front" in Moscow.[41] The critics from Leningrad's *The Life of Art* aligned solidly behind the film. Vladimir Nedobrovo thought it the best film of the year; Adrian Piotrovskii, a dialectical ideal; O. Adamovich, a "great revolutionary film."[42] Reactions were markedly different in Moscow.

This is not to say that Moscow's film critics were joined in lock-step against the picture. Ippolit Sokolov, for one, gave *The Fragment* the review it deserved in *Cinema*. He praised its brilliant technique, its stylistic unity, its powerful emotional appeal, and, especially, Nikitin's triumphant performance.[43] Other reviews were mixed. *Izvestiia*'s critic N. Osinskii (the pseudonym of Prince Valerian Obolenskii) reviewed the film fairly favorably, going so far as to call it "one of the best" of the season. He thought nonetheless that Ermler was wavering between the "modernist" Leningrad film cohort and the realism of Moscow's studios. He praised Nikitin's acting as effectively realistic but criticized Ermler's negative treatment of Soviet life, and the fact that Filimonov's burgeoning class consciousness was less vivid than his recovery of memory.[44] *Soviet Screen*'s B. Alpers also admired some aspects of the picture, namely its construction, acting, and human interest. He did, however, warn against its "psychologism" and Dovzhenkian influences.[45]

Ia. Rudoi, however, was unequivocally critical in the same journal, writing: "Why is it counted the highest artistic achievement to give a picture a thick layer of symbolism? . . . This obviously leads to a break with realistic forms in the mind of the mass viewer." Rudoi went on to say that cinematic material should not be shrouded in a "fog of symbolism" (as he believed it was in *The Fragment of the Empire*) because it would estrange the viewer.[46] By 1930, the film was regularly included in lists of formalist films, even, sadly, in one compiled by the picture's early admirer Sokolov, who now saw *The Fragment of the Empire* as the epitome of the "most basic danger in Soviet cinema."[47]

The Fragment of the Empire was a turning-point in Ermler's career for many reasons. His final and best silent film, *The Fragment* brought Ermler his long-sought acceptance in the Leningrad film community. Ermler does not mention his Order of Lenin (or any of his many awards) in his memoirs; the greatest honor of his life seems to have been the telegrams of congratulations he received from Kozintsev and Eisenstein on his achievement in *The Fragment of the Empire*. His pride at this, recorded thirty years after the fact, is truly touching.[48]

But the movie brought him problems as well. *The Fragment* was the first of Ermler's films troubled by delays and cost overruns,[49] and Ermler's stress level was high. This revealed itself most vividly when the ordinarily professional Ermler, "foaming at the mouth," waved a revolver in Nikitin's face and threatened to shoot him for insubordination on the set.[50] With this wildly melodramatic flourish, one of the great collaborations between actor and director in Soviet cinema ended.[51]

The breach with Nikitin proved irrevocable, but it was not the only problem Ermler faced as a result of this film. *The Fragment of the Empire*, the film that was Ermler's ticket into the inner circle of the Leningrad cinema community, was also the film that led to his estrangement from his Party. One can only imagine the blow that the "war on formalism" – directed as it was against this picture – must have been. Ermler was known in the film community as a "true believer," and he could not forget that he owed his education and his career to the Revolution. Ermler never alluded to the scandal over *Fragment of the Empire*, or to his reasons for quitting cinema temporarily, but it is not really surprising that he announced his retirement and entered the Communist Academy.

A promising start toward the creation of a viable alternative to the bourgeois entertainment cinema ended with a film that was both a considerable achievement and a bitter defeat for its director. Ermler returned to the cinema front in 1932 and with difficulty finally made a film "to order" – *Counterplan*, with Sergei Iutkevich as co-director.[52] With apparently less difficulty, he followed *Counterplan* with two of the most notorious films of the thirties: *Peasants* (1934) and *The Great Citizen* (in two parts, 1938–39). By early 1934, Mikhail Shneider described Ermler as a leader in the struggle against the "bourgeois inheritance of anec-dotalism, adventurism, psychologism, etc."[53] Yet despite the fact that his *œuvre* of the twenties proved a dead end for him personally, the influence of those films on Soviet popular cinema proved quite substantial.[54]

The rhetoric of the early KEM manifestos aside, Ermler was, like Protazanov, an instinctive realist in the tradition of Russian realism and the Moscow Art Theater. Like Protazanov, Ermler knew talent and how to develop it when he found it. But I am not arguing that Ermler was no more than a Protazanov with a pistol, despite strong similarities in professional style. Ermler's *œuvre* has historical significance as a cinematic "document" of both the social problems of the twenties and the critique of NEP society connected with the Party's left wing. He successfully combined entertainment value with didacticism, a feat not to be taken lightly. And however idiosyncratic his view of city and rural life, Ermler was one of the few major directors who consistently used "the people" as central characters in his films.

But as well as Ermler fulfilled most of the commonly accepted norms for a Soviet entertainment film, in the end he found himself in much the same position as Boris Barnet. For critics like director Pavel Petrov-Bytov, who had fired Ermler from his first job in cinema, the ultimate goal was a "workers' and peasants' cinema." Merely deploying peasants and workers as characters in films, as Ermler did, was not enough to constitute a true workers' and peasants' cinema. That issue remained to be resolved.

CHAPTER 9 FOR WORKERS AND PEASANTS ONLY – FACTORY AND TRACTOR FILMS

We have no workers' and peasants' cinema. I state this boldly. Let anyone prove otherwise.   (Pavel Petrov-Bytov, 1929[1])

Boris Barnet and Fridrikh Ermler illustrate the idiosyncracies of Soviet popular cinema in the twenties in several ways. Both men were rather flamboyant, even romantic, figures – boxers and Chekists did not ordinarily become major film directors. In Hollywood, this was the stuff from which press agents constructed legends; not so in the USSR, though Barnet and Ermler played their roles on and off the set quite well.

Their films illustrate that it was possible to make the difficult genres of comedy (*The House on Trubnaia Square*) and melodrama (*Katka the Apple Seller* and *The Parisian Cobbler*) "truly" Soviet. These pictures engaged Soviet life head-on and made Protazanov's work look a little glib by comparison, providing inadvertent reinforcement to the frequent accusations that Protazanov was a "pseudo-Soviet" director. Barnet's and Ermler's movies gave Soviet audiences realistic narratives peopled with vivid characters from the lower echelons of Soviet society – the proletariat, the peasantry, and the *meshchane*.

What did workers think about these films? Although there is evidence that *Katka the Apple Seller* was a modest hit, we cannot determine audience reactions for most pictures with any degree of certainty. Did peasants like them? More importantly, did they ever see them? Based on scattered references to the repertory recommended for rural areas, it seems unlikely, but again, this is a question for which little evidence is available at present. Yet we do know what the "greater and lesser pedants of Soviet cinema" thought. While the enlighteners did not judge films like *The Parisian Cobbler* to be as objectionable as "formalist pictures" such as Kozintsev and Trauberg's *New Babylon* (which was charged with surrendering the masses "to the power of street singers [and] Harry Piel"), they still considered them "inappropriate" for workers and peasants.[2]

In the case of Barnet's films, the reasons were extra-cinematic in part. Barnet had been typecast as a "Mezhrabpom director," maker of *Miss Mend* (times three) and *The Girl with the Hatbox*, so it mattered little whether the content of *The House on Trubnaia Square* was "Soviet" or not. Ermler's case was different. Despite his proletarian origins and Party credentials, Ermler had displayed an unsettling affinity for old-style "intellectuals" and other outcasts, figures who were at best only marginally positive role models for the new society. Furthermore, his understanding of the problems Soviet society faced was perhaps too acute, his depiction of these problems too pointed. So the "pedants" and the "proletarianists" struggled on to find a director, a script, a film that would measure up to their vision of the "real" Soviet cinema – an idealized cinema for idealized masses.

WORKERS

Theory

Throughout the twenties, Soviet terminology carefully divided the "masses" into two groups, workers and peasants. As anyone familiar with the origins and evolution of the working class in Russia knows, this was sometimes an artificial distinction. The working class was still numerically small, about three million (barely 2 percent of the population). Workers' ties with the countryside were persistent, and some film plots, both revolutionary and popular, were built around the *khodok*, the peasant who comes to the city to find work (for example, *Katka the Apple Seller, The End of St. Petersburg, The House on Trubnaia Square*).[3]

Yet despite the problems associated with the rigid division of "worker" and "peasant," it is the framework that informed the cinematic debates. The enlighteners – those cinema activists who believed that the primary function of cinema in a socialist society was educational – had early decided that they knew what workers needed, as this 1924 *Cinema Gazette* editorial indicates:

the worker and worker-intellectual consumer demands *intelligibility, simplicity, logic, lifelikeness, orderliness, everyday life* [byt]. The worker does not suffer ... affectations, idiosyncrasy, mysticism. The world view of the working class, Marxism, is the most well defined and harmonious of existing world views. Only one style, realism, corresponds ... to this world view.[4]

The world view of the working class was to be realized through a bland diet of films about "physical culture, the new way of life, raising standards for industrial labor, history of the revolutionary movement," etc.[5]

The audience preference study conducted by Troianovskii and Egiaza-rov was for the most part class-blind, but the few audience studies which focused on workers generally confirmed the above points, and especially that workers preferred "realism" in their movies. These surveys also vividly demonstrated the chasm that lay between critics and the pro-letariat.

The Association of Revolutionary Cinematography (ARK) sometimes arranged workers' screenings for the purpose of comparing workers' responses to specific films to those of their own membership, that is, industry professionals. Eisenstein's *Battleship Potemkin* (1926), one of the most famous films in cinema history, was duly acclaimed by Soviet critics at the time of its release. Moreover, it appears that there was a campaign afoot to promote the film to the "masses" and to exaggerate its box office.[6]

The workers' screening of *Potemkin* at ARK seriously undermines the credibility of claims that the picture was popular with "ordinary" viewers. While worker reaction was not unanimously negative, those *ARKovtsy* who had enthusiastically supported the film were probably disappointed nonetheless. It must be noted that a few of the workers' comments about the movie seem contrived. For example, a miner named Shipukov found the "happy" ending in which the mutineers appear victorious "unrealistic," while one Poveskii wondered about the absence of revolutionary organizations from the picture. Other remarks ring truer. The audience was apparently sophisticated enough to recognize that cinematically the film was "magnificent," but many complained at the same time that it was "unclear" and difficult to follow.[7] At a later ARK-sponsored screening, workers exhibited more enthusiasm, but the report also mentioned periodic outbursts of inappropriate laughter, which indicate either lack of comprehension or failure to suspend dis-belief.[8]

Aleksandr Razumnyi's Civil War melodrama *The Difficult Years* (released in December 1925), is a very different film from *Potemkin*. Razumnyi directed steadily throughout the twenties, though only two of his films (*Mother*, 1920 and *Commander Ivanov*, 1923) attracted much critical attention, and that attention was essentially negative. Long forgotten, *The Difficult Years* was speedily dismissed by critics as a mediocrity, which makes the results of the ARK workers' screenings very interesting indeed. ARK's "audience sociologist" Aleksandr Dubrovskii asked Association members to grade the film as "good," "satisfactory," or "poor." Of sixty-nine respondents, only fifteen (22 percent) marked it "good." *The Difficult Years* was also shown to two sizeable groups of workers, with 600 and 500 questionnaires returned, respectively. The responses of these two groups were virtually identical to each other and overwhelmingly positive: 94 percent of the first group and 95 percent of the second rated the film "good."[9]

Why did the proletarian audience like this picture? *The Difficult Years* had no big-name stars. Sovkino did not promote it. The plot was simple: a man identified as a "worker-Bolshevik" must decide whether to turn his traitorous son over to the revolutionary tribunal. He does so.[10] But this story of a family torn apart by the Civil War was one with built-in human interest and powerful emotional reverberations for many viewers. And the movie's central conflict presages a major conflict in Soviet life, the subordination of private life to public life.

The ARK studies of viewer responses to *Potemkin* and *The Difficult Years* confirm what other audience surveys do: workers and critics did not like the same pictures. They certainly demonstrate the dichotomy between mass and elite opinion that we have seen time and again. But does this prove the existence of a specifically proletarian taste culture? The answer seems to be "no"; results from working-class studies are virtually identical to Troianovskii and Egiazarov's analysis of the Soviet audience.[11] Soviet viewers liked movies with amusing, exciting, or emotive stories. They did not like movies that were "difficult," regardless of how successful they were cinematically – or how acclaimed they were critically.

Yet the enlighteners stubbornly persisted in treating the proletariat as a special group with special needs. If this "truth" were not apparent from the evidence, then they argued that the evidence was faulty, and more studies were needed. Filmmakers who believed that workers wanted "only" entertainment from movies did not "respect those whom they serve[d]," and needed to be reeducated.[12]

In 1927, calls for control over the repertory for workers became urgent, increasing in intensity and frequency by early 1928. Fears were expressed that worker audiences were being indoctrinated in bourgeois values as a result of their fanatical devotion to foreign films.[13] Some critics of the present state of affairs believed there was a desperate shortage of films on "union and industrial life."[14] This supposed shortage might be overcome in a number of ways: by workers suggesting themes for films, writing scripts (collectively, of course), and finally, by actually making movies.[15] (It was hoped that amateur filmmaking could become as popular a pastime as amateur theatricals in the worker clubs, but given the paucity of resources available to professional filmmakers – and the demands of the censorship – amateur cinema could only be a pipe-dream.) In the meantime, it was reluctantly admitted that some "apolitical" films like *The Collegiate Registrar* could be shown (ostensibly to teach workers about Pushkin!).[16]

The March 1928 Party Conference on Cinema Affairs made the creation of "new genres" for the "toiling masses" a priority; these were to include more films on "industrialization and rationalization" as well as increased production of educational films.[17] The "masses" themselves were soon marshalled to refine these vague formulas. In July 1929, the 1st Workers' Cinema Conference was convened, with 215 delegates who hardly represented society at large: 83 percent male; 45 percent Party/Komsomol.[18] The worker Gorshkov angrily asked why hard currency was being wasted on foreign "trash"; the worker Levykin demanded that "hits" be replaced by films that show "all our achievements in industry and agriculture, all the victories of the working class on the front of socialist construction."[19] A delegation from a candy factory asked for "more films to teach us how to live," that is, films about antediluvian remains from the tsarist past like alcoholism, anti-Semitism, and hooliganism.[20] But the most revealing sign of the times was that after a great deal of self-serving rhetoric about how Soviet workers did not like to spend money on bad films or be "deceived" by flashy advertisements (things bourgeois viewers supposedly welcomed), a decision was reached to control what workers saw by controlling advertising.[21]

Practice

Advertising was not all that extensive in the twenties so it is unlikely that it was a major obstacle inhibiting the enlighteners' efforts to cultivate the worker audience. More critical was the existence of commercial and commercially oriented theaters, which served as a magnet for worker audiences due to the deficiencies of the club network. Nonetheless, many workers did much of their movie-watching at their union clubs, so the cinema propagandists who wished to educate the tastes of the working-class audience naturally focused their efforts there. Yet only half of the working class population even belonged to clubs. An additional factor limiting proletarian exposure to cinema was the shortage of projectors; the clubs' low operating budgets meant that "cinefication" was a costly line item. In 1923, for example, only 25 percent of the clubs showed films regularly.[22] Although "cinefication" of the club network had improved steadily throughout the decade, climbing to 1,788 clubs in 1927, it was not complete by 1929 (see table 8, below).[23] (It is interesting to note that one of the few major feature films to include a scene shot in a workers' club, Barnet's *The House on Trubnaia Square*, showed a revolutionary spectacle as the evening's entertainment, not a movie.)[24]

Clubs with projection capability would typically limit screenings to two a week, a feature film and an industrial *kulturfilm* (or, alternatively, a series of shorts).[25] Sovkino charged the clubs very favorable rental rates for films, but at a cost.[26] Since Sovkino's revenues from clubs were extremely low (only 14 percent of its income in 1927), the clubs did not receive new features until at least one month after the first run in the central theatres – and only a limited number of foreign films among them (but at least 10 percent by contract).[27] The result was that Abram Room's Civil War adventure *Death Bay* arrived in workers' clubs in Novorossiisk one year after its first run, while *The Thief of Baghdad* never played any club anywhere.[28] In general, the club repertory was only 25 percent foreign, as compared to 68 percent at commercial theatres.[29]

Screenings at the clubs were either free or heavily discounted, which presented workers with a clear financial incentive to see films at the clubs, but again, low cost came at a price. In contrast to the accoutrements of the best big-city theatres – orchestras, buffets, plush seats – clubs featured hard seats, a lecturer instead of music, and frequent interruptions for reel changes.[30] Prints wore out quickly due to poor treatment, so month-old pictures were fairly ragged. The screenings rarely started on time.[31] Given the much more attractive viewing conditions as well as the newer and more varied repertory at the commercial theatres, it should not be surprising that workers preferred to see movies in regular theatres, despite the cost of tickets.[32]

These theatres were businesses, not schools for cultural enlightenment, and their business was entertainment. Films about "industrialization and rationalization" were not likely to be booked, and images of workers and factory life were rare in this commercial bill of fare. Although self-styled people's director Pavel Petrov-Bytov claimed that a worker's "punch" would be a "long overdue" response to the cinema avant-garde, it was in fact in "formalist" films that images of proletarian life were most likely to be found.[33] Movies like Eisenstein's *Strike*, Pudovkin's *Mother* and *The End of St. Petersburg*, and Ermler's *The Fragment of the Empire* presented the most positive and detailed cinematic portrayals of workers and factories in Soviet fiction cinema. (Depending on one's definition of fiction, the films of Dziga Vertov could be added to this list as well.)[34] But with the possible exception of *The Fragment of the Empire* and the definite exception of *Mother* (to be discussed below), unsophisticated audiences did not find these "factory films" especially appealing or accessible.

Petrov-Bytov's judgments would have been more accurate if applied to popular cinema, where "worker-heroes" were few and far between. Most heroes in popular pictures were, as we have seen, noblemen, criminals, white-collar workers, Red Army officers, intellectuals, or vaguely déclassé elements. Worker-heroes were most likely to be found in films about the Revolution and Civil War, like Protazanov's *The Forty-First*, Razumnyi's *The Difficult Years* or Abram Room's *Death Bay*, but in such films the focus was on the revolutionary intrigue, not on workers as producers.[35] In films about contemporary life, worker-heroes tended to be craftsmen, like Kirik in *The Parisian Cobbler* or Kolia, the stonemason, in Room's *Third Meshchanskaia Street*. Similarly, women workers were usually depicted in socially marginal occupations like milliner (*The Girl with the Hatbox*), street vendor (Katka in *Katka the Apple Seller* and Zina in *The Cigarette Girl from Mosselprom*), or servant (Parasha in *The House on Trubnaia Square*). (By the film's end, however, finding factory work was usually part of the heroine's political awakening.)[36]

There are so few films to consider in this category that the judgment as to which was "most popular" with both critics and audiences can be made confidently: Pudovkin's *Mother*, a movie which also enjoys the distinction of being one of the few cases in which critical and popular opinion coincided. Pudovkin, like Barnet, had his start as an actor in the Kuleshov collective and had appeared in *The Extraordinary Adventures of Mr. West*.[37] And like Barnet in *Miss Mend*, Pudovkin took a role in *Mother*. But unlike Barnet, Pudovkin is remembered as one of the stars of the avant-garde, not as a popular filmmaker.[38] His future reputation is not obvious in his early film work, however. In 1925, prior to making *Mother* for the Mezhrabpom studio, Pudovkin had directed *Chess Fever*, a short comedy starring Vladimir Fogel, and a scientific film *The Mechanics of the Brain*.[39]

Mother was a free adaptation of Maksim Gorkii's famous novel about the 1905 Revolution and is considered the forerunner to the Socialist Realist films of the thirties. Two of the most popular actors of the silent screen starred: Vera Baranovskaia in the title role with Nikolai Batalov as her son, whose revolutionary activities spark her political awakening and lead to both their deaths.[40] The film had all the ingredients of a popular classic: a simple but dramatic story based on a well-known book, two big-name actors, and Pudovkin's skillful adaptation of some of the new montage techniques to a fairly conventional narrative film. *Mother* received much critical acclaim (including an accolade from Douglas Fairbanks) and was widely distributed, though there were some complaints about the lack of advertising.[41] Its ninth-place posting on Troianovskii and Egiazarov's "top ten" chart (just edging out *The Mark of Zorro*) seems plausible.[42] *Mother* also earned Pudovkin long-lasting good will, which served him well as he turned to more experimental work in the late twenties and early thirties.

There is also no doubt which popular film with workers as the main characters was most anathematized: Abram Room's *Third Meshchanskaia Street*, again starring Nikolai Batalov.[43] Although Room later abandoned cinematic realism for the "formalist" camp (*The Ghost That Does Not Return*, 1930; *A Strict Young Man*, 1936), his early films subscribed to most of the conventions of narrative filmmaking (*Death Bay*, for example). Known in the West as *Bed and Sofa*, *Third Meshchanskaia Street* is a chamber piece about a ménage à trois (indeed, Sovkino changed the title for distribution in the USSR to *Ménage à trois*).[44] This *ménage* (which has been necessitated by Moscow's housing shortage) consists of the stonemason Kolia (Batalov), Kolia's war buddy, the printer Volodia (Vladimir Fogel), and the petty-bourgeois homemaker Liuda (Liudmila Semenova), who becomes wife to both men. Both a comedy and a melodrama, *Third Meshchanskaia Street* depicts Liuda's pitiful attempts to find a measure of happiness with the two cads and her eventual moral awakening. Pregnant, she refuses their demands that she have an abortion and leaves them and the corrupting influences of the big city (Moscow) to make a new life for herself in the country.[45]

This film became a *cause célèbre* prior to its release. The "déclassé specialists" in ARK hailed it as "one of the most successful pictures of Soviet production" – citing its editing, acting, staging, and cinematography.[46] At the same time, it was demonized as "psychopathological" and worse.[47] The reasons for this were immensely complicated, and some of them were extra-cinematic.[48] In terms of the film text itself, however, critics took umbrage at the way in which these two "worker-heroes" were portrayed – as amoral and materialistic denizens of a purely private world. That they were so portrayed by two of the best actors in Soviet cinema made these "negative" characters all the more unforgettable and Room's crime all the more unforgiveable.

Third Meshchanskaia Street opened in Moscow on 15 March 1927. By the end of the month, it had disappeared from the city's first-run theatres. It had the dubious distinction of making Troianovskii and Egiazarov's "most hated" list (along with the film *The Prostitute*), earning only a 25 percent approval rating. Yet it posted a very creditable box-office with nearly 1.3 million viewers in its first six months, and it received Agitprop's imprimatur as a suitable film for workers.[49] Not surprisingly (given its alleged orientations), "bourgeois" viewers were reported to like it.[50]

Mother and *Third Meshchanskaia Street* represent the opposite ends of the workers' film spectrum. Pudovkin followed his effort with *The End of St. Petersburg* (1927), a film commissioned for the tenth anniversary of the October Revolution, which is a much more abstract rendition of the themes begun in *Mother*.[51] Room attempted to rectify his "great mistake" with *Potholes* (1928), the story of an idealized working-class family whose idyllic life is temporarily shattered by a "bad" woman.[52] (Audiences supposedly spurned Harry Piel's latest pictures to flock to *Potholes*.)[53] More typical of the workers' film genre were three pictures answering the call for movies fighting alcoholism, anti-Semitism, and hooliganism. These were, respectively, *Saba* (Mikhail Chiaureli, 1929), *Cain and Artem* (Pavel Petrov-Bytov, 1929), and *Lace* (Sergei Iutkevich, 1928).

Of these three films Chiaureli's *Saba* provides the best illustration of the workers' film, so much so that some *ARKovtsy* thought it too realistic.[54] *Saba* was a beautifully photographed and well-acted melodrama starring Sandro Dzhaliashveli, which traces with precision the worker-protagonist's decline into abject alcoholism. We watch the disintegration of his family, as Saba's petty cruelties to his wife Maro (Veriko Andzhaparidze) and young son Vakhtang (L. Dzhaliashvili) mount. Finally, the drunken Saba (who works as a tram driver), steals a tram, and accidentally runs over his young son. After being brought to trial, Saba reforms, and now sober, is reunited with his family.[55] The sophisticated Soviet critics were appalled at the base appeal to sentiment in this film, but the movie makes its point effectively and painfully.[56] Audiences love to weep on occasion, and this film is a skillfully crafted tear-jerker.

Pavel Petrov-Bytov emerged by the end of the decade as the fiction film's Dziga Vertov, that is, a relentless opponent of "bourgeois" filmmaking. Unfortunately, since he was not a talent of Vertov's stature, his moralizing seems unpleasantly self-aggrandizing. Petrov-Bytov was a director of some repute and had a respectable career in the twenties, making six films from 1925 to 1930; *Cain and Artem*, based on a story by Maksim Gorkii, is the best known of his early work. Cain (E. Gal) is a Jewish shoemaker who saves the life of the Volga boatman Artem (Nikolai Simonov) both literally and figuratively. *Cain and Artem* is a movie about an "awakening," but, in this case, the protagonist's transformation is not a revolutionary one. Through his association with Cain, Artem gradually comes to accept Jews as brothers. The film is competent, but does not tap into emotional reservoirs in the same way *Saba* does. Yet the dismissive reviews *Cain and Artem* received probably had more to do with the way Petrov-Bytov had criticized the critics than with the film itself.[57] Anatolii Lunacharskii stood virtually alone in praising it.[58]

Sergei Iutkevich's *Lace*, an industrial film about, of all things, a lace-making factory, packs three campaigns into a mere seven reels. It attacks drunkenness, hooliganism, and the Komsomol and promotes the usefulness of the wall newspaper (*stengazeta*) as a means of social propaganda. It also features a strong female in the central role, the *komsomolka* Marusia (Nina Shaternikova, Iutkevich's wife), who singlehandedly revitalizes the factory's flaccid Komsomol cell to fight the forces of evil.[59] Local hooligans – who according to a title "need to be crushed morally and even physically" – have been stealing lace from the factory and disturbing peaceful family outings through their rowdy, drunken behavior. By the end, however, their leader is a communist convert, and factory club activities now include a shooting gallery with hooligans as targets.

These many themes are deftly interwoven, and Shaternikova was convincing as the unflaggingly energetic Marusia. Signs of Iutkevich's association with the avant-garde (the FEKS collective of Grigorii Kozintsev and Leonid Trauberg) are plainly visible in the film's formal elements (notably its beautiful but unorthodox cinematography and editing), and *Lace* could just as easily be categorized a formalist, rather than a popular, film. It was, however, so overwhelmingly "correct" politically that the message took precedence over the form for once.[60]

If judged by the standards of European cinema at the time, or even by those of Soviet cinema during the NEP, these three films were unexceptional. But if one judges them by the heavily politicized standards of filmmaking during the Cultural Revolution, they are quite exceptional. Each attempts, however modestly, to put a human face on the rhetoric of the campaigns – and thereby to preserve some of the attributes of popular filmmaking.

PEASANTS

Theory

The world of "peasant cinema" was even more phantasmagorical than that of "worker cinema" in the twenties. It was certainly not for want of a customer, however, since about 120 million people (some 82 per cent of the population) lived in the countryside. Most of these citizens were peasants.

The Russian farming class of the NEP can be safely categorized as a peasantry, with a culture far removed in time and place from farmers of northwestern Europe in the twenties. The stereotypical image of the Russian peasant, familiar from stories, photographs, paintings, and movies, is that of a folkloric people who had scarcely entered the nineteenth century, let alone the twentieth. Like all stereotypes this one is exaggerated, but not by much, and certainly not for the poorer strata of the peasantry. Recent studies of the Russian and Ukrainian rural classes in the early Soviet period have, not surprisingly, focused on land tenure and collectivization; glimpses of peasants as people can be found in works analyzing other aspects of Soviet life as well.[61]

Although the precise figures for literacy among the rural masses are subject to some dispute, it is safe to say that peasant audiences were largely illiterate. They certainly did not read *Soviet Screen* or write letters to *Cinema*; many, if not most, could not even read the intertitles of a film. Neither did they have the visual "literacy" necessary to follow the wordless syntax of a silent film, nor much opportunity to develop it. According to one report, peasants saw one film every four years on the average, compared to one film a month for city-dwellers.[62] (The figure for urban movie-going is a little low, but still within the parameters of the available studies.)

ARK rarely concerned itself with peasant viewers and did not, as far as I know, organize peasant screenings. Since 1924, that had been the domain of the Cinema Section of the Main Committee on Political Education (Glavpolitprosvet) of the Commissariat of Enlightenment (Narkompros) and its "voluntary" arm, the Society of Friends of Soviet Cinema (ODSK). Early Glavpolitprosvet reports of peasant reactions to movies are fascinating, but, though they seem quaint, they are similar to those reported first reactions of European audiences to their first screenings some thirty years earlier.[63]

Aleksandr Katsigras, whose views we have already heard in connection with the entertainment or enlightenment debate, was the most prominent student of the peasant viewer. His findings were very discouraging. Katsigras reported that when first exposed to cinema, peasants saw only fleeting shadows and flickering lights which were so mesmerizing that the narrative was either completely incomprehensible or escaped their notice entirely.[64] Katsigras observed that even more sophisticated peasant audiences found it difficult to follow straightforward narratives (like Aleksandr Razumnyi's *Grandfather Knysh's Gang*, 1924), focusing instead on irrelevant background details.[65] Peasants rejected another Razumnyi film, *Commander Ivanov* (which had been popular with workers) as not very realistic, once again singling out physical detail, rather than story, characterization, acting, humor, etc.[66] Furthermore, peasants did not have the same attention span as city audiences, so the typical six-reel film (about 75 minutes if cranked at twenty frames per second) was too long.[67]

Other evidence was slightly more encouraging. Peasants wanted to see movies that opened their circumscribed world, movies about city life, industry, foreign places. They preferred historical and adventure films.[68] According to one early study, they liked Perestiani's *Little Red Devils*, the phenomenally popular Civil War adventure beloved by all strata of the Soviet audience. They also enjoyed Aleksandr Sanin's *Polikushka* (1919), an adaptation of Lev Tolstoi's grim exposé of rural poverty which ends in the alcoholic protagonist's suicide out of despair at having lost a packet of money entrusted to him. His child drowns in the bathtub when his distraught wife rushes to her husband's body.[69] *Polikushka* was a fascinating combination of dreary naturalism, extreme theatricality, and even a little supernaturalism (Polikushka's ghost appears at the end, after he has been posthumously vindicated). It had the added attraction of starring the famous Moscow Art Theatre actor Ivan Moskvin in his first screen role. *Polikushka* was reputed to have enjoyed acclaim abroad as well as in the countryside.[70]

Given the ambiguity of the data, it is impossible for us definitively to evaluate the character of the rural audience, or the exact degree of its "backwardness." But, slight though it is, the weight of the evidence suggests that peasants sought entertainment from movies like everyone else.[71] Glavpolitprosvet's Cinema Section came to more or less the same conclusion. If cinema bored peasants quickly, it fascinated them, too, and this "magic lantern" could be exploited to promote Soviet culture in the countryside.[72]

There is a paradoxical combination of self-deception and condescension in most discussions of the peasant viewer. On the one hand, peasants (like workers) were seen as especially "serious" viewers. Appropriate themes therefore echoed those deemed suitable for workers: the struggles against moonshine liquor (*samogon*) and arson, promotion of *shefstvo* (a factory's "adoption" of a village for agitational purposes), and the "social role of the press" are just a few examples.[73] The "better" fiction films – like *Potemkin*, *Stepan Khalturin*, *The Palace and the Fortress*, and *Death Bay* – might also be shown.[74] Yet for the most part these "serious" audiences were going to need extremely simple, abbreviated films (no more than four reels, about 48 minutes) with very slow editing.[75] Pavel Petrov-Bytov, though exceptionally blunt, expressed the typically arrogant attitude of the enlighteners toward the peasant audience. He wrote that it consisted of the "peasant woman, thinking with her ponderous, sluggish brain . . . " (Her mate had "gone to make a living in town," but surely he was little better in Petrov-Bytov's eyes.)[76]

Practice

On 1 January 1928, on the eve of the Cultural Revolution in cinema, 2,312 projectors served the entire countryside (see table 8). Of these, 80 percent were travelling projectors (*peredvizhki*), the fruits of the long and bitterly contested struggle between Sovkino and Glavpolitprosvet's Cinema Section to bring movies to the rural masses. The following 1 January, under the pressure of Cultural Revolution and an edict from the Council of People's Commissars, this figure had increased substantially (to 4,121), but the *peredvizhki* still accounted for 78 percent of the total.[77]

The cinefication campaign, discussed earlier in connection with the entertainment and enlightenment debate, could serve as a paradigm for the labyrinthine world of Soviet cultural politics.[78] Behind the enlighteners' genuine desire to bring movies to the masses lay a political struggle, in the broadest sense of the words. The Glavpolitprosvet–Sovkino imbroglio over cinefication was certainly not a case of the Party against the people (or vice versa). Nor was it just a case of intra-Party feuding, though we have seen evidence of factionalism among the Party members who held key positions in the cinema bureaucracy. It was a power struggle at its most elemental, a struggle to control very limited resources. Behind the endless disquisitions over projectors, projectionists and lecturers, and the physical and moral quality of the repertory lay a conflict about money, and specifically, hard currency.

As shown in the entertainment and enlightenment debate, Sovkino

Table 8. *"Cinefication" patterns, 1927–29*

	Distribution of projectors			
	Commercial theatres	Clubs	Travelling/rural	Total
1927	1,500 (33%)	1,788 (40%)	1,200 (27%)	4,488
1928	1,434 (25%)	1,964 (34%)	2,312 (41%)	5,710
1929	1,596 (20%)	2,466 (30%)	4,121 (50%)	8,183

Sources: Vladimir Shneiderov, "Sovetskaia kinopromyshlennost," *Sovetskoe kino*, 1927, no. 7, pp. 31–32; M. P. Efremov, "O prokatnom politike Sovkino," *Kino i kultura*, 1929, no. 4, p. 3.

and Glavpolitprosvet saw the world in very different ways, both of which were, however, "real."[79] Sovkino claimed that the travelling projectors brought in fewer than 5 rubles a day, less than a third of the take from the workers' clubs, where it had heavily discounted the rental as a public service.[80] The *peredvizhki*, most of which were equipped with their own generators because of the lack of electricity, were expensive and unreliable. When they broke down (often due to improper handling by poorly trained projectionists), there was a perennial shortage of spare parts. In addition, Soviet-made projectors wore films out at a faster-than-normal rate, and only slightly more than half of them were working on any given day.[81] Furthermore, Sovkino did not have the wherewithal to import film stock in quantities great enough to print adequate numbers of positive copies for the burgeoning urban market.[82] All in all, Sovkino's opinion was that development of rural cinema was premature.

Glavpolitprosvet's responses indicated that while there was a great deal of truth in Sovkino's version of the situation, there was room for disagreement as to the reasons. If the market were unprofitable, then it was due to Sovkino's lack of business sense and alienation from the mass viewer. How could a repertory of ideologically faulty and "anti-artistic" pictures such as Dmitrii Bassalygo's comedy *Mr. Lloyd's Voyage* be expected to make money?[83] If Sovkino claimed that the educational films (*kulturfilmy*) it sent to the countryside also were unprofitable, that could be explained, too. Only 5 percent of Sovkino's *kulturfilmy* were on agrarian subjects.[84] Aleksandr Katsigras believed that Sovkino inflated losses and overpriced films, charging more than double what they should and focusing on the richest villages.[85] Sovkino should be charged with usury for taking from 7 to 12 kopeks per meter per month in rental, in addition to 25 percent of the box-office.[86] Sovkino was also accused of poor management of the distribution of the *peredvizhki* so that one village might, inexplicably, have two arrive simultaneously, while another would not have had a projector in months.[87]

Peasants watched movies in conditions even worse than those in the workers' clubs. Their "auditoriums" were makeshift at best. There was no music. A lecturer not only explained the picture in a very tendentious way, he also read the titles (often this "lecturer" was the projectionist). The movie was usually from the dregs of the feature film repertory – films too bad ever to be shown to city audiences or popular films so worn out that some two dozen favorite titles circulated the rural network in versions that were short by more than a reel. (It is interesting that the popular historical melodrama *Stepan Khalturin* was one of these.)[88] Few foreign films ever made it to the villages: less than 4 percent of the titles shown in 1926–27, 7 percent the following year.[89]

The films specially made for rural distribution were made on shoe-string budgets (5–10,000 rubles).[90] One of the rare peasant films to gain a favorable press was *Father* (Leonid Molchanov, 1926), a four-reeler which fit the recipe for the rural picture exactly. *Father* has not survived, but *Soviet Fiction Films* describes it as a melodrama about "class war in the countryside in the middle of the twenties." A young peasant girl defies her father (a despicable, autocratic *kulak*) by falling in love with a Komsomol member. Unable to throw off the shackles of her father's "despotism," she ends her life.[91] Viktor Shklovskii explained its appeal: "The film *Father* is shot simply, elementarily, from one point of view, and is edited from a single long piece, which explains its attraction for the peasant viewer."[92]

Rich peasants were staple villains of Soviet fiction films. Soviet directors of all political stripes found the *kulak* a useful type long before the war against this element of the peasantry began in earnest as part of collectivization. Before the Cultural Revolution, movie *kulaks* were usually convenient accomplices to the main villain; there was always a *kulak* eager to assist in a dirty deed – like the *kulak* who helps Vladimir in Protazanov's *His Call*. During the collectivization campaign, *kulaks* occupied center stage in rural films, whether avant-garde or "popular."

Peasants also appeared frequently in the historical melodramas, where they were horribly abused serfs, used to serve as a rationale to show violence on the screen. (Such scenes appear in Aleksandr Ivanovskii's *The Decembrists* and Grigorii Roshal's *The Skotinins*.) Peasants could also serve as comic foils, like those in *The Miracle Worker* (Aleksandr Pan-teleev, 1922) or Iakov Protazanov's *Don Diego and Pelageia*. (In *The Miracle Worker*, Lenin's "favorite film," the peasants hide a pig in their mistress's bed in one scene and throw horse manure through a window in another.)[93]

True rural films were very rare. Protazanov's *His Call* and Ermler's *The Parisian Cobbler* are good examples of what I would dub the "pseudo-rural" film. They are set in the countryside, but peasant life is absent. The main characters are clearly "lower class" but live a deracinated existence. *Don Diego and Pelageia*, certainly the frankest depiction of rural life in the popular films of the twenties, features a vivid peasant character, but even so Pelageia's role is a secondary one. The film focuses on foolish Don Diego, the eager Komsomol members, and the virtuous Party secretary.

In fact the only major Soviet film about peasant life made prior to the Cultural Revolution was Olga Preobrazhenskaia's *Peasant Women of Riazan* (1927, co-directed with Ivan Pravov). Preobrazhenskaia was the leading woman director of fiction films in the twenties. A pre-revolutionary film star (famed for her role in Protazanov's 1913 hit *The Keys to Happiness*), Preobrazhenskaia became Russia's first female direc-tor in 1916, an event so unbelievable that theatre managers altered the posters for *The Lady Peasant* to read "O. Preobrazhensk*ii*."[94] Preobra-zhenskaia made six movies from 1919 to 1927, including a popular children's film, *Kashtanka* (1926), but *Peasant Women* is usually con-sidered her masterpiece in the silent era.[95]

The film is an examination of *snokhachestvo*, sexual abuse of daughters-in-law, a persistent problem in village life. The women of the title, Anna (R. Puzhnaia) and Vassilisa (Emma Tsesarskaia), represent tradition and change. After her husband leaves for the Front in World War I, Anna is raped (and impregnated) by her father-in-law in an especially brutal scene. (It goes without saying that this vicious man is a *kulak*, although in reality, *snokhachestvo* was by no means confined to the wealthy peasantry.) Consumed by shame when her much-loved husband returns and rejects her, Anna can think of no recourse other than to commit suicide by drowning herself. This extremely depressing tale is counterbalanced by that of Anna's vigorous and independent-minded sister-in-law, Vassilisa. Vassilisa chooses to defy her father and traditional opinion by openly living with her lover, a poor peasant who is also the village radical. They work for communism together.

Preobrazhenskaia refused to sensationalize sensational material by resorting to cheap tricks, and *Peasant Women* is a Soviet melodrama of the highest order. It played two months in at least one Moscow theatre, unusual for a Soviet production, almost unheard of for a "rural" film.[96] Workers were reported to like it.[97] O. Barshak, a functionary in the Society of Friends of Soviet Cinema (ODSK) which supported the cinefication campaign, confidently predicted that peasants would like it. In the Association of Revolutionary Cinematography (ARK), however, the film was attacked as "unrealistic" because the peasants were too clean, and the Civil War and Soviet power were nowhere to be seen. *Peasant Women* was also excoriated as "negative" for letting the rapist go unpunished and for allowing the heroine to resolve her shame by taking her own life.[98] These irrelevant charges were repeated in the press, and more were added.[99] One of the best films of rural life suffered the same fate as most of the best efforts of Soviet popular cinema – and a worse fate than those movies which were mediocre or even poor.

The hysterical outcry against *Peasant Women of Riazan* and the cowardice exhibited in ARK, were symptoms of the increasing tensions on the cinema front evident by late 1927. With the onset of the Cultural Revolution the following spring, with its call for films about collectivization to support the collectivization campaign, agitation intensified and the number of "peasant films" increased. Not surprisingly, directors from the avant-garde answered the "call" early.[100] It is also no surprise that their efforts could not pass the stylistic litmus test, and films such as Eisenstein's *The Old and the New* (1929) failed mainly for reasons of form, not content. Eisenstein certainly exhibited the requisite degree of enthusiasm for collectivization in his movie, but he relied too much on what at the time was called "thingism" (*veshchizm*) – the shots of the spinning parts of the milk separator are an obvious example.[101] Dovzhenko's *Earth* (1930) is a much more curious example of the collectivization film – the politically correct story of a handsome young village Party activist murdered by an evil and dissolute *kulak* opposed to collectivization is undercut by a deeply subversive subtext related to its form. The lyrical imagery and slow rhythms of this film, totally unlike Eisenstein's, belie the purported theme and in effect serve as a paen to a way of life soon to be no more.[102]

Few major directors of popular cinema attempted this kind of film. Barnet's only feature film of the period, his 1931 collectivization melodrama *The Ice Breaks*, did not add to his reputation. After the disastrous reception of *The Fragment of the Empire*, Ermler temporarily withdrew from the cinema front to ruminate in the Communist Academy.

Protazanov concentrated on making "safe" and relatively apolitical films like *St. Jorgen's Feast Day* and *Ranks and People*. The only rural film made during the Cultural Revolution which was touted as a major success was Boris Svetozarov's *Tanka the Bar Girl* (1928, released 1929), and its example is an instructive one.

Svetozarov made four movies in the silent period and continued directing through the forties, but mainly "popular-scientific" films. *Tanka* was his only hit. The plot sounds comical: a *kulak*'s tavern is threatened by serious competition – a drama club organized by the schoolteacher (who is both a *komsomolets* and chair of the village soviet). The *kulak*, of course assisted by a hooligan, concocts a plan to murder the teacher. His stepdaughter Tanka and a Young Pioneer warn the teacher and foil the plot. The tavern becomes a tearoom, and the villagers are saved.[103]

Two aspects of this film may explain its alleged success at a time when so many other, undoubtedly better, films failed. First, and perhaps most interesting, it does not deal with collectivization; Svetozarov deployed his *kulak* in much the same way that Protazanov might have. Second, it combines a plethora of campaigns – against alcoholism, hooliganism, and the *kulachestvo* – in much the same way that Sergeii Iutkevich did in his industrialization film *Lace*. The result was that *Tanka* was hailed as a model for the new rural film, receiving no fewer than five reviews in *Cinema* at a time when movies were allocated less and less space in the cinema press.[104]

It should now be fairly clear that the title of this chapter is ironic. In the first decade of Soviet filmmaking "factory and tractor" films were rare, especially in popular cinema. Few may be considered successful as art, entertainment, or politics. Boris Barnet and Fridrikh Ermler had shown that it was possible to "Sovietize" established cinematic genres like comedy and melodrama, but, despite the exhortations of the enlighteners, filmmakers found it very difficult to create new "genres" built around themes drawn from peasant and proletarian life.

But as tentative as these early efforts were, they are quite important. They foreshadowed the shape of popular cinema in the next decade when melodramas about socialist construction and musicals about happy farmers would flourish under the rubric of "Socialist Realism." (Sergei Gerasimov's *Komsomolsk* is a good example of the former; Ivan Pyrev's *The Rich Bride* or *Tractor Drivers*, of the latter.) Under the aegis of Socialist Realism, the genre films of the thirties became even more fantastic than anything made in the twenties.

CONCLUSION

The fundamental functions of cinematography are fighting, political functions. From
them comes the struggle for the viewer, without whom cinematography cannot exist.
  But what happened? What happened was that we lost the viewer.
                                                    (Sergei Iutkevich, 1935[1])

From 1932 to 1934, the Soviet arts bureaucracies were completing the
arduous process of institutional restructuring begun during the Cultural
Revolution. In January 1935, another major film conference was held in
the USSR, the All-Union Creative Conference on Cinematographic
Affairs. Unlike its 1928 counterpart, the Party Conference on Cinema
Affairs, this meeting was an assemblage of filmmakers, not politicians.
Criticism, self-criticism, and fervent embrace of the tenets of Socialist
Realism were the order of the day (and of the decade). Director Sergei
Iutkevich proved himself neither more nor less noble than others, and his
remarks, excerpted above, typified the tenor of the event.[2] The Revo-
lution was over at last.

But ends can also be beginnings. By 1931, it had become apparent to
those "above" that the Cultural Revolution had served its purpose. Film
was now truly in the service of the state. New cadres were in place
(though not firmly enough to present any danger), and filmmakers at least
had an idea of what kinds of films they were not to make under any
circumstances. As the fervor of this second revolution subsided and the
smoke cleared from the cinema front, the extent of the devastation was
obvious.

The scene was eerily reminiscent of the situation ten years earlier when
this story began. In some respects, it seemed even worse. Film production and importation had once again ground to a virtual halt. Technically, the studios were woefully equipped for the transition to sound, a
transition they would have to make completely on their own since
self-reliance was the clarion call of the Second Five Year Plan (as it had

been for the First). Not only were early Soviet sound systems inadequate and expensive, the enormous cost of reequipping the country with sound projectors meant that the future of sound cinema in the USSR was problematic. As a result, Soviet studios continued to produce silent films until 1935, and made silent versions of sound films to the end of the thirties, a circumstance without parallel in other film-producing European countries.

A significant number of the "old specialists" of Russian cinema had fled abroad during the Civil War. Those who remained were in a precarious position, their patrons in the state film trust (renamed Soiuzkino) and in Narkompros gone. Anatolii Lunacharskii died in 1933, and Ilia Trainin left film for the law.[3] Consequently, many bourgeois specialists were hounded out of their positions in the studios or in the press. Among the more prominent examples, directors Cheslav Sabinskii, Vladimir Gardin, and Konstantin Eggert saw the abrupt ends to their careers (and Eggert was arrested during the Terror).[4] Critic Ippolit Sokolov was subjected to particularly savage public attacks, but he found refuge in the state film institute, VGIK, outliving his antagonist Vladimir Kirshon, who was executed in 1938.[5]

The luminaries of the avant-garde also found themselves in an unenviable position. Never the recipients of much official support, they now had none. (Maiakovskii was dead, and Adrian Piotrovskii and Sergei Tretiakov were among those "repressed" at the end of the decade.) Those who would not or could not recant and adapt their styles to the new aesthetics were lucky if they could find work in documentary studios or at VGIK. Kuleshov and Vertov refused to compromise, and their careers as feature filmmakers had essentially ended by 1935. Eisenstein had the benefit of his international reputation to help ease the transition, but his struggle to continue working, which exacted a heavy toll on his health, is well known.

As we have seen in these pages, the vaunted pluralism of the NEP was grudging at best. Yet, while it did not compare to the cultural ferment of Russia's "Silver Age" or even to that of the Civil War, it was surely better than the rigid confines of the new thematics and aesthetics. Though not formally adopted until the Writers' Congress of 1934, the credo of Socialist Realism – with its call for positive heroes, unambiguous support of regime goals, and depiction of "life as it should be" – had for some years been a foregone conclusion. Filmmakers were exhorted to make "movies for the millions," but would the "millions" want to see them? Could Soviet citizens possibly find collective farmers and factory workers as entertaining as Protazanov's dashing thieves and bumbling NEPmen?

But though darkness appeared to have fallen, there was also "light in the darkness" (borrowing from the Russian title of Mary Pickford's film *The Love Light*). Despite the persistent tendency to view Stalinist culture in the thirties as a decisive break with that of the NEP,[6] the history of popular cinema demonstrates that this was far from true. "Russian" cinema had survived the Russian Revolution, and it survived the Stalin Revolution too. While the changes which occurred in the late twenties and early thirties were sweeping (especially from the perspective of censorship and import policies), there are still marked similarities between the popular film culture of the NEP and that of the Stalin era.[7]

Like the rest of Stalinist culture, Soviet cinema of the thirties has been *terra incognita* for historians until quite recently. Both Western and Soviet scholars have seen it as a subject not really worthy of intensive study, and sometimes for the same reasons. (It was, after all, "bad" art.) Yet as the taboos in Soviet cultural history crumble, the importance of understanding what happened in the thirties is becoming increasingly apparent. Research to date, though quite preliminary in nature, indicates that Stalinist cinema was a far more complex phenomenon than has been previously believed. Its history will require extensive analysis for adequate elucidation.[8]

By reviewing the basic themes of this work, however, it is possible to advance some hypotheses and to suggest some avenues for further investigation. Cinema culture was certainly transformed by the Cultural Revolution, but not in the way the enlighteners had hoped. Popular cinema was reconfigured through an ingenious synthesis of old and new elements, in which the continuities counterbalanced the changes.[9] And in several important respects, Stalinist cinema resolved weaknesses inherent in the cinema of the NEP – though we may not like the solutions devised or the means used to achieve them.

First, cinema continued to be a genuinely popular form of entertainment. Despite the decline in production and the shrinking of the repertory of titles in circulation, movies were more popular in the thirties than they had been in the twenties. The "cinefication" campaign resumed, and attendance rose throughout the decade. Box-office figures in the thirties were phenomenal. Nikolai Ekk's *A Start in Life* earned 15 million rubles, far exceeding the previous record, *Miss Mend*'s 3.1 million.[10] This can be explained in part by the dramatically improved distribution network and by the fact that since there were fewer films on the screen, people went to see the same pictures as often as five times![11] It also can be explained by the films themselves, which might be characterized as "Stalinized" versions of the commercial movies of the twenties (just as those films had been "Sovietized" versions of *their* predecessors).

The public debate over "entertainment or enlightenment" ended in the thirties, as did all genuine public debate. But the ideas engendered in the entertainment/enlightenment debate lived on – coopted and synthesized by the Stalinists. So though choice was drastically restricted by the political climate and the depredations of the censorship (which may have led to more films being suppressed than released),[12] in practice the broad patterns of cinematic repertory were quite similar to those of the NEP. Viewers continued to see a mix of edifying and lighthearted fare, the latter of which seemed to satisfy both the basic human need for entertainment and Stalin's need to portray Soviet life as "more joyful."

The fate of the *inostranshchina*, so obvious on the surface, is also quite ambiguous. Importation of foreign films ceased, yet Western influences did not in fact vanish, as anyone familiar with Grigorii Aleksandrov's films is well aware. This may in large part be attributed to Stalin. Recent research has indicated that Stalin's obsession with movies and his dabbling with the minutiae of filmmaking reached bizarre proportions.[13] The dictator loved Western films and made sure they were available to his favorite filmmakers, though not to the public. So the *inostranshchina* lived on (if indirectly) in Aleksandrov's films *The Happy Guys*, *Volga Volga*, and *The Shining Path*, but especially in *The Circus*, where Aleksandrov's wife Liubov Orlova plays the persecuted American singer Marion Dixon, who finds happiness and true love with a Soviet aviator-cum-circus performer. These films, which represent a skillful Stalinization of Hollywood style, were enormously popular with audiences.[14]

The ties between NEP cinema culture and that of the Stalin era are also evident when comparing genres, although the impact of those changes which did occur should not be underestimated. The melodrama had been difficult to execute in the twenties because of the prejudice against depicting private life in films. In the thirties, this tension between the conflicting demands of public and private life had vanished from the screen, because private life was now indistinguishable from public duty. Contemporary melodrama became almost completely subsumed in the tractor and factory films, as heroes sought to combat "wreckers," who were just as likely to be close friends or family members as they were to be foreigners or Trotskyites.

As was the case in the twenties, however, a safer avenue for sating audience demand for melodrama lay in the historical films. In the thirties, costume dramas were more often adaptations of Russian literary classics, rather than screen versions of revolutionary episodes set in the eighteenth and nineteenth centuries. Iakov Protazanov's adaptation of Aleksandr Ostrovskii's play *Without a Dowry* is a good example of a film with a dual function: it satisfied the audience's need for melodramatic escapism, and the regime's need to reacquaint the public with Russia's glorious literary past. In other cases, historical films were grandiose nationalist epics with strong elements of "adventure," such as Eisenstein's *Aleksandr Nevskii* or Olga Preobrazhenskaia and Ivan Pravov's *Stepan Razin*.

True adventure films, on the other hand, ran into political problems in the thirties. The Revolution/Civil War motif in films continued, but after *Chapaev* (1934) there was little action in them, because directors had to suppress any residual notions about revolutionary spontaneity. Films on this subject could be dangerous, too, as Dovzhenko found out with *Shchors*, which was remade several times as the Party line on the Ukrainian Civil War hero changed.[15] As a result, the revolutionary films of the thirties tended to be stilted and fairly boring. Real action was more often than not mixed with numerous shots of a smiling Stalin seated side by side with Lenin, as in Sergei Iutkevich's *The Man with the Gun*. Aviator films, like Iulii Raizman's *Pilots* and Mikhail Kalatozov's *Valerii Chkalov*, proved a more satisfying option for adventure-minded directors, because the formula was not as sanctified as those for the revolutionary pictures.

Quite ironically, the popular genre which had been most troubled of all in the twenties – comedy – sometimes sparkled in an era that was grim indeed. The problem comedy faced in the twenties had been that comedies were supposed to be funny and socially engaged at the same time; in the thirties they were under no such restrictions. Total divorcement from reality was now clearly preferable – and enabled films to be "socially engaged" by embodying public myths, rather than by criticizing public problems. Aleksandrov's musical comedy *Volga Volga* (made at the nadir of the Terror) is an excellent example: it is so outrageously cheerful that it still elicits laughter (for the right reasons), and it was a box-office smash.

The old stereotypes also persisted, as did the trend evident throughout the twenties to keep them as "black and white" as possible. The difference in the thirties is an important one, of course: "graying," difficult in the previous decade, was now completely impossible. But what made this stricture more palatable was the fact that the "star" problem was resolved. Although many of the old guard had not survived due to death (Fogel), emigration (Sten, Malinovskaia, Chekhov), or failure to make the transition to sound, communist modesty and other ideological scruples no longer served as impediments to the promotion of stars. Igor Ilinskii continued to play in carefully selected vehicles to great acclaim (as did Nato Vachnadze), and Nikolai Batalov finally became the star he had long deserved to be.[16] But the glamour queen of the thirties screen was a new face: Liubov Orlova, whose "Slavic" beauty and aura of glowing optimism inspired a generation of Soviet women.

The cadre of directors had always been a combination of types, and that continued as well. Despite the departure of numerous *spetsy* from the cinema front, and the annihilation of the avant-garde in spirit, many from the old guard continued to work – and in ways not easily predicted. The unflappable Iakov Protazanov found it easy to adapt, and though he abandoned overtly Western topics, he still managed to turn out crowd-pleasers. Directing for more than three of the most troubled decades in Russian history, Protazanov still managed a wholly consistent *œuvre*. Fridrikh Ermler turned his considerable talents to more troubling purpose, yet he, too, was able to preserve artistic integrity. Considering the effectiveness of his silent films, it is not surprising that two of the most powerful and terrifying movies of the thirties are his: *Peasants* and *The Great Citizen*. Boris Barnet, on the other hand, eschewed topicality to become an even better director than he had been in the twenties, as his lyrical anti-war film *Outskirts* shows.[17]

The fates of Aleksandr Dovzhenko, Vsevolod Pudovkin, and Abram Room – erstwhile "fellow travellers" of the realist school – and of the staunch formalists Grigorii Kozintsev and Leonid Trauberg also illustrate the unpredictability of movie-making in the thirties. Dovzhenko and Room continued to direct, albeit with increasing difficulty, and Room even succeeded in completing (but not in releasing) what can only be called an avant-garde film, *A Strict Young Man*. Pudovkin made the popular historical epics *Minin and Pozharskii* and *Suvorov*. As for the *enfants terribles* of the avant-garde, Kozintsev and Trauberg produced three of the most beloved movies of the thirties: *The Youth of Maksim*, *The Return of Maksim*, and *The Vyborg Side*.

Numerous new directors, benefitting from the purges of the Cultural Revolution, also came to the forefront. Sergei Gerasimov became a durable and prolific director, and Ivan Pyrev and Grigorii Roshal were unexpectedly elevated to the first rank, a position which sometimes strained their respective talents. But like Grigorii Aleksandrov, who had been Eisenstein's co-director in the twenties, most of these directors were not really "new" and provide yet another link to the past. Sergei Gerasimov had been an excellent actor, playing villains in Kozintsev and Trauberg's silent films, while Pyrev and Roshal had already begun · directing by the late twenties. The creative biographies of all these directors deserve as much attention as Eisenstein's in order to explore the ways in which artists attempted to preserve their personal and professional honor in the face of crushing adversity – and how they sometimes managed to do so.[18]

Describing Soviet popular cinema during the NEP, demonstrating the process of change and the persistence of tradition, and evaluating the degree to which popular cinema was transformed in the next epoch – these are the yeoman's tasks of history, and I hope I have succeeded in them. I would like to return, however, to questions raised at the outset of this book, namely: the function of the NEP in the process of the transformation of Soviet culture, the reality (as opposed to the rhetoric) of class dynamics in the twenties, and finally, the impact of continued Western and "Russian" influences on the life of a revolutionary society.

In his provocative recent monograph, *Culture and Power in Revolutionary Russia*, Christopher Read argues that the NEP can be considered a "breathing space" only with benefit of historical hindsight. It was dramatically more pluralistic than what followed, but much less amenable to diversity than was the Civil War era. It was a true transition – in Read's words, a period of "limited control" between "arbitrariness" and "rigid control," not part of a cycle of "centralization-liberalization-centralization."[19] The history of popular cinema during the NEP provides compelling evidence for this thesis – else why the persistent efforts to exert some measure of control over perfectly apolitical individuals? These were, after all, the very directors able to make profitable films in a time when commercial enterprise and cost-accounting were supposedly being encouraged.

But who was attempting to exert control? It is impossible to write about NEP culture without making any reference to the historiographical debate over whether the Stalin Revolution was a "revolution from above" or one "from below."[20] In *Soviet Cinema in the Silent Era*, I supported the "revolution from below" thesis. I now think this interpretation, at least insofar as it applies to the film industry, needs to be modified. I still see no evidence that the regime had any interest in controlling cinema in the way it was controlled in the thirties, unless one were to exaggerate the importance of Glavpolitprosvet's Cinema Section. But at the same time, it is impossible to find any groundswell of support from real proletarians (as opposed to "proletarianists") for the program of the enlighteners. There was no clamor for *kulturfilmy* or for simple-minded "peasant" and "worker" films, unless that clamor were carefully orchestrated. Indeed, available evidence indicates that workers' tastes differed little from those of the bourgeoisie, except that they were perhaps less exacting in their artistic standards.

What we do see, though, is a revolution *from the middle* in the film world, which coincided for a brief time with the one from above. Many film directors, critics, and other interested parties (especially those in Glavpolitprosvet's Cinema Section) were dissatisfied with the commercialism of the NEP for reasons both idealistic and self-serving. Often these factors were inextricable: while it would not be appropriate to impugn the sincerity of directors like Vertov and Petrov-Bytov, it is at the same time necessary to point out that they simply could not compete under the conditions of NEP cinema. (Nor, as it turned out, could either of them compete under the conditions of the thirties.)

This leads us directly to the next question: is "class culture" a reality or a Marxian pipe-dream? What was labelled "bourgeois" or "petty-bourgeois" in the twenties does indeed seem to support the values of the middle class. Most of the directors of "bourgeois" films were themselves "bourgeois." It is also true that the only major proletarian director of popular films, Fridrikh Ermler, made movies which were quite distinctive. But can we characterize his films as "proletarian" because he came from a working-class background? Contemporary critics did not think so.

Leftist theoreticians of popular culture today, like their counterparts in Glavpolitprosvet's Cinema Section, believe that the popularity of things bourgeois among all classes is manufactured, the product of a kind of cultural "capitalist encirclement."[21] Nonetheless, we see an extra-class appeal in the popular films of the NEP, an appeal which Stalin recognized. After all, Stalin exploited certain attributes of middle-class culture better than most capitalists ever could, a fact which became apparent in the thirties – and even more so in the post-World War II era.[22] Whether we give the values of this culture – pragmatism, optimism, elitism, materialism – "class" attributes or not, the fact is that they were at odds with revolutionary utopianism. In the twenties, this culture conflicted with the dreams of a significant body of disgruntled "true believers"; and from 1928 to 1932, with the goals of the regime as it sought to rekindle revolutionary enthusiasm. But after 1932, these attributes fit perfectly with society's needs, at least as they were construed by Stalin. As we know from his policies in the thirties, Stalin sought to strike a balance between upheaval and stability, and commercial cinema, with its rich tradition, was a prime candidate to promote the latter. It was not only entertaining, it was "Russian," and its time had come.

While the "Russianness" of Soviet culture is becoming increasingly apparent through recent research, the importance of continuing Western influences in Soviet society in the twenties is more difficult to evaluate, especially given that the Soviet people existed in a state of virtual isolation for most of the six decades which followed. We have seen that the angst the *inostranshchina* provoked in the twenties connects the history of Soviet popular cinema with the "high culture" of the nineteenth century, when the first generation of revolutionary intellectuals struggled to define Russia as a nation. But this debate also provides a compelling link between the twenties and today, as the forces unleashed by democratization have all but overwhelmed Soviet society.

In the cinema world, insulated so long from the pressures of profit-making and audience demand, the price of *perestroika* has been high. Once again, foreign films dominate Soviet screens. Once again, the Soviet film industry has been placed on the cost-accounting system. Once again, the only Soviet-made films which can compete with Hollywood movies are not seen as "truly Soviet," but as a product of a "petty-bourgeois" mentality. (Now, however, this is viewed solely as a betrayal of "Russianness," rather than of the revolutionary ethos.) And once again, some Soviet filmmakers and critics – and even a few disgusted viewers – are calling for ... control.[23]

NOTES

Introduction

1 Quoted in Jay Leyda, *Kino: A History of the Russian and Soviet Film* (London: Allen & Unwin, 1960; rpt. New York: Collier, 1973), pp. 20–21. Although there are very few references in this book to Leyda's classic work, I do not intend to minimize its importance as an introduction to the subject.

2 Accounts in English on the history of pre-revolutionary Russian cinema include: Leyda, *Kino*, pp. 1–92; Richard Stites, *Soviet Popular Culture: Entertainment and Society in Russia since 1900* (Cambridge: Cambridge University Press, 1992), chap. 1; Peter Kenez, *Cinema and Soviet Society, 1917–1953* (New York: Cambridge University Press, 1992), chap. 2; Yuri Tsivian, "Early Russian Cinema: Some Observations," in Richard Taylor and Ian Christie, eds., *Inside the Film Factory: New Approaches to Russian and Soviet Cinema* (London: Routledge, 1991), pp. 7–30. For documents, see Yuri Tsivian *et al.*, *Silent Witnesses: Russian Films, 1908–1919* (London: British Film Institute, 1989) and Richard Taylor and Ian Christie, eds., *The Film Factory: Russian and Soviet Cinema in Documents, 1896–1939*, trans. Richard Taylor (Cambridge, MA: Harvard University Press, 1988). The best studies by Soviet film historians (in addition to Tsivian) on the pre-revolutionary period include: B.S. Likhachev, *Istoriia kino v Rossii (1896–1926): Materialy k istorii russkogo kino*, pt. 1, *1896–1913* (Leningrad: Academia, 1927); Likhachev, "Materialy k istorii kino v Rossii (1914–1916)," *Iz istorii kino* 3 (1960): 37–103; S. Ginzburg, *Kinematografiia dorevoliutsionnoi Rossii* (Moscow: Iskusstvo, 1963); and N.M. Zorkaia, *Na rubezhe stoletii: U istokov massovogo iskusstva v Rossii, 1900–1910 godov* (Moscow: Nauka, 1976). For a filmography, see Veniamin Vishnevskii, *Khudozhestvennye filmy dorevoliutsionnoi Rossii: Filmograficheskoe opisanie* (Moscow: Goskinoizdat, 1945).

3 See Louis Forestier, *Velikii nemoi (Vospominaniia kinooperatora)* (Moscow: Goskinoizdat, 1945).

4 Amply illustrated in Tsivian *et al.*, *Silent Witnesses*.

5 Wonderful descriptions of the extant films can be found in ibid.

6 Russian emigrés made significant contributions to French silent cinema. See Richard Abel, *French Cinema: The First Wave, 1915–1929* (Princeton, NJ: Princeton University Press, 1984), *passim*.

7 See Lynn Mally, *Culture of the Future: The Proletkult Movement in Revolutionary Russia* (Berkeley: University of California Press, 1990).

8 The bibliography of Eisensteiniana alone would serve to illustrate this point, and two books about Eisenstein and his work are on the way, one by David Bordwell and Vance Kepley, Jr. (in progress) and the other by Ian Christie and Richard Taylor, eds., *Eisenstein Rediscovered* (London: Routledge, forthcoming).

9 For a history of the historiography which confirms this point, see Ian Christie's introduction to Taylor and Christie, *Film Factory*. Interestingly, there has been little difference in emphasis between Western and pre-*glasnost* Soviet accounts of the cinema of the twenties (but vast differences, of course, in the interpretation of the thirties).

10 As we shall see, box-office data are fragmentary and sometimes suspect, since it could be politically expedient to claim that a certain film was a failure (or a success).

11 For an excellent brief summary of these definitions, see Régine Robin, "Stalinism and Popular Culture," in Hans Günther, ed., *The Culture of the Stalin Period* (London: Macmillan, 1990), pp. 16–17.

12 In the twenties, fine films were produced in the Ukrainian and Georgian studios in particular, but the majority of them were very much "national" in orientation and deserve treatment apart from the Russian example. The heated distribution politics of the period also restricted the circulation of Ukrainian and Georgian films in the RSFSR and vice versa. For these reasons, discussion of non-Russian films in this book will be based on those films (like Perestiani's *Little Red Devils*) which appealed to Russian audiences in much the same way as did other "foreign" films – as great entertainment.

13 This is based on attendance for the biggest "hit," *The Thief of Baghdad*; see S. Krylov, *Kino vmesto vodki: K vsesoiuznom partsoveshchaniiu po voprosam kino* (Moscow: Moskovskii rabochii, 1928), p. 30. Krylov claimed that *Potemkin* had surpassed it, which I suspect indicates that a concerted effort was made to dragoon people into the theatres to see this most "revolutionary" of revolutionary films.

14 P.A. Bliakhin, "Politika Sovkino," *Vokrug Sovkino: Stenogramma disputa organizovannogo TsK VLKSM, TsS ODSK i redaktsiei gazety Komsomolskaia pravda 8–15 okt. 1927* (n.p.: Teakinpechat, 1928), p. 8; L. M. Budiak and V. P. Mikhailov, *Adresa moskovskogo kino* (Moscow: Moskovskii rabochii, 1987), p. 19. In addition to the theatres, there were also some 3,200 projectors in clubs and for the travelling rural shows, but the total of 4,600 projectors should be compared to the 20–21,000 projectors in the US at the same time.

15 In addition to works listed in the preface, I would like to draw attention to Marc Ferro, *Cinema and History*, trans. Naomi Greene (Detroit, MI: Wayne State University Press, 1988); Sheila Fitzpatrick, *Education and Social Mobility in the Soviet Union, 1921–1934* (Cambridge: Cambridge University Press, 1979); Mark von Hagen, *Soldiers in the Proletarian Dictatorship: The Red Army and the Soviet Socialist State, 1917–1930* (Ithaca, NY: Cornell University Press, 1990).

1 A historical overview "from below"

1 Ippolit Sokolov, "Rabotat na massovogo kino-zritelia," *Kino i zhizn*, 1929, no. 2.
2 Adrian Piotrovskii, *Kinofikatsiia iskusstv* (Leningrad: Izd. avtora, 1929), p. 12.
3 Others were owned by cooperatives and other associations and so were also not state entities.
4 Trotskii linked vodka-drinking and movie-going in a different way in his 1923 *Pravda* article "Vodka, the Church, and the Cinema," trans. Taylor and Christie, *Film Factory*, pp. 94–97. Stalin gave the linkage a new twist during the Cultural Revolution, at which time it was noted that cinema revenues were minuscule compared to those from vodka (22 million rubles to 500 million). See. e.g., Krylov, *Kino vmesto vodki* and "Kino na borbu s alkologizmom," *Kino*, 1928, no. 42, p. 2.
5 Youngblood, *Soviet Cinema in the Silent Era, 1918–1935* (Ann Arbor, MI: UMI Research Press, 1985; rpt. Austin: University of Texas Press, 1991), appendix 1. Unless otherwise indicated, production figures come from this source, which was based on analysis of *Sovetskie khudozhestvennye filmy: Annotirovannyi katalog*, vols. 1 and 11 (Moscow: Iskusstvo, 1960–61).
6 Tsentralnyi gosudarstvennyi arkhiv literatury i iskusstva (TsGALI), f. 939, op. 1, ed. khr. 282, "Prikaz po vserossiiskomu foto-kino otdelu Glavpolit-prosveta, 6 maia–10 iiunia 1922," p. 9.
7 "O novykh postannovakh, 1922 g.," *Kino-zhizn*, 1922, no. 3, p. 1. For a general analysis of import patterns, see Vance Kepley, Jr. and Betty Kepley, "Foreign Films on Soviet Screens, 1922–1931," *Quarterly Review of Film Studies* 4, no. 4 (Fall 1979): 429–42.
8 Richard Taylor, *The Politics of the Soviet Cinema, 1917–1929* (Cambridge: Cambridge University Press, 1979), pp. 68–70; Vance Kepley, Jr., "The Origins of Soviet Cinema: A Study in Industry Development," *Quarterly Review of Film Studies* (Winter 1985): 22–38; rpt. Taylor and Christie, *Inside the Film Factory*, pp. 60–79.
9 See Vance Kepley, Jr., "The International Worker's Relief and the Cinema of the Left, 1921–1935," *Cinema Journal* 23, no. 1 (Fall 1983): 7–23.
10 "Nuzhno-li obedinenie?" *Kino-gazeta*, 1924, no. 14, p. 1.
11 Vladimir Erofeev, "Dovolno portit kartiny," *Kino-gazeta*, 1924, no. 49, p. 2. Also see "Ne monopoliia a kontrol," ibid., no. 15.
12 "Pochemu k nam vvoziat khlam?" *Kino-gazeta*, 1924, no. 17, p. 1.
13 Huntly Carter, *The New Theatre and Cinema of Soviet Russia* (New York: International Publishers, 1925), p. 240. Carter went on to describe the Palace Theatre as looking "like a dust hole with the lid off," p. 241. Within a few years, only fifty theatres were still operating in Moscow.
14 "Novosti s zapada," *Kino-gazeta*, 1924, no. 23, p. 2; Daniil Gessen, "Dovolno?" *Kino-nedelia*, 1924, no. 14, p. 1; Grigorii Boltianskii, "Provintsialnyi kino-byt," *Kino-nedelia*, 1924, no. 34, p. 12.
15 "Nuzhno organizovat prokat," *Kino-gazeta*, 1924, no. 46, p. 1.
16 Carter, *New Theatre*, p. 241. In 1924 the tax on tickets was lowered to 10

percent; see "Resheniia Sovnarkoma," *Kino-gazeta*, 1924, no. 21, p. 1 and "Sni-zhenie teatralnogo naloga," *Kino-gazeta*, 1925, no. 4/5, p. 1.

17 "Rezoliutsiia soveshchaniia rabotnikov kinematograficheskikh organizatii SSSR po voprosu monopolii," *Kino-nedelia*, 1924, no. 9, p. 2; *Deiatelnost Vserossiiskogo foto-kinematograficheskogo aktsionnernogo o-va sovetskogo kino Sovkino s 1-go marta 1925 po 1-oe oktiabria 1927* (Moscow: Sovkino, 1928), p. 3. See Taylor and Christie, *Film Factory*, pp. 114–15, for Sovnarkom's decree establishing Sovkino.

18 Youngblood, *Soviet Cinema*, appendix 1; Kepley, "International Worker's Relief"; Vladimir Korolevich, "Dovolno kolumbov," *Sovetskii ekran*, 1926, no. 49, p. 5; Vladimir Shneiderov, "Sovetskaia kino-promyshlennost," *Sovetskii ekran*, 1927, no. 7, pp. 31–32.

19 I.P. Trainin, *Kino-promyshlennost i Sovkino: Po dokladu na 8–ii konferentsii moskovskogo gubrabisa, 1925* (Moscow: Kino-izdatelstvo RSFSR, 1925), p. 16.

20 Ibid., pp. 13, 15–17.

21 Kepley, "International Worker's Relief" and A. Gak, "K istorii sozdaniia Sovkino," *Iz istorii kino*, 1962, vol. v, p. 32.

22 My generalization on typical runs is based on studying advertisements in the press; this impression was confirmed as late as 1929. See N. Volkov, "Sovetskie filmy," *Izvestiia*, 18 November 1929.

23 Ilia Trainin, "Sovetskaia filma i zritel," *Sovetskoe kino*, 1925, no. 4/5.

24 TsGALI, f. 2494, op. 1, ed. khr. 272, "Stenogramma diskussii po obsuzhdeniiu kinofilma *Novyi Vavilon* i otchet po izucheniiu vospriiatiia filma zritelei (1929)."

25 There is ample evidence attesting to the box-office returns of all the films listed with the exception of *Honor*; its addition to the "bestseller" list is somewhat speculative, since it is based solely on self-promotion. See e.g., advertisements in *Izvestiia*, 9, 23, and 24 November 1926.

26 I am acutely aware, however, that making the distinction between an "avant-garde" and a "popular" film may be tricky. For an excellent disquisition on this subject, see J. T. Heil, "Theme and Style and the 'Literary Film' as Avant-Garde," *Avant-Garde*, 1990, no. 5/6, pp. 137–62.

27 See Kepley and Kepley, "Foreign Films," p. 437; L., "Prokat i teatry," *Kino-zhurnal ARK*, 1925, no. 9, p. 21; Krylov, *Kino vmesto vodki*, p. 30.

28 Budiak and Mikhailov, *Adresa moskovskogo kino*, p. 242; conversation with Maia Turovskaia, December 1990.

29 Mikhail Boitler, *Kino-teatr: Organizatsiia i upravlenie* (Moscow: Kinopechat, 1926); Boitler, *Reklama i kino-reklama* (Moscow: Kinopechat, 1926); Carter, *New Theatre*, p. 238; Budiak and Mikhailov, *Adresa sovetskogo kino*, p. 121. (Boitler was the managing director of the Malaia Dmitrovka.)

30 G. Boltianskii, "Provintsialnyi kino-byt," *Kino-nedelia*, 1924, no. 34; "Deiatelnost teatrov Godkino," *Kino-gazeta*, 1925, no. 4, p. 3; Klechatyi, "Kino-teatry Moskomprom" *Kino*, 1925, no. 3, p. 4; "Po moskovskim kino-teatram," *Kino*, 1925, no. 7, p. 4; Kh. Khersonskii, "Ot luchiny k lampochke Ilicha," *Sovetskii ekran*, 1928, no. 32; S. Frederick Starr, *Red and Hot: The Fate of Jazz in the Soviet Union* (New York: Oxford University Press, 1983), p. 64; Budiak and Mikhailov, *Adresa moskovskogo kino*, p. 237.

31 A. I. Troianovskii and R. I. Egiazarov, *Izuchenie kino-zritelia: Po materialam issledovatelskoi teatralnoi masterskoi* (Moscow: Gosizdat Narkompros, 1928), p. 42.

32 According to Budiak and Mikhailov, *Adresa moskovskogo kino*, p. 246, the Krasnaia Presnia was the first proletarian first-run theatre.

33 "Po provintsii: Krasnodarskii okrug," *Sovetskoe kino*, 1927, no. 1, p. 22.

34 K. G[anzenko], "Zabyvaemye zakony," *Sovetskii ekran*, 1925, no. 14.

35 F. M. Nazarov, "Itogi zimnego sezona Rostova na Donu," *Kino-gazeta*, 1925, no. 3, p. 5.

36 V. Ardov, "Chudesa kino: Uplotnennyi seans," *Kino*, 1925, no. 4/5 , p. 10; Nazarov, "Itogi zimnego sezona." The practice was not unheard of in Moscow, however; for amusing accounts see TsGALI, f. 2494, op. 1, ed. khr. 40, "Protokoly zasedanii organizatsionnoi kommissii i detsko-shkolnoi sektsii (1926)," pp. 21–22 and S. Bugoslavskii and V. Messman, *Muzyka v kino* (Moscow: Kinopechat, 1926), pp. 23–25. According to Kristin Thompson, fast cranking to maximize profits was also a practice in US theatres (letter to author June 1991).

37 A. Lvov, *Kinematograficheskaia iazva izlechima* (Report to the Central Committee of the RKP(b), 26 March 1924).

38 F. Kandyba, "Obezdolennyi teatr Kharkova," *Kino*, 1925, no. 2; V.G., "Penzenskaia kino-zhizn," ibid., no. 4/5, p. 3.

39 G. Pavlov, "Kino na okraine," *Sovetskii ekran*, 1927, no. 1.

40 See, e.g., Charli, [untitled], *Kino-zhizn*, 1922, no. 2, p. 4; "Nasha anketa," ibid., no. 3, p. 6; advertisements in the final issue, 1923, no. 5.

41 The role of ARK in Soviet cinema in the twenties is discussed in detail in Youngblood, *Soviet Cinema, passim.*

42 *Cinema Gazette* (Kino-gazeta) was founded at a time of skyrocketing inflation. Its first issue, dated 11 September 1923, sold for 20 rubles. Two months later the price was 100 rubles; by mid-December, 12 gold kopeks.

43 By way of contrast, in 1919 the American movie magazine *Moving Picture World* had a paid circulation of 400,000; see David Bordwell, Janet Staiger, and Kristin Thompson, *The Classical Hollywood Cinema: Film Style and Mode of Production to 1960* (New York: Columbia University Press, 1985), p. 99.

44 *Cinema Creation* (Kino-tvorchestvo) was published in Paris, 1923–26. One other newspaper, *Cinema Week* (Kino-nedelia), which is an important source of information for the earlier period, ceased publication in 1925.

45 Troianovskii and Egiazarov, *Izuchenie kino-zritelia*, p. 45.

46 TsGALI, f. 645, op. 1, ed. khr. 389, "Svodki anketnye materiala po izucheniiu vpechatlenii zritelei kino-kartin," p. 26.

47 Others in this category were Aleksandr Dubrovskii, Aleksandr Anoshchenko, Nikolai Shpikovskii, Sergei Iutkevich, Boris Gusman, Ilia Trauberg, and Viktor Pertsov. The cinema watchdogs disapproved of such "nepotism"; see, e.g., Krylov, *Kino vmesto vodki*, pp. 21–26.

48 The only other stars approaching Ilinskii in popularity, using this criterion, were Nato Vachnadze (the queen of Georgian cinema) and Vera Malinovskaia.

49 Krylov, *Kino vmesto vodki*, p. 3.

50 A team of Soviet film scholars at the All-Union Scientific Institute for Research in

Film Art (VNIIK, Moscow) is investigating box-office records. Maia Turovskaia is project director.

51 TsGALI, f. 2494, op. 1, ed. khr. 60, "Ankety obsledovanii moskovskikh kinoteatrov o sostoianii muzykalnogo soprovozhdeniia kinofilmov"; TsGALI, f. 645, op. 1, ed. khr. 389, "Svodki anketnye materialy," pp. 3–4; TsGALI, f. 2494, op. 1, ed. khr. 40, "Protokoly zasedanii organizatsionnoi komissii i detsko-shkolnoi sektsii."

52 See TsGALI, f. 2494, op. 1, ed. khr. 40, "Protokoly zasedanii organizatsionnoi komissii i detsko-shkolnoi sektsii (1926)"; Iu. Menzhinskaia, "O detskom kino," *Kino-front*, 1927, no. 2 , p. 3; L. Sukharebskii, *Uchebnoe kino* (Moscow: Teakinopechat, 1929). There is a considerable literature on the subject of children and film; see, e.g., P. I. Lublinskii, *Kinematograf i deti* (Moscow: Pravo i zhizn, 1925); Vladimir Vainshtok and Dmitrii Iakobson, *Kino i molodezh* (Moscow: Gosizdat, 1926); A. M. Gelmont, ed., *Kino, deti, shkola: Metodicheskii sbornik* (Moscow: Rabotnik prosveshcheniia, 1929).

53 Troianovskii and Egiazarov, *Izuchenie kino-zritelia*, p. 36; A. Dubrovskii, "Opyty izucheniia zritelia: Anketa ARK," *Kino-zhurnal ARK*, 1925, no. 4/5, pp. 6–9.

54 Troianovskii and Egiazarov, *Izuchenie kino-zritelia*, p. 38.

55 Ibid., pp. 32–33.

56 Dubrovskii, "Opyty izucheniia zritelia."

57 A. I. Krinitskii, *Zadachi sovestkogo kino* (n.p.: Teakinopechat, 1929), pp. 23–25. Krinitskii did, however, blame advertisements for playing to these unfortunate proclivities.

58 Troianovskii and Egiazarov, *Izuchenie kino-zritelia*, pp. 40–41. See also TsGALI, f. 645, op. 1, ed. khr. 389, "Svodki anketnye materialy," p. 14.

59 Dubrovskii, "Opyty izucheniia zritelia"; M. Zaretskii, "Rabochii podrostok kak zritel kino," *Kino-zhurnal ARK*, 1925, no. 3, pp. 20–22.

60 Troianovskii and Egiazarov, *Izuchenie kino-zritelia*, p. 44.

61 Ibid., p. 36; Zaretskii, "Rabochii podrostok"; Vainshtok and Iakobson, *Kino i molodezh*, p. 22.

62 Vainshtok and Iakobson, *Kino i molodezh*, p. 19, report that 62 percent of young male proletarians went to the movies for entertainment; they are obviously using Zaretskii's results, "Rabochii podrostok." Only half of Troianovskii and Egiazarov's sample gave "pleasure" and "relaxation" as their chief motivation for film attendance, *Izuchenie kino-zritelia*, p. 47.

63 TsGALI, f. 645, op. 1, ed. khr. 389, "Svodki anketnye materialy," p. 16. This study also found a substantial group of hard-core film-goers – 25 percent attended eight or more times a month.

64 Efraim Lemberg, *Kinopromyshlennost v SSSR: Ekonomika sovetskoi kinematografii* ([Moscow]: Teakinopechat, 193[0]), pp. 169, 171, 174.

65 Zaretskii, "Rabochii podrostok."

66 A. Kurs, *Samoe mogushchestvennoe* (Moscow: Kinopechat, 1927), p. 14.

67 Ibid., p. 51. Kurs disapproved of the current state of affairs, but he was an honest reporter.

68 Khrisanf Khersonskii, "Khochu snimatsia," *Kino-front*, 1927, no. 5, pp. 4–7.

69 Ippolit Sokolov, "Na putiakh k zvukovomu kino," *Sovetskii ekran*, 1929, no. 44.
70 The literature in English on the Cultural Revolution is extensive; see, e.g., Sheila Fitzpatrick, ed., *Cultural Revolution in Russia, 1928–1931* (Bloomington: Indiana University Press, 1978).
71 TsGALI, f. 2496, op. 1, ed. khr. 25, "Sovkino finansovo-kommercheskii plan na 27/28," p. 1; Mikhail Berestinskii, "Chto skazali o Sovkino na dispute v TsDRI," *Kino*, 1927, no. 43, p. 5.
72 D. Liianov, "Na proizvodstve Sovkino," *Kino*, 1927, no. 14, p. 4. Unemployment among filmworkers had long been a problem; see G. D., "Zhizn kino-rabotnikov: Beseda s zavnospredrabisom V. I. Pokrovskim," *Kino*, 1925, no. 10, p. 5.
73 "Protsess kino-rabotnikov," *Kino*, 1927, nos. 15–18, *passim*.
74 TsGALI, f. 645, op. 1, ed. khr. 385, "Glavnoe upravlenie po delam khudozhestvennoi literatury i iskusstva (1928–29)," p. 195.
75 Krylov, *Kino vmesto vodki*, pp. 28–30; I. Davydov, "Order na zhizn," *Sovetskoe kino*, 1928, no. 1, p. 6. The attacks against Sovkino are detailed in Youngblood, *Soviet Cinema*, chap. 5.
76 Osip Beskin, "Neigrovaia filma," *Sovetskoe kino*, 1927, no. 7, pp. 9–11; "K smotru kino-sezona," *Sovetskii ekran*, 1929, no. 20.
77 B. S. Olkhovyi, ed., *Puti kino: Pervoe vsesoiuznoe soveshchanie po kinematografii* (Moscow: Teakinopechat, 1929), pp. 429–44; the resolutions are translated in Taylor and Christie, *Film Factory*, pp. 208–15. Discussions of the conference can be found in Taylor, *Politics*, pp. 106–13; Youngblood, *Soviet Cinema*, pp. 155–61; Peter Kenez, "The Cultural Revolution in Cinema," *Slavic Review* 47, no. 3 (Fall 1988): 418–19.
78 S. Kosior, "K itogam voprosov kino," *Revoliutsiia i kultura*, 1928, no. 6, pp. 5–7.
79 *Tematicheskii plan Sovkino na 1928/29 g. utverzhdennyi plenumom khudozhestvennogo soveta ot 11 zasedaniem pravleniia Sovkino ot 13/VIII s.g.* ([Moscow] 1928), esp. pp. 3–6.
80 In *Kino*, 1928, see: (for the quotation) "Davno pora," no. 20; "Soobshcheniia Glavrepertkoma," ibid.; "Eshche odna seriia sniatykh kartin," no. 21; "Udachnaia operatsiia: Ekran ochishchen ot khlama," no. 47.
81 The worst attacks were usually launched against people, not films; see, e.g., N. Bodrov, "Litso opportunistov," *Kino* 1930, no. 54, p. 3.
82 See, e.g., Grigorii Boltianskii, "Kino-kadry i ODSK," *Kino i zhizn*, 1930, no. 8.
83 Uspenskii, son of a tsarist bureaucrat, had lived abroad 1907–21. (The fact that he had taken so long to return was clearly held against him.) On his suicide, see A. Milkin, "Pod svoe tiazhestvo," *Kino*, 1929, no. 15, p. 3 and the untitled obituary in *Sovetskii ekran*, 1929, no. 16, p. 4. On the purge of Teakinopechat, see the notices in *Kino*, 1930, no. 2: "Chistka apparata Teakinopechat," p. 1 and no. 26: "Itogi chistki Teakinopechat," p. 1. The ARK archive reveals that the plans to transform *Soviet Screen* into a "mass" organ were in place at the end of 1927; see TsGALI, f. 2494, op. 1, ed. khr. 65, "Plan raboty pravleniia ARK, dek. 1927," p. 44.
84 B. Alpers should probably be included in this list as well, but from time to time he exhibited insights about film that were completely beyond the ken of Bek, Popov,

and Rudoi. See, for example, Alpers, "*Arsenal* Dovzhenko," *Sovetskii ekran*, 1929, no. 16, p. 5.

85 The history of suppressed films of the thirties and forties is being written by Soviet scholars. Abram Room's *A Strict Young Man* (1936) serves as one of the best-known examples; see J. T. Heil, "No List of Political Assets: The Collaboration of Iurii Olesha and Abram Room on *Strogii iunosha*," *Slavistische Beiträge* 248 (December 1989).

86 *Proletarian Cinema* bore as little relation to *Cinema Front* as the old ARK bore to ARRK. *Cinema and Culture* did not outlive the year 1929.

2 The entertainment or enlightenment debate

1 Quoted by Khrisanf Khersonskii, "Khochu snimatsia."

2 See the discussions of this issue in Abel, *French Cinema* and in Thomas Saunders, "Hollywood in Berlin: American Cinema and Weimar Culture," unpublished ms.

3 As rural cinema workers soon found out, some preparation of the uninitiated (and illiterate) peasantry was necessary, but far less than teaching them to read. See, e.g., A. Katsigras, "Voprosy derevenskoi kino-raboty," *Sovetskoe kino*, 1925, no. 6, pp. 35–36 and Katsigras, "Opyty fikatsii zritelskikh interesov," in I. N. Bursak, ed., *Kino* (Moscow: Proletkino, 1925), pp. 50–51.

4 Lenin first wrote about cinema in *Pravda*, 26 May 1913; see A. M. Gak, ed., *Samoe vazhnoe iz vsekh iskusstv: Lenin o kino* (Moscow: Iskusstvo, 1973), p. 13.

5 *Kinematograf: Sbornik statei* (Moscow: Gosudarstvennoe izd-vo, 1919), pp. 3–4. For a translation of Lunacharskii's contribution to the volume, see Taylor and Christie, *Film Factory*, pp. 47–49.

6 See, e.g., Kay Sloan, *The Loud Silents: Origins of the Social Problem Film* (Urbana: University of Illinois Press, 1988), a study of pre–World War I American films.

7 Another good example of this tendency can be seen in the activities of the artists known as the Wanderers. See Elizabeth Kridl Valkenier, *Russian Realist Art: The State and Society, the Peredvizhniki and Their Tradition* (Ann Arbor, MI: Ardis, 1977).

8 For an example, see Margaret A. Rose, *Marx's Lost Aesthetics: Karl Marx and the Visual Arts* (Cambridge: Cambridge University Press, 1984).

9 On *Vpered*, see Zenovia Sochor, *Revolution and Culture: The Bogdanov–Lenin Controversy* (Ithaca, NY: Cornell University Press, 1988); on the Proletkult, see Mally, *Culture of the Future*.

10 Patrick Brantlinger, *Bread and Circuses: Theories of Mass Culture as Social Decay* (Ithaca, NY: Cornell University Press, 1983). Also see Jeffrey Brooks, *When Russia Learned to Read* (Princeton, NJ: Princeton University Press, 1985) and Stites, *Soviet Popular Culture*.

11 S. Zilbershtein, "Nikolai II o kino," *Sovetskii ekran* (12 April 1927), p. 10, quoted in Taylor, *Politics*, p. 1.

12 Editorial, *Kino-fot*, 1922, no. 4, p. 1; B. Arvatov, "Agit-kino," *Kino-fot*, 1922, no. 2, p. 2; Albert Syrkin, "Mezhdu tekhniki i ideologiei (O kino-poputchikakh i partiinom rukovodstve)," *Kino-nedelia*, 1924, no. 37, p. 1. For a later example see

Osip Beskin, "Mesto kino," *Sovetskoi kino*, 1926, no. 1, p. 1. Note the front page placement for three of these four articles.

13 See the discussion in Youngblood, *Soviet Cinema*, e.g., pp. 81–82.

14 Richard Taylor discusses the "art or entertainment" debate in early Soviet cinema in "*The Kiss of Mary Pickford*: Ideology and Popular Culture in Soviet Cinema," in Anna Lawton, ed., *The Red Screen: Politics, Society, Art in Soviet Cinema* (London: Routledge, 1992). Lawton gives a historical overview in "'Lumière' and Darkness: The Moral Question in the Russian and Soviet Cinema," *Jahrbücher für Geschichte Osteuropas* 38, no. 2 (1990): 244–54.

15 V. Meshcheriakov, "Kino dlia derevni (Rabota kino-sektsii Glavpolitprosveta)" in S. Syrtsov and A. Kurs, eds., *Sovetskoe kino na podeme* (Moscow: Kinopechat, 1926), p. 98

16 Lunacharskii's most recent biographers – A. Elkin, *Lunacharskii* (Moscow: Molodaia gvardiia, 1967) and Timothy Edward O'Connor, *The Politics of Soviet Culture: Anatolii Lunacharskii* (Ann Arbor, MI: UMI Research Press, 1983) – ignore his film work entirely.

17 *Locksmith and Chancellor* (1923, Vladimir Gardin); *The Bear's Wedding* (1926, Konstantin Eggert); *Poison* (1927, Evgenii Ivanov-Barkov); *The Salamander* (1928, Grigorii Roshal).

18 See fig. 31.

19 A. V. Lunacharskii, *Kino na zapade i u nas* (n.p.: Teakinopechat, 1928). Other writings have been collected in *Lunacharskii o kino: Stati, vyskazyvaniia, stsenarii, dokumenty*, comp. K. D. Muratova (Moscow: Iskusstvo, 1965). Also see the bibliography *A. V. Lunacharskii o literature i iskusstve: Bibliograficheskii ukazatel, 1902–1963* (Leningrad: [Izd. bibl. AN SSSR] 1964).

20 From 1931 to 1947, Trainin worked for the USSR Institute of law; in the final two years of his life, he held a post at the Academy of Sciences. The third edition of the Soviet encyclopedia *Bolshaia sovetskaia entsiklopediia* lists Trainin as a "prominent jurist," with no professional activity before 1931. All other biographical information comes from the Soviet Data Bank project, University of Pittsburgh, courtesy of William Chase.

21 See the discussion of Lunacharskii's role in the *Vpered* group and his relationship to Bogdanov in O'Connor, *Politics of Soviet Culture*, pp. 7–11; see Mally, *Culture of the Future*, pp. 145, 147, for references to Trainin's role in the Proletkult.

22 I. Trainin, "Puti kino," *Kino-nedelia*, 1924, no. 40/41, pp. 8–10; A. V. Lunacharskii, "Tezisy A. V. Lunacharskogo: Revoliutsionnaia ideologiia i kino," ibid., no. 46, p. 11 (translated in Taylor and Christie, *Film Factory*). Trainin's and Lunacharskii's views on cinema are discussed in more detail in Youngblood, "Entertainment or Enlightenment? Popular Cinema in Soviet Society, 1921–1931," in Stephen White, ed., *New Directions in Soviet History* (Cambridge: Cambridge University Press, 1992), upon which this chapter is based.

23 A. V. Lunacharskii, "Mesto kino sredi drugikh iskusstv," *Sovetskoe kino*, 1925, no. 1, pp. 5–7; I. Trainin, "Na puti k vozrozhdeniiu," ibid., pp. 8–14.

24 Trainin, "Sovetskaia filma i zritel," *Sovetskoe kino*, 1925, no. 4/5, pp. 10–18 and continued in no. 6, pp. 16–23.

25 Ibid., pp. 30–31.
26 Al. Voznesenskii, *Iskusstvo ekrana* (Kiev: Sorabkoop, 1924), p. 103.
27 Ibid., p. 103; "K sovetskomu realizmu," *Kino-gazeta*, 1924, no. 42, p. 1.
28 M. Veremienko, "O kulturfilme," *Sovetskoe kino*, 1927, no. 4, pp. 14–15; G. Boltianskii, "Kino v derevne," in Bursak, *Kino*, p. 41.
29 Kristin Thompson, *Exporting Entertainment: America in the World Film Market, 1907–1934* (London: BFI Publishing, 1985); Abel, *French Cinema*; Saunders, "Hollywood in Berlin."
30 Biographical data on Katsigras and Meshcheriakov come from the Soviet Data Bank.
31 From *Sovetskoe kino*, 1925: on foreign pictures: D. Liianov, "Blizhe k massam," no. 1, pp. 37–38 and "Ob upriamoi deistvitelnosti i bolnykh nervakh," no. 2/3, pp. 18–22; on critics: A. Kurs, "Kino-kritika v SSSR," no. 4/5, pp. 22–28; on ARK: N. Iakovlev, "O levom rebiachestve v kino," no. 1, pp. 25–27; on Sovkino: A. Katsigras, "Voprosy derevenskoi kino raboty," no. 6, pp. 34–38.
32 In *Sovetskoe kino*, 1925, see: P.A., "Organizatsiia proizvodstva: kino-syria i apparatury v SSSR," no. 2/3, pp. 7–12; N. Shapovalenko, "Ekonomicheskii analysis kino-seansa," ibid., pp. 73–74; K. G., "Obshchestvo druzei sovetskogo kino," no. 6, p. 59; Valentin Turkin, "Sostoianie kino obrazovanie v SSSR," no. 2, pp. 68–72; I. Strashun, "O sanprosvetitelnom filme," no. 1, pp. 20–22.
33 In *Sovetskoe kino*, 1925, see: A. Abrosimov, "O prodvizhenii kino v derevnii," no. 1, pp. 44–48; G. Lebedev, "Kino-agropropaganda," no. 2/3, pp. 37–39; A. Katsigras, "Voprosy kinofikatsii derevnii," no. 4/5, pp. 50–58. The campaign will be discussed further in chapter 9.
34 B.L., "O filme dlia derevni," *Kino*, 1925, no. 13 is an especially witty satire.
35 A. Katsigras, *Kino-rabota v derevne* ([Moscow] Kinopechat [1926]), pp. 120–25.
36 Ibid., p. 49; V. P. Uspenskii, *ODSK (Obshchestvo druzei sovetskogo kino)* (Moscow: Kinopechat, 1926), p. 12.
37 Meshcheriakov, "Kak aktsionernoe obshchestvo Sovkino obratilos litsom k derevne," in V. Meshcheriakov, M. Veremienko, and A. Katsigras, *Kino-iazva (Ob uprazhneniiakh Sovkino nad derevnei)* (Leningrad: Izd. zhurnal *Sovetskoe kino*, 1926), pp. 3–14.
38 See, e.g. O. M. Brik, "Kommercheskii raschet," *Kino*, 1926, no. 34, p. 3 and Alexander Dubrovsky, "Soviet Cinema in Danger," in Taylor and Christie, *Film Factory*, pp. 49–50.
39 See translations of Vertov's essays in Taylor and Christie, *Film Factory*, pp. 69, 116, 150.
40 See Ippolit Sokolov, "*Shestaia chast mira*," *Kino-front*, 1927, no. 2, pp. 9–12 and Dziga Vertov, letter, ibid., no. 4, p. 32. Vertov's tribulations are extensively discussed in Youngblood, *Soviet Cinema*, passim.
41 Vladimir Maiakovskii, "Karaul!" *Novyi Lef*, 1927, no. 2, pp. 23–25 (translated in Taylor and Christie, *Film Factory*, pp. 160–61).
42 Translated in Taylor and Christie, *Film Factory*, p. 173.
43 M. Efremov, "Nashi sredstva i zadachi," *Kino*, 1927, no. 47, p. 27.
44 I. P. Trainin, *Kino na kulturnom fronte* ([Leningrad] Teakinopechat, 1928),

pp. 35–36. Based on internal evidence, this appears to be a pre- rather than post-conference polemic.

45 Ibid., pp. 42–43.

46 Ibid., p. 45.

47 A. V. Lunacharskii, "Cinema – the Greatest of the Arts," in Taylor and Christie, *Film Factory*, pp. 155–56. This article originally appeared in *Komsomolskaia pravda*.

48 Olkhovyi, *Puti kino*; Meshcheriakov, whose speech appears pp. 99–104, also made frequent interjections from the floor.

49 Fitzpatrick, *Education and Social Mobility*, pp. 133–35.

50 TsGALI, f. 2498, op. 1, ed. khr. 32, "Biulletin informbiuro Soiuzkino," p. 2.

51 See chapter 2, table 4 and Youngblood, *Soviet Cinema*, appendices 1 and 2.

52 For another angle on this issue, see Kenez, *Birth of the Propaganda State*.

53 See, e.g., Trainin, *Kino na kulturnom fronte*, p. 45.

54 TsGALI, f. 2497, op. 1, ed. khr. 80, "Gosudarstvennoe vsesoiuznoe foto-kino obedinenie Soiuzkino," p. 51; John Barber, "Working Class and Political Culture in the 1930s," in Günther, *Culture of the Stalin Period*, p. 10.

3 The *inostranshchina* in Soviet cinema

1 Khersonskii, "Khochu snimatsia," p. 4.

2 Lev Kuleshov, "Amerikanshchina," *Kino-fot*, 1922, no. 1, pp. 14–15. I have used Ronald Levaco's translation in *Kuleshov on Film* (Berkeley: University of California Press, 1974), pp. 127–30, because I like the coinage "Americanitis," but Richard Taylor has also translated it in Taylor and Christie, *Film Factory*, pp. 72–73.

3 On this practice (not isolated to the USSR), see, e.g., Viktor Shklovskii, *Motalka: O kino-remesle (Knizhka ne dlia kinematografistov)* (Moscow: Teakinopechat, 1927), p. 28 and "Novyi kurs Sovkino," *Sovetskii ekran*, 1929, no. 1, p. 2.

4 Kepley and Kepley, "Foreign Films," p. 431. The Kepleys used Steven Hill's figures for Soviet productions, which are lower than mine because Hill eliminated "shorts" from his analysis. But since the imports included a fair number of 2-reel comedies, exclusion of Soviet "shorts" makes the comparison even more unfavorable than it was in reality.

5 Thomas Saunders has come to a different conclusion in "Hollywood in Berlin." He has found evidence that German theatre managers were such bad businessmen that they did not know how much money they made (or lost) from screening foreign films.

6 Krylov, *Kino vmesto vodki*, pp. 19–20. (Shvedchikov was fighting for Sovkino's survival at this point, so his figures may have been exaggerated.)

7 Krylov, *Kino vmesto vodki*, p. 42.

8 L., "Prokat i teatry," p. 21; Kepley and Kepley, "Foreign Films," p. 437.

9 Vainshtok and Iakobson, *Kino i molodezh*; Troianovskii and Egiazarov, *Izuchenie kino-zritelia*, p. 31.

10 Nataliia Tolstova, "Deti o svoem kino," in Gelmont, *Kino, deti, shkola*, pp. 102–3,

107–8. The sample consisted of 912 children aged from 10 to 15 years. The audience was 55 percent proletarian, and 66 percent male.

11 N. Bodrov, "Nashi kino-nekhvati," *Kino-zhurnal ARK*, 1926, no. 1, pp. 19–20.

12 *The Sea Hawk* earned sixth place, *The Mark of Zorro* tenth in Troianovskii and Egiazarov, *Izuchenie kino-zritelia*, p. 31. George Seitz's *Speed* (1922), which was not imported until 1927, attracted over 1.5 million viewers in its first six months, a very substantial box-office; see Krylov, *Kino vmesto vodki*, p. 30.

13 See, e.g., ads in *Izvestiia*, 12 November 1924.

14 See *Vecherniaia Moskva*, 13 November 1929.

15 S. Bratoliubov, *Na zare sovetskoi kinematografii: Iz istorii kinoorganizatsii Petrograda-Leningrada, 1918–1925 goda* (Leningrad: Iskusstvo, 1976), pp. 52–53.

16 R., "*Vasilii Griaznov*," *Izvestiia*, 30 March 1924, p. 4; the ads appear on p. 5, but this film is not listed in *Sovetskie khudozhestvennye filmy*. The King of the Circus was retitled *The Hero of the Arena* for its Soviet screenings; complete information on the imports can be found in *Kino i vremia*: E. Kartseva, "Amerikanskie nemye filmy v sovetskom prokate," vol. 1 (1960); N. Egorova, "Nemetskie nemye filmy v sovetskom prokate," vol. IV (1965); Iu. Greiding, "Frantsuzkie nemye filmy v sovetskom prokate," vol. IV (1965).

17 "Po provintsii," *Sovetskoe kino*, 1926, no. 8, p. 24. "Armored Car" (*bronevik*) is the name of the theatre; *Light in the Darkness* (Svet vo teme) was the Soviet title for Pickford's film *The Love Light*.

18 Troianovskii and Egiazarov, *Izuchenie kino-zritelia*, p. 92.

19 Khersonskii, "Khochu snimatsia," p. 4; letter from M. Shashkin in "Slovo za chitatelem," *Kino*, 1926, no. 17/18, p. 4.

20 See, e.g., "Slovo za chitatelem," *Kino*, 1926, nos. 12, 13, 15, 16, 17/18.

21 See *Kino-fot*, 1922, no. 4, *passim*.

22 V. Serpukhovskii, "Kino dlia detei," *Pravda*, 6 April 1924, p. 6.

23 "Krasnoiarsk," *Kino*, 1927, no. 38, p. 1.

24 In the videocassette version of *Mary Pickford's Kiss* available in the US, this line has been rendered "the Soviet Doug."

25 See, e.g., in *Kino*, 1926: "K priezdu Ferbenksa i Pikforda," no. 29, pp. 1–2; "Ferbenks i Pikford v SSSR!," no. 30, pp. 1, 3.

26 See, e.g., "Sto protsentov agitatsii," *Kino*, 1925, no. 15, p. 1; "Pervoe pismo," *Kino*, 1926, no. 12, p. 2.

27 L. R-al, "Chto my videli i khotim videt," *Kino*, 1925, no. 23.

28 V. Solskii, "Kino na zapade," *Sovetskoe kino*, 1925, no. 2/3, p. 61.

29 Kuleshov, "Amerikanshchina."

30 "Sto protsentov agitatsii."

31 Solskii, "Kino na zapade"; R-al, "Chto my videli"; Viktor Shklovskii, "Za stolbi," *Sovetskii ekran*, 1929, no. 3.

32 Walter Benjamin, *Moscow Diary*, ed. Gary Smith, trans. Richard Sieburth (Cambridge, MA: Harvard University Press, 1986), p. 54.

33 D. Liianov, "Amerika i Evrope," *Sovetskoe kino*, 1925, no. 4/5, p. 69.

34 I. Urazov, "Vtoroi konets palki," *Sovetskii ekran*, 1927, no. 11, p. 3.

35 V. Turkin, "Povodiia kontsy," *Sovetskii ekran*, 1927, no. 15, p. 4. This subject will be explored further in chapter 5.

36 These Soviet analyses of the appeal of American movies echo the reception of American films in Western Europe, at least as Victoria de Grazia has summarized it: they were "better technically (in set design, lighting, and editing), but also because the acting style was more natural and spontaneous, the narrative more compelling, and the rendering of daily life more accurate." See de Grazia, "Mass Culture and Sovereignty: The American Challenge to European Cinemas, 1920–1960," *Journal of Modern History* 61 (March 1989): 53–87.

37 "Bez otveta," *Kino*, 1926, no. 9, p. 2.

38 V. Turkin, "Bez kino-aktera net kino-kultury," *Sovetskii ekran*, 1928, no. 49, p. 4. Fogel committed suicide in 1929.

39 Evgenii Chvialev, *Sovetskie filmy za granitsei: Tri goda za rubezhom* ([Leningrad] Teakinopechat, 1929), p. 15. Though Lary May puts the 1928 total of projectors at 28,000, *Screening Out the Past: The Birth of Mass Culture and the Motion Picture Industry* (Oxford: Oxford University Press, 1980), p. 164, Kristin Thompson confirms the accuracy of Chvialev's figures (letter to author, June 1991).

40 Pi.D., "Nuzhen uchet," *Kinozhurnal ARK*, 1926, no. 2, p. 20. While I could not confirm the accuracy of these breakdowns from the standard American sources (May, *Screening Out the Past*, chap. 7 or Bordwell, Staiger, and Thompson, *Classical Hollywood Cinema*, pt. 2), Leo Mur, who had worked in Hollywood before the Revolution, came up with a virtually identical comparison in his book *Bumazhnye bronenostsy* (Moscow: Teakinopechat, 1929), p. 10.

41 Ippolit Sokolov, "Khoroshii stsenarii," *Kino-front*, 1926, no. 9/10, p. 8.

42 G.B., "Armiia sovetskogo kino," *Sovetskii ekran*, 1928, no. 46. This writer acknowledged that there may have been fewer in administration/service, perhaps as low as 20,000. Leo Mur's accounting in "Metody raboty amerikanskikh kinorezhisserov," *Kino-zhurnal ARK*, 1925, no. 3, pp. 5–6 is quite similar.

43 Ippolit Sokolov, "Ratsionalizatsiia kinoproizvodstva," *Kino i zhizn*, 1930, no. 28, pp. 15–16.

44 V. Arden, "Kino khudozhnik na zapade i v SSSR," *Kino-zhurnal ARK*, 1926, no. 2, p. 16.

45 May, *Screening out the Past*, p. 177.

46 For a detailed discussion of the reaction in Germany, see Saunders, "Hollywood in Berlin"; for a general discussion of the situation in Western Europe, see de Grazia, "Mass Culture and Sovereignty."

47 Kristol, "Dovolno skazok o nevygodnosti," *Sovetskoe kino*, 1926, no. 2, pp. 6–7.

48 Plots of these films are summarized in *Sovetskie khudozhestvennye filmy: Amerikanka iz bagdada*, no. 963; *Vor, no ne bagdadskii*, no. 336; *Znak Zorro na sele*, no. 460; *Dzhimmi Khiggins*, no. 848; *Kolumb zakryvaet Ameriku*; no. 990; *Miss Keti i mister Dzhek*, no. 480; *Naezdnik iz uailda vesta*, no. 273.

49 All information about content of films comes from my own viewing notes, unless otherwise indicated.

50 V. Shklovskii, "Mister Vest ne na svoemost," *Kino-nedelia*, 1924, no. 21.

51 I. Trainin, "Puti kino."

52 S. Valerian, "*Krest i mauzer*," *Izvestiia*, 19 November 1925; see the advertisement for *Namus*, *Izvestiia*, 9 November 1926.

53 S. M. V., "Proiavitel," *Kino*, 1928, no. 32, p. 3.

54 See, e.g., the ad in *Izvestiia*, 30 March 1924.

55 See, e.g., *Pravda*, 30 September 1924.

56 "Po SSSR," *Kino-nedelia*, 1925, no. 1, p. 25.

57 See the ads in *Izvestiia*, 12 November 1924.

58 Troianovskii and Egiazarov, *Izuchenie kino-zritelia*, p. 31. *Potemkin* and *Mother* came in at nos. 1 and 9, respectively. The remaining three places were held by American films, *The Thief of Baghdad* (5), *The Sea Hawk* (6), and *The Mark of Zorro* (10). The data can be ranked two ways. Based on the ratio of favorable to unfavorable responses (rather than the number of favorable mentions), the top ten is ordered somewhat differently: *The Collegiate Registrar*, *The Mark of Zorro*, *The Bear's Wedding*, *The Thief of Baghdad*, *The Case of the Three Million*, *Potemkin*, *The Decembrists*, *Mother*, *The Sea Hawk*, and *The Forty-First*.

59 N[ikolai] V[olkov], "Kartiny sezona," *Izvestiia*, 16 October 1926.

60 Kurs, *Samoe mogushchestvennoe*, p. 67.

61 G. D., "My zagranitse, zagranitse nam (Beseda s zaveduiushchim eksportno-importnym otdelom K. I. Feldmanom)," *Kino*, 1925, no. 3; Chvialev, *Sovetskie filmy*, pp. 22–32; Vl[adimir] E[rofeev], "*Dvorets i krepost* v Berline," *Kino*, 1925, no. 9, p. 2; Viktor Shklovskii, "Kolonizatsiia kino," *Sovetskii ekran*, 1928, no. 34, p. 5.

62 I. Urazov, "*Krylia kholopa*," *Kino*, 1926, no. 47, p. 2; M. Bystritskii, "S tochki zreniia teorii," ibid., 1927, no. 2, p. 3.

63 See *Kinotvorchestvo*, 1925, no. 10/12.

64 E. Kaufman, "Sovetskaia kartina na vneshnem rynke," *Kino-front*, 1927, no. 5, pp. 28–29. According to Kristin Thompson (letter to author, June 1991), Soviet films reached the height of their popularity in Germany later than this, so Kaufman's list is only preliminary.

65 Chvialev, *Sovetskie filmy*, pp. 36–37; the seven were *Potemkin*, *The End of St. Petersburg*, *The Wings of a Serf*, *The Bear's Wedding*, *Mother*, *The Collegiate Registrar*, and *By the Law*.

66 E. Kaufman, "Nash eksport-import," *Kino-zhurnal ARK*, 1925, no. 10.

67 See *Deiatelnost Vserossiiskogo foto-kinematograficheskogo aktsionernogo o-va*, p. 24 and K. Shvedchikov, "Sovkino otvechaet," *Kino-front*, 1928, no. 1, pp. 31–32. The price-fixing theory can be confirmed in Germany, anyway; see Bruce Murray, *Film and the German Left in the Weimar Republic: From Caligari to Kuhle Wampe* (Austin: University of Texas Press, 1990).

68 G. Dashevskii, "Amerikanskaia kinopromyshlennost v borbe za mirovuiu gegemoniiu," *Kino-front*, 1927, no. 5, p. 31. Product placement continues to be an important commercial aspect of filmmaking today.

69 Beskin, "Neigrovaia filma," p. 10.

70 A. V. Goldobin, *Kak pisat stsenarii dlia kino-kartin* (Moscow: Moskovskoe teatralnoe izd-vo, 1925), p. 11.

71 Lev V-s, "Rabochii zritel o zagranichnykh komediiakh," *Kino*, 1928, no. 9, p. 5.

72 Efr[aim] Lemb[erg], "Aktualneishchaia problema: Voprosy kino na pedagogi-cheskom sezde," *Sovetskoe kino*, 1928, no. 1, p. 15.

73 B.S., "Sud na Garri Pilem," *Pravda*, 16 June 1927, p. 6.

74 "Tekstilshchiki o Garri Pile," *Kino*, 1927, no. 35, p. 10.

75 In *Vokrug Sovkino*: see remarks by Lvovskii, p. 28; Khanin, pp. 29–30; Kirshon, pp. 32–34.

76 R. Pikel, "Ukhaby na kino-fronte," *Revoliutsiia i kultura*, 1928, no. 3/4, p. 46.

77 "Udachnaia operatsiia," p. 6.

78 "O sovetskom kino-importe," *Sovetskii ekran*, 1929, no. 40.

79 G. Nakatov, "Zagranichnye kino-gazy," *Sovetskoe kino*, 1926, no. 2, p. 2.

80 V. Kirshon, *Na kino-postu* (Moscow: Moskovskii rabochii, 1928), pp. 43–45.

81 V. Pertsov, "Mest zarezannykh kadrov (Zagranichnaia kartina na sovetskom ekrane)," *Sovetskoe kino*, 1926, no. 2, pp. 16–17.

82 V.S., "Protiv Ameriki," *Kino*, 1926, no. 23, p. 2.

83 S. D. Vasilev, *Montazh kinokartiny* (Leningrad: Teakinopechat, 1929), p. 87. This practice was satirized in *Cinema* with a cartoon of a film editor busily cutting objectionable material out of foreign films; see *Kino*, 1926, no. 12.

84 O. M. Brik, "Kartiny kotorye nam ne pokazyvaiut," *Sovetskoe kino*, 1926, no. 2, p. 9.

85 "Rabkor" Bystritskii, "Znak Zorro," *Kino*, 1925, no. 23, p. 2. It is not clear whether this man and the critic "M. Bystritskii" are one and the same.

86 A. Dubrovskii, "Atele i natura," *Sovetskii ekran*, 1926, no. 27, p. 5.

87 Beskin, "Neigrovaia filma," pp. 9–10.

88 B[oris] G[usman], "*Aelita*," *Pravda*, 1 October 1924; Khrisanf Khersonskii, "*Aelita*," *Izvestiia*, 2 October 1924. Interestingly enough, the emigré journal *Kinotvorchestvo* found *Aelita* "tendentious"; see "Russkoe proizvodstvo," 1926, no. 15/16.

89 S. Valerian, "*Krest i mauzer*," *Izvestiia*, 19 November 1925.

90 Kh. Khersonskii, "*Chortovo koleso*," *Pravda*, 27 March 1926.

91 M.Z., "*Bluzhdaiushchie zvezdy*," *Kino*, 1928, no. 9, p. 3; for a discussion of this film, which primarily concerned anti-Semitism, see J. Hoberman, "A Face to the *Shtetl*: Soviet Yiddish Cinema, 1924–36," in Taylor and Christie, *Inside the Film Factory*, p. 132.

92 Chvialev, *Sovetskie filmy*, p. 10.

93 "Opasnosti *Garemov iz Bukhary*," *Sovestkii ekran*, 1927, no. 42; Beskin, "Neigro-vaia filma."

94 "Vkratse," *Kino*, 1927, no. 37, p. 1.

95 Vasilev, *Montazh kino-kartiny*, p. 92.

96 A. Rustemoe, "Proizvodstvo i Sovkino," *Kino*, 1925, no. 2, p. 3. Also see Vasilev, "O peremontazhe," *Kino-gazeta*, 1925, no. 8, p. 1.

97 "Proverki kassoi," *Kino*, 1925, no. 3; I. Urazov, "Pobeda politiki i tsifry," *Sovetskii ekran*, 1927, no. 1, p. 3; G. Arustanov, "Rentabelnost," *Sovetskoe kino*, 1927, no. 8/9, p. 10.

98 "Nasha pochta," *Sovetskii ekran*, 1928, no. 42.

99 Kirshon, *Na kino-postu*, p. 46.

100 *Deiatelnost Vserossiiskogo aktsionernogo o-va*, p. 20.

101 See, e.g., V. Shneiderov, "Organizatsionnye formy kinopromyshlennosti," *Sovetskoe kino*, 1927, no. 8/9, p. 8; Urazov, "Pobeda politiki i tsifry"; N. Iakovlev, "Uzlovye voprosy," *Kino*, 1927, no. 46, p. 1; "Doloi!" *Sovetskii ekran*, 1928, no. 26, p. 3.

102 "Nado rashirit front borby," *Sovetskii ekran*, 1927, no. 35; S. V. Serpinskii, *Chto takoe kino* (Moscow: Gosizdat, 1928), pp. 49–50.

103 The slogan first appeared in *Kino*, 1926, no. 26, p. 2.

104 "Ideologiia i kassa," *Sovetskii ekran*, 1927, no. 43, p. 3.

105 K. Shutko, "Mezhrabpom-film," *Sovetskii ekran*, 1928, no. 39.

106 Beskin, "Neigrovaia filma," p. 10.

107 "Mezhrabpomfilm – organizatsiia nuzhdaiushchaiasia v korennoi perestroike," *Kino*, 1930, no. 5, p. 2.

108 Vertov, letter to *Kino-front*, 1927, no. 4, p. 32; Viktor Geiman, "Protiv prikazchikov burzhuaznogo iskusstva za izucheniia tvorcheskikh metodov sovetskogo kino," *Kino*, 1930, no. 48, p. 3.

109 *Kino*, 1928, no. 11, p. 2.

110 B[oris] G[usman], "*Banda batki Knysha*," *Pravda*, 4 June 1924; A. Fevralskii, "Shest vostochnykh kartin," *Pravda*, 21 May 1926.

111 G.R., "*Mashinist Ukhtomskii*," *Izvestiia*, 28 April 1926; N. Lebedev, "Novaia filma Proletkino (*Borba za ultimatum*)," *Izvestiia*, 23 December 1922.

112 In *Izvestiia*, see: Kh. Khersonskii, "Kino i sedmomu," 12 November 1924; S. V[aleria]n, "*Na zhizn i na smert*," 11 September 1925; M. Olshevits, "*Vodovorot*," 10 January 1928. These views did not necessarily correspond to those of the spectators; for example, workers were reported to like *Evdovkiia Rozhnovskaia*, see "Rabochie o kartine *Evdokiia Rozhnovskaia*," *Pravda*, 1 November 1924.

113 St. As-ov, "Pobeda kino," *Izvestiia*, 20 February 1923. The "Gold Series" refers to big-budget films produced by the Thiemann and Reinhardt studio before the Revolution.

114 Mikh. Koltsov, "*Ego prizyv*," *Pravda*, 17 February 1925; Kh. Khersonskii, "*Ego prizyv*," *Izvestiia*, 19 February 1925.

115 Vladimir Solskii, "Diskussii o Sovkino," *Kino-front*, 1927, no. 11/12, pp. 9–10.

116 I. Kr., "*Dva dnia*," *Izvestiia*, 10 January 1928; N. Volkov, "*Pravo na zhizn*," *Izvestiia*, 13 December 1928; Kh[risanf] Kh[ersonskii], "*Katka bumazhnyi ranet*," *Pravda*, 5 January 1927.

117 I.N., "Nasha, i zapadnoe kino," *Sovetskii ekran*, 1929, no. 19 and TsGALI, f. 2494, op. 1, ed. khr. 234, "Stenogramma lektsii S. A. Bugoslavskogo 'Organizatsiia zvuka tonfilma (1929)'," pp. 4–5.

118 Although during the Cultural Revolution ARK/ARRK attempted to become a "proletarian" society, it was in fact a nest of "bourgeois specialists." Glavpolitprosvet's Cinema Section is the film world's equivalent to RAPP. A good short introduction to Socialist Realism can be found in Margaret Bullitt, "Toward a Marxist Theory of Aesthetics: The Development of Socialist Realism in the Soviet Union," *The Russian Review* 35, no. 1 (January 1976).

4 Genres and hits

1 Viktor Shklovskii, "O mezhdu prochem," *Sovetskii ekran*, 1926, no. 20, p. 2.

2 Mikhail Shneider, "Genealogiia sovetskoi kartiny," *Sovetskii ekran*, 1927, no. 7, p. 14. Shneider considered the exemplars of the style to be Protazanov first and foremost, followed by his "sons," Zheliabuzhskii, Ivanovskii, Tarich, and Eggert.

3 Obviously, any attempt at a genre categorization of films will have its limitations, and this attempt is no exception.

4 One of the few who did was Valentin Turkin, "Povodiia kontsy," *Sovetskii ekran*, 1927, no. 15, p. 4.

5 See, e.g., Dubrovskii, "Opyty izucheniia zritelia," p. 9; B.T., "Plach o smekhe," *Sovetskii ekran*, 1929, no. 3.

6 V[ladimir] E[rofeev], "Pervyi ekran: *Kombrig Ivanov*," *Kino-gazeta*, 1923, no. 8, p. 2.

7 See "Grustnoe v smeshnom," *Sovetskii ekran*, 1927, no. 32, p. 3; and Pochtar, "Smekh i ideologiia," *Kino*, 1927, no. 2, p. 4.

8 Sokolov, "Kak sozdat sovetskuiu komediiu," *Kino-front*, 1927, no. 4, p. 14; Brik, "Na podstupakh v sovetskoi komedii," *Kino-front*, 1927, no. 3, p. 14. It is also possible, of course, that this remark is indicative of Brik's total cynicism; see the characterization of Brik in Vassily Rakitin, "The Avant-Garde and the Art of the Stalinist Era," in Günther, *Culture of the Stalin Period*, p. 185.

9 See Sokolov, "Kuda idet sovetskogo kino," *Sovetskii ekran*, 1926, no. 37; TsGALI, f. 2496, op. 1, ed. khr. 23, "Tematicheskii plan Sovkino postanovki khud. filmov na 1927/1928 g.," p. 38.

10 "Sovetskaia komicheskaia," *Kino*, 1927, no. 16, p. 2.

11 See *Tematicheskii plan Sovkino na 1928/29 g.*, p. 6.

12 See Vlada Petrić, "A Subtextual Reading of Kuleshov's Satire *The Extraordinary Adventures of Mr. West in the Land of the Bolsheviks*," paper delivered at the Loyola University conference on Soviet film satire, New Orleans, 1990.

13 Khrisanf Khersonskii, "Pombykh iz pultresta," *Izvestiia*, 5 December 1924; for a typical review, see Ia.M., "*Papirosnitsa ot Mosselproma*," *Kino-nedelia*, 1924, no. 44, p. 8.

14 See, e.g., A[leksandr] D[ubrov]skii, "*Pokhozdeniia Oktiabriny*," *Kino-zhurnal ARK*, 1925, no. 3, p. 34 (these comments were made in the context of a review about another "failed" comedy); Sokolov, *Kino-stsenarii*, p. 55. (It is also possible that A. D-skii was critic A. Dvoretskii.)

15 Edgar Arnoldi, *Komicheskoe v kino* (Moscow: Kinopechat, 1928), p. 4 (this book features an apologetic introduction by Vladimir Nedobrovo explaining why Arnoldi used so many American examples to illustrate his points); Kirshon, "Listki iz bloknota," *Kino-front*, 1927, no. 13/14, p. 10.

16 Dubrovskii, "Opyty izucheniia zritelia," p. 8.

17 S. Ermolinskii, "*Potselui Meri*," *Pravda*, 6 September 1927.

18 Kirshon, *Na kino-postu*, p. 10; V.N., "*Potselui Meri*," *Zhizn iskusstva*, 1927, no. 48, p. 11.

19 "K soveshchaniiu po delam kino v TsK VKP(b)," *Kino-front* 1927, no. 9/10.

20 See, e.g., M. Bystritskii, "Besprizornaia (Po povodu *Potselui Meri*)," *Kino*, 1927, no. 38, p. 3; R. Pikel, "Ideologiia i kommertsiia," *Kino*, 1927, no. 41, p. 2.

21 E. Arnoldi, *Avantiurnyi zhanr v kino* (Leningrad: Teakinopechat, 1929), pp. 72–74, 90–91.

22 Ibid., p. 61.

23 Budiak and Mikhailov, *Adresa moskovskogo kino*, p. 31.

24 "Pervaia filma revoliutsii," *Kino-gazeta*, 1923, no. 12, p. 1.

25 Khersonskii, "*Krasnye diavoliata*," *Izvestiia*, 25 November 1922.

26 See advertisements in *Izvestiia*, November and December 1922.

27 "Filmy priemye dlia rabochikh klubov," *Kino-zhurnal ARK*, 1925, no. 2, pp. 41–42; Zaretskii, "Rabochii podrostok," p. 22; Sokolov, "NOT v kinoproizvodstve," p. 11.

28 See, e.g., P.A., "*Oshibka Vasiliia Guliaeva* (*Veter*)," *Kino*, 1926, no. 43; Ippolit Sokolov, "*Veter*," ibid., no. 45, p. 3.

29 As a perfect example of the name recognition problem, *Sovetskie khudozhestvennye filmy* lists only this actress's surname.

30 A. German, "*Tripolskaia tragediia*," *Kino*, 1926, no. 15, p. 15 and in the same issue "Slovo za chitatelem"; "Krov na ekrane," *Sovetskii ekran*, 1927, no. 32, p. 4–6.

31 S. Valerian, "*Krest i mauzer*," *Izvestiia*, 19 November 1925.

32 Nikolai Lebedev, "*Slesar i kantsler*," *Pravda*, 13 December 1923.

33 Advertisement in *Izvestiia*, 19 November 1925.

34 Viktor Shklovskii, "Retsenzent," *Sovetskii ekran*, 1925, no. 35, p. 7.

35 See, e.g., A. Dvoretskii, "*Abrek Zaur* i prochee," *Sovetskii ekran*, 1926, no. 5, pp. 4–5; P. Neznamov, "Kovboi v papkakh," *Kino*, 1926, no. 14, p. 2.

36 *Wings of a Serf*, like *Cross and Mauser*, played more than one theatre, the first and second Sovkino theatres. See advertisements in *Pravda*, 23 November 1926. For a detailed discussion of the historical film, see Youngblood, "'History' on Film: The Historical Melodrama in Early Soviet Cinema," *Historical Journal of Film, Radio & Television* 11, no. 2 (June 1991): 173–84.

37 "Tov. Zinovev o sovetskoi filme," *Kino-nedelia*, 1924, no. 7, p. 2.

38 See Youngblood, "'History' on Film."

39 Kirshon, *Na kino-postu*, p. 64 and V. M. Mikhailov, "Bolshe, deshevle, luche!," *Sovetskii ekran*, 1929, no. 35, claimed it cost 340,000 rubles; Vladimir Korolevich, who levied the bankruptcy charge, gave a lower figure of 250,000 rubles in "Dovolno kolumbov," *Sovetskii ekran*, no. 49, 1926, p. 5.

40 "*Dekabristy*," *Kino*, 1927, no. 3, p. 4.

41 Vl. Nedobrovo, "*Dekabristy*," *Zhizn iskusstva*, 1927, no. 5, p. 15; Korolevich, "Sankt-Peterburg i Leningrad," *Sovetskoe kino*, 1926, no. 8, pp. 16–17; Arsen, "*Dekabristy*," *Kino-front*, 1927, no. 5, pp. 15–17.

42 Gusman, "*Dekabristy*," *Pravda*, 1 March 1927; Troianovskii and Egiazarov, *Izuchenie kino-zritelia*, p. 31. There are two ways to interpret their findings, but *The Decembrists* holds fourth place either way.

43 Mikhailov, "Bolshe, deshevle, luche!"

44 Maiakovskii, "Speech in Debate on 'The Paths and Policy of Sovkino,'" in

Taylor and Christie, *Film Factory*, p. 171. The complete minutes of the meeting at which Maiakovskii made these remarks appear in *Vokrug Sovkino*.

45 "Pushkinisty o *Poete i tsare*," *Sovetskii ekran*, 1927, no. 43, p. 4. This was followed by several pages of negative commentary.

46 Adrian Piotrovskii, *Khudozhestvennye techeniia v sovetskom kino* (Leningrad: Teakinopechat, 1930), pp. 2, 11.

47 Kirshon, *Na kino-postu*, p. 31.

48 See, e.g., M. Babenchikov, "Kino-geroi-byt," *Sovetskii ekran*, 1927, no. 39, p. 37; Pikel, "Ideologiia i kommertsiia"; P. Neznamov, *Poet i tsar*," p. 3.

49 K. Iukov, "Puti i pereputia sovetskogo kino," *Kino-front*, 1927, no. 9/10, p. 3.

50 Youngblood, *Soviet Cinema*, appendix 2.

51 Adrian Piotrovskii, *Khudozhestvennye techeniia*, p. 18.

52 TsGALI, f. 2014, op. 1, ed khr. 24, "Dogovor Grebnera s Lunacharskom o sovmestnoi napisanii literaturnogo stsenariia *Salamandra*," p. 1.

53 Troianovskii and Egiazarov, *Izuchenie kino-zritelia*, p. 31.

54 See, e.g., Gekht, "Kino-parad," *Sovetskii ekran*, 1926, no. 30, p. 3; L. Kosovitskii, "Slovo za chitatelem," *Kino*, 1926, no. 14, p. 5.

55 Chvialev, *Sovetskie filmy*, p. 37; "Opasnost *Garemov iz bukhary*." (*The Harem from Bukhara* [original title *Minaret of Death*] was among films labelled a "bear's wedding.")

56 I. Falbert, "Zolotaia seriia (*Medvezhia svadba*)," *Kino*, 1926, no. 6, p. 2, and Gekht, "Kino-parad."

57 Katsigras, *Kino-rabota v derevne*, pp. 48–49.

58 Beskin, "Neigrovaia filma"; Shklovskii, "O mezhdu prochem"; TsGALI, f. 2494, op. 1, ed. khr. 32, "Protokoly obshchikh sobranii chlenov ARK (1926)," pp. 6–7. Unlike the other cases of price politics cited herein, exact figures were never used, which means that this particular claim could well have been exaggerated for political reasons.

59 S. Ermolinskii, "*Iad*," *Pravda*, 6 September 1927.

60 See, e.g., Iakov Lev [Nikolai Iakovlev], "*Iad*," *Kino*, 1927, no. 37, p. 3; F.A., "Kak delalsia stsenarii *Iada* (Iz nashego obsledovaniia)," ibid.; S.I., "*Iad*," *Kino-front*, 1927, no. 11/12, pp. 29–30; K. Denisov, "O stsenariiakh," *Kino-front*, 1927, no. 4, p. 12.

61 Rakitin, "Art of the Stalinist Era," p. 178.

62 O. Beskin, "Nekotorye cherty iz zhizni Sovkino," *Sovetskoe kino*, 1928, no. 1, p. 2; Kirshon, *Na kino-postu*, p. 32.

63 The history of this film from the German side is covered in Murray, *Film and the German Left*, pp. 135–37.

64 A.S., "*Salamandra*," *Izvestiia*, 19 December 1928.

65 He also played himself in *Overcrowding*, which Aleksandr Panteleev directed from Lunarcharskii's script.

66 Kh. Khersonskii, "*Salamandra*," *Pravda*, 30 December 1928; Lev Shatov, "*Salamandra*," *Kino*, 1928, no. 51.

67 Kh. Khersonskii, "*Na zhizn i na smert* i *Kollezhskii registrator*," *Kino-zhurnal ARK*, 1925, no. 10, p. 27.

68 See, e.g., the advertisement for the film in *Kino*, 1925, no. 18; Chvialev, *Sovetskie filmy*, p. 37.
69 Sokolov, "NOT v kino-proizvodstve," p. 11.
70 *Three Lives* was based on a book by the Georgian novelist Tsereteli, but whether this adaptation was true or false troubled Russian critics not at all. (Pushkin, however, was an altogether different matter for Russians.)
71 Budiak and Mikhailov, *Adresa moskovskogo kino*, p. 31; A. Fevralskii, "Shest vostochnykh kartin," *Pravda*, 21 May 1926.
72 Sokolov, "NOT v kino-proizvodstve," p. 11; N.L., "*Tri zhizni*," *Kino-zhurnal ARK*, 1925, no. 1, p. 31.
73 Khersonskii, "*Namus*," *Kino*, 1926, no. 43, p. 2; "*Namus*," *Kino-front*, 1926, no. 4/5, pp. 29–30.

5 Images and stars

1 V. Turkin, *Kino-akter* (Moscow: Teakinopechat, 1929), p. 178.
2 I consider "actor" to be a gender-neutral term when it is used generically.
3 Fogel made twelve films from 1924 to his death in 1929, which is certainly enough work to qualify him for star status. Fogel did not, however, fit the star mold in other crucial respects. Based on my reading of the press, directors admired him for his abilities, not for his personality or "drawing" power, and Fogel's films were never promoted as "his" films.
4 On Vertov, see Dziga Vertov, *Kino-Eye: The Writings of Dziga Vertov*, ed. Annette Michelson, trans. Kevin O'Brien (Berkeley: University of California Press, 1984) and Vlada Petrić, *Constructivism in Film: The Man with the Movie Camera, a Cinematic Analysis* (Cambridge: Cambridge University Press, 1987).
5 Typage was widely misunderstood in its own time to mean a *rejection* of the professional actor, when even Eisenstein always blended professional and non-professional casts. Ippolit Sokolov wrote extensively on typage; two of his best articles are "Amplua – tipazh – maska: Kharakter obraza," *Kino-front*, 1927, no. 3, pp. 18–22 and "Metody igry pered kino-apparaturom," ibid., no. 5, pp. 10–14, and no. 6, pp. 11–13.
6 The most recent translation of Eisenstein is S. M. Eisenstein, *Selected Works*, vol. 1, *Writings: 1922–1934*, ed. and trans. Richard Taylor (Bloomington: Indiana University Press, 1988). The Hungarian film critic Béla Balázs, who enjoyed considerable prestige in the USSR, also rejected "theatrical" actors as inherently uncinematic (although he was a well-known opponent of Eisenstein's theories of film editing). For Balázs's views on typage (at least to the extent they were known in the Soviet film community) see, e.g., B. Balázs, *Kultura kino* (Leningrad: Gosizdat, 1925), pp. 32–34.
7 Kh[risanf] K[ersonskii], "Ishchem liudei ekrana," *Kino-zhurnal ARK*, 1925, no. 10, pp. 29–30.
8 Translations of Kuleshov may be found in a number of sources, including Taylor and Christie, *Film Factory*, but his seminal works are included in *Kuleshov on Film*. Another example of the enduring popularity of modish theories about physical

education and exercise in the field of film acting can be found in N. Oznobishin, *Fizkultura kino-aktera: Prakticheskoe rukovodstvo* (Moscow: Teakinopechat, 1929). Oznobishin includes numerous diagrams which illustrate the exercises necessary for developing acting techniques.

9 The notable exception to Kuleshov's basic theories in the KEM group was Fedor Nikitin, trained at the Moscow Art Theatre; see chapter 8. For a general discussion of early Soviet film schools, see Vance Kepley, Jr., "Building a National Cinema: Soviet Film Education, 1918–1934," *Wide Angle* 9, no. 3 (1987): 4–20.

10 Iurii Tarich was an exception to the unwritten rule that the old specialists stayed on the sidelines of cultural polemics. Tarich spoke against typage and in favor of using only professional actors in cinema at an ARK meeting. See TsGALI, f. 2494, op. 1, ed. khr. 64, "Stenogramma diskussii o tipazhe v kino (1926)," pp. 3–10.

11 Biographical data on actors in this chapter are drawn from their entries in *Kino-slovar* and *Kino: Entsiklopedicheskii slovar*, unless otherwise indicated.

12 Vsevolod Pudovkin, in particular, was drawn to stage actors. Nikolai Batalov and Vera Baranovskaia starred in *Mother*, but it was widely reported, especially abroad, that the film was shot without professional actors. See the discussion in TsGALI, f. 2494, op. 1, ed. khr. 64, "Stenogramma diskussii," p. 30.

13 See Krupskaia's remarks in the survey "*Oktiabr*," *Kino*, 1928, no. 12, p. 4.

14 Aleksandra Khokhlova, Kuleshov's leading actress, also suffered from the insistence that only "beautiful women" could appear on the screen, and Kuleshov was told at one point that he would not make more films unless he dropped her. See, e.g., Turkin, *Kino-akter*, pp. 82–83; Kirshon, *Na kino-postu*, pp. 53–54; and Kuleshov, "O nashem kinoaktere," *Kino*, 1927, no. 21, p. 3.

15 See, e.g., B. Alpers, "*Staroe i novoe*," *Sovetskii ekran*, 1929, no. 40.

16 Ippolit Sokolov, "Sostoianie stsenarnogo dela," *Kino-front*, 1927, no. 13/14, pp. 22–23.

17 See, e.g., "Standarty sovetskikh bytovykh kartin," *Sovetskii ekran*, 1928, no. 27, p. 11.

18 Obviously all cinema is subject to censorship, whether explicit or implicit. But commercial and moral "censorship" at least has a basis in taste cultures and societal norms, which in my opinion makes it much more palatable than externally imposed dictates such as these.

19 There is an interesting discussion of this issue as it relates to the films *Strike* and *Third Meshchanskaia Street*, in Judith Mayne, *Kino and the Woman Question: Feminism and Soviet Silent Film* (Columbus: Ohio State University Press, 1989); for a contemporary Soviet viewpoint, see Turkin, "Povodiia kontsy."

20 It is perhaps worth adding that these critics were all male. The limited possibilities for screen heroines was a worrisome matter to a few critics – and definitely to actresses. Vladimir Korolevich in *Zhenshchina v kino* (n.p.: Teakinopechat, 1928), p. 23 admired Hollywood actress Nita Naldi, Barbara La Marr, Mary Pickford, May Murray, and Greta Garbo (who had emigrated to Hollywood by then). Ada Voitsik, Galina Kravchenko, and Tatiana Lukashevich bitterly com-

plained about the portrayal of women in Soviet films in "Protiv poshlosti," *Kino*, 1928, no. 36, p. 3.

21 See B. Kolomarov, *Zlodei v kino* (Moscow: Teakinopechat, 1929), p. 27. Kolomarov listed as among his favorite Soviet villains: Sergei Gerasimov (who was especially good in Kozintsev and Trauberg's *The Devil's Wheel* and *Alone*), Valerii Solovtsov, Naum Rogozhin, and Iakov Gudkin.

22 Solokov's book on Gish, *Analiz igry kinoaktera: Masterstvo Lilian Gish* (Leningrad: Teakinopechat, 1929), got him into a great deal of trouble, and its publication during the Cultural Revolution was certainly ill-timed.

23 Scenarists for these films were: Aleksei Faiko and Fedor Otsep (*The Cigarette Girl from Mosselprom*) Anatolii Lunacharskii and Georgii Grebner (*Poison*), and Nikolai Saltykov and Abram Room (*Wind*).

24 Turkin did, however, recognize and admire Fridrikh Ermler's talent for casting in *The Parisian Cobbler*. See Turkin, "O zhivykh liudiakh," *Sovetskii ekran*, 1929, no. 20, p. 7.

25 See, e.g., A. Cherkasov, "Masterstvo artista v kino," *Kino-front*, 1927, no. 5, p. 2.

26 Ivan Koltsov, "Kommertsiia nevpopad," *Kino*, 1928, no. 14, p. 4 (Koltsov disapproved this practice); Vladimir Korolevich, *Nata Vachnadze* (Moscow: Kino-izd-vo RSFSR Kinopechat, 1926; reprinted twice in 1927); P. Neznamov, *Nata Vachnadze* (Moscow: Teakinopechat, 1928). (Russian film critics "russified" Vachnadze's first name, rendering it "Nat*a*" rather than "Nato.")

27 Eugenia Semyonova Ginzburg, *Journey into the Whirlwind*, trans. Paul Stevenson and Max Hayward (New York: Harcourt Brace Jovanovich, 1967), p. 202.

28 Korolevich, *Zhenshchina v kino*, p. 88.

29 For unfavorable references to Ilinskii's style, see Benjamin, *Moscow Diary*, p. 84; Shklovskii, "Za stolby"; N. Volkov, "Novye kino-kartiny," *Izvestiia*, 12 June 1927. (Volkov labelled Ilinskii an imitation Keaton in the film *A Cup of Tea*.) For favorable evaluations: Vadim Shershenevich, *Igor Ilinskii* (Moscow: Kino-izd-vo RSFSR Kinopechat, 1926; reprinted twice in 1927); Sergei Iutkevich, *Igor Ilinskii* (Moscow: Teakinopechat, 1929).

30 O. Brik, "Kino v teatre Meierkholda," *Sovetskii ekran*, 1926, no. 20, pp. 6–7.

31 See e.g., Turkin, *Kino-akter*, p. 70 (Turkin compared Ilinskii very favorably with Chaplin).

32 A. Room, "Rezhisser ... v koridore!" *Kino*, 1927, no. 21, p. 2. Batalov had to leave off shooting *Third Meshchanskaia Street* at 11 a.m. daily to head for his rehearsals at the Moscow Art Theatre.

33 Anna Sten came to Hollywood to be a "Russian Garbo," but ended up in character roles instead. Khersonskii wrote a nasty exposé, accusing her of gentrifying her background and falsifying her age for the Western press; see Khersonskii, "Dve biografii," *Proletarskoe kino*, 1933, no. 11/12, pp. 39–43.

34 Meierkhold received 5,000 rubles for ten days of work; Kachalov 12,500 for twenty-five. Typical "star" salaries would have been 200 and 500 rubles, respectively. See D. Semenov, "Mezhrabpom khvataet zvezdy," *Kino*, 1928, no. 38, p. 4.

35 TsGALI, f. 2494, op. 1, ed. khr. 33, "Protokoly zasedanii akterskoi podsektsii

ARK, 1 fev. -15 iiun. 1926," p. 31; K. Gavriushin, *Ia khochu rabotat v kino: Posobie pri vybore professii* (Moscow: Kino-izdatelstvo RSFSR, 1925), p. 37; Korolevich, "Kino i 'zagovor imperatritsy'," p. 9. Gavriushin's figures on average daily wages run a little higher than ARK's (notwithstanding that Gavriushin is identified as an ARK member in his book).

36 A. Goldman, *U poroga kino-proizvodstva (Zametki o kinoaktera)* (Leningrad: Tea-kinopechat, 1929), pp. 19, 24–25, 30–31.

37 Korolevich, "Kino ili 'zagovor imperatritsy'," pp. 8–9; "Reguliarnaia armiia kino-rabotnikov," *Sovetskii ekran*, 1927, no. 23.

38 The "high culture" cachet of theatre was pronounced in early Soviet culture, despite the rhetoric about cinema as the art of the future.

39 TsGALI, f. 2494, op. 1, ed. khr. 33, "Protokoly zasedanii," p. 30.

40 Vladimir Korolevich, "Samaia deshevlaia veshch," *Sovetskii ekran*, 1926, no. 46, p. 13.

41 Goldman, *U poroga kino-proizvodstva*, p. 6.

42 Khokhlova dissented from this viewpoint; because of the nepotism scandals plaguing the Soviet film industry, it is worth remembering that her director, Kuleshov, was also her husband. See "Nozhnitsy ili akter?" *Sovetskii ekran*, 1926, no. 41, pp. 6–7.

43 See Igor Ilinskii, *Sam o sebe* (Moscow: Iskusstvo, 1984).

44 S.I., "Novye liudi," *Kino-front*, 1927, no. 3, pp. 3–7; "Kino-akter," *Kino*, 1927, no. 21, p. 2. Yet the list of "best" actors included three who were not "new people" – Eggert, Baranovskaia, and Okhlopkov – and the rest (Batalov, Ilinskii, Ktorov, and Kuindzhi) all came from the theatre! (I suspect the article by "S. I." was written by Ippolit Sokolov, using his initials in reverse.)

45 Kuleshov fought back in "O nashem kinoaktere," p. 3. Charges against Lili Brik were in connection with her film *The Glass Eye* (an interesting experimental work); those against Barnet, in connection with *The House on Trubnaia Square*.

46 See e.g., L.V., "Chto skazal ARK o pisme Leningradskikh rezhisserov," *Kino*, 1927, no. 27, p. 5; "Rezoliutsiia ARK," ibid., "Sovetskaia obshchestvennost ne pozvolit sryvat rabotu professionalnykh organizatsii," *Kino*, 1928, no. 25, p. 2; "Akter ili tipazh" and "Soiuz otvechaet," ibid., no. 26, p. 2.

47 Cherkasov, "Masterstvo artista v kino," pp. 2–4.

48 "Bolnoe mesto v kino," *Kino-front*, 1927, no. 5, p. 1.

49 Khersonskii, "Khochu snimatsia," p. 6. Cherkasov, in "Masterstvo artista," expressed similar doubts.

50 A.Zh., "Obshchestvennyi sud na tipazhem," *Kino*, 1928, no. 31, p. 4.

51 N.I. Sakharov, "Pochemu vy khotite stat kino-akterom?" *Sovetskii ekran*, 1929, no. 37.

52 Iurii Gromov, "Za novyi byt geroev filmy," *Sovetskii ekran*, 1929, no. 35, p. 6.

53 Petr Sakharov, "Nenuzhnaia buza," *Sovetskii ekran*, 1929, no. 4.

54 Mikhail Levidov, "Naschet geroev: V kino i v literature," *Sovetskii ekran*, 1928, no. 49; F. Nikitin, "Nam nuzhna novaia sovest," ibid., no. 47.

55 B. Alpers, "*Prazdnik sviatogo Iorgena*," *Kino i zhizn*, 1930, no. 25, p. 7. Alpers felt

compelled to add that this popularity lay with the public who "demands nothing but entertainment," from movies.

6 Iakov Protazanov, the "Russian Griffith"

1 Ia. Galitskii, "Protazanov," on the page of poems and caricatures entitled "Shpilkoi v ekrane," *Sovetskii ekran*, 1927, no. 49, p. 2. Because the syntax and punctuation of the poem make little sense when rendered in English prose, this is a rather free translation.

2 For descriptions of Protazanov's pre-revolutionary work see Leyda, *Kino*; Tsivian, *Silent Witnesses*; M. N. Aleinikov, ed., *Iakov Protazanov: O tvorcheskom puti rezhissera*, 2nd edn., rev. (Moscow: Iskusstvo, 1957); Mikhail Arlazorov, *Protazanov* (Moscow: Iskusstvo, 1973); Ginzburg, *Kinematografiia dorevoliutsionnoi Rossii*. On Protazanov's French films, see Abel, *French Cinema*, pp. 19–20.

3 Aleinikov, "Zasluzhennyi master sovetskogo kino," in Aleinikov, *Protazanov*, p. 27. Aleinikov says that Protazanov was homesick, but adds no supporting detail.

4 Mark Kushnirov, *Zhizn i filmy Borisa Barneta* (Moscow: Iskusstvo, 1977), p. 44.

5 He made his first talkie, *Tommy*, in 1931.

6 This phrase was used in the editorial "Za ratsionalizatsiiu proizvodstva," *Kino-front*, 1926, no. 7/8, p. 1, specifically to refer to pre-revolutionary producers Khanzhonkov and Drankov, but Protazanov, too, was a Moscow merchant.

7 Unless otherwise noted, biographical details are drawn from Arlazorov, *Protazanov*, pp. 5–30 and from "Protazanov o sebe," in Aleinikov, *Protazanov*, pp. 287–309. A more complete exposition of Protazanov's background and a different formulation of issues discussed here can be found in Youngblood, "The Return of the Native: Yakov Protazanov and Soviet Cinema," in Taylor and Christie, *Inside the Film Factory*, pp. 103–23.

8 "Protazanov o sebe," p. 287. Aleinikov, in "Zasluzhennyi master," p. 6 says that Protazanov mainly attended the Moscow Art and Malyi theatres, noted for their realism.

9 Arlazorov, *Protazanov*, pp. 22–23; O. L. Leonidov, "Iakov Aleksandrovich Protazanov," in Aleinikov, *Protazanov*, p. 345.

10 Arlazorov contradicts Protazanov's account by saying that "Gloria" was purchased by Thiemann and Reinhardt, *Protazanov*, p. 29. (The studio's name was actually "Gloria," spelled with Roman letters, not its Russian equivalent, *slava*.)

11 "Protazanov o sebe," p. 297.

12 Protazanov attributed his success with actors to the high regard he felt for them; see "Protazanov o sebe," pp. 307–08.

13 Preobrazhenskaia, who will be discussed in chapter 9, went on to become Russia's first woman director and an important director in the Soviet period too.

14 Aleinikov, "Zasluzhennyi master," p. 20.

15 See Jeffrey Brooks, *When Russia Learned to Read*, esp. his comments on Verbitskaia's readership, pp. 158–60. Also see Zorkaia, *Na rubezhe stoletii*, pp. 165ff.

16 See Leyda's description of the reception of this film, *Kino*, p. 63; unfortunately

Leyda did not credit his source, but it was probably Likhachev, *Kino v Rossii*. See also Arlazorov, who reports that box-office receipts were "insane," pp. 47–48; and "Protazanov o sebe," p. 229. Aleinikov rather obviously disapproves of *The Keys to Happiness* and stresses that Protazanov adapted classics as well; see "Zasluzhennyi master," p. 16.

17 Aleinikov, "Zasluzhennyi master," p. 17 and Arlazorov, *Protazanov*, p. 60, both make a point of how much Protazanov liked money. Protazanov admitted this himself in "Protazanov o sebe," p. 297.

18 Arlazorov, *Protazanov*, pp. 72–73.

19 *Satan Triumphant*, described by Leyda, *Kino*, p. 88, though tame by current standards, does not fit the image that Soviet scholars have painstakingly crafted of Protazanov as maker of healthy entertainment pictures. The movie is, however, included in the apparently complete filmography in Aleinikov, *Protazanov*, pp. 387–412. Also see Tsivian, *Silent Witnesses*, p. 422.

20 Aleinikov calls *Father Sergius* a pre-revolutionary film, giving its date of release as 1917, although his own filmography contradicts this. The discrepancy can probably be explained by confusion between production and release dates; in any case it is certainly a pre-revolutionary film in style. See "Zasluzhennyi master," p. 26 and Tsivian, *Silent Witnesses*, p. 484.

21 Arlazorov, *Protazanov*, pp. 80–82, making reference to Frida Protazanova's diaries (no date is given for the departure from Moscow, and I have not been able to determine it from any other source). Protazanov himself is completely silent on this subject.

22 Protazanov's long-time friend and colleague Aleinikov confirms this and reports that Protazanov was fond of saying "My pictures speak for me." See Aleinikov, "Zasluzhennyi master," p. 27.

23 The reason for Protazanov's sudden move to Berlin remains a mystery; even Arlazorov refuses to speculate, *Protazanov*, p. 90.

24 Vladimir Gardin, Cheslav Sabinskii, Aleksandr Ivanovskii and others were in much the same position.

25 The novel is available in English translation: Aleksei Tolstoi, *Aelita, or the Decline of Mars* (Ann Arbor, MI: Ardis, 1985). For a discussion of the popularity of science fiction at this time, see Richard Stites, *Revolutionary Dreams: Utopian Vision and Experimental Life in the Russian Revolution* (Oxford: Oxford University Press, 1989), chap. 8; for a different point of view on *Aelita*, see Ian Christie, "Down to Earth: *Aelita* Relocated," in Taylor and Christie, *Inside the Film Factory*, pp. 80–102.

26 B[oris] G[usman], "*Aelita*," *Pravda*, 1 October 1924.

27 *Aelita: Kino-lenta na temu romana A.N. Tolstogo* (n.p.: [1924]), p. 45.

28 Rotha, *The Film Till Now*, (London: Spring Books, 1967; rpt. 1930 edn), p. 228; for Soviet reactions see esp. N[ikolai] L[ebedev], "*Aelita*," *Kino-gazeta*, 1924, no. 39, p. 2; and "Poputchiki ili prisoedinishsia," ibid., no. 43, p. 1. These sentiments did not, however, constrain *Kino-gazeta* from running advertisements for *Aelita*, see e.g., no. 43, p. 7. The term "ralliés" was introduced into Soviet cultural politics by Trotskii; "ralliés" were "the pacified Philistines of art," lesser

beings than "fellow travellers." See Lev Trotskii, *Literature and Revolution* (Ann Arbor: University of Michigan Press, 1960), p. 37.

29 A. V. Goldobin, "Blizhiishie zadachi kino," *Proletarskoe kino*, 1925, no. 1, pp. 4–5; "Proletarskaia literatura i kino," *Kino-nedelia*, 1925, no. 3, p. 5; Syrkin, "Mezhdu tekhniki i ideologiei."

30 Although *Cinema Week* implied they were typical, these viewers probably were carefully selected; see "Chto govoriat ob *Aelite*," *Kino-nedelia*, 1924, no. 37, p. 6.

31 Sokolov wrote about the film in his book *Kino-stsenarii*, p. 64 and his articles "Material i forma," p. 15 and "Kuda idet sovetskogo kino?" p. 3.

32 *Aelita* is listed among films cuttingly labelled "first-class Russian cigarettes" (*papirosy vyshego sorta*) in *Novyi lef*, 1928, no. 2, p. 28.

33 Dubrovskii, "Opyty izucheniia zritelia," p. 8.

34 At least according to Khrisanf Khersonskii, "*Ego prizyv*," *Izvestiia*, 19 February 1925.

35 See A. Kurs, "O kino-obshchestvennosti, o zritele i nekotorykh nepriiatnykh veshchakh," *Kino-zhurnal ARK*, 1925, no. 3, pp. 3–4; Sokolov, "Material i forma," p. 17; B. Malkin, "Mezhrabpom-rus," *Sovetskoe kino*, 1926, no. 8, p. 9; G. Boltianskii, "Kino v derevne," p. 41; Kh[risanf] Kh[ersonskii], "*Ego prizyv*," *Kino-zhurnal ARK*, 1925, no. 3, pp. 31–32; Mikhail Koltsov, "*Ego prizyv*," *Pravda*, 17 February 1925.

36 See advertisements in *Pravda*, 17 February 1925.

37 Sokolov, "NOT v kino-proizvodstve," p. 11; Gekht, *Kino-parad*," p. 3, says viewers liked it because it was well shot, had good actors, and a plot with romantic interest.

38 Kh. Khersonskii, "Komicheskaia i komedii," *Kino-zhurnal ARK*, 1925, no. 11/12, pp. 27–28.

39 Troianovskii and Egiazarov, *Izuchenie kino-zritelia*, p. 32. and TsGALI, f. 645 (Glaviskusstvo), op. 1, ed. khr. 389, "Svodki anketnogo materiala," pp. 3–4. The composition of the latter audience was 40 percent Party/Komsomol; in terms of occupation: 28 percent proletarians, 22 percent white-collar workers, 30 percent students.

40 A. Lunacharskii, "Pobeda sovetskogo kino," *Izvestiia*, 10 October 1926; in "*Kartiny sezona*," Nikolai Volkov also wrote a favorable review, where he declared the film up to "good Western standards." For unfavorable references see: M. Zagorskii, "Tapioka – Ilinskii – teatr – kino," *Sovetskii ekran*, 1926, no. 38, p. 5; Arnoldi, *Avantiurnyi zhanr*, p. 68.

41 S. Eizenshtein [Eisenstein], "Za rabochii boevik," *Revoliutsiia i kultura*, 1928, no. 3/4, p. 54; also see Kurs, *Samoe mogushchestvennoe*, pp. 63–64.

42 Kurs, *Samoe mogushchestvennoe*, p. 59, noted resignedly: "*The Case of the Three Million* is a successful picture. I don't want to argue with the viewer. The viewer is always right. In general, one shouldn't argue with the viewer. One needs to study him."

43 *Izvestiia*, 26 February 1927.

44 Troianovskii and Egiazarov, *Izuchenie kino-zritelia*, p. 31.

45 See Beskin, "Neigrovaia filma," p. 10 for a somewhat backhanded compliment; in

Kino, 1927, see: "Na temu grazhdanskoi voiny (O *Sorok pervom*)," no. 11, p. 4; and Khersonskii, "*Sorok pervyi*," no. 12, p. 3.

46 Arsen, "*Sorok pervyi*," *Kino-front*, 1927, no. 6, pp. 15–19. I have not been able to learn "Arsen's" real name.

47 See Shutko, "Mezhrabpom-film," *Sovetskii ekran*, 1928, no. 39, p. 6; K. Feldman, "Itogi goda Mezhrabpom-filma," ibid., no. 42, p. 6; Prim, "Generalnaia liniia Mezhrabpom-filma," ibid., 1929, no. 20, p. 6.

48 Nikolai Volkov, "*Chelovek iz restorana*," *Izvestiia*, 21 August 1927. As examples of the extremely negative reviews of this film see in *Kino*, 1927: P. Neznamov, "Chekhov – krupnym planom," no. 34, p. 4; M. Shneider, "Po tu storonu 17-go goda: *Chelovek iz restorana*," no. 36, no. 3; R. Pikel, "Ideologiia i kommertsiia," no. 41, p. 2. Also see Feldman, "Itogi goda Mezhrabpom-filma," and V. Kirshon, *Na kino-postu*, p. 12.

49 According to legend, anyway; I have yet to find this piece in *Pravda*. See L.V., "O sovetskoi komedii: Disput v dome pechati," *Kino*, 1928, no. 19, p. 6.

50 N. Iakovlev, "Pervaia komediia: *Don Diego i Pelageia*," *Sovetskii ekran*, 1927, no. 51, p. 3.

51 TsGALI, f. 2492 (ARK), op. 1, ed. khr. 99, "Stenogramma sobranie chlenov ARK po obsuzhdeniiu kino-filme *Don Diego i Pelageia Demina [sic]*, 1 dek. 1927," pp. 3–4. On Vertov's problems with *One-Sixth of the World* see TsGALI, f. 2492, op. 1, ed. khr. 69, unpublished letter from Sovkino to *Cinema Front*; Ippolit Sokolov, "*Shestaia chast mira*," *Kino-front*, 1927, no. 2, pp. 9–12; Sokolov, untitled letter, *Kino-front*, 1927, no. 7/8, pp. 31–32; summary in Youngblood, *Soviet Cinema*, pp. 138–42.

52 For reviews of *Don Diego i Pelageia* see "Rezoliutsiia po kartine *Don Diego i Pelageia*," *Kino-front*, 1928, no. 2, p. 6 and A. Aravskii, "*Don Diego i Pelageia*," ibid., pp. 20–21; L.V., "O sovetskoi komedii"; B. Gusman, "Po teatram i kino," *Revoliutsiia i kultura*, 1928, no. 3/4, pp. 13–14; M. Bystritskii, "Shag vpered (*Don Diego i Pelageia*)," *Kino*, 1928, no. 3, p. 3; N. Volkov, "*Don Diego i Pelageia*," *Izvestiia*, 4 March 1928. There is an interesting discussion of the film preserved in TsGALI, f. 2494, op. 1, ed. khr. 99, "*Don Diego i Pelageia Demina*." In addition to the fear cited above that the film might be misused by enemies of the Soviet Union, there was a heated debate about the recent "excesses" and abuses of film critics.

53 See "Lef i kino: Stenogramma soveshchaniia," *Novyi Lef*, 1927, no. 11/12, p. 54, for Tretiakov's remarks. These were echoed by Osip Brik, ibid., pp. 63–64. Vladimir Korolevich had earlier defined *Khanzhonkovshchina* as "boyar style and the good old days" (referring to the pre-revolutionary producer Khanzhonkov). See Korolevich, "Dlia Ars i Arsikov," *Sovetskii ekran*, 1927, no. 5/6, p. 11.

54 Dwight MacDonald, "Eisenstein, Pudovkin, and Others," *The Miscellany* (March 1931).

55 See Bliakhin, "K itogam kino-sezona 1927–28 goda," p. 10; Piotrovskii, *Khudozhestvennye techeniia*, p. 14; in *Kino*, 1928: Sokolov, "Prichiny poslednikh neudach," no. 46, pp. 4–5; L. Averbakh, "Eshche o reshitelnom," no. 45, p. 3. With the exception of Averbakh, who headed RAPP, these men were well-established

film critics, but of differing backgrounds. Bliakhin (who was the scenarist for *Little Red Devils*) and Sokolov liked entertainment films, while Piotrovskii thought of film as "art" and was attacked as a "formalist."

56 See, e.g., Prim, "Generalnaia liniia Mezhrabpom-filma"; "Tam, gde delaiut krizis kinematografii," *Kino*, 1928, no. 50, p. 2; "Kino," *Na literaturnom postu*, 1930, no. 2, p. 65; Ia. Rudoi, "Zametki o tvorcheskikh putiakh sovetskogo kino," *Kino i zhizn*, 1930, no. 24.

57 There was, however, a very long line to see *The White Eagle* the first time I saw it, in 1979 in Moscow. The audience had come to see Meierkhold.

58 N. Volkov, "Kachalov i Meierkhold na ekrane," *Pravda*, 18 October 1928. Volkov did not think too much of the picture, but this is far from the worst review.

59 E. Kuznetsov, "Kak vy zhivete?" *Kino*, 1932, no. 45. Others believed to be living too well included Vsevolod Pudovkin, Oleg Leonidov, Osip Brik, and Natan Zarkhi, an odd company with little in common.

60 "Nasha kino-anketa," *Na literaturnom postu*, 1928, no. 1, pp. 71–76 and no. 2, pp. 50–54. Protazanov's response, bringing up the rear, appears on p. 54.

61 Nikolai Volkov disagreed, finding no traces of the satirical elements which existed in the original stories, see "Sovetskie filmy."

62 Ibid.

63 Kh. Khersonskii, "*Chiny i liudi*," *Kino*, 1929, no. 40, p. 5; A.V., "*Prazdnik sviatogo Iorgena*," ibid., 1930, no. 51, p. 4.

64 B. Alpers, "*Prazdnik sviatogo Iorgena*," pp. 7–8.

65 Viktor Shklovskii, *Za sorok let* (Moscow: Iskusstvo, 1965), p. 94 (from *Ikh nastoiashchee*, 1927); also see Lunacharskii, *Kino na zapade*, p. 76.

7 Boris Barnet: Soviet actor/Soviet director

1 Boris Barnet, "Au seuil de la comédie soviétique," in François Albèra and Roland Cosandey, eds., *Boris Barnet: Ecrits, documents, études, filmographie* (Locarno: Editions du Festival internationale du film de Locarno, 1985), p. 41 [orig. *Kino*, 19 April 1927, but I have translated from the French].

2 This account of Barnet's early years is drawn from François Albèra, "Boris Barnet, une chronique," in Albèra and Cosandey, *Barnet*, pp. 11–13; Barnet, "Comment je suis devenu réalisateur," in ibid., pp. 36–41; and Kushnirov, *Zhizn i filmy*, pp. 3–19.

3 There are a number of discrepancies between Albèra's and Kushnirov's accounts, but Albèra has confirmed the accuracy of Kushnirov's version, given here, in a letter to me (January 1991).

4 Kushnirov, *Zhizn i filmy*, p. 4.

5 Ibid., pp. 5–9.

6 Barnet, "Comment je suis devenu réalisateur,' p. 37.

7 Ibid.

8 Ibid., pp. 16–17. On Shershenevich's "serious" literary career, see Anna Lawton, *Vadim Shershenevich: From Futurism to Imaginism* (Ann Arbor, MI: Ardis, 1981).

9 Ibid., pp. 37–38. Kushnirov's account of Barnet's Kuleshov years has been translated in Albèra and Cosandey, *Barnet*, pp. 86–102.

10 Barnet, "Comment je suis devenu réalisateur," pp. 39–40; Kushnirov, *Zhizn i filmy*, pp. 30–31.

11 Ardis has just published S. D. Ciordan's excellent translation of *Mess Mend* (Ann Arbor, MI: 1991).

12 Barnet, "Comment je suis devenu réalisateur," p. 40; Kushnirov, *Zhizn i filmy*, p. 37.

13 My assessment of the implicit connection between Protazanov and Barnet coincides with Kushnirov's; see *Zhizn i filmy*, pp. 43–47. Kushnirov notes, however, that there was no particular friendship between the two men, citing differences in temperament.

14 Ada Gorodetskaia, Barnet's first wife, died not long after they were married.

15 *Sovetskie khudozhestvennye filmy*'s plot summaries for the three films have been translated in Albèra and Cosandey, *Barnet*, pp. 199–202.

16 See Noel Burch, "Harold Lloyd contre le Docteur Mabuse," in ibid., p. 106.

17 Unfortunately, I do not know if that figure is for each of the three parts, which were screened separately, or for the three parts combined, but I assume it is for the former. See Krylov, *Kino vmesto vodki*, p. 30.

18 See advertisements in *Pravda* from 26 October 1926 through the end of the year. *Miss Mend* was replaced at the Ars by Conrad Veidt in *Lucretia Borgia* (see the advance announcement in *Izvestiia*, 24 November 1926).

19 See, e.g., "*Miss Mend*," *Sovetskoe kino*, 1926, no. 8, p. 31; Khrisanf Khersonskii, "Lakirovannoe varvarstvo ili 'Miss, vyidite na minutku'," *Kino*, 1926, no. 49. Khersonskii also attacked *Miss Mend* in *Kino-front* and the third part in *Kino*, 1926, no. 50, both of which reviews are translated in part in Albèra and Cosandey, *Barnet*, pp. 202–04.

20 See TsGALI, f. 2492, op. 1, ed. khr. 26, "Protokoly obshchikh sobranii chlenov ARK (1926)," pp. 15–16. Khrisanf Khersonskii was comparing *Miss Mend*'s promotion to *Mother*'s.

21 Prim, "Generalnaia liniia Mezhrabpom-filma," p. 6.

22 V. Solskii, "Kino-zadachi i kino-opasnosti," p. 50. Solskii claimed that *Miss Mend* failed at the box-office, an outrageous falsification.

23 Again, Albèra and Cosandey have translated the plot summary from *Sovetskie khudozhestvennye filmy* in *Barnet*, p. 207.

24 For example, Shershenevich once defined montage this way: "The art of carelessly cutting and carving. To edit a foreign film is to render it unprofitable." Shershenevich, "Kino-slovar," *Kino-kalendar* (1927).

25 Barnet, "La jeune fille au carton à chapeau," in Albèra and Cosandey, *Barnet*, p. 208 [orig. *Sovetskii ekran*, 1927, no. 12].

26 Kushnirov asserts that it was loved by "all," which seems quite believable as far as the general public was concerned. He also claims that the critics liked it too, which emphatically is not the case. See *Zhizn i filmy*, p. 67.

27 Kushnirov, *Zhizn i filmy*, p. 67.

28 Barnet, "Au seuil de la comédie soviétique."

29 Iakov Lev [Nikolai Iakovlev], "*Devushka s korobkoi*," *Kino*, 1927, no. 18, p. 2 (translated in Albèra and Cosandey, *Barnet*, pp. 210–11, but here I am translating from the original); Beskin, "Neigrovaia filma."

30 Iakov Lev, "*Devushka s korobkoi*"; Beskin, "Neigrovaia filma," also used the film as a paradigm for Mezhrabpom's alleged deficiencies. For an analysis of the relationship between *Third Meshchanskaia Street* and Sovkino's demise, see Youngblood, "The Fiction Film as a Source for Soviet Social History: The *Third Meshchanskaia Street* Affair," *Film & History* 19, no. 3 (September 1989): 50–60.

31 S. Ermolinskii, "*Devushka s korobkoi*," *Pravda*, 11 May 1927, p. 6; N. Volkov, "Novye kartiny," *Izvestiia*, 17 May 1927.

32 Kushnirov, *Zhizn i filmy*, p. 77.

33 S. Ermolinskii, "Kino v oktiabre," *Pravda*, 9 November 1927.

34 *Sovetskie khudozhestvennye filmy*'s plot summary appears in Albèra and Cosandey, *Barnet*, p. 212.

35 Boris Barnet, "Moscou en Octobre," in Albèra and Cosandey, *Barnet*, p. 213 (orig. *Sovetskii ekran*, 1927, no. 42).

36 See the ad in *Pravda*, 9 November 1927.

37 Khersonskii, as always, proved himself the master of invective. See "*Moskva v oktiabre*," *Kino*, 1927, no. 47, p. 3 (trans. in Albèra and Cosandey, *Barnet*, p. 214).

38 For a discussion of the contemporary critical reception of *October* and *The End of St. Petersburg*, see Youngblood, *Soviet Cinema*, pp. 151–52 and 174–75. I am not passing judgment on the artistic value of these films.

39 I am not alone in this assessment. Ian Christie has faithfully championed Barnet, and it was Christie's criticisms of my previous evaluation of Barnet (in *Soviet Cinema*) that provoked me to rethink Barnet, and to see his films again. See Christie's article "Barnet tel qu'en lui-même? ou L'exception et la règle" in Albèra and Cosandey, *Barnet*, pp. 74–85.

40 This interpretation of *The House on Trubnaia Square* is a marked departure from *Soviet Cinema*, where I labelled the film "tiresome."

41 See "Kumovstvo na kino-fabrike," *Kino*, 1928, no. 14, p. 6.

42 Another sign that this might be true is that *The House* was connected with the historical melodrama *The Captain's Daughter*, a film that it in no way resembles, except for the fact that Shklovskii served as scenarist for both. See Sokolov, "Prichiny poslednykh neudach."

43 Barnet had hoped Nikolai Batalov would take the role of the chauffeur; see Kushnirov, *Zhizn i filmy*, p. 86.

44 This plot line is faintly reminiscent of Gogol's *Revizor*, as Richard Stites has reminded me.

45 *Sovetskie khudozhestvennye filmy*'s plot summary appears in Albèra and Cosandey, *Barnet*, pp. 214–16.

46 "*Dom na Trubnoi*," *Kino*, 1928, no. 38, p. 6; see Youngblood, "'History' on Film," for a discussion of *The Wings of a Serf*.

47 K. Feldman, "Na putiakh k sovetskoi komedii," *Kino*, 1928, no. 40, p. 3 (Feldman did, however, state in this article his belief that directors had the right to make mistakes). Interestingly, Feldman reversed his opinion at the end of the Cultural

Revolution and wrote that Barnet had been a successful critic of the NEP bourgeoisie in *The House* and *The Girl*. See Feldman, "A propos d'un film réussi *La débâcle* et d'une critique ratée," in Albèra and Cosandey, *Barnet*, p. 219 [orig. *Sovetskoe iskusstvo*, 1931, no. 33].

48 Kushnirov, *Zhizn i filmy*, p. 98.

49 Albèra and Cosandey, *Barnet*, p. 217 and Kushnirov, *Zhizn i filmy*, p. 100.

50 The subheading for this section is an allusion to the French title for *The Ice Breaks*: *La débâcle*, a less literal but "truer" translation of *ledolom*.

51 I have not seen this film, which did not garner much notice at the time of its release. For a plot description, see *Sovetskie khudozhestvennye filmy*, 1: 431–32. Albèra and Cosandey mistakenly claim in *Barnet*, p. 218, that it had been omitted from the catalogue.

52 Bernard Eisenschitz, "A Fickle Man, or Portrait of Boris Barnet as Soviet Director" in Taylor and Christie, *Inside the Film Factory*, p. 156. (This article originally appeared in French in Albèra and Cosandey, *Barnet*.)

53 Feldman, "A propos d'un film."

54 Kushnirov, *Zhizn i filmy*, p. 103.

55 I discussed *Outskirts* briefly in *Soviet Cinema*; Peter Kenez takes it up in more detail in "Cultural Revolution."

56 Barnet went on to direct fifteen films (and act in four), but the promise of *Outskirts* was never fully realized, no surprise considering the political conditions under which Soviet directors had to work – in the thirties and forties in particular. Chronically depressed in his later years and an alcoholic, he committed suicide in 1965. Discussions of his later work appear in Kushnirov, *Zhizn i filmy*; in a number of the articles in Albèra and Cosandey, *Barnet*; and, in English translation, Eisenschitz, "A Fickle Man."

57 Protazanov did not heedlessly compound his "errors"; his actions seem to have been quite deliberate.

58 I mean to imply here that true artists are "driven" and less likely to be swayed by the vagaries of cultural politics than are purveyors of entertainment.

8 Fridrikh Ermler and the social problem film

1 Nikitin goes on to say that Ermler despised such bombast, and bitterly suggests that Ermler would have responded to his tribute with a "rather coarse witticism." See Nikitin, "Iz vospominaniia kinoaktera," *Iz istorii Lenfilma: Stati, vospominaniia, dokumenty, 1920-e gody*, pt. 2 (Leningrad: Iskusstvo, 1970), p. 111.

2 G. Kozintsev, "Slovo o druge," in I. V. Sepman, ed., *Fridrikh Ermler: Dokumenty, stati, vospominaniia* (Leningrad: Iskusstvo, 1974), p. 295 (originally in *Iskusstvo kino*, 1969, no. 7) and M. Bleiman, "Neskolko zagadok," in Sepman, *Ermler*. The latter is a perceptive tribute to the director by a long-time friend.

3 Unless otherwise attributed, biographical data on Ermler were gleaned from his autobiographical writings: "Kak ia stal rezhisserom," *Iskusstvo kino*, 1969, no. 7, pp. 109–36 (published posthumously); and from Sepman, *Ermler*: "Avtobiograficheskii zametki," pp. 90–96 and a questionnaire he completed in 1925, "Anketnyi

list, no. 71," p. 87. More details can be found in Youngblood, "Cinema as Social Criticism: The Early Films of Fridrikh Ermler," in Lawton, *Red Screen*.

4 Ermler tells two different stories here. This version is the more dramatic, drawn from "Kak ia stal rezhisserom," p. 10. In "Avtobiograficheskie zametki," pp. 92–93, he implies that he returned to the army voluntarily because he was unable to find work in the Petrograd studios.

5 Vera Bakun, "Neskolko slov o lichnom," Sepman, *Ermler*, p. 327. Bakun, a movie actress, was also Ermler's wife.

6 Ermler, "Kak ia stal rezhisserom," p. 113. Sergei Vasilev was to become one of Ermler's early collaborators in KEM, and, with Georgii Vasilev, the co-director of *Chapaev*.

7 Bakun, "Neskolko slov," p. 327.

8 Ia. Gudkin, "Riadovoi kemovskogo otriada," *Iz istorii Lenfilma*, pt. 2: 115.

9 Ibid. Gudkin's memoir is fascinating in its own right and powerfully depicts the poverty of the students at the institute.

10 *Red Partisans* survives (although I have not seen it); *Tea* does not.

11 Meierkhold was not in fact Jewish, but from a russified German family; see Robert C. Williams, *Artists in Revolution: Portraits of the Russian Avant-Garde, 1905–1925* (Bloomington: Indiana University Press, 1977), pp. 85–86. It is also somewhat misleading to call Stanislavskii a *barin*, since most "gentlemen" were usually nobles, whereas Stanislavskii was a member of the merchant caste.

12 "Osnovnoe polozhenie kinoeksperimentalnoi masterskoi," *Iz istorii Lenfilma*, pt. 2: 229. In this volume also see "Ustav kinoeksperimentalnoi masterskoi," p. 231, for an additional statement of KEM's goals.

13 Bleiman, "Neskolko zagadok," p. 277. Bleiman says Ermler was always embarrassed when *Scarlet Fever* was mentioned. (No doubt the scarlet fever epidemic of spring 1924, a notable victim of which was artist Liubov Popova, was not considered a laughing matter.)

14 Bleiman, "*Deti buri*," *O kino: Svidetelskie pokazaniia (1924–1971)* (Moscow: Iskusstvo, 1973), p. 74; orig. *Leningradskaia pravda*, 18 August 1926. This picture, and *Katka the Apple Seller*, were co-directed with Eduard Ioganson, about whom Ermler had little to say.

15 Verka is a typical female criminal of the period. See Louise Shelley, "Female Criminality in the 1920s: A Consequence of Inadvertent and Deliberate Change," *Russian History/Histoire russe* 9, pts. 2/3 (1982): 269.

16 Vadka's personality caused great concern in the studio's artistic council, which had to approve the script. Ermler was instructed not to emphasize the part too much. See "O stsenarii *Katka bumazhnyii ranet* (Iz protokoly khudozhestvennogo soveta kinofabriki Leningradkino, mar.-apr. 1926)," in Sepman, *Ermler*, pp. 106–07.

17 "*Katyka [sic] – bumazhnyii ranet*," *Sovetskoe kino*, 1927, no. 2, pp. 30–31.

18 Khrisanf Khersonskii, "*Katka bumazhnyii ranet*," *Pravda*, 5 January 1927.

19 N[ikolai] V[olkov], "Teatr – muzyka – kino: Novye kinokartiny," *Izvestiia*, 9 January 1927. Volkov did admire the editing and cinematography.

20 K. Ganzenko, "Sovetskii byt na sovetskom ekrane," *Kino-front*, 1927, no. 1, pp. 9–10.

21 Adrian Piotrovskii, "K partsoveshchaniia o kino rabote (ili 'Ob ideologii i kommertsii'), *Zhizn iskusstva*, 1927, no. 37, p. 5.

22 Vladimir Kirshon put the figure at 28,000 rubles; see Olkhovyi, ed., *Puti kino*, p. 79.

23 Nikolai Nikitin, "Prestuplenie Kirika Rudenko," *Krasnaia nov*, 1927, nos. 9–11; reprinted in Nikitin, *Prestuplenie Kirika Rudenko; Pogovorim o zvezdakh: Povesti* (Leningrad: Lenizdat, 1966); mentioned in Robert A. Maguire, *Red Virgin Soil: Soviet Literature in the 1920s* (Ithaca, NY: Cornell University Press, 1987; orig. edn, 1968), p. 314. Both I. V. Sepman and V. P. Borovkov state that the film was based on the story; see Sepman, "Kinematograf Fridrikha Ermlera," in Sepman, *Ermler*, p. 27 and Borovkov, *Fedor Nikitin* (Moscow: Iskusstvo, 1977), p. 54. Adrian Piotrovskii, on the other hand, wrote that it was the first Soviet "novelization" of a film; see Piotrovskii, *Kinofikatsiia iskusstv* (Leningrad: Izd. avtora, 1929), p. 43. The emigré Soviet scenarist Paul Babitsky confirmed Piotrovskii's version in Babitsky and John Rimberg, *The Soviet Film Industry* (New York: Praeger, 1955), p. 130. Adding to the complicated genesis of this story is Eric Naiman's recent discovery that the plot was cribbed without credit from Boris Okhremenko, "Prestuplenie Kirika Basenko," *Komsomolskaia pravda*, 25 September 1926; see Naiman, "The Case of Chubarov Alley: Collective Rape, Utopian Desire and the Mentality of NEP," *Russian History/Histoire russe* 17, no. 1 (Spring 1990): 27, n.87.

24 See Sheila Fitzpatrick, "Sex and Revolution: An Examination of Literary and Statistical Criminality; Data on the Mores of Soviet Students in the 1920s," *Journal of Modern History* 50 (June 1982): 252–78; Shelley, "Female Criminality"; Naiman, "Case of Chubarov Alley."

25 See a discussion of this curious notion that gang rape was an abortifacient in Naiman, "Case of Chubarov Alley," p. 27.

26 Khrisanf Khersonskii, "Kino: *Parizhskii sapozhnik*," *Pravda*, 14 February 1928.

27 Mikhail Shneider, "*Parizhskii sapozhnik*," *Kino-front*, 1928, no. 2, pp. 22–25. Andrei troubled Shneider – was he a negative hero or just "insufficiently positive?" The "almost Khanzhonkovian lack of motivation" was also a source of puzzlement.

28 K. Feldman, "Chto na ekrane," *Sovetskii ekran*, 1928, no. 6, p. 13.

29 TsGALI, f. 2949, op. 1, ed. khr. 213, "Stenogramma zasedaniia rezhisserskoi sektsii ARRKe o stsenarnom krizise."

30 See in Olkhovyi, *Puti kino*, e.g., remarks by Krinitskii, p. 24; Kirshon, p. 79; and Meshcheriakov, p. 103. Trainin, in ibid., p. 139, confirmed Ermler's assertion, p. 324, that Glavrepertkom was slow to approve the film's script, but Trainin said it was due to co-author Boris Leonidov's political difficulties.

31 Khersonskii, "*Parizhskii sapozhnik*," and N. Volkov, "Teatr – muzyka – kino: Po moskovskim ekranam (Kinoobzor)," *Izvestiia*, 11 April 1928.

32 TsGALI, f. 2494, op. 1, ed. khr. 171, "Protokol diskussii obsuzhdeniiu kinofilma *Parizhskii sapozhnik*, 24 ianv. 1928." The Association of Revolutionary Cinematography (ARK) became the Association of Workers in Revolutionary Cinematography (ARRK) in September 1928.

33 See Rafes's remarks in TsGALI, f. 2494, op. 1, ed. khr. 213, "Stenogramma zasedaniia rezhisserskoi sektsii ARRK," p. 9.

34 The ARRK and ODSK resolutions used exactly the same words to criticize the "aestheticism" of the film; see D. Donat, *"Parizhskii sapozhnik"*; and "ODSK o *Parizhskom sapozhnike,"* Kino, 1928, no. 7

35 See, e.g. the attacks on Preobrazhenskaia's *Peasant Women of Riazan* recounted below, chapter 9.

36 Khrisanf Khersonskii, "Kino: *Dom v sugrobakh,"* Pravda, 7 April 1928. K. Feldman confirmed Khersonskii's assertion that the film was never released to first-run theatres in *"Dom v sugrobakh,"* Kino, 1928, no. 14.

37 Volkov, "Teatr – muzyka – kino."

38 TsGALI, f. 2494, op. 1, ed. khr. 149, "Stenogramma diskussii po obsuzhdeniiu kinofilma *Dom v sugrobakh*, 6 apr. 1928."

39 Many films were advertised as being based on "true stories," a device which apparently appealed as much to Soviets then as it does to Americans now.

40 Rotha, *The Film Till Now*, p. 249. *The Museum of Modern Art Department of Film Circulating Programs* (New York: MOMA, 1973) says the scene "remains one of the finest examples of associative editing," p. 21.

41 See the discussion of the "war on formalism" in Youngblood, *Soviet Cinema*, pp. 194–214.

42 In *Zhizn iskusstva*, 1929, see Vladimir Nedobrovo, *"Oblomok imperii,"* no. 36, p. 7 and "Kino pod znakom rekonstruktsii," no. 42, pp. 9–10; Adrian Piotrovskii, "Dialekticheskaia forma v kino i front kino-reaktsii," o. 41, p. 3 and Piotrovskii, "Za materialisticheskuiu dialektiku v kino protiv nastupaiushchii kino-reaktsii," no. 47, pp. 2–3; and O. Adamovich, "Glazami bolshevika: Zametki o tvorchestve Fridrikha Ermlera," no. 47, pp. 4–5.

43 Ippolit Sokolov, *"Oblomok imperii,"* Kino, 1929, no. 38, p. 2.

44 N. Osinskii, *"Oblomok imperii,"* Izvestiia, 3 November 1929. See the discussion of Obolenskii in Stites, *Soviet Popular Culture*.

45 B. Alpers, *"Oblomok imperii."* The beginning scenes of *The Fragment* remind me of Dovzhenko's *Arsenal*.

46 Ia. Rudoi, "Nasha kinematografiia i massovoi zritel," *Sovetskii ekran*, 1929, no. 37, p. 17. Similar remarks were made at the Sovkino screening; see "Iz stenogrammy zasedanii pravleniia kinofabriki Sovkino: Diskussiia po povodu kartiny *Oblomok imperii*, 6 avg. 1929," in Sepman, *Ermler*, pp. 114–20.

47 See e.g., "K itogam kinosezona," *Kino i zhizn*, 1930, no. 15; and Sokolov, "Korni formalizma," *Kino*, 1930, no. 17.

48 Ermler, "Kak ia stal rezhisserom," p. 131.

49 For a full account of the troubled production, see Ermler's "Kak ia stal rezhisserom," pp. 127–28 and "Ob *Oblomke imperii*," in Sepman, *Ermler*, pp. 111–12. After Sergei Eisenstein viewed the rushes and criticized the film harshly, the panicked Ermler scrambled to reshoot as much as he could afford to.

50 Nikitin, "Iz vospominaniia kinoaktera." p. 108. Ermler does not refer to this incident in his brief discussions of the production. (A more detailed account appears in Youngblood, "Cinema as Social Criticism.")

51 Nikitin's memoirs are exceptionally frank; see "Iz vospominaniia kinoaktera," pp. 75–111. The Nikitin–Ermler relationship is a central theme in Youngblood, "Cinema as Social Criticism."

52 See the discussion of *Counterplan* in Youngblood, "Cinema as Social Criticism" and a less kindly view in Kenez, *Cinema and Soviet Society*.

53 Mikhail Shneider, "Fridrikh Ermler," *Kino*, 1934, no. 6.

54 My opinion of Ermler's influence does not seem to be shared by Soviet film scholars. Despite the Sepman volume, it appears that he has yet to be "rehabilitated," and the current political climate is not particularly conducive to a sympathetic reevaluation of a "true believer."

9 For workers and peasants only – factory and tractor films

1 P.P. Petrov-Bytov, "We Have No Soviet Cinema," in Taylor and Christie, *Film Factory*, p. 261 (orig. *Zhizn iskusstva*, 21 April 1929). Petrov-Bytov's point of view was confirmed by the "bourgeois specialist" Mikhail Shneider, "Proizvodstvo i shkola," *Kino-front*, 1927, no. 9/10, p. 11.

2 Petrov-Bytov, "We Have No Soviet Cinema," p. 261.

3 An excellent description of proletarian *byt* in Moscow in the twenties can be found in William J. Chase, *Workers, Society and the Soviet State: Labor and Life in Moscow, 1918–1929* (Urbana: University of Illinois Press, 1988).

4 "K sovetskomu realizmu," *Kino-gazeta*, 1924, no. 42, p. 1.

5 N. Gollender, "Rabota tretei Goskino-fabrika," *Kino-zhurnal ARK*, 1925, no. 3, p. 8. Gollender offered a similar prescription for peasants.

6 This has long been a controversial point; if the attendance figures of over 2.1 million in the first six months were real, they may have represented a partly "captive" audience. See Krylov, *Kino vmesto vokdi*, p. 30.

7 TsGALI, f. 2494, op. 1, ed. khr. 50, "Stenogramma diskussii *Bronenosets Potemkin*." In the ARK discussion after the screening, Aleksandr Dubrovskii, who conducted most of ARK's studies of worker audiences and may therefore be considered something of an expert on the subject, concluded that the film was "boring" for workers due to its paucity of "content."

8 Ibid., "6 fev. 1926."

9 A. Dubrovskii, "Rabochaia auditoriia o *Tiazhelykh godakh*," *Kino-zhurnal ARK*, 1926, no. 2.

10 I have not seen this film, but according to *Sovetskie khudozhestvennye filmy* it is extant. Interestingly, Razumnyi's biography in *Kino: Entsiklopedicheskii slovar* does not list *The Difficult Years* in his filmography.

11 *Izuchenie kino-zritelia*, which has been cited often, did include class breakdowns, but Troianovskii and Egiazarov's key generalizations ignored class distinctions.

12 "Kinotvorchestvo i massovoi zritel," *Kino i zritel*, 1930, no. 18. Articles of this sort were quite common during the Cultural Revolution.

13 Leningradskoi oblastnoi komitet VKP (b). *Rezoliutsiia Leningradskogo oblastnoi partsoveshchaniia po voprosam kinematografii (2–3 marta 1928)*, p. 5.

14 Z. A. Edelson and B. M. Filippov, *Profsoiuzy i iskusstva: Sbornik statei s prilozhe-*

niem rezoliutsii pervoi Leningradskoi mezhsoiuznoi konferentsii po voprosam khudo-zhestvennoi raboty (Leningrad: Izd-vo leningradskogo gubprofsoveta, 1927), p. 146.

15 B. Filippov, "Kino i kultrabota," in ibid., pp. 91–93.

16 Ibid., p. 83.

17 Olkhovyi, *Puti kino*, p. 436.

18 B. Levman, *Rabochii zritel i kino: Itogi pervoi rabochii kino-konferentsii* (n.p.: Tea-kinopechat, 1930), p. 43.

19 Ibid., pp. 15–17.

20 Ibid., p. 41.

21 Ibid., pp. 37–38. The "problem" of advertisements was also discussed on pp. 24–25.

22 By then, 89 percent of the clubs had projectors. See Vance Kepley, Jr., "Cinema and Everyday Life: Soviet Worker Clubs of the 1920s," in Robert Sklar and Charles Musser, eds., *Resisting Images: Essays in Cinema and History* (Philadelphia, PA: Temple University Press, 1990), pp. 113–14. This interesting and well-informed article is the first systematic account of exhibition practices in the clubs.

23 Krylov, *Kino vmesto vodki*, pp. 47–48.

24 Of course, the character Parasha would not have been able to interrupt a movie to such great effect (see the discussion of *The House on Trubnaia Square* in chap. 8). Iutkevich's *Lace* also showed club activities, with not a projector in sight.

25 Kepley, "Cinema and Everyday Life," pp. 114–15.

26 B. Filippov, a leader of the union cinefication campaign, did not find these rates so favorable. See Filippov, "Sovkino i profsoiuzy," *Kino-gazeta*, 1925, no. 1 and Filippov, "Profsoiuzy i Sovkino," *Kino*, 1925, no. 7. M. P. Efremov (Sovkino's deputy director) defended the film trust against Filippov's charges by saying that Sovkino was not responsible for setting prices, not by refuting Filippov's allegations of excess profits; see Efremov, "Po povodu stati 'Profsoiuzy i Sovkino,'" *Kino*, 1925, no. 9.

27 Krylov, *Kino vmesto vodki*, pp. 47–48; Kepley, "Cinema and Everyday Life," p. 118.

28 Krylov, *Kino vmesto vodki*, pp. 22, 85.

29 Ibid., pp. 26–27. I believe Krylov's figures are accurate, but I did come across one report which claimed that 60 percent of the films shown at clubs were foreign; see "Klubnoi prokat," *Sovetskii ekran*, 1927, no. 30, p. 3.

30 As Kepley notes, the lectures filled the time while the reels were being changed in a constructive way, but it is hard for a philistine like me to believe that workers appreciated this "rational learning exercise"; see "Cinema and Everyday Life," p. 121. (The inimitable ambiance of the typical club is well portrayed in Barnet's *The House on Trubnaia Square* and to a lesser extent, in Iutkevich's *Lace*.)

31 A. Lvovskii, "Kino v kultrabote profsoiuzov," in Maltsev, *Sovetskoe kino*, pp. 146–52.

32 Ibid.

33 Petrov-Bytov, "We Have No Soviet Cinema," p. 261.

34 I allude here to charges made by Vertov's contemporaries that the degree of shot

manipulation in his pictures was such that they could not be considered non-fiction.

35 Room's *Death Bay* provided a twist on the "divided families" theme of *The Difficult Years*. In Room's film, the father, a ship's mechanic, is the White, while his son is the Red. Happily for the family, however, the father sees the light and goes over to the Reds.

36 Zina's "getting her man" as the be-all and end-all of *The Cigarette Girl* makes this picture a real oddity in Soviet cinema.

37 Although Pudovkin did not advertise it, he had briefly worked with "bourgeois" director Vladimir Gardin before joining Kuleshov. Pudovkin had gotten this job through the efforts of director Olga Preobrazhenskaia, a distant cousin, who co-directed with Gardin. See Budiak and Mikhailov, *Adresa moskovskogo kino*, p. 322.

38 In this he may be seen as the opposite of Ermler, a popular director with one formalist masterpiece to his credit.

39 *Chess Fever* was co-directed by Nikolai Shpikovskii. After seeing Shpikovskii's 1928 satire *A Familiar Face*, which never played the RSFSR in its time (although it has been shown recently), I suspect that *Chess Fever* is in large part Shpikovskii's work.

40 A feminist reading of this film appears in Mayne, *Kino and the Woman Question*, pp. 91–109; another interesting analysis of *Mother* can be found in Richard Taylor, *Film Propaganda: Soviet Russia and Nazi Germany* (New York: Barnes & Noble, 1979), pp. 81–92.

41 See, e.g., Viktor Shklovskii's glowing review, "Pudovkin," *Kino*, 1926, no. 36, p. 1 or Khrisanf Khersonskii, "Borba faktov," *Kino-front*, 1926, no. 9/10, p. 24, and also the minutes of the ARK discussion of the film, TsGALI, f. 2494, op. 1, ed. khr. 32, "Protokoly obshchego sobraniia chlenov, 6 dek. 1926." Fairbanks's remarks are reported in Budiak and Mikhailov, *Adresa moskovskogo kino*, p. 325.

42 Troianovskii and Egiazarov, *Izuchenie kino-zritelia*, p. 31.

43 The word "popular" here is used to refer to *Third Meshchanskaia Street*'s conventional narrative style; Ermler's *The Fragment of the Empire* probably takes the honors in the "formalist film" category.

44 Yuri Tsivian believes the film satirizes the Brik–Maiakovskii–Brik triangle (letter to author, November 1990).

45 See the feminist analysis of this film in Mayne, *Kino and the Woman Question*, pp. 110–29. I think, however, that Mayne has misjudged where Room's sympathy lies; in my opinion, it is clearly with Liuda.

46 See K. Ganzenko, "Sovetskii byt na sovetskom ekrane," *Kino-front*, 1927, no. 1, pp. 9–12 and "*Tretia Meshchanskaia*," ibid., no. 4, p. 21.

47 See, e.g. N. Iakovlev, "Pervosortnaia meshchanskaia," *Kino*, 1927, no. 5, p. 3 and N. Chuzhak, "Slezivaia komediia: *Liubov v troem*," *Zhizn iskusstva*, 1927, no. 13, pp. 5–6.

48 These have to do with the first stages of the campaign to destroy ARK and Sovkino; see the discussion in Youngblood, "Fiction Film."

49 Troianovskii and Egiazarov, *Izuchenie kino-zritelia*, p. 32; Krylov, *Kino vmesto*

vodki, p. 30; Krinitskii, *Zadachi sovetskogo kino*, pp. 17–18. This is obviously a troubling anomaly, which I overlooked in "Fiction Film." Was *Third Meshchanskaia Street* the film people loved to hate?

50 Krylov, *Kino vmesto vodki*, pp. 4–5.

51 If this film, commissioned for the tenth anniversary of the Revolution, disappointed those who expected another realist work from Pudovkin, they did not say so; they simply pretended that it *was* realistic! See, e.g. Mikhail Levidov, "*Konets Sankt-Peterburga*," *Kino*, 1927, no. 47, p. 2. Khrisanf Khersonskii was alone in pointing out that Pudovkin had embarked on a new artistic course; see Khersonskii, "*Konets Sankt-Peterburga*," *Kino-front*, 1928, no. 1, p. 1.

52 The film is not extant, but a detailed review appears in K.M., "Six Russian Films," *Close Up* (October 1928), pp. 22–26. (The reviewer found it difficult to believe that the director of *Bed and Sofa* could have made such a potboiler.) Soviet critic Mikhail Shneider attacked it in a similar fashion; see "*Ukhaby*," *Kino-front*, 1928, no. 1, pp. 19–22.

53 TsGALI, f. 2356, op. 1, ed. khr. 8, report by P. Bauer, "V kino: Byt na ekrane," p. 61.

54 TsGALI, f. 2494, op. 1, ed. khr. 279, "Stenogramma diskussii po obsuzhdeniiu kinofilma *Saba* (1929)."

55 When I saw *Saba* at VGIK, the final reel was missing (although I was not aware of it). It appeared, therefore, the little boy had died, and that there was no resolution of the conflict, which gave the film quite a different message. The finale of the film as given here is drawn from *Saba*'s entry in *Sovetskie khudozhestvennye filmy*, 1: 342 and has been confirmed by Kristin Thompson, who has seen a print with this ending (letter to author, June 1991).

56 See, e.g., Khrisanf Khersonskii, "*Saba* – igrovaia kulturfilma," *Sovetskii ekran*, 1929, no. 7 and Khersonskii, "*Saba*," *Kino*, 1929, no. 39. Khersonskii, who frequently wrote multiple reviews, wielded considerable influence.

57 See, e.g., Khersonskii, "*Kain i Artem*," *Kino*, 1929, no. 49.

58 A. Lunacharskii, "*Kain i Artem*," *Izvestiia*, 20 November 1929.

59 Again, I mention Shaternikova's relationship to Iutkevich only because of the perception in the twenties that the film industry was riddled with such examples of nepotism.

60 For reviews, see, e.g., K. G[anzenko], "O *Kruzhevakh*," *Kino*, 1928, no. 17, and Kh. Khersonskii, "*Kruzheva*," *Sovetskii ekran*, 1928, no. 16, p. 10.

61 See, e.g., Dorothy Atkinson, *The End of the Russian Land Commune, 1905–1930* (Stanford, CA: Stanford University Press, 1983); Robert Conquest, *Harvest of Sorrow: Soviet Collectivization and the Terror-Famine* (New York: Oxford University Press, 1986); Kenez, *Birth of the Propaganda State*. Lynne Viola's *Best Sons of the Fatherland: Workers in the Vanguard of Collectivization* (New York: Oxford University Press, 1987) adopts the point of view of the proletarian "25,000ers," but one can indirectly catch glimpses of peasant mores from her book.

62 "Kino na borbu s alkogologizmom," *Kino*, 1928, no. 42, p. 2.

63 The reports of European "first response" have never been substantiated.

64 Katsigras, "Opyty fiksatsii zritelskikh interesov," in Bursak, *Kino*, p. 51. See also

Katsigras, "Izuchenie derevenskogo kino-zritelia," *Sovetskoe kino*, 1925, no. 2/3, p. 50.
65 Katsigras, "Opyty fiksatsii," p. 50.
66 L. Kosmatov, "Krestianskaia filma," *Kino-gazeta*, 1924, no. 34. Nikolai Iakovlev, however, reported the contrary. See "Kino dlia derevne," *Kino-zhurnal ARK*, 1925, no. 3, pp. 38–39.
67 V.G., "Kak ne sleduet prodavit derevne filmu," *Kino*, 1925, no. 4/5, p. 2, and V. Katkov, "Eshche o derevenskoi kartine," ibid., no. 8, p. 4.
68 S. Deev-Khomiakovskii, "Chto oni khotiat videt," *Kino*, 1927, no. 49, p. 2.
69 *Sovetskii ekran* (9 June 1925), cited in Peter Kenez, "Peasant and Movies," *Historical Journal of Film, Radio, and Television*, forthcoming.
70 Balázs, *Kultura kino*, p. 50.
71 V.K., "Zabytaia tema," *Kino*, 1925, no. 10, p. 2.
72 Ibid., and Boltianskii, "Kino v derevne," pp. 31–47. Boltianskii, who headed Goskino's newsreel division and was himself a documentary filmmaker, saw the countryside as a captive audience for non-fiction films.
73 V.G., "Kak ne sleduet"; M., "Kino v dome krestiane," *Kino*, 1925, no. 1, p. 2; Boltianskii, "Kino v derevne"; B.L., "O filme dlia derevne."
74 Katsigras, *Kino-rabota v derevne*, pp. 46–47.
75 V.G., "Kak ne sleduet"; V. Katkov, "Eshche o derevenskoi kartine"; Nikolai Lebedev, *Kino: Ego kratkaia istoriia, ego vozmozhnosti, ego stroitelstva v sovetskom gosudarstve* (Moscow: Gosudarstvennoe izd-vo, 1924), p. 134.
76 Petrov-Bytov, "We Have No Soviet Cinema," p. 261.
77 M. P. Efremov, "O prokatnoi politike Sovkino," *Kino i kultura*, 1929, no. 4, p. 3; M. Paushkin, "Direktivy Sovnarkoma RSFSR o plane kinofikatsii," *Sovetskii ekran*, 1928, no. 29.
78 A complete bibliography of the polemics on cinefication would be many pages long. See Youngblood, *Soviet Cinema*, *passim*, but esp. pp. 47–55 and 114–17 for details on the politics of the campaign; Kenez, "Peasants and Movies" for a discussion of logistics.
79 Kenez's view of the overall success of the cinefication campaign in "Peasants and Movies" is more positive than mine in *Soviet Cinema*. Additional research on the subject has convinced me that he is right; though dramatic gains were not made until after 1928, growth in the rural network was steady throughout the twenties.
80 Efremov, "O prokatnoi politike," p. 4.
81 Aleksandr Katsigras reported these points as Sovkino-inspired calumnies; see Katsigras, "Kritika uslovii derevenskogo prokata," in Meshcheriakov, *Kino-iazva*, p. 27.
82 Paushkin, "Direktivy Sovnarkoma."
83 A. Katsigras, "Kulturfilma: Organizatsionnye voprosy," *Kino i kultura*, 1929, no. 4, p. 14.
84 1927/28 production year, ibid., p. 17.
85 Katsigras, "Kritika uslovii," pp. 26–27, 29.
86 Ibid., pp. 47, 60. The problem with Katsigras's analysis here is that he forgot to mention ticket prices were only 10–15 kopeks.

87 Stekliannyi glaz, "Obzor pechati," *Sovetskii ekran*, 1929, no. 31, p. 10.
88 M. Veremienko, "Kakie kartiny dalo Sovkino dlia derevni," in Meshcheriakov, *Kino-iazva*, p. 24.
89 TsGALI, f. 645, op. 1, ed. khr. 385, "Glavnoe upravlenie po delam khudo-zhestvennoi literatury i iskusstva," p. 194.
90 "Ocherednye zadachi: Proizvodstvo i kinofikatsiia," *Kino-zhurnal ARK*, 1925, no. 6/7, p. 2.
91 *Sovetskie khudozhestvennye filmy*, 1: 155.
92 Viktor Shklovskii, "O krestianskoi lente," *Kino*, 1926, no. 10, p. 2.
93 M. Ulianova, "Zadachi kino," in Bursak, *Kino*, p. 3. Ulianova was Lenin's sister.
94 TsGALI, f. 2356, op. 1, ed. khr. 46a, O. Preobrazhenskaia, "Avtobiografiia," pp. 1–3.
95 S. Ermolinskii, however, deemed *Kashtanka* unsuitable for children. See his review in *Pravda*, 11 December 1926. Preobrazhenskaia made her last film in 1941, although she continued to draw criticism; by the time she made *Stepan Razin* in 1939, she had become a very different filmmaker.
96 TsGALI, f. 2494, op. 1, ed. khr. 149, "Stenogramma diskussii *Dom v sugro-bakh*," p. 17.
97 TsGALI, F. 2492, op. 1, ed. khr. 77, "Protokoly zasedanii tsentralnogo biuro foto-kino sektsii TsK Rabis, no. 9, 7 apr. 1928," p. 22.
98 TsGALI, f. 2494, op. 1, ed. khr. 94, "Stenogramma diskussii po obsuzhdeniiu kinofilma *Baby riazanskie*, 17–22 noia. 1927." Barshak caustically noted that the film's critics had "absolutely no understanding of the countryside."
99 P. Neznamov, for example, excoriated it as "partyless and inter-class," in Neznamov, "*Baby riazanskie*," *Kino*, 1927, no. 52. It was also attacked in "*Baby riazanskie*," *Sovetskoe kino*, 1927, no. 8/9.
100 As J. T. Heil notes in "Theme and Style," p. 137, n. 2, one of the most unusual features of the Soviet avant-garde in the twenties was that they were "not in opposition to the dominant ideology, but worked to legitimize it, unlike most members of avant-garde movements in the West."
101 See, e.g., Alpers, "*Staroe i novoe*."
102 This film had a very confused press; see, e.g., Ippolit Sokolov, "*Zemlia*," *Kino*, 1930, no. 21, pp. 4–5. More details on the reaction can be found in Young-blood, *Soviet Cinema*, p. 211; an interesting analysis of the film appears in Vance Kepley, *In the Service of the State: The Cinema of Alexander Dovzhenko* (Madison: University of Wisconsin Press, 1986), chap. 6.
103 I have drawn the plot description from *Sovetskie khudozhestvennye filmy*, 1: 298; Allan Wildman, who saw *Tanka* in Helsinki, confirmed its accuracy (conversation, July 1990). I discuss this picture in more detail in "The Fate of Soviet Popular Cinema during the Stalin Revolution," *The Russian Review* 50, no. 2 (April 1991): 156.
104 See, e.g., "Obsuzhdaem *Tanku*," *Kino*, 1929, no. 35 and Ashmarin, "*Tanka – seredniachka*," ibid., no. 37.

Conclusion

1   Iutkevich in S. Dinamov, ed., *Za bolshoe kino-iskusstvo* (Moscow: Kinofotoizdat, 1935), p. 83.

2   See Youngblood, *Soviet Cinema*, pp. 230–32 for a brief discussion. Dinamov, *Za bolshoe kino-iskusstvo*, serves as the public record of the conference; excerpts have been translated in Taylor and Christie, *Film Factory*, pp. 348–55.

3   Trainin may thereby have saved his life; Boris Shumiatskii, the head of Soiuzkino, was shot in 1938.

4   *Kino: Entsiklopedicheskii slovar* says Eggert survived to 1955, though his entry in "Rezhissery sovetskogo khudozhestvennogo kino" gives his date of death as "193?"

5   Mikhail Shneider, who was also persecuted mercilessly during the Cultural Revolution, made a brief appearance in the film press in the thirties before vanishing again.

6   For example, even though Hans Günther recognizes tensions in NEP culture, he sees these as emanating solely from the conflict between folk culture and the avant-garde, ignoring the existence of commercial culture. He writes in his introductory essay to *Culture of the Stalin Period*, p. xix: "the avant-garde type of culture which was imposed by a revolutionary elite coexisted with the deep-rooted mentalities and cultural patterns of the Russian peasants and workers. There existed an enormous gap between the two cultures which remained unbridged during the 1920s." This is true as far as it goes, but perhaps more to the point, the commercial culture of the period, which did attract workers and may have attracted peasants, served "to bridge the gap."

7   And in other aspects of popular culture as well, as Richard Stites convincingly demonstrates in *Soviet Popular Culture*.

8   This challenge is being taken up by Peter Kenez, *Cinema and Soviet Society*, and by Richard Taylor, whose work to date includes: *The Film Factory*, pp. 286–401; "Boris Shumyatsky and the Soviet Cinema in the 1930s: Ideology as Mass Entertainment," *Historical Journal of Film, Radio & Television* 6, no. 1 (1986): 43–64; rpt. Taylor and Christie, *Inside the Film Factory*, pp. 193–216; and an anthology of papers presented at the 1990 Inter-University History Film Consortium Conference on "Soviet Cinema: Continuity and Change," to be published by the Routledge Soviet Cinema series. A good summary of the period appears in François Albèra, "Le cinéma soviétique des années trente aux années quatre-vingt," in E. Etkind *et al.*, eds., *Histoire de la littérature russe XX-ième siècle* (Paris: Fayard, 1990), pp. 641–51.

9   By taking this line of analysis, I do not in any way wish to minimize the implications of the drastic diminution of artistic freedom that occurred at this time, not to mention the death and imprisonment of critics, scenarists, directors, and producers.

10 Maia Turovskaia, "Zritelskie predpochiteniia 30-kh godov," paper delivered to the IREX-Goskino Cinema Commission conference on "Reality and Realism in American and Soviet Cinema in the 1930s," Washington, DC, December 1990.

11 Ibid.; Kenez, *Cinema and Society*, chap. 8.

12 Soviet scholar Ekaterina Khokhlova (Aleksandra Khokhlova's granddaughter) and critic Viacheslav Shmyrov have separate studies under way.

13 See Kenez, *Cinema and Society*, chaps. 6 and 8.

14 This theme is carried through to the present day in Youngblood, "'Americanitis': The *Amerikanshchina* in Soviet Cinema," *Journal of Popular Film & Television* 19, no. 4 (Winter 1992).

15 See the fascinating discussion of the production history of this film in Kepley, *In the Service of the State*, chap. 9.

16 Batalov died in 1937, apparently from tuberculosis.

17 Nonetheless, Barnet and Ermler made far fewer films than directors like Gerasimov or Aleksandrov. Since both had serious health problems (Barnet was an alcoholic and Ermler had a heart condition), it is difficult to determine the reasons for their declining rate of production.

18 With Dovzhenko, of course, this has been done, in Kepley's *In the Service of the State*.

19 Christopher Read, *Culture and Power in Revolutionary Russia: The Intelligentsia and the Transition from Tsarism to Communism* (New York: St. Martin's, 1990), pp. 142, 232. Mally makes a similar point in *Culture of the Future*, but she does not go so far as to claim that the fate of the Proletkult is paradigmatic.

20 See Fitzpatrick, *Cultural Revolution in Russia* and the forum on Stalinism in *Russian Review* 45, no. 4 (October 1986): 357–414, in which Fitzpatrick, Kenez, Stephen F. Cohen, Geoff Eley, and Alfred G. Meyer participated.

21 Bruce Murray discusses this question with reference to Weimar cinema in *Film and the German Left*, introduction; Steven Ross with reference to American cinema in "Struggles for the Screen: Workers, Radicals, and the Political Uses of Silent Film," *American Historical Review* 96, no. 2 (April 1991): 333–67.

22 See Vera Dunham, *In Stalin's Time: Middle Class Values in Soviet Fiction* (Cambridge: Cambridge University Press, 1976) and Sheila Fitzpatrick, "Middle Class Values and Soviet Life in the 1930s," in Terry L. Thompson and Richard Sheldon, eds., *Soviet Society and Culture: Essays in Honor of Vera S. Dunham* (Boulder, CO: Westview Press, 1988).

23 This book was already in press when the USSR was in its death throes.

FILMOGRAPHY

Russian and Soviet titles cited in the text

(Translated title, Russian title, director,
year of production/year of release [if different], studio)

Abrek Zaur [Abrek Zaur]. Boris Mikhen, 1926, Goskino

Aelita [Aelita]. Iakov Protazanov, 1924, Mezhrabpom-Rus

Aleksandr Nevskii [Aleksandr Nevskii]. Sergei Eizenshtein, 1938, Mosfilm

Alone [Odna]. Grigorii Kozintsev and Leonid Trauberg, 1931, Soiuzkino

The American Girl from Baghdad [Amerikanka iz bagdada]. Nikolai Klado, 1931, Uzbekgoskino

Andrei Kozhukhov [Andrei Kozhukhov]. Iakov Protazanov, 1917, Ermolev

Arsen Dzhordzhiashveli [Arsen Dzhordzhiashveli]. Ivan Perestiani, 1921/1922, Kinosektsiia Narkompros Gruzii

Arsenal [Arsenal]. Aleksandr Dovzhenko, 1929, VUFKU

Battleship Potemkin see *Potemkin*

The Bear's Wedding [Medvezhia svadba]. Konstantin Eggert, 1925/26, Mezhrabpom-Rus

Bed and Sofa, see *Third Meshchanskaia Street*

Borderlands, see *Outskirts*

By the Law [Po zakonu]. Lev Kuleshov, 1926, Goskino

Cain and Artem [Kain i Artem]. Pavel Petrov-Bytov, 1929, Sovkino

The Captain's Daughter [Kapitanskaia dochka]. Iurii Tarich, 1928, Sovkino

The Case of the Three Million [Protsess o trekh millionakh]. Iakov Protazanov, 1926, Mezhrabpom-Rus

Chapaev [Chapaev]. Georgii Vasilev and Sergei Vasilev, 1934, Lenfilm

Chess Fever [Shakhmatnaia goriachka]. Vsevolod Pudovkin and Nikolai Shpikovskii, 1925, Mezhrabpom-Rus

Children of the Storm [Deti buri]. Fridrikh Ermler and Eduard Ioganson, 1926/27, Leningradkino

The Cigarette Girl from Mosselprom [Papirosnitsa ot Mosselproma]. Iurii Zheliabuzhskii, 1924, Mezhrabpom-Rus

The Circus [Tsirk]. Grigorii Aleksandrov, 1936, Mosfilm

The Collegiate Registrar [Kollezhskii registrator]. Iurii Zheliabuzhskii and Ivan Moskvin, 1925, Mezhrabpom-Rus

Columbus Discovers America [Kolumb zakryvaet Ameriku]. B. Fedorov, 1931/32, Soiuzkino

Commander Ivanov [Kombrig Ivanov]. Aleksandr Razumnyi, 1923, Proletkino

Convict's Song [Pesn katorzhanina]. Iakov Protazanov, 1911, Thiemann and Reinhardt

Counterplan [Vstrechnyi]. Fridrikh Ermler and Sergei Iutkevich, 1932, Rosfilm

Cross and Mauser [Krest i mauzer]. Vladimir Gardin, 1925, Goskino

A Cup of Tea [Chashka chaia]. Nikolai Shpikovskii, 1927, Sovkino

Death Bay [Bukhta smerti]. Abram Room, 1926, Goskino

The Decembrists [Dekabristy]. Aleksandr Ivanovskii, 1926/27, Leningradkino

The Devil's Wheel [Chortovo koleso]. Grigorii Kozintsev and Leonid Trauberg, 1926, Leningradkino

The Difficult Years [Tiazhelye gody]. Aleksandr Razumnyi, 1925, Goskino

Don Diego and Pelageia [Don Diego i Pelageia]. Iakov Protazanov, 1927/28, Mezhrabpom-Rus

Earth [Zemlia]. Aleksandr Dovzhenko, 1930, VUFKU

The End of St. Petersburg [Konets Sankt-Peterburga]. Vsevolod Pudovkin, 1927, Mezhrabpom-Rus

Evdokiia Rozhnovskaia [Evdokiia Rozhnovskaia]. Sergei Mitrich, 1924, Goskino

The Extraordinary Adventures of Mr. West in the Land of the Bolsheviks [Neobychainye prikliucheniia mistera Vesta v strane bolshevikov]. Lev Kuleshov, 1924, Goskino

The Eyes of Andoziia [Glaza Andozii]. Dmitrii Bassalygo, 1926, Proletkino

The Fall, see *The Ice Breaks*

Father [Otets]. Leonid Molchanov, 1926, Goskino

Father Sergius [Otets Sergii]. Iakov Protazanov, 1917, Ermolev

The Female Muslim [Musulmanka]. Dmitrii Bassalygo, 1925, Proletkino and Bukhkino

The Forty-First [Sorok pervyi]. Iakov Protazanov, 1926/27, Mezhrabpom-Rus

Forward, Soviet! [Shagai Sovet!]. Dziga Vertov, 1926, Goskino

The Fragment of the Empire [Oblomok imperii]. Fridrikh Ermler, 1929, Sovkino

The Ghost That Does Not Return [Privedenie kotoroe ne vozrashchaetsia]. Abram Room, 1929/30, Sovkino

The Girl with the Hatbox [Devushka s korobkoi]. Boris Barnet, 1927, Mezhrabpom-Rus

Grandfather Knysh's Gang [Banda batki Knysha]. Aleksandr Razumnyi, 1924, Goskino

The Great Citizen [Velikii grazhdanin]. 2 pts. Fridrikh Ermler, 1938 & 1939, Lenfilm

The Great Consoler [Velikii uteshitel]. Lev Kuleshov, 1933, Mezhrabpomfilm

The Happy Guys [Veselye rebiata]. Grigorii Aleksandrov, 1934, Moskinokombinat

The Harem from Bukhara, see *The Minaret of Death*

His Call [Ego prizyv]. Iakov Protazanov, 1925, Mezhrabpom-Rus

Honor [Namus]. Amo Bek-Nazarov, 1926, Goskinprom Gruzii

The Horseman from the Wild West [Naezdnik iz uailda vesta]. Aleksandr Tsutsunava, 1925, Goskinprom Gruzii

The House in the Snowdrifts [Dom v sugrobakh]. Fridrikh Ermler, 1927/28, Sovkino
The House on Trubnaia Square [Dom na Trubnoi]. Boris Barnet, 1927/28, Mezhrabpom-Rus
The Ice Breaks [Ledolom]. Boris Barnet, 1931, Mezhrabpomfilm
The Ice House [Ledianoi dom]. Konstantin Eggert, 1928, Mezhrabpom-Rus
Jimmy Higgins [Dzhimmi Khiggins]. Georgii Tasin, 1928, VUFKU
Jolly Fellows, see *The Happy Guys*
Katka the Apple Seller [Katka bumazhnyi ranet]. Fridrikh Ermler and Eduard Ioganson, 1926, Sovkino
Katka's Reinette Apples, see *Katka the Apple Seller*
Kashtanka [Kashtanka]. Olga Preobrazhenskaia, 1926, Sovkino
The Keys to Happiness [Kliuchi schastia]. Iakov Protazanov and Vladimir Gardin, 1913, Thiemann and Reinhardt
Komsomolsk [Komsomolsk]. Sergei Gerasimov, 1938, Lenfilm
Lace [Kruzheva]. Sergei Iutkevich, 1928, Sovkino
The Lady Peasant [Baryshnia krestianka]. Olga Preobrazhenskaia, 1916, Vengerov and Gardin
Little Red Devils [Krasnye diavoliata]. Ivan Perestiani, 1923, Kinosektsiia Narkomprosa Gruzii
The Living Corpse [Zhivoi trup]. Fedor Otsep, 1929, Mezhrabpomfilm and Prometheusfilm
Locksmith and Chancellor [Slesar i kantsler]. Vladimir Gardin, 1923, VUFKU
The Man with a Gun [Chelovek s ruzhem]. Sergei Iutkevich, 1938, Lenfilm
The Man with the Movie Camera [Chelovek s kinoapparatom]. Dziga Vertov, 1928/29, VUFKU
The Man from the Restaurant [Chelovek iz restorana]. Iakov Protazanov, 1927, Mezhrabpom-Rus
The Mark of Zorro in the Village [Znak Zorro na sele]. Boris Lagunov and Boris Nikiforov, 1927, Trudkino
Mary Pickford's Kiss [Potselui Meri Pikford]. Sergei Komarov, 1927, Mezhrabpom-Rus and Sovkino
Machinist Ukhtomskii [Mashinist Ukhtomskii]. Aleksei Dmitriev, 1926, Krasnaia zvezda (PUR)
The Mechanics of the Brain [Mekhanika golovnogo mozga]. Vsevolod Pudovkin, 1926, Mezhrabpom-Rus
Minaret of Death [Minaret smerti]. Viacheslav Viskovskii, 1925, Sevzapkino and Bukhkino
Minin and Pozharskii [Minin i Pozharskii]. Vsevolod Pudovkin, 1939, Mosfilm
The Miracle Worker [Chudotvorets]. Aleksandr Panteleev, 1922, Sevzapkino
Miss Katie and Mr. Jack [Miss Keti i mister Dzhek]. A. Durov, 1927, Goskinprom Gruzii
Miss Mend [Miss Mend]. Three parts. Fedor Otsep and Boris Barnet, 1926, Mezhrabpom-Rus
Mother [Mat]. Aleksandr Razumnyi, 1919/20, Moskovskii kinokomitet
Mother [Mat]. Vsevolod Pudovkin, 1926, Mezhrabpom-Rus

Moscow in October [Moskva v Oktiabre]. Boris Barnet, 1927, Mezhrabpom-Rus
Mr. Lloyd's Voyage [Reis mistera Loida]. Dmitrii Bassalygo, 1927, Sovkino
New Babylon [Novyi vavilon]. Grigorii Kozintsev and Leonid Trauberg, 1929, Sovkino
The Ninth of January [Deviatoe ianvaria]. Viacheslav Viskovskii, 1925, Sevzapkino
October [Oktiabr]. Sergei Eizenshtein and Grigorii Aleksandrov, 1927/28, Sovkino
The Old and the New [Staroe i novoe]. Sergei Eizenshtein and Grigorii Aleksandrov, 1929, Sovkino
On Life and Death [Na zhizn i na smert]. Boris Chaikovskii and Pavel Petrov-Bytov, 1925, Sevzapkino
One of Many [Odin iz mnogikh]. Nikolai Khodataev, 1927, Mezhrabpom-Rus
One-Sixth of the World [Shestaia chast mira]. Dziga Vertov, 1926, Goskino
Outskirts [Okraina]. Boris Barnet, 1933, Mezhrabpomfilm
Overcrowding [Uplotnenie]. Aleksandr Panteleev, 1918, Petrogradskii kinokomitet
The Palace and the Fortress [Dvorets i krepost]. Aleksandr Ivanovskii, 1923/24, Sevzapkino
The Parisian Cobbler [Parizhskii sapozhnik]. Fridrikh Ermler, 1927/28, Sovkino
Peasant Women of Riazan [Baby riazanskie]. Olga Preobrazhenskaia and Ivan Pravov, 1927, Sovkino
Peasants [Krestiane]. Fridrikh Ermler, 1934, Lenfilm
Pilots [Letchiki]. Iulii Raizman, 1935, Mosfilm
The Poet and the Tsar [Poet i tsar]. Vladimir Gardin, 1927, Sovkino
Poison [Iad]. Evgenii Ivanov-Barkov, 1927, Sovkino
Polikushka [Polikushka]. Aleksandr Sanin, 1918/19, Rus
Potemkin [Bronenosets Potemkin]. Sergei Eizenshtein, 1925/26, Goskino
Potholes [Ukhaby]. Abram Room, 1927/28, Sovkino
The Prostitute [Prostitutka]. Oleg Freilikh, 1926/27, Belgoskino
The Queen of Spades [Pikovaia dama]. Iakov Protazanov, 1916, Ermolev
Ranks and People [Chiny i liudi]. Iakov Protazanov, 1929, Mezhrabpomfilm
Red Imps, see *Little Red Devils*
Red Partisans [Krasnye partizany]. Viacheslav Viskovskii, 1924, Sevzapkino
The Return of Maksim [Vozrashchenie Maksima]. Grigorii Kozintsev and Leonid Trauberg, 1937, Lenfilm
The Rich Bride [Bogataia nevesta]. Ivan Pyrev, Ukrainfilm, 1938
The Right to Life [Pravo na zhizn]. Pavel Petrov-Bytov, 1928, Sovkino
The Road to Damascus [Put v Damask]. Lev Sheffer, 1927, Sovkino
The Road to Life, see *A Start in Life*
Saba [Saba]. Mikhail Chiaureli, 1929, Goskinprom Gruzii
The Salamander [Salamandra]. Grigorii Roshal, 1928, Mezhrabpomfilm and Prometheusfilm
Satan Triumphant [Satana likuiushchii]. 2 pts. Iakov Protazanov, 1917, Ermolev
Scarlet Fever [Skarlatina]. Fridrikh Ermler, 1924, Sevzapkino
A Severe Youth, see *A Strict Young Man*
Shchors [Shchors]. Aleksandr Dovzhenko, 1939, Kiev
The Shining Path [*Svetlyi put*]. Grigorii Aleksandrov, 1940, Mosfilm

The Skotinins [Gospoda Skotininy]. Grigorii Roshal, 1926/27, Sovkino

The Sold Appetite [Prodannyi appetit]. Nikolai Okhlopkov, 1928, VUFKU

St. Jorgen's Feast Day [Prazdnik sviatogo Iorgena]. Iakov Protazanov, 1930, Mezhrab-pomfilm

The Station Master, see *The Collegiate Registrar*

A Start in Life [Putevka v zhizn]. Nikolai Ekk, 1931, Mezhrabpomfilm

Stepan Razin [Stepan Razin]. Olga Preobrazhenskaia and Ivan Pravov, 1938, Mosfilm

Stepan Khalturin [Stepan Khalturin]. Aleksandr Ivanovskii, 1925, Sevzapkino

A Strict Young Man [Strogii iunosha]. Abram Room, 1936/never released, Ukrainfilm

Strike [Stachka]. Sergei Eizenshtein, 1924/25, Goskino and Proletkult

The Struggle for the Ultimatum. [Borba za ultimatum]. Dmitrii Bassalygo, 1923, Proletkino

The Suram Fortress [Suramskaia krepost]. Ivan Perestiani, 1922/23, Kinosektsiia Narkomprosa Gruzii

Suvorov [Suvorov]. Vsevolod Pudovkin, 1941, Mosfilm

The Tailor from Torzhok [Zakroishchik iz Torzhka]. Iakov Protazanov, 1925, Mezhrabpom-Rus

Tanka the Bar Girl [Tanka traktirshchitsa]. Boris Svetozarov, 1928/29, Sovkino

Tea [Chai]. Viacheslav Viskovskii, 1924, Sevzapkino

A Thief, but Not from Baghdad [Vor, no ne bagdadskii]. Vladimir Feinberg, 1926, Goskino

Third Meshchanskaia Street [Tretia Meshchanskaia]. Abram Room, 1927, Sovkino

Three Lives [Tri zhizni]. Ivan Perestiani, 1924/25, Goskinprom Gruzii

The Three Millions Trial, see *The Case of the Three Million*

Tip Top in Moscow [Tip Top v Moskve]. Aleksandr Ivanov, 1928, Sovkino

Tommy [Tommi]. Iakov Protazanov, 1931, Mezhrabpomfilm

Tractor Drivers [Traktoristy]. Ivan Pyrev, 1939, Mosfilm

The Tripole Tragedy [Tripolskaia tragediia]. Aleksandr Anoshchenko, 1926, VUFKU

Two Days [Dva dnia]. Georgii Stabovoi, 1927, VUFKU

Valerii Chkalov [Valerii Chkalov]. Mikhail Kalatozov, 1941, Lenfilm

Vasilii Griaznov [Vasilii Griaznov]. 1924 (obscure)

Volga Volga [Volga Volga]. Grigorii Aleksandrov, 1938, Mosfilm

The Vyborg Side [Vyborgskaia storona]. Grigorii Kozintsev and Leonid Trauberg, 1939, Lenfilm

The Wandering Stars [Bluzhdaiushchie zvezdy]. Grigorii Gricher-Cherikover, 1926/27, VUFKU

War and Peace [Voina i mir]. Vladimir Gardin and Iakov Protazanov, 1915, Thiemann and Reinhardt

We Don't Need Blood [Ne nado krovi]. Iakov Protazanov, 1917, Ermolev

The Whirlpool [Vodovorot]. Pavel Petrov-Bytov, 1927, Sovkino

The White Eagle [Belyi orel]. Iakov Protazanov, 1928, Mezhrabpomfilm

Wind [Veter]. Lev Sheffer and Cheslav Sabinskii, 1926, Sovkino

The Wings of a Serf [Krylia kholopa]. Iurii Tarich, 1926, Sovkino

Without a Dowry [Bespridannitsa]. Iakov Protazanov, 1937, Mezhrabpomfilm

The Youth of Maksim [Iunost Maksima]. Grigorii Kozintsev and Leonid Trauberg, 1935, Lenfilm

Foreign titles cited in the text

(Original title, Russian title, director,
year of production/year of release in the USSR, producer)

Bella Donna [Bella Donna]. George Fitzmaurice, 1923/1926, Famous Players Laskey

Das Kabinett des Dr. Caligari [Kabinet d-ra Kaligari]. Robert Wiene, 1919/1920, Decla-Bioscope

Don Q – Son of Zorro [Chelovek s krutom]. Donald Crisp, 1925/unknown, Elton

Dr. Caligari's Cabinet, see *Das Kabinett des Dr. Caligari*

The King of the Circus [Geroi areny]. G. P. MacGowan, 1920, Universal

The Last Laugh, see *Der letzte Mann*

Der letzte Mann [Chelovek i livreia]. F. W. Murnau, 1924/1927, UFA

The Love Light [Svet vo teme]. Frances Marion, 1921/1926, United Artists

Lucretia Borgia [Lukretsia Bordzhia]. Richard Oswald, 1922/1923, Richard Oswald-film

The Mark of Zorro [Znak Zorro]. Fred Niblo, 1920/1925, Elton

Robin Hood [Robin Gud]. Allan Dwan, 1923/1925, Elton

Rosita [Rozita]. Ernst Lubitsch, 1923/1926, United Artists

Society Scandal [Skandal v obshchestve]. Allan Dwan, 1924/1926, Famous Players Laskey

The Sea Hawk [Morskoi iastreb]. Frank Lloyd, 1924/1926, First National

The Son of Zorro, see *Don Q – Son of Zorro*

Speed [Spid]. George Seitz, 1922/1927, Pathé

The Thief of Baghdad [Bagdadskii vor]. Raoul Walsh, 1924/1925, United Artists

A Woman of Paris [Parizhanka]. Charles Chaplin, 1923/1925, United Artists

BIBLIOGRAPHY

Primary Sources

A.S. "*Salamandra.*" *Izvestiia*, 19 December 1928

A.V. "*Prazdnik sviatogo Iorgena.*" *Kino*, 1930, no. 51

A.Zh. "Obshchestvennyi sud na tipazhem." *Kino*, 1928, no. 31

Abrosimov, A. "O prodvizhenii kino v derevnii." *Sovetskoe kino*, 1925, no. 1

Adamovich, O. "Glazami bolshevika: Zametki o tvorchestve Fridrikha Ermler." *Zhizn iskusstva*, 1929, no. 47

Aelita: Kino-lenta na temu romana A. N. Tolstogo. n.p.: [1924]

"Akter ili tipazh." *Kino*, 1928, no. 26

Aleinikov, M. N., ed. *Iakov Protazanov: O tvorcheskom puti rezhissera*, 2nd edn. rev. Moscow: Iskusstvo, 1957

Alpers, B. "*Arsenal* Dovzhenko." *Sovetskii ekran*, 1929, no. 16

"*Staroe i novoe.*" *Sovetskii ekran*, 1929, no. 40

"*Oblomok imperii.*" *Izvestiia*, 3 November 1929

"*Prazdnik sviatogo Iorgena.*" *Kino i zhizn*, 1930, no. 25

Aravskii, A. "*Don Diego i Pelageia.*" *Kino-front*, 1928, no. 2

Arden, V. "Kino khudozhnik na zapade i v SSSR." *Kinozhurnal ARK*, 1926, no. 2

Ardov, V. "Chudesa kino: Uplotnennyi seans." *Kino*, 1925, no. 4/5

Arnoldi, Edgar. *Komicheskoe v kino.* Moscow: Kinopechat, 1928.

Avantiurnyi zhanr v kino. Leningrad: Teakinopechat, 1929

Arossev, A. *Soviet Cinema.* Moscow: n.p., 1935

Arsen. "*Dekabristy.*" *Kino-front*, 1927, no. 5

"*Sorok pervyi.*" *Kino-front*, 1927, no. 6

Arustanov, G. "O politike bez (osobennogo) iskusstva: Otvet tov. Traininu. *Kino*, 1925, no. 6

"Rentabelnost." *Sovetskoe kino*, 1927, no. 8/9

Arvatov, B. "Agit-kino." *Kino-fot*, 1922, no. 2

Ashmarin [n.f.n.]. "*Tanka* – seredniachka." *Kino*, 1929, no. 37

As-ov, St. "Pobeda kino." *Izvestiia*, 20 February 1923

Averbakh, L. "Eshche o reshitelnom." *Kino*, 1928, no. 45

B.L. "O filme dlia derevni." *Kino*, 1925, no. 13

B.S. "Sud na Garri Pilem." *Pravda*, 16 June 1927

B.T. "Plach o smekhe." *Sovetskii ekran*, 1929, no. 3

Babenchikov, M. "Kino-geroi-byt." *Sovetskii ekran*, 1929, no. 39
"*Baby riazanskie.*" *Sovetskoe kino*, 1927, no. 8/9
Bakun, Vera. "Neskolko slov o lichnom." In Sepman, *Ermler*
Balázs, Béla. *Kultura kino.* Leningrad: Gosizdat, 1925
Barnet, Boris. "Au seuil de la comédie soviétique." In Albèra and Cosandey, *Boris Barnet*
"La jeune fille au carton à chapeau." In ibid.
"Moscou en Octobre." In ibid.
Benjamin, Walter. *Moscow Diary.* Ed. Gary Smith. Trans. Richard Sieburth. Cambridge, MA: Harvard University Press, 1986
Berestinskii, Mikhail. "Chto skazali o Sovkino na dispute v TsDRI." *Kino*, 1927, no. 43
Beskin, Osip. "Mesto kino." *Sovetskoe kino*, 1926, no. 1
"Neigrovaia filma." *Sovetskoe kino*, 1927, no. 7
"Nekotorye cherty iz zhizni Sovkino." *Sovetskoe kino*, 1928, no. 1
"Bez otveta." *Kino*, 1926, no. 9
Bleiman, Mikhail. *O kino: Svidetelskie pokazaniia (1924–1971).* Moscow: Iskusstvo, 1973
"*Deti buri.*" In ibid.
"Neskolko zagadok." In Sepman, *Ermler*
Bliakhin, P. A. "Politika Sovkino." In Olkhovyi, *Vokrug Sovkino*
"K itogam kino-sezona 1927–28 goda." *Kino i kultura*, 1929, no. 2
Bodrov, N. "Nashi kino-nekhvati." *Kino-zhurnal ARK*, 1926, no. 1
"Litso opportunistov." *Kino*, 1930, no. 54
Boitler, Mikhail. *Reklama i kino-reklama.* Moscow: Kinopechat, 1926
Kino-teatr: Organizatsiia i upravlenie. Moscow: Kinopechat, 1926
"Bolnoe mesto v kino." *Kino-front*, 1927, no. 5
Boltianskii, Grigorii. "Kino v derevne." In Bursak, *Kino*
"Provintsialnyi kino-byt." *Kino-nedelia*, 1924, no. 34
"Teatr kulturfilmy." *Sovetskoe kino*, 1926, no. 1
"Kino-kadry i ODSK." *Kino i zhizn*, 1930, no. 8
Brik, O. M. "Kartiny kotorye nam ne pokazyvaiut." *Sovetskoe kino*, 1926, no. 2
"Kommercheskii raschet." *Kino*, 1926, no. 34
"Kino v teatre Meierkholda." *Sovetskii ekran*, 1926, no. 20
"Na podstupakh v sovetskoi komedii." *Kino-front*, 1927, no. 4
Bugoslavskii, S. and V. Messman. *Muzyka v kino.* Moscow: Kinopechat, 1926
Bursak, I. N., ed. *Kino.* Moscow: Proletkino, 1925
Bystritskii [n.f.n]. "*Znak Zorro.*" *Kino*, 1925, no. 23
Bystritskii, M. "S tochki zreniia teorii." *Kino*, 1927, no. 2
"Besprizornaia (Po povodu *Potselui Meri*)." *Kino*, 1927, no. 38
"Shag vpered (*Don Diego i Pelageia*)." *Kino*, 1928, no. 3
Carter, Huntly. *The New Theatre and Cinema of Soviet Russia.* New York: International Publishers, 1925
The New Spirit in the Russian Theatre, 1917–28. London: Brentano's, 1929
Charli. [untitled]. *Kino-zhizn*, 1922, no. 2

Cherkasov, A. "Masterstvo artista v kino." *Kino-front*, 1927, no. 5

"Chistka apparata Teakinopechat." *Kino*, 1930, no. 2

"Chto govoriat ob *Aelite*." *Kino-nedelia*, 1924, no. 37

Chuzhak, N. "Slezivaia komediia: *Liubov v troem*." *Zhizn iskusstva*, 1927, no. 13

Chvialev, Evgenii. *Sovetskie filmy za granitsei: Tri goda za rubezhom*. [Leningrad]: Teakinopechat, 1929

Dashevskii, G. "Amerikanskaia kinopromyshlennost v borbe za mirovuiu gegemoniiu." *Kino-front*, 1927, no. 5

"Davno pora." *Kino*, 1928, no. 20

Davydov, I. "Order na zhizn." *Sovetskoe kino*, 1928, no. 1

Deev-Khomiakovskii, S. "Chto oni khotiat videt." *Kino*, 1927, no. 49

"Deiatelnost teatrov Goskino." *Kino-gazeta*, 1925, no. 4

Deiatelnost Vserossiiskogo foto-kinematograficheskogo aktsionnernogo o-va sovetskogo kino Sovkino s 1-go marta 1925 po 1-oe oktiabria 1927. Moscow: Sovkino, 1928

"*Dekabristy*." *Kino*, 1927, no. 3

Denisov, K. "O stsenariakh." *Kino-front*, 1927, no. 4

Dinamov, S., ed. *Za bolshoe kino-iskusstvo*. Moscow: Kinofotoizdat, 1935

"Doloi!" *Sovetskii ekran*, 1928, no. 26

"*Dom na Trubnoi*." *Kino*, 1928, no. 38

Donat, D. "*Parizhskii sapozhnik*." *Kino*, 1928, no. 7

Dubrovskii, Aleksandr. "*Pokhozdeniia Oktiabriny*." *Kino-zhurnal ARK*, 1925, no. 3

"Opyty izucheniia zritelia: Anketa ARK," *Kino-zhurnal ARK*, 1925, no. 4/5

"Rabochaia auditoriia o *Tiazhelykh godakh*." *Kino-zhurnal ARK*, 1926, no. 2

"Atele i natura." *Sovetskii ekran*, 1926, no. 27

"Soviet Cinema in Danger." In Taylor and Christie, *Film Factory*

Dvoretskii, A. "*Abrek Zaur* i prochee." *Sovetskii ekran*, 1926, no. 5

Edelson, Z. A. and Filippov, B. M. *Profsoiuzy i iskusstva: Sbornik statei s prilozheniem rezoliutsii pervoi Leningradskoi mezhsoiuznoi konferentsii po voprosam khudozhestvennoi raboty*. Leningrad: Izd-vo leningradskogo gubprofsoveta, 1927

Editorial. *Kino-fot*, 1922, no. 4

Efremov, M. P. "Po povodu stati 'Profsoiuzy i Sovkino.'" *Kino* 1925, no. 9

"Nashi sredstva i zadachi." *Kino*, 1927, no. 47

"O prokatnoi politike Sovkino." *Kino i kultura*, 1929, no. 4

Egorova, N. "Nemetskie nemye filmy v sovetskom prokate." *Kino i vremia*, vol. IV (1965)

Eisenstein, Sergei, *see* Eizenshtein, Sergei

Eizenshtein, Sergei. "Za rabochii boevik." *Revoliutsiia i kultura*, 1928, no. 3/4

Selected Works, vol. I: *Writings: 1922–1934*. Ed. and trans. Richard Taylor. Bloomington: Indiana University Press, 1988

Ermler, Fridrikh. "Kadr i akter." *Kino*, 1927, no. 9

"Kak ia stal rezhisserom." *Iskusstvo kino*, 1969, no. 7

"Avtobiograficheskii zametki." In Sepman, *Ermler*

"Ob *Oblomke imperii*." In ibid.

Ermolinskii, S. "*Kashtanka*." *Pravda*, 11 December 1926

"*Devushka s korobkoi.*" *Pravda,* 11 May 1927
"*Iad.*" *Pravda,* 6 September 1927
"*Potselui Meri.*" *Pravda,* 6 September 1927
"Kino v oktiabre." *Pravda,* 9 November 1927
Erofeev, Vladimir. "Pervyi ekran: *Kombrig Ivanov.*" *Kino-gazeta,* 1923, no. 8
"Dovolno portit kartiny." *Kino-gazeta,* 1924, no. 49
"*Dvorets i krepost* v Berline." *Kino,* 1925, no. 9
"Eshche odna seriia sniatykh kartin." *Kino,* 1928, no. 21
F.A. "Kak delalsia stsenarii *Iada* (Iz nashego obsledovaniia)." *Kino,* 1927, no. 37
Falbert, I. "Zolotaia seriia (*Medvezhia svadba*)." *Kino,* 1926, no. 6
Feldman, K. "*Dom v sugrobakh.*" *Kino,* 1928, no. 14
"Na putiakh k sovetskoi komedii." *Kino,* 1928, no. 40
"Chto na ekrane." *Sovetskii ekran,* 1928, no. 6
"Itogi goda Mezhrabpom-filma." *Sovetskii ekran,* 1928, no. 42
"A propos d'un film réussi *La débâcle* et d'une critique ratée." In Albèra and
    Cosandey, *Boris Barnet*
"Ferbenks i Pikford v SSSR!" *Kino,* 1926, no. 30
Fevralskii, A. "Shest vostochnykh kartin." *Pravda,* 21 May 1926
Filippov, B. "Sovkino i profsoiuzy." *Kino-gazeta,* 1925, no. 1
"Profsoiuzy i Sovkino." *Kino,* 1925, no. 7
"Kino i kultrabota." In Edelson and Filippov, *Profsoiuzy i iskusstva*
"Filmy priemye dlia rabochikh klubov." *Kino-zhurnal ARK,* 1925, no. 2
Forestier, Louis. *Velikii nemoi (Vospominaniia kinooperatora).* Moscow:
    Goskinoizdat, 1945
G.B. "Armiia sovetskogo kino." *Sovetskii ekran,* 1928, no. 46.
G.D. "My zagranitse, zagranitse nam (Beseda s zaveduiushchim eksportno-import-
    nym otdelom K. I. Feldmanom)." *Kino,* 1925, no. 3
"Zhizn kino-rabotnikov: Beseda s zavnospredrabisom V.I. Pokrovskim." *Kino,*
    1925, no. 10
G.R. "*Mashinist Ukhtomskii.*" *Izvestiia,* 28 April 1926
Galitskii, Ia. "Protazanov." *Sovetskii ekran,* 1927, no. 49
Ganzenko, K. "Obshchestvo druzei sovetskogo kino." *Sovetskoe kino,* 1925, no. 6
"Zabyvaemye zakony." *Sovetskii ekran,* 1925, no. 14
"Sovetskii byt na sovetskom ekrane." *Kino-front,* 1927, no. 1
"*Tretia Meshchanskaia.*" *Kino-front,* 1927, no. 4
"O *Kruzhevakh.*" *Kino,* 1928, no. 17
Gavriushin, K. *Ia khochu rabotat v kino: Posobie pri vybore professii.* Moscow: Kino-
    izdatelstvo RSFSR, 1925
Geiman, Viktor. "Protiv prikazchikov burzhuaznogo iskusstva, za izuchenie tvor-
    cheskikh metodov sovetskogo kino." *Kino* 1930, no. 48
Gekht, S. "Kino-parad." *Sovetskii ekran,* 1926, no. 30
Gelmont, A. M., ed. *Kino, deti, shkola: Metodicheskii sbornik.* Moscow: Rabotnik
    prosveshcheniia, 1929
German, A. "*Tripolskaia tragediia.*" *Kino,* 1926, no. 15
Gessen, Daniil. "Dovolno?" *Kino-nedelia,* 1924, no. 14

Ginzburg, Eugenia Semyonovna. *Journey into the Whirlwind.* Trans. Paul Stevenson and Max Hayward. New York: Harcourt Brace Jovanovich, 1967
Goldman, A. *U poroga kino-proizvodstva: Zametki o kino-aktere.* Leningrad: Teakinopechat, 1929
Goldobin, A. V. "Blizhiishie zadachi kino." *Proletarskoe kino*, 1925, no. 1
Kak pisat stsenarii dlia kino-kartin. Moscow: Moskovskoe teatralnoe izd-vo, 1925
Gollender, N. "Rabota tretei Goskino-fabrika." *Kino-zhurnal ARK*, 1925, no. 3, p. 8
Greiding, Iu. "Frantsuzskie nemye filmy v sovetskom prokate." *Kino i vremia*, vol. IV (1965)
Gromov, Iurii. "Za novyi byt geroev filmy." *Sovetskii ekran*, 1929, no. 35
"Grustnoe v smeshnom." *Sovetskii ekran*, 1927, no. 32
Gudkin, Ia. "Riadovi kemovskogo otriada." In *Iz istorii Lenfilma*
Gusman, Boris. "*Banda batki Knysha.*" *Pravda*, 4 June 1924
"*Aelita.*" *Pravda*, 1 October 1924
"*Dekabristy.*" *Pravda*, 1 March 1927
"Po teatram i kino." *Revoliutsiia i kultura*, 1928, no. 3/4
I. Kr. "*Dva dnia.*" *Izvestiia*, 10 January 1928
I.N. "Nasha, i zapadnoe kino." *Sovetskii ekran*, 1929, no. 19
Ia.M. "*Papirosnitsa ot Mosselproma.*" *Kino-nedelia*, 1924, no. 44
Iakobson, Dm. *Kino i molodezh.* Moscow: Gosizdat, 1926
Iakovlev, Nikolai. "O levom rebiachestve v kino." *Sovetskoe kino*, 1925, no. 1
"Kino dlia derevni." *Kino-zhurnal ARK*, 1925, no. 3
"Pervosortnaia meshchanskaia." *Kino*, 1927, no. 5
"*Devushka s korobkoi.*" *Kino*, 1927, no. 18
"*Iad.*" *Kino*, 1927, no. 37
"Uzlovye voprosy." *Kino*, 1927, no. 46
"Pervaia komediia: *Don Diego i Pelageia.*" *Sovetskii ekran*, 1927, no. 51
"Ideologiia i kassa." *Sovetskii ekran*, 1927, no. 43
Ilinskii, Igor. *Sam o sebe.* Moscow: Iskusstvo, 1984
"Bogatoe nasledstvo." In Aleinikov, *Protazanov*
"Itogi chistki Teakinopechat." *Kino*, 1930, no. 26
Iukov, K. "Puti i pereputia sovetskogo kino." *Kino-front*, 1927, no. 9/10
Iutkevich, Sergei. *Igor Ilinskii.* Moscow: Teakinopechat, 1929
"Iz stenogrammy zasedanii pravleniia kinofabriki Sovkino: Diskussiia po povodu kartiny *Oblomok imperii*, 6 avg. 1929." In Sepman, *Ermler*
"K itogram kinosezona." *Kino i zhizn*, 1930, no. 15
"K priezdu Ferbenksa i Pikforda." *Kino*, 1926, no. 29
"K smotru kino-sezona." *Sovetskii ekran*, 1929, no. 20
"K soveshchaniiu po delam kino v TsK VKP(b)." *Kino-front*, 1927, no. 9/10
"K sovetskomu realizmu." *Kino-gazeta*, 1924, no. 42
K.G. "Obshchestvo druzei sovetskogo kino." *Sovetskoe kino*, 1925, no. 6
K.M. "Six Russian films." *Close Up*, October 1928
Kandyba, F. "Obezdolennyi teatr Kharkova." *Kino*, 1925, no. 2
Kartseva, E. "Amerikanskie nemye filmy v sovetskom prokate." *Kino i vremia*, vol. I (1960)

Katkov, V. "Eshche o derevenskoi kartine." *Kino*, 1925, no. 8
Katsigras, A. "Izuchenie derevenskogo kino-zritelia." *Sovetskoe kino*, 1925, no. 2/3
"Voprosy kinofikatsii derevnii." *Sovetskoe kino*, 1925, no. 4/5
"Voprosy derevenskoi kino-raboty." *Sovetskoe kino*, 1925, no. 6
"Opyty fiksatsii zritelskikh interesov." In Bursak, *Kino*
Kino-rabota v derevne. [Moscow]: Kinopechat, [1926]
"Kritika uslovii derevenskogo prokata." In Meshcheriakov *et al.*, *Kino-iazva*
"Ne pora li?" *Sovetskoe kino*, 1927, no. 2
"*Katyka [sic] – bumazhnyi ranet*." *Sovetskoe kino*, 1927, no. 2
"Kulturfilma: Organizatsionnyi voprosy." *Kino i kultura*, 1929, no. 4
Kaufman, E. "Nash eksport-import." *Kino-zhurnal ARK*, 1925, no. 10
"Sovetskaia kartina na vneshnem rynke." *Kino-front*, 1927, no. 5
Kaufman, I. "Stil igry." *Sovetskii ekran*, 1928, no. 49
Khersonskii, Khrisanf. "*Krasnye diavoliata*." *Izvestiia*, 25 November 1922
"*Aelita*." *Izvestiia*, 2 October 1924
"Kino i sedmomu." *Izvestiia*, 12 November 1924
"Pombykh iz pultresta." *Izvestiia*, 5 December 1924
"*Ego prizyv*." *Kino-zhurnal ARK*, 1925, no. 3
"*Ego prizyv*." *Izvestiia*, 19 February 1925
"*Na zhizn i na smert* i *Kollezhskii registrator*." *Kino-zhurnal ARK*, 1925, no. 10
"Ishchem liudei ekrana." *Kino-zhurnal ARK*, 1925, no. 10
"Komicheskaia i komedii." *Kino-zhurnal ARK*, 1925, no. 11/12
"*Namus*." *Kino*, 1926, no. 43
"Lakirovannoe varvarstvo ili 'Miss, vyidite na minutku.'" *Kino*, 1926, no. 49
"*Chortovo koleso*." *Pravda*, 27 March 1926
"Borba faktov." *Kino-front*, 1926, no. 9/10
"*Sorok pervyi*." *Kino*, 1927, no. 12
"*Moskva v oktiabre*." *Kino*, 1927, no. 47
"Khochu snimatsia." *Kino-front*, 1927, no. 5
"Kino: *Katka bumazhnyi ranet*." *Pravda*, 5 January 1927
"*Konets Sankt-Peterburga*." *Kino-front*, 1928, no. 1
"Kino: *Parizhskii sapozhnik*." *Pravda*, 14 February 1928
"Kino: *Dom v sugrobakh*." *Pravda*, 7 April 1928
"*Kruzheva*." *Sovetskii ekran*, 1928, no. 16
"Ot luchiny k lampochke Ilicha." *Sovetskii ekran*, 1928, no. 32
"Smotr." *Sovetskii ekran*, 1928, no. 38
"*Salamandra*." *Pravda*, 30 December 1928
"*Saba* – igrovaia kulturfilma." *Sovetskii ekran*, 1929, no. 7
"*Saba*." *Kino*, 1929, no. 39
"*Chiny i liudi*." *Kino*, 1929, no. 40
"*Kain i Artem*." *Kino*, 1929, no. 49
"Dve biografii." *Proletarskoe kino*, 1933, no. 11/12
Kinematograf: Sbornik statei. Moscow: Gosudarstvennoe izd-vo, 1919
"Kino." *Na literaturnom postu*, 1930, no. 2
"Kino-akter." *Kino*, 1927, no. 21

Kino-biulletin. Moscow: Narkompros, 1918
"Kinotvorchestvo i massovoi zritel." *Kino i zritel,* 1930, no. 18
Kirshon, Vladimir. "Listki iz bloknota." *Kino-front,* 1927, no. 13/14
Na kino-postu. Moscow: Moskovskii rabochii, 1928
Klechatyi. "Kino-teatry Moskomprom." *Kino,* 1925, no. 3
"Klubnoi prokat." *Sovetskii ekran,* 1927, no. 30
Knigi o kino (1917–1960): Annotirovannaia bibliografiia. Moscow: Izd-vo vostochnoi literatury, 1960
Kolomarov, B. *Zlodei v kino.* Moscow: Teakinopechat, 1929
Koltsov, Ivan. "Kommertsiia nevpopad." *Kino,* 1928, no. 14
Koltsov, Mikhail. *"Ego prizyv."* *Pravda,* 17 February 1925
Korolevich, Vladimir. "Sankt-Peterburg i Leningrad." *Sovetskoe kino,* 1926, no. 8
"Samaia deshevlaia veshch." *Sovetskii ekran,* 1926, no. 46
"Dovolno kolumbov." *Sovetskii ekran,* 1926, no. 49
Nata Vachnadze. Moscow: Kino izd-vo RSFSR Kinopechat, 1926
"Kino i 'zagovor imperatritsy.'" *Kino-front,* 1927, no. 5
"Dlia Ars i Arsikov." *Sovetskii ekran,* 1927, no. 5/6
Zhenshchina v kino. n.p.: Teakinopechat, 1928
Kosior, Stanislav. "K itogam voprosov kino." *Revoliutsiia i kultura,* 1928, no. 6
Kosmatov, L. "Krestianskaia filma." *Kino-gazeta,* 1924, no. 34
Kosovitskii, L. "Slovo za chitatelem." *Kino,* 1926, no. 14
Kozintsev, Grigorii. "Slovo o druge." In Sepman, *Ermler*
"Krasnoiarsk." *Kino,* 1927, no. 38
Krinitskii, A. I. *Zadachi sovetskogo kino.* n.p.: Teakinopechat, 1929
Kristol. "Dovolno skazok o nevygodnosti." *Sovetskoe kino,* 1926, no. 2
"Krov na ekrane." *Sovetskii ekran,* 1927, no. 32
Krupskaia, Nadezhda. *"Oktiabr."* *Kino,* 1928, no. 12
Krylov, S. "Kino na borbu s alkologizmom." *Kino,* 1928, no. 42
Kino vmesto vodki: K vsesoiuznom partsoveshchaniiu po voprosam kino. Moscow: Moskovskii rabochii, 1928
Kuleshov, Lev. "Amerikanshchina." *Kino-fot,* 1922, no. 1
"Ob *Aelite."* *Kino-nedelia,* 1924, no. 47
"O nashem kinoaktere." *Kino,* 1927, no. 21
Kuleshov on Film. Ed. and trans. Ronald Levaco. Berkeley: University of California Press, 1974
Sobranie sochinenii v trekh tomakh, vol. 1, *Teoriia, kritika, pedagogika.* Moscow: Iskusstvo, 1987
"Kumovstvo n kino-fabrike." *Kino,* 1928, no. 14
Kurs, A. "O kino-obshchestvennosti, o zritele i nekotorykh nepriiatnykh veshchakh." *Kino-zhurnal ARK,* 1925, no. 3
"Kino-kritika v SSSR." *Sovetskoe kino,* 1925, no. 4/5
Samoe mogushchestvennoe. Moscow: Kinopechat, 1927
Kuznetsov, E. "Kak vy zhivete?" *Kino,* 1932, no. 45
L. "Prokat i teatry." *Kino-zhurnal ARK,* 1925, no. 9
L.V. "Chto skazal ARK o pisme Leningradskikh rezhisserov." *Kino,* 1927, no. 27

"O sovetskoi komedii: Disput v dome pechati." *Kino*, 1928, no. 19

Lebedev, G. "Kino-agropropaganda." *Sovetskoe kino*, 1925, no. 2/3

Lebedev, Nikolai. "Novaia filma Proletkino (*Borba za ultimatum*)." *Izvestiia*, 23 December 1922

"*Slesar i kantsler.*" *Pravda*, 13 December 1923

"*Aelita.*" *Kino-gazeta*, 1924, no. 39

Kino: Ego kratkaia istoriia, ego vozmozhnosti, ego stroitelstva v sovetskom gosudarstve. Moscow: Gosudarstvennoe izd-vo, 1924

"Lef i kino: Stenogramma soveshchaniia." *Novyi Lef*, 1927, no. 11/12

Lemberg, Efraim. "Aktualneishchaia problema: Voprosy kino na pedagogicheskom sezde." *Sovetskoe kino*, 1928, no. 1

Kinopromyshlennost v SSSR: Ekonomika sovetskoi kinematografii. [Moscow]: Teakinopechat, 193[0]

Lenin, V. I., *Samoe vazhnoe iz vsekh iskusstv: Lenin o kino.* Ed. A. Gak. Moscow: Iskusstvo, 1973

Leningradskoi oblastnoi komitet VKP(b). *Rezoliutsii Leningradskogo oblastnoi partsoveshchaniia po voprosam kinematografii (2–3 marta 1928)*

Leonidov, O. L. "Iakov Aleksandrovich Protazanov." In Aleinikov, *Protazanov*

Levidov, Mikhail. "*Konets Sankt-Peterburga.*" *Kino*, 1927, no. 47

"Naschet geroev: V kino i v literature." *Sovetskii ekran*, 1928, no. 49

Levman, B. *Rabochii zritel i kino: Itogi pervoi rabochii kino-konferentsii.* Moscow: Teakinopechat, 1930

Liianov, D. "Blizhe k massam." *Sovetskoe kino*, 1925, no. 1.

"Ob upriamoi deistvitelnosti i bolnykh nervakh." *Sovetskoe kino*, 1925, no. 2/3

"Amerika i Evropa." *Sovetskoe kino*, 1925, no. 4/5

"Na proizvodstve Sovkino." *Kino*, 1927, no. 14

Likhachev, B. S. *Istoriia kino v Rossii (1896–1926): Materialy k istorii russkogo kino.* Pt. 1: *1896–1913.* Leningrad: Academia, 1927

"Materialy k istorii kino v Rossii (1914–1916)." *Iz istorii kino* 3 (1960)

Lublinskii, P. I. *Kinematograf i deti.* Moscow: Pravo i zhizn, 1925

Lunacharskii, A. V. "Tezisy A. V. Lunacharskogo: Revoliutsionnaia ideologiia i kino." *Kino-nedelia*, 1924, no. 46

"Mesto kino sredi drugikh iskusstv." *Sovetskoe kino*, 1925, no. 1

"Pobeda sovetskogo kino." *Izvestiia*, 10 October 1926

Kino na zapade i u nas. n.p.: Teakinopechat, 1928

"*Kain i Artem.*" *Izvestiia*, 20 November 1929

A. V. Lunacharskii o literature i iskusstve: Bibliograficheskii ukazatel, 1902–1963. Leningrad: [Izd. bibl. AN SSSR] 1964

Lunacharskii o kino: Stati, vyskazyvaniia, stsenarii, dokumenty. Comp. K. D. Muratova. Moscow: Iskusstvo, 1965

"Cinema – the Greatest of the Arts." In Taylor and Christie, *Film Factory*

Lvov, A. *Kinematograficheskaia iazva izlechima.* Report to the TsK RKP(b), 26 March 1924

Lvovskii, A. "Kino i kultrabote profsoiuzov." In Maltsev, *Sovetskoe kino*

M. "Kino v dome krestiane." *Kino*, 1925, no. 1

M.Z. "*Bluzhdaiushchie zvezdy.*" *Kino*, 1928, no. 9
MacDonald, Dwight. "Eisenstein, Pudovkin, and Others." *The Miscellany* (March 1931)
Maiakovskii, Vladimir. "Karaul!" *Novyi Lef*, 1927, no. 2
"Speech in Debate on 'The Paths and Purposes of Sovkino.'" In Taylor and Christie, *Film Factory*
Malkin, B. "Mezhrabpom-rus." *Sovetskoe kino*, 1926, no. 8
Maltsev, K. A. *Sovetskoe kino pered litsom obshchestvennosti.* n.p.: Teakinopechat, 1928
Menzhinskaia, Iu. "O detskom kino." *Kino-front*, 1927, no. 2
Meshcheriakov, V. "Kak aktsionernoe obshchestvo Sovkino obratilos litsom k derevne." In Meshcheriakov *et al.*, *Kino-iazva*
"Kino dlia derevni (Rabota kino-sektsii Glavpolitprosveta)." In Syrtsov and Kurs, *Sovetskoe kino na podeme*
and M. L. Veremienko, and A. Katsigras. *Kino-iazva (Ob uprazhneniiakh Sovkino nad derevene).* Leningrad: Izd. zhurnala *Sovetskoe kino*, 1926
"Mezhrabpom-film – organizatsiia nuzhdaiushaiasia v korennoi perestroike," *Kino*, 1930, no. 5
Mikhailov, V. M. "Bolshe, deshevle, luche!" *Sovetskii ekran*, 1925, no. 35
Milkin, A. "Pod svoe tiazhestvo." *Kino*, 1929, no. 15
"*Miss Mend.*" *Sovetskoe kino*, 1926, no. 8
Mur, Leo. "Metody raboty amerikanskikh kino-rezhisserov." *Kino-zhurnal ARK*, 1925, no. 3
Bumazhnye bronenostsy. Moscow: Teakinopechat, 1929
N.L. "*Tri zhizni.*" *Kino-zhurnal ARK*, 1925, no. 1
"Na temu grazhdanskoi voiny (o *Sorok pervom*)." *Kino*, 1927, no. 11
"Nado rashirit front borby." *Sovetskii ekran*, 1927, no. 35
Nakatov, G. "Zagranichnye kino-gazy." *Sovetskoe kino*, 1926, no. 2
"*Namus.*" *Kino-front*, 1926, no. 4/5
"*Namus.*" *Izvestiia*, 9 November 1926
"Nasha anketa." *Kino-zhizn*, 1922, no. 2
"Nasha kino-anketa." *Na literaturnom postu*, 1928, no. 1
"Nasha pochta." *Sovetskii ekran*, 1928, no. 42
Nazarov, F. M. "Itogi zimnego sezona Rostova na Donu." *Kino-gazeta*, 1925, no. 3
"Ne monopoliia a kontrol." *Kino-gazeta*, 1924, no. 15
Nedobrovo, Vladimir. "*Dekabristy.*" *Zhizn iskusstva*, 1927, no. 5
"*Oblomok imperii.*" *Zhizn iskusstva*, 1929, no. 36
"Kino pod znakom rekonstruktsii." *Zhizn iskusstva*, 1929, no. 42
Neznamov, P. "Kovboi v papkakh." *Kino*, 1926, no. 14
"Chekhov – krupnym planom." *Kino*, 1927, no. 36
"*Poet i tsar.*" *Kino*, 1927, no. 39
"*Baby riazanskie.*" *Kino*, 1927, no. 52
Nata Vachnadze. Moscow: Teakinopechat, 1928
Nikitin, Fedor. "Nam nuzhna novaia sovest." *Sovetskii ekran*, 1928, no. 47
"Iz vospominaniia kinoaktera." *Iz istorii Lenfilma*, pt. 2 (1970)

Nikitin, Nikolai. "Prestuplenie Kirika Rudenko." *Krasnaia nov*, 1927, nos. 9–11.
Rpt. *Prestuplenie Kirika Rudenko; Pogovorim o zvezdakh: Povesti*. Leningrad:
Lenizdat, 1966
"Novosti s zapada." *Kino-gazeta*, 1924, no. 23
"Novyi kurs Sovkino." *Sovetskii ekran*, 1929, no. 1
Nozhnitsy. "Sovkino v role retsenzenta." *Kino*, 1927, no. 39
"Nozhnitsy ili akter?" *Sovetskii ekran*, 1926, no. 41
"Nuzhno organizovat prokat." *Kino-gazeta*, 1924, no. 46
"Nuzhno-li obedinenie?" *Kino-gazeta*, 1924, no. 14
"O novykh postannovakh, 1922 g." *Kino-zhizn*, 1922, no. 3
"O sovetskom kino-importe." *Sovetskii ekran*, 1929, no. 40
"O stsenarii *Katka bumazhnyi ranet* (Iz protokoly khudozhestvennogo soveta kinofa-
briki Leningradkino, mar.–apr. 1926)." In Sepman, *Ermler*
Obolenskii, Valerian. *See* Osinskii, N.
"Obsuzhdaem *Tanku*." *Kino*, 1929, no. 35
"Ocherednye zadachi: proizvodstvo i kinofikatsiia." *Kino-zhurnal ARK*, 1925, no. 6/7
"ODSK o *Parizhskom sapozhnike*." *Kino*, 1928, no. 7
Olkhovyi, B. S., ed. *Puti kino: Pervoe vsesoiuznoe soveshchanie po kinematografii.*
Moscow: Teakinopechat, 1929
Olshevits, M. "*Vodovorot*." *Izvestiia*, 10 January 1928
"ONO ili Sovkino." *Sovetskii ekran*, 1927, no. 38
"Opasnosti *Garemov iz Bukhary*." *Sovetskii ekran*, 1927, no. 42
Osinskii, N. "*Oblomok imperii*." *Izvestiia*, 3 November 1929
"Osnovnoe polozhenie kinoeksperimentalnoi masterskoi." *Iz istorii Lenfilma*, pt. 2 (1970)
Oznobishin, N. *Fizkultura kino-aktera: Prakticheskoe rukovodstvo*. Moscow: Teaki-
nopechat, 1929
P.A. "Organizatsiia proizvodstva: kino-syria i apparatury v SSSR." *Sovetskoe kino*,
1925, no. 2/3
"*Oshibka Vasiliia Guliaeva (Veter)*." *Kino*, 1926, no. 43
Paushkin, M. "Direktivy Sovnarkoma RSFSR o plane kinofikatsii." *Sovetskii ekran*,
1928, no. 29
Pavlov, G. "Kino na okraine." *Sovetskii ekran*, 1927, no. 1
Pertsov, V. "Mest zarezannykh kadrov (Zagranichnaia kartina na sovetskom
ekrane)." *Sovetskoe kino*, 1926, no. 2
"Pervaia filma revoliutsii." *Kino-gazeta*, 1923, no. 12
"Pervoe pismo." *Kino*, 1926, no. 12
Petrov-Bytov, Pavel. "We Have No Soviet Cinema." In Taylor and Christie, *Film
Factory*
Pi.D. "Nuzhen uchet." *Kinozhurnal ARK*, 1926, no. 2
Pikel, R. "Ideologiia i kommertsiia." *Kino*, 1927, no. 41
"Ukhaby na kino-fronte." *Revoliutsiia i kultura*, 1928, no. 3/4
Piliver, I. "K voprosu ob organizatsionno-khoziaistvennykh formakh kino-teatral-
nogo dela v RSFSR." *Sovetskoe kino*, 1927, no. 2
Piotrovskii, Adrian. "K partsoveshchaniia o kino rabote (ili 'Ob ideologii i kommer-
tsii')." *Zhizn iskusstva*, 1927, no. 37

"Dialekticheskaia forma v kino i front kino-reaktsii." *Zhizn iskusstva*, 1929, no. 41
"Za materialisticheskuiu dialektiku v kino protiv nastupaiushchii kino-reaktsii."
     Zhizn iskusstva, 1929, no. 47
Kinofikatsiia iskusstv. Leningrad: Izd. avtora, 1929
Khudozhestvennye techeniia v sovetskom kino. Leningrad: Teakinopechat, 1930
"Po provintsii." *Sovetskoe kino*, 1926, no. 8
"Po provintsii: Krasnodarskii okrug." *Sovetskoe kino*, 1927, no. 1
"Po moskovskim kino-teatram." *Kino*, 1925, no. 7
"Po SSSR." *Kino-nedelia*, 1925, no. 1
"Pochemu k nam vvoziat khlam?" *Kino-gazeta*, 1924, no. 17
Pochtar. "Smekh i ideologiia." *Kino*, 1927, no. 2
"Poputchiki ili prisoedinishsia." *Kino-gazeta*, 1924, no. 43
"Prigovor obshchestvennogo suda nad tipazhem." *Kino*, 1928, no. 32
Prim. "Generalnaia liniia Mezhrabpom-filma." *Sovetskii ekran*, 1929, no. 20
"Proletarskaia literatura i kino." *Kino-nedelia*, 1925, no. 3
Protazanov, Iakov. "Protazanov o sebe." In Aleinikov, *Protazanov*
"Protiv poshlosti." *Kino*, 1928, no. 36
"Protsess kino-rabotnikov." *Kino*, 1927, nos. 15–18
"Proverki kassoi." *Kino*, 1925, no. 3
"Pushkinisty o *Poete i tsare*." *Sovetskii ekran*, 1927, no. 43
R. "*Vasilii Griaznov*." *Izvestiia*, 30 March 1924
R-al, L. "Chto my videli i khotim videt." *Kino*, 1925, no. 23
"Rabochie o kartine *Evdokiia Rozhnovskaia*." *Pravda*, 1 November 1924
"Reguliarnaia armiia kino-rabotnikov." *Sovetskii ekran* 1927, no. 23
"Resheniia Sovnarkoma." *Kino-gazeta*, 1924, no. 21
"Rezhissery sovetskogo khudozhestvennogo kino," *Kino i vremia*, vol. III (1963)
"Rezoliutsiia ARK." *Kino*, 1927, no. 27
"Rezoliutsiia po kartine *Don Diego i Pelageia*." *Kino-front*, 1928, no. 2
"Rezoliutsiia soveshchaniia rabotnikov kinematograficheskikh organizatii SSSR po
     voprosu monopolii." *Kino-nedelia*, 1924, no. 9
Room, Abram. "Rezhisser ...v koridore." *Kino*, 1927, no. 21
Rosenberg, William G., ed., *Bolshevik Visions: First Phase of the Cultural Revolution in
     Soviet Russia*. Ann Arbor, MI: Ardis, 1984
Rotha, Paul, *The Film Till Now*. London: Spring Books, 1967; rpt. 1930 edn
Rudoi, Ia. "Nasha kinematografiia i massovoi zritel." *Sovetskii ekran*, 1929, no. 37
     "Zametki o tvorcheskikh putiakh sovetskoi kinematografii." *Kino i zhizn*, 1930,
     no. 24
"Russkoe proizvodstvo." *Kinotvorchestvo*, 1926, no. 15/16
Rustemoe, A. "Proizvodstvo i Sovkino." *Kino*, 1925, no. 2
S.I. "Novye liudi." *Kino-front*, 1927, no. 3
     "*Iad*." *Kino-front*, 1927, no. 9/10
S.M.V. "Proiavitel." *Kino*, 1928, no. 32
Sakharov, N.I. "Pochemu vy khotite stat kino-akterom?" *Sovetskii ekran*, 1929, no. 37
Sakharov, Petr. "Nenuzhnaia buza." *Sovetskii ekran*, 1929, no .4
Saltanov, Iurii. "Nuzhno sobrat kino set." *Sovetskoe kino*, 1927, no. 5/6

Semenov, D. "Mezhrabpom khvataet zvezdy." *Kino*, 1928, no. 38

Sepman, I.V., ed. *Fridrikh Ermler: Dokumenty, stati, vospominaniia*. Leningrad: Iskusstvo, 1974

Serpinskii, S.V. *Chto takoe kino*, Moscow: Gosizdat, 1928

Serpukhovskii, V. "Kino dlia detei." *Pravda*, 6 April 1924

Shaginian, Marietta. *Mess Mend: Yankees in Petrograd*. Trans. S. D. Cioran. Ann Arbor, MI: Ardis, 1991

Shapovalenko, N. "Ekonomicheskii analiz kino-seansa." *Sovetskoe kino*, 1925, no. 2/3

Shashkin, M. Letter. *Kino*, 1926, no. 17/18

Shatov, Lev. "*Salamandra*." *Kino*, 1928, no. 51

Shershenevich, Vadim. *Igor Ilinskii*. Moscow: Kino-izd-vo RSFSR Kinopechat, 1926

"Kino-slovar." *Kino-kalendar* (1927)

Shklovskii, Viktor. "Mister Vest ne na svoemost." *Kino-nedelia*, 1924, no. 21

"Retsenzent." *Sovetskii ekran*, 1925, no. 35

"O krestianskoi lente." *Kino*, 1926, no. 10

"O mezhdu prochem." *Sovetskii ekran*, 1926, no. 20

"Pudovkin." *Kino*, 1926, no. 36

"Kolonizatsiia kino." *Sovetskii ekran*, 1928, no. 34

"Za stolbi." *Sovetskii ekran*, 1929, no. 3

Za sorok let. Moscow: Iskusstvo, 1965

Za 60 let: Raboty o kino. Moscow: Iskusstvo, 1985

Shneider, Mikhail. "Genealogiia sovetskoi kartiny." *Sovetskii ekran*, 1927, no. 7

"Proizvodstvo i shkola." *Kino-front*, 1927, no. 9/10

"Po tu storonu 17-go goda: *Chelovek iz restorana*." *Kino*, 1927, no. 36

"*Ukhaby*." *Kino-front*, 1928, no. 1

"*Parizhskii sapozhnik*." *Kino-front*, 1928, no. 2

"Fridrikh Ermler." *Kino*, 1934, no. 6

Shneiderov, Vladimir. "Sovetskaia kino-promyshlennost." *Sovetskii ekran*, 1927, no. 7

"Organizationnye formy kinopromyshlennosti." *Sovetskoe kino*, 1927, no. 8/9

Shutko, K. "Mezhrabpom-film." *Sovetskii ekran*, 1928, no. 39

Shvedchikov, K. "Sovkino otvechaet." *Kino-front*, 1928, no. 1

"Slovo za chitatelem." *Kino*, 1926, nos. 12, 13, 14, 15/17

"Snizhenie teatralnogo naloga." *Kino-gazeta*, 1925, no. 4/5

"Soiuz otvechaet." *Kino*, 1928, no. 26

Sokolov, Ippolit. "*Veter*." *Kino*, 1926, no. 43

"NOT v kino-proizvodstve." *Kino-front*, 1926, no. 7/8

"Khoroshii stsenarii." *Kino-front*, 1926, no. 9/10

"Material i forma." *Kino-front*, 1926, no. 9/10

"Kuda idet sovetskogo kino?" *Sovetskii ekran*, 1926, no. 37

Kino stsenarii: Teoriia i tekhnika. Moscow: Kinopechat, 1926

"Amplua–tipazh–maska: Kharakter obraza." *Kino-front*, 1927, no. 3

"Kak sozdat sovetskuiu komediiu." *Kino-front*, 1927, no. 4

Letter. *Kino-front*, 1927, no. 7/8

"Metody igry pered kino-apparaturom." *Kino-front*, 1927, no. 5

"*Shestaia chast mira*." *Kino-front*, 1927, no. 2

"Sostoianie stsenarnogo dela." *Kino-front*, 1927, no. 13/14

"Prichiny poslednikh neudach." *Kino*, 1928, no. 46

"Rabotat na massovogo kino-zritelia." *Kino i zhizn*, 1929, no. 2

Analiz igry kinoaktera: Masterstvo Lilian Gish. Leningrad: Teakinopechat, 1929

"*Oblomok imperii*." *Kino*, 1929, no. 38

"Na putiakh k zvukovomu kino." *Sovetskii ekran*, 1929, no. 44

"Korni formalizma." *Kino*, 1930, no. 17

"*Zemlia*." *Kino*, 1930, no. 21

"Ratsionalizatsii kinoproizvodstva." *Kino i zhizn*, 1930, no. 28

Solskii, V. "Kino na zapade." *Sovetskoe kino*, 1925, no. 2/3

"Kino-zadachi i kino-opastnosti." *Na literaturnom postu*, 1927, no. 4

"Diskussii o Sovkino." *Kino-front*, 1927, no. 11/12

"Soobshcheniia Glavrepertkoma." *Kino*, 1928, no. 20

"Sovetskaia komicheskaia." *Kino*, 1927, no. 16

"Sovetskaia obshchestvennost ne pozvolit sryvat rabotu professionalnykh organizatsii." *Kino*, 1928, no. 25

Sovetskie khudozhestvennye filmy: Annotirovannyi katalog, vols. I and II. Moscow: Iskusstvo, 1960–61

"Standarty sovetskikh bytovykh kartin." *Sovetskii ekran*, 1928, no. 27

Stekliannyi glaz. "Obzor pechati." *Sovetskii ekran*, 1929, no. 31

"Sto protsentov agitatsii." *Kino*, 1925, no. 15

Strashun, I. "O sanprosvetitelnom filme." *Sovetskoe kino*, 1925, no. 1

Stsenaristy sovetskogo khudozhestvennogo kino, 1917–1967. Moscow: Iskusstvo, 1972

Sukharebskii, L. *Uchebnoe kino*. Moscow: Teakinopechat, 1929

Syrkin, Albert. "Mezhdu tekhniki i ideologiei (O kino-poputchikakh i partiinom rukovodstve)." *Kino-nedelia*, 1924, no. 37

Syrtsov, S. and A. Kurs. *Sovetskoe kino na podeme*. Moscow: n.p., 1926

"Tam, gde delaiut krizis v kinematografii." *Kino*, 1928, no. 50

Taylor, Richard and Ian Christie, eds. *The Film Factory: Russian and Soviet Cinema in Documents, 1896–1939*. Trans. Richard Taylor. Cambridge, MA: Harvard University Press, 1988

"Tekstilshchiki o Garri Pile." *Kino*, 1927, no. 35

Tematicheskii plan Sovkino na 1928/29 g. utverzhdennyi plenumom khudozhestvennogo soveta ot 11 zasedaniem pravleniia Sovkino ot 13/VIII s.g. [Moscow] 1928

Tolstoi, Aleksei. *Aelita, or the Decline of Mars*. Ann Arbor MI: Ardis, 1985

Tolstova, Nataliia. "Deti o svoem kino." In Gelmont, *Kino, deti, shkola*

"Tov. Zinovev o sovetskoi filme." *Kino-nedelia*, 1924, no. 7

Trainin, I. "Puti kino." *Kino-nedelia*, 1924, no. 40/41

"Na puti k vozrozhdeniiu." *Sovetskoe kino*, 1925, no. 1

"Ob iskusstve bez politiki." *Kino*, 1925, no. 3

"Sovetskaia filma i zritel." *Sovetskoe kino*, 1925 nos. 4/5 and 6

"Iz opyty Sovkino." *Kino*, 1925, no. 9

"Medvezhia usluga t. Arustanova Goskinproma." *Kino*, 1925, no. 6

Kino-promyshlennost i Sovkino: Po dokladu na 8-ii konferentsii moskovskogo gubrabisa, 1925. Moscow: Kino-izdatelstvo RSFSR, 1925

Kino na kulturnom fronte. [Leningrad] Teakinopechat, 1928
Troianovskii, A. I. and R. I. Egiazarov. *Izuchenie kino-zritelia: Po materialam issledo-vatelskoi teatralnoi masterskoi.* Moscow: Gosizdat Narkompros, 1928
Trotskii, Lev. *Literature and Revolution.* Ann Arbor, MI: University of Michigan Press, 1960
"Vodka, the Church, and the Cinema." In Taylor and Christie, *The Film Factory*
Tsentralnyi gosudarstvennyi arkhiv literatury i iskusstva (TsGALI), f. 645, op. 1, ed. khr. 385, "Glavnoe upravlenie po delam khudozhestvennoi literatury i iskusstva NKP RSFSR, sektsiia kino-radio raboty (1928–29)"
ed. khr. 389. "Svodki anketnye materialy po izucheniiu vpechatlenii zritelei kino-kartin: Issledovatelskaia teatralnaia masterskaia (1926/27)"
TsGALI, f. 939, op. 1, ed. khr. 282. "Prikaz po vserossiiskomu foto-kino otdelu Glavpolitprosveta, 6 maia – 10 iiunia 1922"
TsGALI, f. 2014, op. 1, ed. khr. 24. "Dogovor Grebnera s Lunacharskom o sovmestnoi napisanii literaturnogo stsenariia *Salamandra*"
TsGALI, f. 2356, op. 1, ed. khr. 8, "P. Bauer, 'V kino: Byt na ekrane'"
ed. khr. 46a, "O. Preobrazhenskaia, 'Avtobiografiia.'"
TsGALI, f. 2494, op. 1, ed. khr. 26. "Protokoly obshchikh sobranii chlenov ARK (1926)"
ed. khr. 32. "Protokoly obshchikh sobranii chlenov ARK (1926)"
ed. khr. 33. "Protokoly zasedanii akterskoi podsektsii ARK, 1 fev.–15 iiun 1926"
ed. khr. 40. "Protokoly zasedanii organizatsionnoi komissii i detsko-shkolnoi sektsii, 30 noia. – 8 dek. 1926"
ed. khr. 50. "Stenogramma diskussii *Bronenosets Potemkin*, 30 ianv. 1926"
ed. khr. 60. "Ankety obsledovanii moskovskikh kinoteatrov o sostoianii muzykal-nogo soprovozhdeniia kinofilmov, 1926"
ed. khr. 64. "Stenogramma diskussii o tipazhe v kino, 1926"
ed. khr. 65, "Plan raboty pravleniia ARK, dek, 1927 g."
ed. khr. 69. Unpublished letter from Sovkino to *Cinema Front*
ed. khr. 77. "Protokoly zasedanii tsentralnogo biuro foto-kino sektsii TsK Rabis (1928)
ed. khr. 94. "Stenogramma diskussii po obuzhdeniiu kinofilma *Baby riazanskie*, 17–22 noia. (1927)"
ed. khr. 99 "Stenogramma sobranie chlenov ARK po obuzhdeniiu kino-filme *Don Diego i Pelageia Demina* [*sic*], 1 dek. 1927"
ed. khr. 149 "Stenogramma diskussii po obuzhdeniiu kinofilma *Dom v sugrobakh*, 6 apr. 1928"
ed. khr. 171 "Protokol diskussii obuzhdeniiu kinofilma *Parizhskii sapozhnik*, 24 ianv. 1928"
ed. khr. 213 "Stenogramma zasedaniia rezhisserskoi sektsii ARRKe o stsenarnom krisize"
ed. khr. 234. "Stenogramma lektsii S. A. Bugoslavskogo organizatsiia zvuka v tonfilme (1929)"
ed. khr. 272. "Stenogramma diskussii po obuzhdeniiu kinofilma *Novyi Vavilon* i otchet po izucheniiu vospriiatiia filma zritelei, 21 marta 1929 & 20 maia 1929"

ed. khr. 279 "Stenogramma diskussii po obsuzhdeniiu kinofilma *Saba* (1929)"
TsGALI, f. 2496, op. 1, ed. khr. 23. "Tematicheskii plan Sovkino postanovki khud.
filmov na 1927/1928 g."
ed. khr. 25 "Sovkino finansovo-kommercheskii plan na 27/28"
TsGALI, f. 2497, op. 1, ed. khr. 10. "Gosudarstvennoe vsesoiuznoe foto-kino
obedinenie Soiuzkino"
TsGALI, f. 2498, op. 1, ed. khr. 32. "Biulletin informbiuro Soiuzkino"
Tsivian, Yuri *et al.*, eds. *Silent Witnesses: Russian Films, 1908–1919.* London: British
Institute, 1989
Turkin, Valentin. "Sostoianie kino obrazovanie v SSSR." *Sovetskoe kino*, 1925, no. 2
"Povodiia kontsy." *Sovetskii ekran*, 1927, no. 15
"Bez kino-aktera net kino-kultury." *Sovetskii ekran*, 1928, no. 49
"O zhivykh liudiakh." *Sovetskii ekran*, 1929, no. 20
Kino-akter. Moscow: Teakinopechat, 1929
"Udachnaia operatsiia; Ekran ochishchen ot khlama." *Kino*, 1928, no. 47
Ulianova, M. "Zadachi kino." In Bursak, *Kino*
Urazov, Izmail. "*Krylia kholopa.*" *Kino*, 1926, no. 47
"Pobeda politiki i tsifry." *Sovetskii ekran*, 1927, no. 1
"Vtoroi konets palki." *Sovetskii ekran*, 1927, no. 11
Uspenskii, V. P. *ODSK (Obshchestvo druzei sovetskogo kino).* Moscow: Kinopechat,
1926
[Obituary]. *Sovetskii ekran*, 1929, no. 16
"Ustav kinoeksperimentalnoi masterskoi." *Iz istorii Lenfilma* 2 (1970)
V.G. "Penzenskaia kino-zhizn." *Kino*, 1925, no. 4/5
"Kak ne sleduet prodavit derevne filmu." *Kino*, 1925, no. 4/5
V.K. "Zabytaia tema." *Kino*, 1925, no. 10
V.N. "*Potselui Meri.*" *Zhizn iskusstva*, 1927, no. 48
V.S. "Protiv Ameriki." *Kino*, 1926, no. 23
V-s, Lev. "Rabochii zritel o zagranichnykh komediiakh." *Kino*, 1928, no. 9
Vainshtok, Vladimir and Dmitrii Iakobson. *Kino i molodezh.* Moscow: Gosizdat, 1926
Valerian, S. "*Na zhizn i na smert.*" *Izvestiia*, 11 September 1925
"*Krest i mauzer.*" *Izvestiia*, 19 November 1925
"V zashchitu kino-manii." *Kino*, 1928, no. 21
Vasilev, S. D. "O peremontazhe." *Kino-gazeta*, 1925, no. 8
Montazh kinokartiny. Leningrad: Teakinopechat, 1929
Veremienko, M. "Politprosvet kino-rabota: Detskoe kino (Postanovka voprosa)."
Sovetskoe kino, 1926, no. 2
"Kakie kartiny dalo Sovkino dlia derevni." In Meshcheriakov *et al.*, *Kino-iazva*
"O kulturfilme." *Sovetskoe kino*, 1927, no. 4
Vertov, Dziga. [letter]. *Kino-front*, 1927, no. 4
Kino-Eye: The Writings of Dziga Vertov. Ed. Annette Michelson and trans. Kevin
O'Brien. Berkeley: University of California Press, 1984
Vishnevskii, Veniamin. *Khudozhestvennye filmy dorevoliutsionnoi Rossii: Filmografi-
cheskoe opisanie.* Moscow: Goskinoizdat, 1945
"Vkratse." *Kino*, 1927, no. 37

Vokrug Sovkino: Stenogramma disputa organizovannogo Tsk VLKSM, TsS ODSK i redaktsiei gazety Komsomolskaia pravda 8–15 okt., *1927*, n.p.: Teakinopechat, 1928
Volkov, Nikolai. "Kartiny sezona." *Izvestiia*, 16 October 1926
"Teatr – muzyka – kino: Novye kinokartiny." *Izvestiia*, 9 January 1927
"Novye kartiny." *Izvestiia*, 17 May 1927
"Novye kino-kartiny." *Izvestiia*, 12 June 1927
"*Chelovek iz restorana.*" *Izvestiia*, 21 August 1927
"*Don Diego i Pelageia.*" *Izvestiia*, 4 March 1928
"Teatr – muzyka – kino: Po moskovskim ekranam (Kinoobzor)." *Izvestiia*, 11 April 1928
"*Pravo na zhizn.*" *Izvestiia*, 13 December 1928
"Kachalov i Meierkhold na ekrane." *Pravda*, 18 October 1928
"Sovetskie filmy." *Izvestiia*, 18 November 1929
Voznesenskii, Al. *Iskusstvo ekrana.* Kiev: Sorabkoop, 1924
"Za ratsionalizatsiiu proizvodstva." *Kino-front*, 1926, no. 7/8
Zagorskii, M. "Tapioka – Ilinskii – teatr – kino." *Sovetskii ekran*, 1926, no. 38
Zaretskii, M. "Rabochii podrostok kak zritel kino." *Kino-zhurnal ARK*, 1925, no. 3

Secondary sources

Abel, Richard. *French Cinema: The First Wave, 1915–1929.* Princeton, NJ: Princeton University Press, 1984
Aktery sovetskogo kino. Moscow: Iskusstvo, 1967
Albèra, François. "Le cinéma soviétique des années trente aux années quatre-vingt." In E. Etkind *et al.*, eds., *Histoire de la littérature russe XX–ième siècle* (Paris: Fayard, 1990)
    and Roland Cosandey, eds. *Boris Barnet: Ecrits, documents, études, filmographie.* Locarno: Editions du Festival international du film de Locarno, 1985
    and Ekaterina Khokhlova and Valerie Posener, eds. *Kouléchov et les sièns.* Locarno: Editions du Festival international du film de Locarno, 1990
Arlazorov, Mikhail. *Protazanov.* Moscow: Iskusstvo, 1973
Atkinson, Dorothy. *The End of the Russian Land Commune, 1905–1930.* Stanford, CA: Stanford University Press, 1983
Avins, Carol. *Border Crossings: The West and Russian Identity in Soviet Literature, 1917–1934.* Berkeley: University of California Press, 1983
Babitsky, Paul and Martin Lutich. *The Soviet Movie Industry: Two Studies.* New York: Research Fund on the USSR, 1953
    and John Rimberg. *The Soviet Film Industry.* New York: Praeger, 1955
Bailes, Kendall E. *Technology and Society under Lenin and Stalin: The Origins of the Soviet Technical Intelligentsia, 1917–1941.* Princeton, NJ: Princeton University Press, 1978
Ball, Alan M. *Russia's Last Capitalists: The NEPmen, 1921–1929.* Berkeley: University of California Press, 1987
Barber, John. "Working Class Culture and Political Culture in the 1930s." In Günther, *Culture of the Stalin Period*

Barlow, John D. *German Expressionist Film.* Boston: Twayne, 1982

Bigsby, C. W. E. *Approaches to Popular Culture.* Bowling Green, OH: Bowling Green University Press, 1976

Bordwell, David, Janet Staiger, and Kristin Thompson. *The Classical Hollywood Cinema: Film Style and Mode of Production to 1960.* New York: Columbia University Press, 1985

Borovkov, V. P. *Fedor Nikitin.* Moscow; Iskusstvo, 1977

Brantlinger, Patrick. *Bread and Circuses: Theories of Mass Culture as Social Decay.* Ithaca, NY: Cornell University Press, 1983

Bratoliubov, S. *Na zare sovetskoi kinematografii: Iz istorii kinoorganizatsii Petrograda-Leningrada, 1918–1925 goda.* Leningrad: Iskusstvo, 1976

Brooks, Jeffrey. *When Russia Learned to Read.* Princeton, NJ: Princeton University Press, 1985

"Popular Philistinism and the Course of Russian Modernism." In Gary Saul Morson, ed., *Literature and History: Theoretical Problems and Russian Case Studies* (Stanford, CA: Stanford University Press, 1986)

Budiak, L. M. and V. P. Mikhailov. *Adresa moskovskogo kino.* Moscow: Moskovskii rabochii, 1987

Bullitt, Margaret M. "Toward a Marxist Theory of Aesthetics: The Development of Socialist Realism in the Soviet Union." *The Russian Review* 35, no. 1 (January 1976)

Burbank, Jane. *Intelligentsia and Revolution: Russian Views of Bolshevism, 1917–1922.* Oxford: Oxford University Press, 1987

Burch, Noel. "Harold Lloyd contre le Docteur Mabuse." In Albèra and Cosandey, *Boris Barnet*

Cawelti, John G. *Adventure, Mystery, and Romance: Formula Stories as Art and Popular Culture.* Chicago: University of Chicago Press, 1976

Chase, William J. *Workers, Society, and the Soviet State: Labor and Life in Moscow, 1918–1929.* Urbana: University of Illinois Press, 1988

Christie, Ian. "Barnet tell qu'en lui-même? ou L'exception et la règle." In Albèra and Cosandey, *Boris Barnet*

"Down to Earth: *Aelita* Relocated." In Taylor and Christie, *Inside the Film Factory* and Richard Taylor, eds. *Eisenstein Rediscovered.* London: Routledge, forthcoming

Clark, Katerina. *The Soviet Novel: History as Ritual.* Chicago: University of Chicago Press, 1981

Conquest, Robert. *Harvest of Sorrow: Soviet Collectivization and the Terror-Famine.* New York: Oxford University Press, 1987

de Grazia, Victoria. "Mass Culture and Sovereignty: The American Challenge to European Cinemas, 1920–1960." *Journal of Modern History* 61 (March 1989)

Dunham, Vera S. *In Stalin's Time: Middle Class Values in Soviet Fiction.* Cambridge: Cambridge University Press, 1976

Eisenschitz, Bernard. "A Fickle Man, or Portrait of Boris Barnet as a Soviet Director." In Taylor and Christie, *Inside the Film Factory* (and in French in Albèra and Cosandey, *Boris Barnet*)

Eisner, Lotte H. *The Haunted Screen: Expressionism in German Cinema and the Influence of Max Reinhardt.* Berkeley: University of California Press, 1969

Elkin, A. *Lunacharskii.* Moscow: Molodaia gvardiia, 1967

Ferro, Marc. *Cinema and History.* Trans. Naomi Greene. Detroit, MI: Wayne State University Press, 1988

Fitzpatrick, Sheila. *The Commissariat of Enlightenment: Soviet Organization of Education and the Arts under Lunacharsky, October 1917–1921.* Cambridge: Cambridge University Press, 1970

"The Emergence of Glaviskusstvo: Class War on the Cultural Front, Moscow, 1928–29." *Soviet Studies* 23, no. 2 (October 1971)

"Cultural Revolution in Russia, 1928–1932." *Journal of Contemporary History* 9 (January 1974)

"The 'Soft' Line on Culture and Its Enemies: Soviet Cultural Policy, 1922–27." *Slavic Review* 33 (June 1974)

"Culture and Politics under Stalin: A Reappraisal." *Slavic Review* 35 (June 1976)

Education and Social Mobility in the Soviet Union, 1921–1934. Cambridge: Cambridge University Press, 1979

"Sex and Revolution: An Examination of Literary and Statistical Criminality; Data on the Mores of Soviet Students in the 1920s." *Journal of Modern History* 50 (June 1982)

et al. [Forum on Stalinism]. *The Russian Review* 45, no. 4 (October 1986)

"Middle Class Values and Soviet Life in the 1930s." In Terry L. Thompson and Richard Sheldon, eds., *Soviet Society and Culture: Essays in Honor of Vera S. Dunham* (Boulder, CO: Westview Press, 1988)

ed. *Cultural Revolution in Russia, 1928–1931.* Bloomington: Indiana University Press, 1978

Gak, A. "K istorii sozdaniia Sovkino." *Iz istorii kino*, vol. v (1962)

Gans, Herbert J. *Popular Culture and High Culture: An Analysis and Evaluation of Taste.* New York: Basic Books, 1974

Ginzburg, S. *Kinematografiia dorevoliutsionnoi Rossii.* Moscow: Iskusstvo, 1963

Gleason, Abbott, Peter Kenez, and Richard Stites, eds. *Bolshevik Culture: Experiment and Order in the Russian Revolution.* Bloomington: Indiana University Press, 1985

Günther, Hans, ed. *The Culture of the Stalin Period.* London: Macmillan, 1990

Hall, Stuart and Paddy Whamel. *The Popular Arts.* New York: Pantheon, 1964

Hay, James. *Popular Film Culture in Fascist Italy: The Passing of the Rex.* Bloomington: Indiana University Press, 1987

Heil, J. T. "No List of Political Assets: The Collaboration of Iurii Olesha and Abram Room on *Strogii iunosha.*" *Slavistische Beiträge* 248 (December 1989)

"Theme and Style and the 'Literary Film' as Avant-Garde." *Avante-Garde* 5/6 (1990)

"Isaak Babel and His Film Work." *Russian Literature* 27 (1990)

Henry, Michael. *Le cinema expressioniste allemand: un langage métaphorique.* Paris: Editions du signe, 1971

Hill, Steven P. "A Quantitative View of Soviet Cinema." *Cinema Journal* 11, no. 2 (1972). Rpt. Richard Dyer MacCann and Jack C. Ellis, eds. *Cinema Examined: Selections from Cinema Journal.* New York: E. P. Dutton, 1982

Hoberman, J. "A Face to the *Shtetl*: Soviet Yiddish Cinema, 1924–36." In Taylor and Christie, *Inside the Film Factory*

Iampolskii, Mikhail. "Pestrota i sliakot rossii." *Kinovedcheskie zapiski*, 1989, no. 4

Iangirov, Rashit. "Nezavisimoe kino: Vzgliad v proshloe." In *Assotsiatsiia nezavisimoe kino* (Moscow: Soiuzinformkino, 1990)

Iz istoriia Lenfilma: Stati, vospominaniia, dokumenty, 1920-e gody, pt. 2. Leningrad: Iskusstvo, 1970

Kenez, Peter. *The Birth of the Propaganda State: Soviet Methods of Mass Mobilization, 1917–1929*. Cambridge: Cambridge University Press, 1985

"The Cultural Revolution in Cinema." *Slavic Review* 47, no. 3 (Fall 1988)

Cinema and Soviet Society, 1917–1953. New York: Cambridge University Press, 1992

"Peasants and Movies." *Historical Journal of Film, Radio and Television*, forthcoming

Kepley, Vance, Jr. "The International Worker's Relief and the Cinema of the Left, 1921–1935." *Cinema Journal* 23, no. 1 (Fall 1983)

"The Origins of Soviet Cinema: A Study in Industry Development." *Quarterly Review of Film Studies* (Winter 1985). Rpt. Taylor and Christie, *Inside the Film Factory*

In the Service of the State: The Cinema of Alexander Dovzhenko. Madison: University of Wisconsin Press, 1986

"Building a National Cinema: Soviet Film Education, 1918–1934." *Wide Angle* 9, no. 3 (1987)

"Cinema and Everyday Life: Soviet Workers Clubs of the 1920s." In Sklar and Musser, *Resisting Images*

and Betty Kepley, "Foreign Films on Soviet Screens, 1922–1931," *Quarterly Review of Film Studies* 4, no. 4 (Fall 1979)

Khaichenko, G. A. *Igor Ilinskii*. Moscow: AN SSSR, 1962

Kino: Entsiklopedicheskii slovar. Moscow: Sovetskaia entsiklopediia, 1986

Kinoslovar. 2 vols. Moscow: Sovetskaia entsiklopediia, 1966 and 1970

Koenker, Diane P., William G. Rosenberg, and Ronald Grigor Suny. *Party, State and Society in the Russian Civil War: Explorations in Social History*. Bloomington: Indiana University Press, 1989

Kushnirov, M. *Zhizn i filmy Borisa Barneta*. Moscow: Iskusstvo, 1977

Landy, Marcia. *Fascism in Film: The Italian Commercial Cinema, 1931–1943*. Princeton, NJ: Princeton University Press, 1986

Lawton, Anna. *Vadim Shershenevich: From Futurism to Imaginism*. Ann Arbor, MI: Ardis, 1981

"'Lumière' and Darkness: The Moral Question in the Russian and Soviet Cinema." *Jahrbücher für Geschichte Osteuropas* 38, no. 2 (1990)

ed. *The Red Screen: Politics, Society, Art in Soviet Cinema*. London: Routledge, 1992

Lebedev, Nikolai. *Ocherk istorii kino SSSR*, vol. 1, *Nemoe kino*. Moscow: Goskinoizdat, 1947

Leyda, Jay. *Kino: A History of the Russian and Soviet Film*. London: Allen & Unwin, 1960

Maguire, Robert A. *Red Virgin Soil: Soviet Literature in the 1920s.* Ithaca, NY: Cornell University Press, 1987; rpt. 1968 edn.

Mally, Lynn. "Intellectuals in the Proletkult: Problems of Authority and Expertise." In Koenker *et al.*, *Party, State and Society*

Culture of the Future: The Proletkult Movement in Revolutionary Russia. Berkeley: University of California Press, 1990

Manvell, Roger and Heinrich Fraenkel. *The German Cinema.* New York: Praeger, 1971

May, Lary. *Screening out the Past: The Birth of Mass Culture and the Motion Picture Industry.* Oxford: Oxford University Press, 1980

Mayne, Judith. *Kino and the Woman Question: Feminism and Soviet Silent Film.* Columbus: Ohio State University Press, 1989

Mendelsohn, Harold. *Mass Entertainment.* New Haven, CT: College & University Press, 1966

Monaco, Paul. *Cinema & Society: France and Germany during the Twenties.* New York: Elsevier, 1976

Murray, Bruce. *Film and the German Left in the Weimar Republic: From Caligari to Kuhle Wampe.* Austin: University of Texas Press, 1990

The Museum of Modern Art Department of Film Circulating Programs. New York: MOMA, 1973

Naiman, Eric. "The Case of Chubarov Alley: Collective Rape, Utopian Desire and the Mentality of NEP." *Russian History/Histoire russe* 17, no. 1 (Spring 1990)

O'Connor, Timothy Edward. *The Politics of Soviet Culture: Anatolii Lunacharskii.* Ann Arbor, MI: UMI Research Press, 1983

Petrić, Vlada. *Constructivism in Film: The Man with the Movie Camera; a Cinematic Analysis.* Cambridge: Cambridge University Press, 1987

"A Subtextual Reading of Kuleshov's Satire *The Extraordinary Adventures of Mr. West in the Land of the Bolsheviks.*" Paper presented at the conference on "The Spirit of Satire in Soviet Cinema," Loyola University, New Orleans, 1990

Rakitin, Vassily. "The Avant-Garde and the Art of the Stalinist Era." In Günther, *Culture of the Stalin Period*

Read, Christopher. *Culture and Power in Revolutionary Russia: The Intelligentsia and the Transition from Tsarism to Communism.* New York: St. Martin's, 1990

Rentschler, Eric, ed. *German Film & Literature: Adaptations and Transformations.* New York: Methuen, 1986

Robin, Régine. "Stalinism and Popular Culture." In Günther, *Culture of the Stalin Period*

Rose, Margaret A. *Marx's Lost Aesthetics: Karl Marx and the Visual Arts.* Cambridge: Cambridge University Press, 1984

Rosenberg, Bernard and David Manning White, eds. *Mass Culture Revisited.* New York: Van Nostrand Reinhold, 1971

Ross, Steven J. "Struggles for the Screen: Workers, Radicals, and the Political Uses of Silent Film," *American Historical Review* 96, no. 2 (April 1991)

Saunders, Thomas. "Hollywood in Berlin: American Cinema and Weimar Culture." Unpublished ms.

Sepman, I. V. "Kinematograf Fridrikha Ermlera." In Sepman, *Ermler*

Shelley, Louise. "Female Criminality in the 1920s: A Consequence of Inadvertent and Deliberate Change." *Russian History/Histoire russe* 9, pts. 2/3 (1982)

Sklar, Robert. *Movie-Made America: A Social History of American Movies*. New York: Random House, 1975

"Oh, Althusser! Historiography and the Rise of Cinema." In Sklar and Musser, *Resisting Images*

and Charles Musser, eds. *Resisting Images: Essays on Cinema and History*. Philadelphia, PA: Temple University Press, 1990

Sloan, Kay. *The Loud Silents: Origins of the Social Problem Film*. Urbana: University of Illinois Press, 1988

Sochor, Zenovia. *Revolution and Culture: The Bogdanov–Lenin Controversy*. Ithaca, NY: Cornell University Press, 1988

Starr, Frederick. *Red and Hot: The Fate of Jazz in the Soviet Union*. New York: Oxford University Press, 1983

Stites, Richard. "Stalinism and the Restructuring of Revolutionary Utopianism." In Günther, *Culture of the Stalin Period*

Revolutionary Dreams: Utopian Vision and Experimental Life in the Russian Revolution. Oxford: Oxford University Press, 1989

Soviet Popular Culture: Entertainment and Society in Russia since 1900. Cambridge: Cambridge University Press, 1992

Strong, John W., ed. *Essays on Revolutionary Culture and Stalinism*. Columbus, OH: Slavica, 1990

Taylor, Richard. *The Politics of the Soviet Cinema, 1917–1929*. Cambridge: Cambridge University Press, 1979

Film Propaganda: Soviet Russia and Nazi Germany. New York: Barnes & Noble, 1979

"A 'Cinema for the Millions': Soviet Socialist Realism and the Problem of Film Comedy." *Journal of Contemporary History* 18, no. 3 (July 1983)

"Soviet Socialist Realism and the Cinema Avant-Garde," *Studies in Comparative Communism* 17, no. 3/4 (Fall/Winter 1984/5)

"Boris Shumyatsky and the Soviet Cinema in the 1930s: Ideology as Mass Entertainment." *Historical Journal of Film, Radio and Television* 6, no. 1 (1986). Rpt. Taylor and Christie, *Inside the Film Factory*

"Soviet Cinema as Popular Culture, or the Extraordinary Adventures of Mr. Nepman in the Land of the Silver Screen." *Revolutionary Russia* 1, no. 1 (June 1988)

"*The Kiss of Mary Pickford*: Ideology and Popular Culture in Soviet Cinema." In Lawton, *The Red Screen*

and Ian Christie, eds. *Inside the Film Factory: New Approaches to Russian and Soviet Cinema*. London: Routledge, 1991

Thompson, Denys, ed. *Discrimination and Popular Culture*. 2nd. edn. London: Heinemann, 1973

Thompson, Kristin. *Exporting Entertainment: America in the World Film Market, 1907–1934*. London: BFI Publishing, 1985

Tone, Pier Giorgio. *Strutture e forme del cinema tedesco degli anni Venti: Scrittura filmica e sviluppo capitalistico.* n.p.: Mursia, 1978

Tsivian, Yuri. "Early Russian Cinema: Some Observations." In Taylor and Christie, *Inside the Film Factory*

Turovskaia, Maia. "Zritelskie predpochiteniia 30-kh godov." Paper delivered to the IREX-Goskino Cinema Commission Conference, Washington, DC, December 1990

Valkenier, Elizabeth Kridl. *Russian Realist Art: The State and Society, the Peredvizhniki and Their Tradition.* Ann Arbor, MI: Ardis, 1977

Viola, Lynn. *Best Sons of the Fatherland: Workers in the Vanguard of Collectivization.* New York: Oxford University Press, 1987

Von Hagen, Mark. *Soldiers in the Proletarian Dictatorship: The Red Army and the Soviet Socialist State, 1917–1930.* Ithaca, NY: Cornell University Press, 1990

Williams, Robert C. *Artists in Revolution: Portraits of the Russian Avant-Garde, 1905–1925.* Bloomington: Indiana University Press, 1977

Youngblood, Denise J. *Soviet Cinema in the Silent Era, 1918–1935.* Ann Arbor, MI: UMI Research Press, 1985; rpt. Austin: University of Texas Press, 1991

"The Fiction Film as a Source for Soviet Social History: The *Third Meshchanskaia Street* Affair." *Film & History* 19, no. 3 (September 1989)

"The Fate of Soviet Popular Cinema during the Stalin Revolution," *The Russian Review* 50 (April 1991)

"'History' on Film: The Historical Melodrama in Early Soviet Cinema." *Historical Journal of Film, Radio & Television* 11, no. 2 (June 1991)

"The Return of the Native: Yakov Protazanov and Soviet Cinema." In Taylor and Christie, *Inside the Film Factory*.

"Entertainment or Enlightenment? Popular Cinema in Soviet Society, 1921–1931." In Stephen White, ed. *New Directions in Soviet History.* Cambridge: Cambridge University Press, 1992

"Americanitis: The *Amerikanshchina* in Soviet Cinema." *Journal of Popular Film and Television* 19, no. 4 (Winter 1992)

"Cinema as Social Criticism: The Early Films of Fridrikh Ermler." In Lawton, *The Red Screen*

Zorkaia, N. M. *Portrety.* Moscow: Iskusstvo, 1966

Na rubezhe stoletii: U istokov massovogo iskusstva v Rossii, 1900–1910 godov. Moscow: Nauka, 1976

INDEX